November 2, 1984

Jan,

Although this book was begun before I knew you, its completion owes much to your understanding, insight, compassion, and guidance. You are an important, even critical, enabling force in my life and you are appreciated.

Love,
Anne

RESEARCH DESIGN AND STATISTICS FOR PHYSICAL EDUCATION

Anne L. Rothstein

Herbert H. Lehman College
City University of New York

PRENTICE-HALL, INC., ENGLEWOOD CLIFFS, NEW JERSEY 07632

Library of Congress Cataloging in Publication Data

ROTHSTEIN, ANNE L.
  Research design and statistics for physical
education.

  Bibliography: p.
  Includes index.
  1. Physical education and training—Statistical
methods.   2. Statistics.   I. Title.
GV362.R67 1985   613.7'028   84-15014
ISBN 0-13-774142-1

Editorial/production supervision and
  interior design: Dee Josephson
Cover design: Ben Santora
Manufacturing buyer: Harry Baisley

Printed in the United Staes of America

10   9   8   7   6   5   4   3   2   1

ISBN 0-13-774142-1   01

Prentice-Hall International, Inc., *London*
Prentice-Hall of Australia Pty. Limited, *Sydney*
Editora Prentice-Hall do Brasil, Ltda., *Rio de Janeiro*
Prentice-Hall Canada Inc., *Toronto*
Prentice-Hall of India Private Limited, *New Delhi*
Prentice-Hall of Japan, Inc., *Tokyo*
Prentice-Hall of Southeast Asia Pte. Ltd., *Singapore*
Whitehall Books Limited, *Wellington, New Zealand*

This book is dedicated to my father, William Rothstein, and to my brother, Harold Rothstein, with love and appreciation. Most especially it is dedicated to the memory of my mother, Rose Rothstein.

CONTENTS

Preface   xi

PART I   Descriptive Statistics

Chapter 1   Research Design and Statistics: An Overview   1
    A Preliminary Example   2
    Types of Statistics   3
Chapter 2   Measurement   5
    Levels of Measurement   5
    Nominal Measurement   5
    Ordinal Measurement   6
    Interval Measurement   8
    Ratio Measurement   8
    Characteristics of a Good Measure   9
    Validity   9
    Reliability   9
    Sensitivity   10
    Responsivity to Change   11
Chapter 3   Descriptive Statistics   12
    Grouped versus Ungrouped Data   12
    Measures of Central Tendency   15
    Mean   16
    Median   17
    Mode   22
    Measures of Variability   22

Range   22
Interquartile Range   23
Variance and Standard Deviation   25
Understanding Your Scores   29
Exercises   31

PART II   Research Design

Chapter 4   What Research Is   33
The Research Puzzle   33
The Research Process   36
Problem Identification   36
Problem Refinement   37
Chapter 5   The Experimental Study: An Overview   40
Elements of the Experiment   40
The Problem   41
Variables   41
The Hypothesis   42
The Experimental Plan   42
Good Experimental Design   43
Chapter 6   Research Design I: Control   46
What is Controlled?   47
Maximizing Treatment Variance   47
Controlling Extraneous Variance   49
Minimizing Error Variance   58
Chapter 7   Research Design II: Factors Affecting Validity   60
Factors Affecting Internal Validity   61
History   61
Maturation   63
Pre-testing   65
Hawthorne Effect   65
Instrumentation   66
Statistical Regression   68
Differential Selection of Subjects   69
Experimental Mortality   70
Factors Affecting External Validity   71
Representativeness   72
Interaction of Treatment and Subjects   72
Effect of Pretesting   73
Hawthorne Effect   74
Multiple Treatment Interference   74
Summary   74
Chapter 8   Research Design III: Sampling   76
Sampling   76
Population   77

Sample   77
Potential Problems   79
Power, Sample Size, and Reliability   81
Type I and Type II Error   81

PART III   Inferential Statistics

Chapter 9   Statistical Inference   84
Using Statistical Inference to Compare Two Samples   87
Relationship Among s, SEM, and $s_{\bar{x}_1-\bar{x}_2}$ 88
Estimating s, sem, and $s_{\bar{x}_1-\bar{x}_2}$ 89
Testing Hypotheses   89
Level of Significance   91
Degrees of Freedom   91

Chapter 10   Probability and the Normal Curve   95
Probability   95
Normal Curve   98
Further Use of the Normal Curve   101
Confidence Intervals   107

Chapter 11   Testing the Difference Between Two Means   110
Calculating the *t*-ratio   111
The *t*-test for Dependent Groups   113
Calculating the *t*-ratio   116
Exercises   118

Chapter 12   Determining the Relationship Between Two Means   121
Scattergram   122
Pearson Product Moment Correlation   124
Spearman Rank Order Correlation   126
Further Uses of Correlation   130
Reliability   132
Validity   133
Exercises   135

Chapter 13   Analyzing Categorized Data   137
One-way Chi-square   137
Chi-square for Two Variables   141
Exercises   143

Chapter 14   Analyzing Differences Among Three Groups or More   145
Partitioning the Variance   147
Exercises   151

Chapter 15   Analyzing Repeated Measures   153
Numerical Example   155
Exercises   158

Chapter 16   Analyzing Factorial Designs   160
Analysis of Variance: Concepts and Foundations   160
A numerical Example   165
Exercises   170

Chapter 17   Analyzing Mixed Designs   172
   Preliminary Calculations   177
   Calculating the Sums of Squares   181
   The Analysis of Variance Table   184
   Extension to Other Designs   186
   Interactions   186
   Exercises   189
Chapter 18   Analyzing Covariance Designs   191
   Using the Analysis of Covariance Technique   193
   Organizing the Data   194
   Calculating the Analysis   196
   Adjusting the Treatment Means   198
   Completing the Analysis   199
   Exercises   200
Chapter 19   Considering Significant Findings: Follow-up Tests   202
   Individual Comparisons   202
   Studentized Range Statistic   203
   Newman-Kuels   204
   Tukey's HSD   207
   Duncan's Multiple Range Test   207
   Scheffe's Test   208
   Simple Effects   210
   Exercises   215

PART IV   Special Topics

Chapter 20   Meta-analysis: Using Research to Influence Practice   216
   Research: Application to Practice   217
   Meta-Analysis   217
   What is Meta-analysis?   218
   Critical Factors Approach   220
   Combining Results   220
   Baysian Approach   221
   How to do a Meta-analysis   225
   Calculating Effect Sizes   228
   Two Complex Examples   229
   Uses and Findings of Meta-Analysis to Date   240
   Role of Meta-Analysis in Physical Education   249
   Statistical Analysis of Game Statistics   250
   An Illustration   251
   Summary   252
   References and Bibliography   252
Chapter 21   Using Computers in Research   257
   Computer Literacy   257
   Some Useful Terminology   259

A Little Background   261
How it Works   262
Hardware vs. Software   262
What is a Program?   263
Summary   264
Using Computers in Literature Search   264
Using Computers to do Research   267
Computers in Biomechanics Research   269
Computers in Exercise Physiology Research   271
Computers in Motor Learning Research   272
Use of Computers in Sport Psychology   273
Descriptive Analytic Research on Teaching   274
Using the Computer to Analyze the Results of Research   274
Using the Computer for Word Processing   277
Using the Computer to Enhance Instruction   279
A Personal Note   279
Bibliography   280

Appendix A   Statistical Tables   283
   A1. Areas Under the Normal Curve   283
   A2. Table of Values for *t*-test of Significance   287
   A3. Pearson Product Moment Correlation   287
   A4. Spearman Rank Order Correlation   288
   A5. Chi-Square Values of Significance   288
   A6. *F* Distribution   289
   A7. Studentized Range Statistic   292

Appendix B   Annotated Computer Programs and Output   294
   1. Applesoft   296
   2. SPSSX   326
   3. BMDP   317
   4. SAS   322

Appendix C   Review of Mathematical Skills and Symbolic Directions   336
Appendix D   Answers to Selected Exercises   342

PREFACE

This book is intended as a generic text on research design and statistics which incorporates examples from physical education and sport. It emphasizes application, learning by doing, and learning through example. It is intended for use in connection with formal study and by individuals with minimal knowledge of statistics who require a resource book in this area. It focuses on the thinking, reasoning, and problem-solving nature of research design and statistics, and it views research as a way of looking at the world, and as a mindset that can be learned.

The text focuses primarily on how rather than why. It includes a wide variety of statistical tests, indicates how basic factorial designs can be extended for additional factors and for unequal groups, provides annotated examples of microcomputer and statistical package programs, facilitates the statistical decision-making process by presenting and incorporating a logical, step-by-step approach, and includes an introduction to meta-analysis, that is, statistical synthesis of research findings for the purpose of application.

Chapter 1 provides an overview and preliminary example and an introduction to research design and statistics. Chapters 2 and 3 introduce concepts about measurement and descriptive statistics. Chapters 4 through 8 cover topics in research design: Chapter 4 clarifies the research process and Chapter 5 provides an overview of the experimental study. The other chapters in this section, 6, 7, and 8, present concepts of experimental design as they relate to control, validity, and sampling. Chapter 9 explains statistical inference and uses computer-generated tables to illustrate the concepts of statistical inference. Chapter 10 focuses on probability and the normal curve and uses computer-generated examples and extensive diagrams to facilitate student understanding of the concepts presented. All of these are particularly useful to the beginning researcher.

Chapters 11 through 19 present the statistical tests. Each chapter provides a conceptual framework for the test, includes a detailed, step-by-step example, uses the decision-making process outlined in Chapter 9, and contains additional exercises. Answers to all exercises are provided in Appendix D. An important and unique feature of the book is the inclusion, in Appendix B, of annotated microcomputer programs for most of the tests presented in the book and the presentation of annotated input and output for three commonly used statistical packages, BMDP, SAS, and SPSS. These programs can be used to check answers to the exercises in the book or to analyze data. In Chapter 16, Analysis of Factorial Designs, there is an easily understood introduction to the concept of analysis of variance; Chapter 17 contains sections on interaction and extension of the methods presented to other, more complicated designs. Chapter 19 focuses on follow-up tests, and covers both individual comparisons and simple effects.

It is important to note that in selecting or designing the studies to be used as examples or exercises in this textbook the goal was simplicity rather than perfection. Thus there was no attempt to consider all the complex problems involved in research design for each example. Rather, the goal was to use examples and exercises that beginning researchers might relate to most readily.

Chapters 20 and 21, respectively, cover meta-analysis and use of computers. The chapter on meta-analysis takes the approach that research can influence practice if appropriate synthesis methods are used. A variety of techniques, which come under the general heading of meta-analysis, are described and examples from physical education and related areas are presented. An introduction to principles and procedures is included and the interested reader could perform a meta-analysis based on the information provided. A chapter on computers is viewed as essential in a text on research design and statistics because microcomputers have facilitated applications that were not feasible several years ago and promise to continue to affect the conduct of research and statistical analysis in important ways. Chapter 21 provides an easily understood introduction to computers and computer applications. A general section on computers includes information on the use of computers in several areas within physical education and sport. Annotated research and statistical analysis programs are provided in Appendix B and are available on disk for several microcomputers. Annotated input and output for several commonly used statistical packages is also presented.

Input from and assistance of others has been essential in the initiation and completion of this book, although the final responsibility for the material contained here is my own. I must thank A. M. Gentile, whose intuitive grasp of statistics and method of sharing her knowledge and insights with her students provided the foundation upon which this book is structured. Ree Arnold, a good friend and colleague, has contributed to this book through our planning for workshops and our discussions about research, statistics, statistical analysis, and computers. Preliminary versions of this text have been field-tested through the efforts of a former student who is now a good friend and colleague, Emily Wughalter, who provided valuable assistance with the SAS statistical examples in Appendix B and also some interesting research design and statistics questions and answers. My many senior honors students and graduate students at Lehman College and my friends and colleagues completing theses and dissertations presented provocative research problems that contributed to my thinking and also provided some of the examples used in this text. The graduate and undergraduate students in my research classes, who challenged me to make difficult concepts clear, and who used and commented on early drafts of this book, deserve thanks. Tina Caraszi, who assisted with the typing of manuscript and tables, played an important role in the completion of this project.

I particularly appreciated the time and efforts of Jo Safrit, whose thorough review of the manuscript led to many worthwhile changes and additions. Dee Josephson, production editor, has played an important role in the completion of this book and I appreciate her assistance, concern, and support. To my close friends, who understood why I often had to work instead of play, and to Jan Anderheggen, whose support helped me to finish this project, go my appreciation and thanks. To Carol Wolfgram, whose encouragement, confidence, and support have been unflagging, go may deepest appreciation and gratitude.

A.L.R.

CHAPTER ONE
RESEARCH DESIGN AND STATISTICS: AN OVERVIEW

This book will approach research design and statistics with an emphasis on doing and finding out and with the view that statistics can be enjoyable. Statistics and research design can help us to explain observations about teaching, learning, and performance in physical education and sport. They can help us to answer questions about physical education. At the very least, familiarity with these topics can help us to understand the ways in which statistics are used by the media to influence us.

The notion that statistics is a form of higher mathematics is a myth. In fact, success at statistics takes little more than the ability to add, subtract, divide, and multiply in logical fashion. The most complex formula in statistics can be reduced to a series of logical operations involving these four procedures.

Research design and statistics involves the study of certain tools that enable us to systematically investigate, describe, and interpret phenomena in physical education. Statistics is one of the tools. Research design is another. Measurement techniques is the third. Each of these tools thus represents a way of finding out about sport and physical education. You have had or will have courses in kinesiology, exercise physiology, motor learning, sport psychology, and/or sport sociology. Associated with each of these subjects are facts and theories that elucidate behavior in sport. The facts and theories were derived through the use of measurement, research, and statistics tools.

Further, you use these tools every day. Much of the information you receive is based upon measurement, research, and statistics. Among the common uses of these tools are baseball statistics, grade-point average, gross national product, Gallup polls, fitness testing, the Census, and the cost-of-living index. In addition, you are bombarded with claims based upon "research and statistics" every day in advertising. "Nine out of ten dentists who recommend gum, recommend Trident." How many dentists did they question to find ten who recommended chewing gum to their patients? "The group that used X toothpaste had 47% fewer cavities." Fewer than what? What percent fewer cavities did the other group have? When you get into your car in the morning and it won't start, you consider alternative reasons—maybe the battery is dead, no gas, bad starter—and systematically eliminate each possibility until you discover the cause. You have done research. You have "guessed" at the cause and have tested your "guess." When you discover that you are correct, you act.

Before continuing, let us briefly define each of the terms we have used.

Measurement A numerical score derived from an observation which generally reflects the extent to which an individual or object possesses a particular characteristic.

Research Systematic procedures for observing and recording information about phenomena. These procedures are detailed in such a way that anyone could carry out the same observations and obtain the same information.

Statistics A single numerical score which characterizes an entire set of scores. Thus, if you measure the height of a group of individuals and take the average height, the average height is a statistic which characterizes the entire group of people you measured.

So, research is a plan for systematically observing some phenomenon which you will measure. Research dictates that you measure one or more individuals and that, in some cases, you compare the scores of one person or group to those of another person or group. (Research involving one person is called a *case study*.) In these instances you must calculate statistics—representative scores— for each group. A simple example which demonstrates the use of measurement, research, and statistics should be helpful.

A PRELIMINARY EXAMPLE

Teacher A at B high school designs a new way to teach the tennis serve. The teacher believes this new method is much better than the old one but wishes to subject it to a test. The teacher decides that the Hewitt Tennis Achievement Test (Hewitt, 1966) will be a good way to measure serve performance. So the measure of tennis performance is the score the student obtains on the test. Having taken care of the problem of measurement of tennis serve performance, the teacher turns attention to the research design. In order to have a fair test, students who are equal in serve performance (possibly all beginners) should be randomly assigned to either the *traditional* serve instruction group or the *new* serve instruction group. Having made this random assignment, the teacher instructs both groups. After the instruction period and the practice period are over (these periods can be as long as the teacher wishes but must be equal for both groups), the teacher administers the Hewitt Tennis Achievement Test and records the scores of each student. Finally, using the scores of the students in each group, the teacher calculates statistics. The one you are most familiar with is the *average* (statisticians like to call this the *mean*). If the mean score for the students in the traditional group is lower than that for the students in the new group, the teacher may conclude that the new method is better and may use it in the future instead of the traditional method.

In testing the effectiveness of the traditional versus the new method of teaching the tennis serve, the teacher did the following:

Identified the problem. (How can I teach the tennis serve more effectively?)

Reviewed available information and past experience with teaching the tennis serve.

Decided that the *new* method was better than the *traditional* method.

Designed a research study to test the *new* method against the *traditional* method. (This included selecting a method of measurement.)

Conducted the study according to previously chosen systematic procedures to assure a fair test.

Gathered scores on the test of serve performance.

Analyzed the scores. (By calculating the average for each group.)

Reached a conclusion about which was the better method.

In fact, the analysis of the scores or measures obtained would normally have a more stringent basis than just the average scores, and in the third section of the book we will consider other ways of evaluating research studies. For now the average is the easiest statistic to calculate.

So, we see in the example that research, statistics, and measurement are intertwined and that together they enable us to answer questions about sport and physical education. These questions may center on the acquisition of skill (motor learning), the behavior of individuals in group settings (sport sociology), the characteristics of individuals (sport psychology), attaining and maintaining physical fitness (exercise physiology), efficiency of movement (kinesiology), prevention and treatment of injury (sports medicine), design and implementation of learning experiences (curriculum), or the clarification and interpretation of past events (sports history). The design and conduct of experimental research will be considered in the second section of this book.

TYPES OF STATISTICS

Traditionally the study of statistics has been divided into two parts, descriptive statistics and inferential statistics. *Descriptive statistics* is concerned with characterizing a particular set of observations which have been made on things or people. We may describe the average height of college seniors, the frequency of incomplete grades in various academic departments, the frequency of males and females in different majors, the median income of college professors, or the variability of ages of college students. In describing the items indicated we might use numerical, tabular, or graphic devices. However, the purpose of descriptive statistics is to summarize information and observations in a simple and meaningful way. Chapter 3 discusses the mean (average score), median (middle score), and mode (most frequent score) as well as the standard deviation, the range, and the interquartile range. These are all examples of descriptive statistics. Each statistic tells us something important about the group of scores it describes; in combination these statistics are very powerful, but we must know how to interpret their meaning.

Descriptive statistics provide information to characterize groups of measures, but in research we need more. The researcher must be able to generalize the scores of a small group of individuals (a sample) to the larger group from which they come (the population). *Inferential statistics* provides the tools to make these generalizations. The researcher, typically, wants to make predictions about a large group of individuals by studying only a small sample of the total group. The purpose of inferential statistics is to predict or estimate characteristics of a population from a knowledge of only a sample of the population. This can be accomplished with a known margin of error; that is, the researcher knows what the probability is that the estimate or prediction is wrong.

Inferential statistics always involves:

1. Statement of a guess about what will happen if you do something to a group of individuals.
2. Collection of data from a sample of the population to be studied.
3. Analysis of the results using some inferential statistical test.

The second section of this book (Chapters 4 to 8), which is concerned with research techniques and methods, details what happens in steps 1 and 2. The third section (Chapters 9 to 19) focuses on the various statistical tests you will use in step 3 to draw inferences from a sample about a population. A final section, Chapters 20 and 21, considers two special topics in research, meta-analysis and computers.

CHAPTER TWO
MEASUREMENT

A measurement is a numerical score derived from observation of a behavior or characteristic. A behavior or characteristic that can take different values is called a *variable*. If, for example, in your exercise physiology class each student takes the Harvard Step Test to determine cardiovascular endurance, then we say we have data on the variable cardiovascular endurance. If we determine the eye color of each person in this class, then we have data on the variable eye color. ("Data" is just a fancy name for a set of measurements.) In similar manner we can obtain data on the variables of motivation, social status, class in school, college major, height, weight, tennis ability, strength, endurance.

LEVELS OF MEASUREMENT

In measurement, we derive numerical scores by assigning numbers to observations according to preset rules. When your performance on the Harvard Step Test is measured, you are assigned a number which reflects your cardiovascular endurance. Your scoring in a tennis game is guided by rules. All measurement is (or should be) guided by explicit or implicit rules.

Different rules apply at different levels of measurement. There are four such levels, each useful in its own way and each dictating certain types of statistical procedures. These levels are nominal, ordinal, interval, and ratio.

Nominal Measurement

Nominal measurement may be thought of as measurement "in name only." At this, the lowest level of measurement, people or objects are categorized by such things as sex, political affiliation, eye color, hair color, and body type. In order to categorize, we must list the categories and then assign each person or thing to the appropriate category. In a recent statistics class we counted the number of individuals with blue, brown, hazel, or green eye color. The "other" category was added in case the eye colors selected did not account for all the members of the class.

EYE COLOR

BLUE	BROWN	HAZEL	GREEN	OTHER
ⅦⅠ	Ⅶ	⦀	‖	⦀⦀
Ⅰ	Ⅶ			
(6)	(10)	(3)	(2)	(4)

In nominal measurement (1) the list of categories must be exhaustive; they must account for all observations; (2) the categories must be mutually exclusive; each observation must fit into only one category; and (3) the categories cannot be placed into any meaningful order.

Ordinal Measurement

The second level of measurement is *ordinal measurement*. The numbers assigned to the observations reflect differing amounts of the characteristic. In a race, for example, prizes are awarded for amount of speed in finishing, in terms of order of finish: first place, second place, third place. In high school, based on amount of accomplishment in your studies, you occupied an ordinal position in the class rankings. A ladder tournament in tennis or other sport reflects the order of ability of the participants. In ordinal measurement the size of the number assigned to the observation indicates a position with relation to the other observations; however, the distances between the points on the ordinal scale are not equal.

One way to compare individuals is to rank them on different measures and then juxtapose the ranks for the various measures. Suppose that a group of physical education majors participated in ladder tournaments in tennis, badminton, table tennis, and one-on-one (basketball). In a ladder tournament players challenge each other according to preset rules, and after a certain date their positions in the ladder are final and taken to represent their level within the group. The ranks on the ladder are presented in Table 2.1.

As you can see, we have placed the subjects in order in relation to their ranks in the tennis ladder. We then found the subject who achieved the highest position in badminton (it was E) and put a 1 opposite the name of this student in the badminton column. Who was the student who did worst in badminton? (If you said student H, you would be correct.) In similar manner we will record rankings for basketball and for table tennis. These rankings do not imply that the person who is number 1 is equally as distant from number 2 as number 2 is from number 3; they mean merely that the position (or raw score) of each

TABLE 2.1   Ranks in Ladder Tournaments

STUDENT	RANK, TENNIS LADDER	RANK, BADMINTON LADDER	RANK, BASKETBALL LADDER	RANK, TABLE TENNIS LADDER
A	1	4	8	3
B	2	3	5	7
C	3	2	7	1
D	4	6	6	6
E	5	1	1	4
F	6	5	2	5
G	7	7	3	8
H	8	8	4	2

person 1 in the respective ladder was better than that of person 2, and that the position of person 2 was better than that of person 3, and so on.

Problems can arise when ordinal measurement is used in comparing different groups. Suppose that we have two tennis coaches who are scheduling their players to play first singles, second singles, third singles, and so on. Each coach should assign his or her players in order of actual player ability (an ordinal measure). Some coaches do this by having players continually play off against each other as in a ladder tournament. For example, the individuals of the two schools are scaled according to the arrangement shown in Figure 2.1. In school 1, through ordinal measurement (a ladder tournament), we know that student A is better than student B and that student B is better than student C. Figure 2.1 shows that, in relation to student C, student A is far better than student B— but ordinal measurement does not give us this information. Ordinal measurement tells us that someone is *better* than someone else, not *how much better*. (The comparative scaling in Figure 2.1 was determined by a different testing procedure that yielded actual, comparable scores, not through an ordinal measure such as a ladder tournament.)

Another bit of information shown by Figure 2.1 but not revealed by simple rank-order comparison is that the number 1 singles player in School 2 (player W) is not as good as the number 2 player (player B) in school 1. Rank order relates only to the *other members of the same group;* it does not mean that you are equal in ability to a member of another group who holds the same rank. This has sometimes created a problem for college admissions offices. Is the rank of number 1 in High School A equivalent to a rank of Number 1 in High School B? In High School C? It has also troubled the individuals who rank

```
School 1  | A        B   C        D           |
            High                      Low
School 2  |              W      X Y      Z     |
            High                      Low
```

FIGURE 2.1   Comparative Scaling of Tennis Ability

amateur tennis players. If you win a particular tennis tournament but there are no ranked players entered, is that worth as much as winning a tournament in which highly ranked players are entered? Accordingly, a system has been developed which weights the tournaments with respect to the level of the players. In diving competition, dives are assigned a degree-of-difficulty weighting, so that an individual cannot win simply by choosing easier dives to perform.

Regardless of these pitfalls, ordinal measurement does prove useful in many instances. However, the researcher, teacher, or coach who uses this method of comparing individuals or groups would do well to keep the possible misinterpretations in mind.

Interval Measurement

Interval measurement encompasses the givens for the nominal and ordinal scales—different numbers reflect different things, and observations are ordered along some dimension—and it adds the aspect that the intervals between adjacent points on the scale have equal value. That is, the numbers reflect *how much better than;* they afford the opportunity for comparison between different scale points. A common example is that of temperature: the difference between 50° F and 60° F is the same as the difference between 80° F and 90° F. However, 50° F is not half as warm as 100° F, because in interval measurement there is no true zero point on the scale; rather it is arbitrary. The commonly used and abused measure, IQ, is another example of an interval scale. You can say that the difference between IQs of 100 and 110 is the same as the difference between IQs of 80 and 90, but you cannot say that an IQ of 90 is twice an IQ of 45, because the IQ scale has no true zero. Many measurements in physical education are interval in nature.

Ratio Measurement

In *ratio measurement* we assume that the scale has an absolute zero. Examples of ratio scales are height, weight, and time. Ten minutes is twice as long as 5 minutes and half as long as 20 minutes. A person who executes

TABLE 2.2   Comparison of the Four Scales of Measurement

SCALE	CHARACTERISTICS	EXAMPLES
Ratio	Numbers represent equal units from absolute zero. Observations can be compared as ratios or percentages.	Distance, time, weight
Interval	Numbers represent equal units (intervals). Distances between observations can be compared.	Year, temperature, IQ
Ordinal	Numbers indicate rank order of observations.	Percentiles, ladder tournament, tennis rankings
Nominal	Numbers represent categories. Numbers do not reflect differences in magnitude. Numbers do not distinguish groups.	Sex, nationality, eye color, class in college

a high jump of 7 feet jumps twice as high as someone who clears 3'6". If I run a mile in 6 minutes and you run it in 3, you have run twice as fast. Table 2.2 summarizes the major differences among the four scales of measurement (Hopkins and Glass, 1978, p. 12).

CHARACTERISTICS OF A
GOOD MEASUREMENT

Whenever you want to observe a phenomenon, you must choose a means of measurement. In order to obtain accurate and useful data, you must choose the means of measurement with care. There are several characteristics that a good observation measure should have: validity, reliability, sensitivity, and responsiveness to change.

Validity

When we say that a measure is *valid*, we mean that it measures what it is supposed to measure. If a person does well on the test, he or she will do well in the skill we are predicting. For example, if I administer a tennis test to a group of students, I expect that those who do well on the test will do well in a tennis tournament and those who do poorly on the test will do poorly in the tennis tournament. The test is designed to "predict" tennis-playing ability. If it does, indeed, identify the good players and the poor players, then we say it has good predictive validity. If not, then it is not a valid test; it does not reflect tennis ability. In short, validity is a test's ability to predict performance in other situations.

Reliability

A measure is *reliable* if it measures behavior in a consistent way. The test can be counted on to give us similar results each time we use it. Suppose we administer a test to 10 individuals, and they score as indicated in Table 2.3, Test I; then we administer the same test a week later, and they score as indicated for Test II.

TABLE 2.3   Student Scores on Two Test Administrations

STUDENT	TEST I	TEST II
1	90	95
2	85	89
3	84	85
4	83	85
5	80	79
6	75	78
7	75	74
8	74	73
9	73	70
10	70	65

Even though the absolute values of the scores have changed, the relative order of the individuals has not. The test therefore measures behavior consistently. The score we obtain on one administration of the test is similar to the score we obtain on a second administration. An interesting analogy is presented by Phillips (1973):

> Imagine a man aiming a rifle in the general direction of a target that is several hundred feet away. I say "in the general direction" because there is a huge sheet of white gauze that hides not only the target but a considerable area around it. Our marksman takes aim then, at a spot that he hopes is the bullseye. He fires five shots—and scatters them all over the cloth screen.
>
> . . . Another marksman takes aim at the same spot as the first did. He "groups" his shots . . . thereby missing the target completely.
>
> . . . Finally, a third marksman decides where he thinks the target is, aims at its supposed center and pumps off five shots that are as close together as those of the second marksman and are also perfectly placed on the target. (page 55)

In this example, reliability is illustrated by the two groupings. Each shot lands in almost the same place; you can bet on it, just as you can expect a reliable test to yield consistent scores. The proximity to the target illustrates the concept of validity. It does no good to be reliable, to group your shots, if they are off target. It matters not if a test is reliable if it does not measure what you wish to test. High reliability and high validity do not necessarily occur together. However, low reliability and low validity always do. A test can be reliable without being valid, but it can't be valid without being reliable.

Sensitivity

When we say a measure is *sensitive*, we mean that if the characteristic we are measuring is present at all, even in the most minute amounts, the measure will detect it. Sensitivity is particularly critical when we are attempting to measure learning or retention of that which has been learned. In addition, it is also important in measuring improvement in variables, such as in physical fitness or weight loss.

People like to feel they are improving; they like to be successful. Improvement and success are highly motivating. If we use gross measures of performance (these may also be thought of as least sensitive), we are unlikely to detect small improvements. Suppose, for example, that a child is throwing balls at a target which has only a small center point. If the child hits the center, then a point is scored; a hit anywhere else scores zero. If only the child's score were reported, no improvement over zero would be shown except for a hit, even though the child might be throwing the ball closer to the center point. If instead of one center point we had used concentric circles, each having a lower value as we moved from center to outer circle, then as the child became more accurate, the score would go up. Instead of hit or miss we would have a sensitive measure of the improvement the child was making.

Responsivity to Change

If a measure is responsive to change, then you will obtain different scores as you improve; people of different ability will get different scores, and the score they obtain will reflect their ability. This means that in one way the measure must be sensitive, but it also means that the measure must be designed in a way that allows for improvement to occur. If a measure of behavior has a narrow range, there will be little room for improvement. So you want to design it to provide more room for change.

References

HOPKINS, K. D. and GLASS, G. V. *Basic statistics for the behavioral sciences.* Englewood Cliffs: Prentice-Hall, 1978.

PHILLIPS, J. L. Jr. *Statistical thinking (2nd ed.).* San Francisco: W. H. Freeman, 1982.

CHAPTER THREE
DESCRIPTIVE
STATISTICS

Once you have collected your data and want to characterize what you have observed, you will use descriptive statistics. In particular, you will use measures of *central tendency* and *variability*. If you have a large number of observations, say 100 or more scores, you may also use *grouping* techniques to reduce the mass of data to more manageable size.

This chapter will discuss, first, the grouping of data, including the concepts of ungrouped data, simple frequency distributions, and grouped data; second, measures of central tendency and their use with ungrouped and grouped data, and finally, measures of variability.

GROUPED VERSUS
UNGROUPED DATA

We may treat data in three different ways to prepare them for summarizing through use of descriptive statistics. (1) We may use them in raw form, usually after organizing the scores in descending order (from highest to lowest). (2) We may count the number of times each different score occurs. This is a *simple frequency distribution.* (3) We may define categories or classes which contain more than one score value. This is a *grouped frequency distribution.* Let us look at an example to clarify the differences among these treatments.

A teacher of tennis has surveyed 50 entering students to determine the level of tennis class they should register for. The scores on the diagnostic test range from a high of 40 to a low of 0. The scores of the 50 students have been ordered from the highest to lowest in Table 3.1. Column 1 gives the student's case

TABLE 3.1   Raw Data and a Simple Frequency Distribution

CASE	SCORE (X)	FREQUENCY (f)	fX
50	40	2	80
49	40		
48	39	1	39
47	38	1	38
46	37	2	74
45	37		
44	36	1	36
43	35	1	35
42	34	1	34
41	32	1	32
40	31	2	62
39	31		
38	29	2	58
37	29		
36	28	3	84
35	28		
34	28		
33	27	1	27
32	25	6	150
31	25		
30	25		
29	25		
28	25		
27	25		
26	24	1	24
25	22	1	22
24	21	1	21
23	19	1	19
22	18	1	18
21	15	2	30
20	15		
19	14	2	28
18	14		
17	13	1	13
16	10	3	30
15	10		
14	10		
13	9	2	18
12	9		
11	8	1	8
10	7	1	7
9	6	1	6
8	5	1	5
7	4	1	4
6	3	2	6
5	3		
4	2	2	4
3	2		
2	1	2	2
1	1		
	$\Sigma X = 1013$		$\Sigma fX = 1013$

number. The student's score on the test is given in column 2. The scores in column 2 represent a distribution of raw data. In column 3, headed f for frequency, scores which are the same have been counted and their number entered. In column 4, headed fX, the score has been multiplied by the number of times it appears (f). The sum of the second column is the same as the sum of the fourth column, because all the scores have been accounted for in the fX multiplication.

Instead of using the actual scores as the labels for the categories, we might wish to group the observations by collapsing the scale. This requires the establishment of *class intervals*—categories which define the upper and lower limits of the scores that are counted as part of that interval. Grouping is helpful when there are a large number of scores which are widely spread and when some of the scores appear infrequently. A number of conventions are used in "grouping" scores, but truthfully the grouping is more art than science. It is intended to provide a meaningful overall picture of the data (when used with graphing techniques) as well as to facilitate the calculation of descriptive statistics. (It is important to note, as will be shown, that some information and precision are lost when the observations are grouped.)

The process of organizing data into a grouped frequency distribution like that shown in Table 3.2 consists of a number of steps:

1. Organize the scores in descending order.
2. Determine the *range*, the distance from the highest score to the lowest score $+1$. For the scores on the previous page this is $(40 - 1) + 1$ or 40.
3. Traditionally, between 10 and 20 class intervals (c.i.) are used. It is suggested that the size of the class intervals be determined by dividing the range by 15 (because it is halfway between 10 and 20). So, $40/15 = 2.67$. By rounding this to the nearest whole number we determine that the c.i. size should be 3. It is suggested also that the size of the class interval be an odd number (3, 5, 7). This will be helpful in statistical calculations, since the representative score (X) will be a whole number.
4. Since the lowest score is 1 and the interval selected is 3, the lowest c.i. should be 0–2, the next interval 3–5, and so on, until we progress to the last interval, 39–41. (The lower limit of each class interval can be a multiple of the c.i. size, so that checking the work is easier.)
5. We then count the number of scores which fall in each c.i. and write this number in the column f(frequency). The sum of this column, Σf, equals the number of cases in the distribution (N).
6. The other columns are the cumulated frequencies (cf), the percentage each frequency represents (%), and the percent each cumulated frequency represents $(c\%)$. The percent is calculated by dividing the frequency in the column by the total N and multiplying by 100. The cumulative percent is obtained in the same way, but the cf column is used.
7. The column labeled X is the "representative score" used in calculations. This number is the midpoint of the class interval. In column fX the representative score has been multiplied by the frequency of scores in the c.i. Adding the numbers in this column gives an approximation of the sum of the scores. Note that the total here is 1016, while the total in Table 3.1 is 1013.

To test your understanding of the concepts presented here, use the scores

TABLE 3.2   Grouped Frequency Distribution

CLASS INTERVAL	f	cf	X	fX	%	c%
39–41	3	50	40	120	6	100
36–38	4	47	37	148	8	94
33–35	2	43	34	68	4	84
30–32	3	41	31	93	6	82
27–29	6	38	28	168	12	76
24–26	7	32	25	175	14	64
21–23	2	25	22	44	4	50
18–20	2	23	19	38	4	46
15–17	2	21	16	32	4	42
12–14	3	19	13	39	6	38
9–11	5	16	10	50	10	32
6– 8	3	11	7	21	6	22
3– 5	4	8	4	16	8	16
0– 2	4	4	1	4	8	8

$$\Sigma fX = 1016$$

shown below to organize a grouped frequency distribution. You might also wish to construct a simple frequency distribution. [*Hint:* Before beginning, you will want to put the scores in order. Also you might begin with a low class interval of 6–8.]

```
24  23   9  31  16  16  21  26  26  19  35  33  40  29  28  23  21  42  37  25  24  13
23  25  32  22  22  14  39  17  38  20  21  18  43   8  19  20  27  18  27  20  30  26
25  25  34  25  36  34  38  36  36  12  12  27  28  34  32  30  21  25  23  13  34  33
37  35  15  15  24  25  23  31  29  29  26  24  25  23
```

MEASURES OF CENTRAL TENDENCY

Measures of central tendency may be thought of as typical scores. They represent points in the set or distribution around which scores seem to center. They are by far the most widely used statistics, both for the researcher and for the general public. How often have you heard statements about average rainfall, average SAT scores, average income, average rate of inflation, average family size, average weight, batting average? Such measures are used in order to condense information.

The three commonly used measures of central tendency are defined as follows:

Mean   The statistic that represents the balance point of the distribution. It is the sum of all the scores in the distribution divided by the number of scores in the distribution.

Median   The middle score in the distribution. The score below which 50% of the cases fall. It is obtained by ordering the scores and finding the score which is in the exact middle position.

Mode   The score which appears most frequently. It may be thought of as the most popular score. It is obtained by counting the frequency of each score value and then choosing the one that has the highest frequency.

Mean

In order to determine the mean, symbolized by $\overline{X}$ (called X-bar), add together all the scores and divide by the number of scores. In mathematical notation a single score is indicated by the symbol X, and the Greek symbol Σ (capital sigma) represents "sum of." Therefore we can use the symbol $\Sigma\ X$ to indicate that we add together all the scores. The number of scores is indicated by the symbol N. Putting the symbols together, we obtain the equation

$$\overline{X} = \frac{\Sigma\ X}{N} \tag{3.1}$$

If we use the scores

10, 9, 9, 8, 7, 7, 7, 6, 4, 3

we may express the mean as follows:

$$\overline{X} = \frac{10 + 9 + 9 + 8 + 7 + 7 + 7 + 6 + 4 + 3}{10}$$

$$= \frac{70}{10} \tag{3.2}$$

$$= 7$$

Using equation (3.1), we find that

$$N = 10, \qquad X = 70$$

Therefore, substituting:

$$\overline{X} = \frac{\Sigma\ X}{N}$$

$$= \frac{70}{10} \tag{3.3}$$

$$= 7$$

To demonstrate the nature of the mean as the balance point of the distribution we can consider it as the fulcrum or center. Two ways of illustrating this are shown in Figure 3.1(a) and (b).

```
                7
         9      7
10       9  8   7  6     4  3
        ─────────────────────────
         +8      X̄   −8
```

FIGURE 3.1(a)   Mean as Balance Point of Distribution

We can demonstrate that the mean is the center or balance point by calculating the difference between each score and the mean. The sum of the differences on one side should equal the sum of the differences on the other side, shown in Figure 3.1(a) and (b).

X	$X - \overline{X}$	
10	3	
9	2	
9	2	+8
8	1	
7	0	
7	0	
7	0	
6	−1	
4	−3	
3	−4	−8
	Sum = 0	

FIGURE 3.1(b)   Use of the Deviation Score

Through use of the deviation score, as in Figure 3.1(b), we can express the notion that the mean is, indeed, the balance point of the distribution, because the sum of the deviations from the mean $(X - \overline{X})$ is zero. If the scores are regarded as units, then we can think of the mean as the center of gravity. Each unit is given the same weight, and we might think of them as being arranged on a see-saw balanced on the mean.

Median

We defined the median as the point that represents the exact middle in the distribution. As many scores lie above the median as lie below. If a distribution is symmetrical, the median will be the same as the mean. For the scores considered previously,

10, 9, 9, 8, 7, 7, 7, 6, 4, 3

the median would be that score which divides the upper 5 scores from the lower 5 scores. In this instance the median is not an actual score but one which would lie midway between the highest score of the lower half and the lowest score of the upper half. It is helpful to visualize each score as having a case number, as illustrated in Figure 3.2.

Case number	1	2	3	4	5	6	7	8	9	10
Score	10	9	9	8	7	7	7	6	4	3

FIGURE 3.2   Scores with Their Case Numbers

The median *case* would be determined as in equation (3.4):

$$\text{Mdn case} = \frac{N + 1}{2}$$

$$= \frac{10 + 1}{2}$$

$$= \frac{11}{2}$$

$$= 5.5$$

(3.4)

The median *score* is that score that is or *would be* at that case number. For the distribution presented in Figure 3.2 the score would be calculated as in equation (3.5):

$$\text{Mdn score} = \frac{\text{case 6} + \text{case 5}}{2}$$

$$\text{Mdn score} = \frac{7 + 7}{2}$$

$$= \frac{14}{2}$$

$$= 7$$

(3.5)

If the distribution has an odd number of cases (e.g., 9, 11, 15) rather than an even number (e.g., 10, 16, 20), then the median case will be associated with an actual score value. For the set of scores

14, 13, 10, 9, 8, 8, 7, 6, 4, 4, 1

there are 11 cases. Therefore, the median case is calculated as in equation (3.6):

$$\text{Mdn case} = \frac{11 + 1}{2}$$

$$= \frac{12}{2} \tag{3.6}$$

$$= 6$$

The sixth case is the middle case. If you count, you will find that there are 5 cases above the sixth case and 5 cases below it. Thus, arranging the scores with their case numbers, as in Figure 3.3, we find that the score corresponding to the sixth case is 8. In this instance we do not have to calculate the actual score as we did in equation (3.5) because it is a real score:

Mdn score = 8

Case number	1	2	3	4	5	6	7	8	9	10	11
Score	14	13	10	9	8	8	7	6	4	4	1

FIGURE 3.3   Scores with Their Case Numbers

If we refer to the grouped frequency distribution presented in Table 3.2, we find that we have lost the original data and cannot find the median score using the procedure presented above. Note that the above procedure can be used only for raw data for data organized into a simple frequency distribution.

There is a procedure for locating the median in grouped frequency distributions; we present it here because it is a generic procedure and will be applied to finding percentiles, deciles, and quartiles. The procedure to be illustrated assumes that the cases in each class interval are evenly distributed throughout the class. In addition the *real limits* of the scores in any class go from .5 below the lower limit to .5 above the upper limit. Thus, for the first four class intervals presented in Table 3.2 the *real limits* would be:

8.5–11.5
5.5– 8.5
2.5– 5.5
−.5– 2.5

In fact, the limits would not coincide, the lower limit would be .5 and the upper limit would be .49. This is not a crucial point, and we can operate as though they were both .5.

If we assume that the cases in any class interval are evenly distributed, then we can estimate the position of the median in the class it falls in by considering what proportion of the cases in that class must be added to all cases occurring in classes below. This procedure is stated statistically by equation (3.7):

$$Mdn = LL + \left[\frac{\%(N) - f_b}{f_w}\right] i \qquad (3.7)$$

where LL = the real lower limit of the class interval containing the case of interest

N = the total number of cases

$\%$ = the percentile you are interested in; for the median, you are interested in the 50th percentile or .50

f_b = all cases which occur below the class interval containing the case of interest (this is found in the cf column)

f_w = all cases within the class interval containing the case of interest (this is found in the f column)

i = the width of each class interval (found by subtracting the real lower limit from the real upper limit)

To find the median for the distribution presented in Table 3.2 we would proceed as follows:

1. Find the case you are interested in by multiplying its percentile by N. For the median work $.50(N)$. For the distribution in Table 3.2 multiply $.50(50) = 25$th case.
2. Find the class interval that contains the 25th case by scanning the cf column until you find where the 25th case would be. (You should discover the case in the class interval 21–23.)
3. Now substitute the appropriate numbers in equation (3.7):

$$Mdn = 20.5 + \left[\frac{25 - 23}{2}\right] 3$$

$$= 20.5 + \left[\frac{2}{2}\right] 3 \qquad (3.8)$$

$$= 20.5 + [1]3 = 20.5 + 3 = 23.5$$

Now, we can use a different frequency distribution, like that in Table 3.3.

TABLE 3.3   Illustrative Distribution

CLASS INTERVAL	f	cf	X	fX
30–34	3	30	32	96
25–29	5	27	27	135
20–24	6	22	22	132
15–19	8	16	17	136
10–14	4	8	12	48
5– 9	3	4	7	21
0– 4	1	1	2	2
				570

Find the median case:

$$\text{case} = .50(N)$$

$$= .50(30) \tag{3.9}$$

$$= 15$$

Find the median score:

$$\text{Mdn} = LL + \left[\frac{.50(N) - f_b}{f_w}\right] i$$

$$= 14.5 + \left[\frac{15 - 8}{8}\right] 5$$

$$= 14.5 + \left[\frac{7}{8}\right] 5 \tag{3.10}$$

$$= 14.5 + [.875]5$$

$$= 14.5 + 4.375$$

$$= 18.875$$

We demonstrate the placement of the median score graphically in Figure 3.4 by juxtaposing the case numbers of the scores in the 15–19 interval with the

Cases	8	9	10	11	12	13	14	15	16
Scores	14.5	15.125	15.750	16.375	17	17.625	18.25	18.875	19.5

FIGURE 3.4   Distribution of Scores within the Interval

score units. In order to find out how much each case is worth, we divide the score units by the number of cases they must be distributed over. In this class interval each case is worth .625 score units. Adding the .625 to each case, we find that case number 15 is associated with a score of 18.875, the same value found in the problem.

We could do the same for any of the class intervals, and we would find that the score units remain the same (5) but the number of cases in the interval changes. Thus, the amount we add proportionally changes, based on the number of cases. Try it out for one of the other intervals. Try the 10–14. What is each score worth? The 30–34. What is each score worth?

Mode

The mode has been defined as the most frequently occurring score value in a distribution. In any large distribution there will be one score which occurs more frequently than any other; this is the mode. Sometimes there will be more than one mode; in this case the distribution is called bimodal. If a small sample has more than one mode, this can usually be discounted. In a large distribution, however, this means that the sample is not homogeneous and that the scores observed represent two merged samples. In grouped frequency distributions the mode is the representative score of the class interval that has the most cases.

MEASURES OF VARIABILITY

We have explored the mean, median, and mode as ways of describing the center of a set of scores. However, it is nearly impossible to interpret what these statistics indicate without having some notion of the variability or scatter of the scores. Several distributions may have the same mean but differ markedly in variability. The measures of variability we shall consider may be defined briefly as follows:

> **Range**   This represents the total distance in scores from the highest to the lowest in the distribution. It is affected by spurious scores (scores that are extremely high or extremely low in relation to the majority of scores).
>
> **Interquartile range**   A measure that provides a more stable measure of the spread of scores by using the 75% and 25% scores to determine the range. It is not affected by extreme scores, and it can be useful.
>
> **Variance and standard deviation**   The most widely used and respected measures of variability or spread. They are based on deviation scores, as illustrated in Figure 3.1(b). The concepts are central to many inferential statistical tests and are based on the notion of the sum of squares (the squared deviations of scores from the mean).

Range

In order to determine the range of a distribution, we subtract the lowest score from the highest score:

$$\text{Range} = X_H - X_L \tag{3.11}$$

Some textbooks suggest that the formula be modified by adding 1 to the result in order to account for the error of 1 score when using this formula. Since this statistic is subject to many modifications and is not useful for further calculations, either formula may be used. Equation (3.12), in which 1 is added, is probably most correct, and if you are going to remember only one of them, it is probably the best:

$$\text{Range} = X_H - X_L + 1 \tag{3.12}$$

For the following scores

    12, 11, 9, 9, 8, 7, 6, 6, 6, 4, 3, 2

the range is

$$\text{Range} = 12 - 2 + 1$$

$$= 10 + 1 \tag{3.13}$$

$$= 11$$

Interquartile Range

The interquartile range is calculated by using the procedures for determining the median to calculate the 25% and the 75%. The procedure would be as follows:

1. Determine the score which corresponds to 25% by using equation (3.14):

$$LL + \left[\frac{.25(N) - f_b}{f_w} \right] i \tag{3.14}$$

    You should recognize this as the formula you used to determine the median, except that the .50 is replaced by the .25.
2. Determine the score which corresponds to the 75% by using equation (3.14) and replacing .25 by .75.
3. Using the scores calculated in steps 1 and 2, where the score corresponding to the 25% = Q_1 and the score corresponding to the 75% = Q_3, substitute in equation (3.15), the difference is the interquartile range.

$$Q = Q_3 - Q_1 \tag{3.15}$$

Using the distribution in Table 3.4, we calculate as in equations (3.16)–(3.20).

TABLE 3.4   Distribution of Scores

X	CUM. FREQ. (cf)
12	12
11	11
9	10
9	9
8	8
7	7
6	6
6	5
6	4
4	3
3	2
2	1

$$Q_3 \text{ case} = .75(12) = 9 \tag{3.16}$$

$$Q_3 \text{ score} = 8.5 + \left[\frac{9-8}{1}\right]1 = 8.5 + 1 = 9.5 \tag{3.17}$$

$$Q_1 \text{ case} = .25(12) = 3 \tag{3.18}$$

$$Q_1 \text{ score} = 3.5 + \left[\frac{3-2}{1}\right]1 = 3.5 + 1 = 4.5 \tag{3.19}$$

$$Q = Q_3 - Q_1 = 9.5 - 4.5 = 5 \tag{3.20}$$

Using the grouped frequency distribution presented in Table 3.3, we would proceed in similar fashion.

$$\text{case} = \text{prop}(N)$$

$$Q_3 \text{ case} = .75(30) = 22.5 \text{ case} \tag{3.21}$$

$$Q_1 \text{ case} = .25(30) = 7.5 \text{ case} \tag{3.22}$$

$$\text{score} = LL + \left[\frac{\%(N) - c_b}{c_w}\right]i$$

$$Q_3 \text{ score} = 24.5 + \left[\frac{22.5 - 22}{5}\right]5$$

$$= 24.5 + \left[\frac{.5}{5}\right]5 \tag{3.23}$$

$$= 24.5 + [.1]5$$

$$= 24.5 + .5$$

$$= 25$$

$$Q_1 \text{ score} = 9.5 + \left[\frac{7.5 - 4}{4}\right] 5$$

$$= 9.5 + \left[\frac{3.5}{4}\right] 5 \tag{3.24}$$

$$= 9.5 + [.875]5$$

$$= 9.5 + 4.375$$

$$= 13.875$$

$$Q = Q_3 - Q_1$$

$$Q = 25 - 13.875 = 11.125 \tag{3.25}$$

Variance and Standard Deviation

The variance and the standard deviation are related because the standard deviation is the square root of the variance. Since the variance is based upon the concept of the sum of squares and since this concept is crucial in the consideration of inferential statistics in the third section of the text, this notion, sum of squares, will be introduced here.

In order to introduce this concept the notions of deviation from the mean and the squared deviation from the mean are presented in Table 3.5. The first column of the table contains the actual scores; the second column the deviations from the mean and the sum of those deviations (0). The third column $(X - \overline{X})^2$ represents the squared deviations from the mean, and the sum of that column (44) represents the *sum of squares*—statistical shorthand for the *sum of the squared deviations from the mean.*

When we work with people's scores and we begin to use techniques of statistical inference, we will be interested in measuring the magnitude of individual differences, for example, as they affect the scores that are obtained in performance. The deviation from the mean (before squaring) evaluates the effect of these individual differences, but the sum of squared deviations from the mean, or the sum of squares, has the effect of weighting those differences which are farther from the mean, through squaring them, thus providing an index of the strength, or magnitude, of those differences.

TABLE 3.5   Scores, Deviations, and Squared Deviations[a]

SCORE (X)	$(X - \bar{X}) = \chi$	$(X - \bar{X})^2 = \chi^2$
10	3	9
9	2	4
9	2	4
8	1	1
7	0	0
7	0	0
7	0	0
6	−1	1
4	−3	9
3	−4	16
	$\Sigma (X - \bar{X}) = 0$	$\Sigma (X - \bar{X})^2 = 44$

[a]X represents a score; χ, the difference between X and $\bar{X}$; χ^2 represents a squared deviation of a score from the mean.

Conceptually, the sum of squared deviations from the mean, or the sum of squares, is easy to visualize. You take the difference between each score and the mean and square the differences. (As a check you might wish to add the χ column to be certain it adds to 0.) When you add the squared differences, you get the sum of squares. Thus:

$$\Sigma (X - \bar{X})^2 = 3^2 + 2^2 + 2^2 + 1^2 + 0^2 + 0^2 + 1^2 + -3^2 + -4^2$$

$$= 9 + 4 + 4 + 1 + 0 + 0 + 0 + 1 + 9 + 16 = 44$$

(3.26)

The procedure for obtaining the sum of squares by the deviation method provides the notion of the conceptual basis for the sum of squares, but it can be quite cumbersome to calculate, particularly when the mean of the distribution is not a whole number but is a decimal, such as 25.37. In this case you would have to deal with adding and subtracting decimals and squaring decimals and might more readily make mistakes. Fortunately, there are equivalent methods for determining the sum of squares which uses the raw scores directly, without going through the step of computing the deviation scores and then squaring and adding. They are:

$$\Sigma (X - \bar{X})^2 = \Sigma X^2 - \frac{(\Sigma X)^2}{N}$$

(3.27)

or

$$\Sigma (X - \bar{X})^2 = \Sigma X^2 - N(\bar{X}^2)$$

(3.27a)

TABLE 3.6   Scores, Squared Scores, and Sums

X (SCORES)	X² (SQUARED SCORES)
10	100
9	81
9	81
8	64
7	49
7	49
7	49
6	36
4	16
3	9
$\Sigma\, X = 70$	$\Sigma\, X^2 = 534$

Verbally (3.27), the sum of squares is the sum of the squared scores ($\Sigma\ X^2$) less the squared sum of the scores (($\Sigma\ X)^2$) divided by the number of scores (N) or (3.27a) the sum of the squared scores less the number of scores times the squared mean ($\overline{X}^2$). (Note: the placement of parentheses is used to dictate the order of operations.)

Using the scores in Table 3.6, we modify the procedure by summing the scores and the squared scores separately. This is shown in Table 3.6.

Then we calculate as in equation (3.28).

$$\Sigma\ (X - \overline{X})^2 = \Sigma\ X^2 - \frac{(\Sigma\ X)^2}{N}$$

$$= 534 - \frac{(70)^2}{10}$$

$$= 534 - \frac{4900}{10} \tag{3.28}$$

$$= 534 - 490$$

$$= 44$$

You will recall that the sum of the squared deviation scores was also 44. Thus, the two methods are equivalent. This, then, is the preferred procedure for calculating the sum of squares, which forms the basis for computing both the variance and the standard deviation.

The *variance* may be thought of as the mean sum of squared deviations from the mean: We can therefore obtain it by calculating as in equation (3.29):

$$s^2 = \frac{\Sigma X^2 - \frac{(\Sigma X)^2}{N}}{N} \tag{3.29}$$

or

$$s^2 = \frac{\Sigma X^2 - N(X^2)}{N} \tag{3.29a}$$

where s^2 is the statistical notation for variance.
Continuing from equations (3.28) and (3.29):

$$s^2 = \frac{44}{10} = 4.4 \tag{3.30}$$

$$s^2 = \frac{534 - 10(7^2)}{10}$$

$$= \frac{534 - 490}{10} = \frac{44}{10} = 4.4 \tag{3.30a}$$

If you recall, the variance was the mean squared deviation from the mean of the set of scores. Although the variance will be very useful in statistical inference, it is not really comparable to the mean which we calculated earlier, because it is the squared deviation. In order to obtain a more useful *descriptive* score, which can be used to clarify and interpret the mean of a set of scores, we need to obtain the square root of the variance. Thus, taking equation (3.29) or (3.29a) for the variance:

$$s^2 = \frac{\Sigma X^2 - \frac{(\Sigma X)^2}{N}}{N} \quad \text{or} \quad s^2 = \frac{\Sigma X^2 - N(\overline{X}^2)}{N}$$

we take the square root of both sides and obtain:

$$s = \sqrt{\frac{\Sigma X^2 - \frac{(\Sigma X)^2}{N}}{N}} \tag{3.31}$$

or

$$s = \sqrt{\frac{\Sigma X^2 - N(\overline{X}^2)}{N}} \tag{3.31a}$$

where s is the statistical notation for standard deviation. Thus, using the data from equation (3.28) in equation (3.31), we see:

$$s = \sqrt{\frac{534 - \frac{(70)^2}{10}}{10}} \tag{3.32}$$

$$= \sqrt{\frac{44}{10}}$$

$$= \sqrt{4.4}$$

$$= 2.098$$

or

$$s = \sqrt{\frac{534 - 10(7^2)}{10}} \tag{3.32a}$$

$$= \sqrt{\frac{534 - 490}{10}}$$

$$= \sqrt{\frac{44}{10}}$$

$$= \sqrt{4.4}$$

$$= 2.098$$

UNDERSTANDING YOUR SCORES

The purpose of descriptive statistical techniques, used to calculate the mean, median, mode, standard deviation, range, and IQR, is to reduce many scores to one or several scores which represent all the scores in the set. Measures of central tendency represent a focal point for the distribution in terms of balance (mean), midpoint (median), or frequency (mode). Measures of variability represent the spread of the distribution in terms of deviations from the mean (standard deviation), actual score values (range), or quartiles (IQR).

Every sample contains scores which vary in value; we will see later that these variations are the result of what we will call *error*. It is useful to think of error as *unidentified variation*, since in some cases we can identify and partition (separate out) some of this variability. It is useful to do this when feasible because of the concomitant reduction in the error.

Each raw score can be thought of as consisting of two components:

1. The *representative score* (mean) which is the same for every person in the sample, and
2. A *deviation score* which sums up all the individuating influences.

It is the deviation score which represents the "error" and which may be partitioned by identifying factors which contribute to the differences among individuals. An example, adapted from one presented by Diamond (1959), should be helpful.

Assume that we have obtained grip-strength scores of 12 males and 12 females using a hand dynamometer. The data are presented in Table 3.7 in a frequency-distribution format.

Using the overall mean as the starting point and ignoring the scores as separated by sex, we can calculate the variability of the set of scores. We have done that, and it is included in Table 3.7 as the standard deviation. You can see that the s for the total group is 22.53.

It would be helpful if we could identify other factors which would enable us to further partition the individual difference (error) portion which is represented by the standard deviation. (More properly, as we shall see later, we should use the sum of the squared deviations from the mean. The point to be made, however, can be illustrated more easily using a measure which is familiar.) In choosing a factor which might account for some of the variability which we observe in the

TABLE 3.7   Grip-Strength Scores of Men and Women

CLASS INTERVAL	SCORE	$f(M)$	$f(W)$	$f(M + W)$
126–134	130	1	0	1
116–125	120	2	0	2
106–115	110	0	0	0
96–105	100	3	1	4
86– 95	90	4	2	6
76– 85	80	2	2	4
66– 75	70	0	1	1
56– 65	60	0	3	3
46– 55	50	0	2	2
36– 45	40	0	1	1
Mean		99.17	69.17	84.17
Median		95.5	65.50	87.00
Mode		90	60	90
Std. Dev.(s)		15.52	18.01	22.53

raw data, we consider, as one possible alternative, information from the area of exercise physiology which suggests that some of the variability in the scores might be accounted for by the gender of the subject. Thus, if we separate the subjects by gender, we reduce the variability which is attributed to error. Observe that the variability for the females is 18.01, while the variability for the males is 15.52. Both of these are much less than that reported for the total group.

Thus, the variability in the raw scores can be attributed to three components:

1. Representative score (mean),
2. Gender component, and
3. Individual component (error).

By factoring out the gender component, we can reduce the variability which is attributed to error. We will see, in discussing research design, that this technique is important in minimizing error variance in experimental studies.

EXERCISES

For each of the following sets of data find the $\overline{X}$, Mdn, and Mo. [*Hint:* To find the Mdn you must order the data first.] Then for each set calculate the range, the interquartile range, and the standard deviation.

1. 21, 30, 20, 28, 9, 11, 16, 19, 20, 27, 24, 15, 7, 18, 23, 27, 19, 21, 20, 20, 26, 14, 24, 16, 12, 13, 29, 15, 17, 18

2. 13, 15, 17, 16, 17, 14, 12, 13, 16, 19, 20, 21, 17, 16, 15, 14, 15, 14, 15, 12, 15, 11, 15, 12

3. 3, 6, 8, 17, 17, 11, 13, 10, 14, 10, 9, 7, 18, 23, 22, 21, 21, 11, 11, 17, 19, 12, 14, 15, 17

4. a. 8, 6, 8, 7, 9, 8, 6, 8, 7, 8
    b. 10, 11, 12, 11, 9, 10, 11, 11

5. a. 4, 9, 3, 7, 5, 10, 8, 4, 3, 7
    b. 12, 7, 9, 10, 5, 6, 7, 5, 4, 3

6. a. 5, 4, 7, 3, 6
    b. 4, 2, 5, 1, 3

7. a. 2, 8, 9, 5, 7, 3, 11, 1, 10, 8, 6
    b. 5, 9, 2, 12, 7, 4, 13, 8, 10, 5
    c. 2, 2, 4, 6, 8, 8, 4, 2, 6, 3
    d. 6, 2, 3, 4, 7, 2, 5, 9, 8, 10
    e. 2, 3, 5, 11, 15, 13, 12, 12, 11, 2, 3, 4
    f. 2, 6, 4, 9, 5, 7, 4, 7, 9, 10, 13, 20, 18, 4

8. a. 63–65   2   b. 100–104   3   c. 25   1
        60–62   3   95– 99   5   24   2
        57–59   6   90– 94   7   23   3
        54–56   10   85– 89   9   22   4
        51–53   12   80– 84   21   21   6
        48–50   9   75– 79   19   19   7
        45–47   4   70– 74   14   18   4
        42–44   3   65– 69   8   17   3
        39–41   1   60– 64   6   16   2
                             55– 59   5   14   2
                             50– 54   3   12   1

REFERENCES

DIAMOND, S. *Information and error.* New York: Basic Books, 1958.

CHAPTER FOUR
WHAT RESEARCH IS

Research is life! It is curiosity! It is excitement! Research looks at the world as a source of information and of answers to questions that begin: why? how? what? Research involves putting together the pieces of a puzzle so that reasonable answers to specific questions may be found. Research, in an informal sense, is the basis of living. We learn from our successes and failures because we use an informal research process to evaluate our current activities.

THE RESEARCH PUZZLE

The idea of research as a puzzle is worth following, since it reveals research as an enterprise that can be viewed at different levels and in which pieces must fit together to form scenes or parts of scenes. In addition, it carries the notions of play and fun, of research as a game, as a search for the right pieces.

In research an important role is played by theory. Theories are the glue that holds the pieces of the research puzzle together. Theory also helps in the question-development, design, analysis, and discussion phases of the research study. It is unlikely that a particular study is unrelated to previous research or to theory. Researchers must be certain to review previous research on the topic before designing the study. There is always some research, perhaps on a related aspect, that will help in choosing subjects, tasks, measures. This is where a research program (to be discussed later)—a commitment to a series of research studies in a single area—is useful. The researcher or group of researchers can study various aspects of a theory or research area.

The introduction of the schema theory of motor behavior (Schmidt, 1975) and the research efforts which followed furnish a good example of how theory-based research can contribute to knowledge. It must be acknowledged that the theory was a good one in terms of ease of generating research, since it provided many postulates which could be easily translated into individual research studies. Over 200 studies have tested various aspects of schema theory since it was first presented. Students interested in following the development, extension, and testing of a theory should trace the research related to this theory. One way of doing this for schema theory is to locate a recent article on it and begin to trace the studies cited there. Another way, much quicker, is to conduct a computerized literature search. *Psychological Abstracts* may also be used to locate articles related to schema theory.

Let us now consider a jigsaw puzzle model as it might be applied to research in physical education (Rothstein, 1979, 1980). Most studies fall into a particular area of study within physical education: exercise physiology, sport psychology, motor behavior, motor development, sport sociology, biomechanics, sport history, sport philosophy, and so on. Rarely does a single study integrate areas, though this approach is on the increase. In contrast, the learner must be considered wholistically; at the learner's level it is impossible to separate adequately the various aspects. What is needed is to bring the diverse areas to bear on a particular aspect of performance. This problem can be envisioned as a huge jigsaw puzzle which has a particular title—for example, "Peak performance in sport." Research in many of the areas indicated above has yielded information relevant to the explanation of peak performance. The idea is to search out this information, piece by piece (study by study), and slowly build a picture out of the physiological, psychological, developmental, behavioral, sociological, biomechanical, and philosophical information relevant to peak performance. Perhaps parts of the picture are too light (not sufficient information); perhaps some of the information clashes (contrary studies). More likely some important pieces are missing which would clarify the picture. This lack signals areas in which further research is needed.

This puzzle is a large one, encompassing many areas of research in physical education. Each section of the large puzzle, however, can be used to create a puzzle of its own in relation to the question. For example, in exercise physiology peak performance can be evaluated by a number of different methods (e.g., chemical, physical). The smaller puzzle, like the larger one, may have gaps, inconsistencies, missing areas, pieces that don't quite fit. Research studies in this area should be designed to fill in gaps, clarify inconsistencies, and help to integrate the areas of the puzzle. These studies may be done by different individuals or by an individual or a group engaged in a research program.

A *research program* may be characterized as a group of studies on a single topic, or on closely related topics, undertaken by an individual or by a group working together. The individual or group may be described as filling in the pieces in a particular segment of a small puzzle by following a line of inquiry to a logical conclusion. Studies suggest further studies based on new and related questions, using slightly different techniques, slightly different subjects, slightly different tasks. It is similar to what lawyers do in a courtroom when they examine and cross-examine a witness. The idea is to tease out all the useful information that can be obtained from a line of questioning (research) so that reasonable and accurate conclusions can be drawn.

One approach to learning about research is by doing research—by starting with a small study on a topic of particular interest or by assisting a faculty member or other researcher with a study. The idea is to use research tools and techniques to find answers. Research is the process of finding answers to questions through observing, recording, organizing, and analyzing information. This information may be in various forms: verbal, visual, or numerical.

In the most general form, research involves the collection of information for the purpose of confirming or refuting guesses. You do this every day. You wake up and have a headache, so you reflect upon your past experience with headaches. Having decided that the symptoms resemble a sinus headache, you gather additional data. The weather report indicates that the weather is changing and a storm is predicted. You have identified a problem—why do you have a headache? You have gathered information about the problem— what reasons have been true in the past? could they be true now? You have selected the best "guess," the hypothesis that best fits the present situation—if I have a headache, then the weather must be changing. You have gathered information to test your hypothesis—listened to the weather report. You have analyzed the information—a storm is coming. You have concluded that your guess was correct and that you have a sinus headache. Therefore you take appropriate medication.

Later that same day you attend basketball practice. You begin your usual warm-up and then go over to take some foul-shot practice. You are not doing as well as usual. You use the same procedure as earlier to discover what you are doing wrong. You review the main points of the foul shot; you select one possible reason for your drop in performance; you evaluate your performance or ask someone else to do it for you; you analyze the information; you conclude that your elbow is in the wrong position; and you modify your performance.

Although you don't think of your analysis of everyday events as research, because you don't systematically proceed step-by-step and maintain careful records, you are doing research. You have a question, you observe what is going on, record (in your head) the information, organize the findings, and treat the findings in order to come up with an answer to your question or problem.

THE RESEARCH PROCESS

The difference between what you do for yourself and what researchers do is based on the need to be able to generalize the findings to more than just one person. Your findings are right for you but may not be correct for someone else because you are an individual and differ from other individuals in important ways.

In order to insure that their findings will be generalizable to large groups of individuals, researchers must be systematic, critical, and objective in their work. The *scientific method* is an abstraction of the process used by most persons who do research. If you approached ten different researchers and asked each one, "How do you do research?" you would get what would seem, on the surface, to be many different answers. If you extracted the core of each description, however, you would be likely to find a common thread, which would be the scientific method. This common thread also runs through the examples provided earlier. The scientific method is generally thought to consist of the following steps:

1. Problem identification
2. Information gathering
3. Hypothesis formulation
4. Design of study
5. Gathering of data
6. Analysis of data
7. Conclusion

Problem Identification

Perhaps the most difficult part of research for beginners is in the problem-identification stage. Many students who must do a research paper or who wish to engage in research for an independent study or thesis requirement find themselves without a problem that interests them. They ask their advisor, "What should I study?" The advisor may respond, "What are you interested in?" The student will reply, "I don't know." (Does this sound familiar?) It is unfortunate that many students have forgotten how to ask WHY?

> Why does this group do so much better at tennis than that group?
> Why did that team have a big lead going into the second half of the game and then lose by such a large margin?
> Why do I have so much difficulty hitting fast balls?
> Why do I do well in sprints but so poorly in long distance races?
> Why is it so much harder to concentrate on your opponent's home court?

Another related question prefix is, HOW can I?

How can I improve my tennis ability?
How can I motivate students to come to practice?
How can I increase my cardiovascular endurance?

None of these questions can be the direct basis for a research study in its present form, but each of them, and any that you can think of, can be worked around and distilled into acceptable research questions. Research can be performed for the purpose of trying out new methods of teaching skills or developing physical fitness; satisfying the researcher's curiosity; establishing the existence of some phenomenon; or exploring the conditions under which something occurs (Sidman, 1960).

Problem Refinement

Once a broad area or question has been identified, the problem must be refined so that it leads more directly to a research study. The problem must be refined so that the limits of the study can be clearly identified. This is not a quick and easy process. Let us use the question, Why does this group do so much better at tennis than that group?

1. Identify all the possible reasons you can think of that may explain why the groups are different.
   a. Past experience
   b. Playing environment
   c. Teaching method used
   d. Amount of practice time
   e. Sex of class
   f. Skill of teacher
   g. Equipment used
   h. Amount of instruction
   i. Visual skills of students
   j. Movement skills of students
   k. Time of day of class
   l. ....
   m. ....

2. Systematically go through the list that you have created and evaluate the feasibility of the reasons. You might get comments like this:
   a. Both beginning classes
   b. Both play on same courts
   c. Not certain of method (ask instructor)
   d. Same amount of practice
   e. Mixed classes
   f. ....
   g. ....

3. After reviewing each possibility, you will find some that seem different in the two classes. From among these you would choose one on the basis of your interest in that area. Suppose you have selected practice or teaching method. You would need to describe the critical differences between the two. The example uses teaching method.

Method 1   Teacher first presents short game with students playing close to net and then gradually moves the students back, concentrating on backhand stroke.

Method 2   Teacher uses traditional method, begins with long game, drilling forehand, backhand, serve, with some game practice. Short game not presented until the very end.

4. You have now identified the experimental variable, the specific treatment that you will manipulate in your experiment. Next you need to decide what you will measure as the index of performance. You need to choose something that can be measured objectively but that is likely to reflect tennis ability—something that is a good measure of what has been learned in the class. After much thought and searching you decide on a test which involves setting up situations and measuring the accuracy of placement of different shots. You call this the ABC Tennis Test. (If you made this test up, you would need to test it for reliability and validity before you could be certain of its usefulness. These topics will be covered later.)

5. You state the question in the form of a specific research question: "Does teaching method affect performance in tennis?" The question contains an experimental variable and a suggestion of what will be measured.

6. Your next step is to operationally define each of the terms so that the definition reflects how you will produce the condition (experimental variable) or how you will measure the outcome (dependent variable).

    New Method   (Describe how you will teach)
    Traditional Method   (Describe how you will teach)
    Performance   (Describe your ABC Tennis Test)

After accomplishing these steps you have a research question. You then proceed to *develop a hypothesis*. This is an if . . . then statement specifying the relationship between the experimental variable and the dependent variable. Your hypothesis for this study might be:

If traditional and new methods of teaching tennis are used, then the group using the new method will perform better.

The *design of the study* involves specifying rather precisely whom you will study, how you will assign them to groups, what you will tell them, what will be the same for the groups, how you will impose the experimental variable, how you will test them, and how you will collect and analyze the data. Also how long the study will run, where the groups will meet, opportunity for practice, and how they will practice.

Finally, you conduct the study, gather the data, analyze what you observe, and conclude whether either method was better. After you have completed the study, it is traditional to report the results of your findings publicly in verbal or written form.

An important aspect of research that we will deal with in subsequent chapters is research design. An understanding of this area is important to doing, reading, and applying research findings. *Research design* involves the study of how to plan the research study so that it is accurate in its findings and general in its scope. *Accuracy* refers to the degree to which your results reflect the experimental treatment rather than extraneous factors or error. *General in scope* indicates that the findings are applicable beyond the particular group of subjects in your study.

Before we consider specific elements of research design, a short introduction to experimental research is in order. The next chapter discusses the system and language of research to facilitate your understanding of the material to come.

REFERENCES

ROTHSTEIN, A.L. "Motor learning-patterns of advanced performers." In A. Stillman (Ed.), *Proceedings of 1978 fall conference.* Eastern Association of Physical Education for College Women, 1979, 28–38.

ROTHSTEIN, A. L. "Puzzling the role of research in practice." *Journal of Physical Education, Recreation and Dance,* 1980, *51,* 39–40.

SCHMIDT, R. A. "A schema theory of discrete motor skill learning." *Psychological Review,* 1975, *82,* 225–260.

SIDMAN, M. *Tactics of scientific research: Evaluating experimental data in psychology.* New York: Basic Books, 1960.

CHAPTER FIVE
THE EXPERIMENTAL
STUDY: AN OVERVIEW

This chapter is an introduction to the experimental study. It will help you to understand the specific aspects of research design that we consider next.

The goal of experimental research is *prediction and control.* The experiment achieves this goal by evaluating the effect of one or more treatments (independent variables) on the behavior of the subjects (as reflected by the dependent variable or variables). The relationship between the treatment and the observed behavior is one of cause and effect.

The nature of this cause-and-effect relationship enables the researcher to make statements which are *predictive.* These statements are hypotheses: if X, then Y. Statistical tests enable the researcher to estimate the predictive power of the findings with reference to a particular hypothesis. When behavior can be predicted with consistency in a variety of situations, then there is the potential for *control* of behavior. If the experimenter wishes to elicit a particular behavior, Y, the conditions associated with the behavior, X, can be recreated. This is possible, in theory, because of the nature of the experiment: the researcher assumes that the changes in the dependent variable were the result of the manipulations of the independent variable. Good experimental design increases the probability that this assumption is true.

ELEMENTS OF THE
EXPERIMENT

Every experiment, regardless of the topic under study, has certain elements in common. We shall define each of these elements and give examples.

The Problem

The problem is a question, a felt need, an issue which needs to be resolved, a difficulty. A problem may start with: "I wonder what would happen if . . . ," "Why does . . . ," "Which method of . . . ," "How can . . . ," "How come . . . ." Problems do not lead directly to research but must be developed into research questions. In order to do this you must first begin to specify, restrict, and define the elements within the problem. What is meant by a particular term? What stage of learning are you interested in? How can performance be measured? How long should training or practice continue? In whom am I interested?

These latter questions have the effect of limiting and delimiting the study. *Limiting the study* refers to the boundaries within which conclusions can be made. Are there errors in the methods, in the equipment, in the sampling? *Delimiting the study* refers to the study's scope. Is the study too narrow; did you restrict the type of subjects?

Limitations are avoidable by careful attention to research design and methods. Delimitations are a necessary part of experimental design; each study cannot be all things to all people, cannot provide answers to all questions. Answers to questions come in small doses. Many answers must be combined in order to adequately solve problems. Each study should *relate* to the broader question or problem but cannot answer the whole question or solve the whole problem.

Variables

Inherent in the identification of a specific problem to be investigated is the specification of the variables. These variables are called independent variables, dependent variables, control variables, subject variables, and organismic variables.

Independent variable   This is the set of events which is manipulated by the experimenter—the condition(s) imposed on the subjects. Independent variables are assumed to influence the behavior of the subjects and so the outcome of the study.

Dependent variable   This is the behavior which is measured by the experimenter. It is called dependent because we assume that the value that it takes is the result of (is dependent on) the manipulations of the independent variable.

Control variable   This is a variable which needs to be held constant so that its effect is the same for all conditions.

Subject variable   This variable can be used as an independent variable but is a constant characteristic of the individual. That is, subject variables cannot be manipulated or imposed on the subjects, but subjects can be assigned to experimental groups on the basis of these variables, and subject variables can be analyzed statistically. They may be related to organismic variables.

Organismic (intervening) variable   This is a variable that cannot be observed directly (motivation, arousal, perception) but must be inferred.

The Hypothesis

The hypothesis is a best guess. The phrase "best guess" may be misleading, since development of the hypothesis implies that the researcher has become familiar with the major theories, research studies, and other information bearing upon the topic of the research question. This thorough analysis of previous work in the field leads to the hypothesis and ultimately to the research plan. Thus, the hypothesis you formulate about the relationship between or among variables may not be a "guess" at all. The phrase "best guess" is used here to convey the notion that the outcome of a study is always somewhat uncertain. Otherwise, why do the study? The hypothesis is only a prediction. The more you know, however, the better your prediction and the more likely your hypothesis.

Once you have identified a specific problem and have stated it as a question (implying that you have consulted sources to obtain information about the particular problem or question), you can formulate the hypothesis. More specifically, the hypothesis is an "if X, then Y" statement which indicates the relationship between the independent variable and the dependent variable, where X symbolizes the independent variable and Y symbolizes the dependent variable. If, for example, the problem involved the usefulness of different training schedules for improving cardiovascular fitness, the hypothesis might be:

> If different training schedules are employed, then cardiovascular fitness will differ.

Here the independent variable is training schedule and the dependent variable is cardiovascular fitness.

In further developing the hypothesis and clarifying the study, the researcher formulates *operational definitions*. These provide the set of operations or procedures that will be used to produce (in the case of independent variables) or measure (in the case of dependent variables) elements in the study. An operational definition of training schedule might be:

> Training schedule is the number of days per week that an individual participates in an exercise program.

An operational definition of cardiovascular fitness might be:

> Cardiovascular fitness is the score attained on the Harvard Step Test.

The Experimental Plan

The construction of an experimental plan involves identification of the subjects, specification of the testing equipment, explanation of the precise experimental or research design, and specification of the methods and procedures to be employed in the study.

The identification of the subjects requires information on who, how many, age, sex, previous training, educational level, and so on. The specific information required depends on the particular problem and variables to be studied.

Specification of testing equipment should include any written tests, specific equipment (treadmill, computer equipment, videotape equipment, bicycle ergometers) together with makes and model numbers where appropriate, software or other programs or methods used to control the operation of equipment, and an indication of the placement of the equipment in the experimental setting and the subjects' relation to it.

The experimental design should indicate what the variables are and what specific values they can take. For most purposes it is helpful to think of each independent variable as a *factor* and to think of the values it can take as the *levels* of that factor. Thus, in our previous example the factor is training schedule and the levels that it can take (as inferred from the operational definition) are no days per week, 1 day per week, 3 days per week, 5 days per week, and 7 days per week. Thus, in later chapters we can talk of *factorial* designs as having one, two, or three factors, each having a specific number of levels. We will also specify designs as 2×3 factorial, $2 \times 2 \times 3$ factorial, where each number represents a different factor (independent variable) and indicates how many levels that particular factor takes in the study. The design also indicates the dependent variable and specifies how it is to be measured.

The plan should also indicate the specific procedures used to conduct the study and to produce the particular experimental conditions. It is useful to think of the procedures section of the experimental plan as a cookbook that another experimenter could follow, in conjunction with the rest of the plan, in exactly reproducing the conditions of your study in order to replicate what you have done. This section is also useful to individuals who wish to evaluate the goodness of your experimental design and plan for the purpose of ascertaining the reliability and validity of your findings.

Finally, it is necessary to include information on the treatment of the data. This includes information on how the raw measures will be reduced or translated into scores to be analyzed, what specific packages (if computerized) will be used to statistically treat the data, and what comparisons will be used in follow-up tests of the findings.

When other researchers consider the quality of your experiment, they will be concerned with the goodness of your design and will want to be certain that you have eliminated any errors that might confound or confuse the results of your study. Recall that the goal of the experiment is prediction and control and that we want to be able to indicate that the independent variable has *caused* the behavioral effects we observe.

GOOD EXPERIMENTAL DESIGN

A good experiment is one which provides the highest probability that the changes observed in the dependent variable are caused by manipulations of the independent variable. While we never *know* that this is true, we can increase the probability of its being true by following several rules in designing the study (Cox, 1958).

First, *systematic error should be avoided.* The only difference between or among the experimental groups should be the treatment (independent variable) imposed by the experimenter. Other differences are considered to be error and should be avoided. This means that different treatment groups should *not* have different experimenters, should *not* meet at different times of the day, should *not* be tested in different rooms, should *not* use different equipment, should *not* be different from each other in some way, and so on. If some of these differences were present, in addition to the experimental treatment, and a significant difference were noted, it would be impossible to determine whether the observed difference was the result of the experimental variable or of the systematic difference that was not controlled.

Second, *the precision of the findings should be maximized.* If the study is designed with this rule in mind, then the estimate of treatment differences obtained will differ from the "true" treatment differences only randomly. (This relationship between the sample mean and the true mean is further defined in the chapter on statistical inference using a dice-throw example.) Precision can be increased by reducing the variability of the subjects. For example, the study can use homogeneous groups of subjects rather than heterogeneous groups. Instead of using children of mixed ages in each group, the study can be limited to children of a single age group. We will see later that age may also be used as an additional independent variable.

Precision can also be increased by increasing the accuracy of measurement through fine calibration of equipment, extensive training of observers, and automatic recording of measures. A related technique for increasing precision involves increasing the number of subjects or the number of observations per subject or both.

Finally, precision can be increased through design of the study. This approach is considered at great length in the chapters on research design which follow.

A third requirement is that *the results should be generalizable beyond the particular experiment.* This requirement is met through careful attention to the relationship between the subjects used in the experiment and the larger group to which the results will be applied. If the subjects in the study are not representative of the larger population, then the results will reflect only the specific subjects used in the study rather than a larger population. Although this problem has usually been related to sampling procedures, more recently consideration has been extended to the study of using volunteer versus paid versus required subjects in experiments. In reviewing the literature for their recent study, Arnett and Rikli (1981) found that volunteers tend to be more intelligent, more sociable, more persistent, more arousal-seeking, and more in need of social approval than non-volunteers. In addition, volunteers score better on tasks involving speed, agility, strength, power, and endurance, are more verbal, are better educated, and tend to be higher in social class. Volunteers also tend to be more accommodating than nonvolunteers. Clearly, this is an important area for researchers to consider, since much of the research in physical education is conducted on volunteer and paid subjects but is intended to apply to the general population. A related problem which should be noted is that most of the research in physical education has been conducted on male subjects. It is unlikely that these findings are generalizable to female subjects. Fortunately, many researchers are recognizing this problem, and more research is being conducted using female subjects.

A keyword in science is parsimony, economy of explanation. Behavior should be explained as economically as possible. A similar notion in experimental design is simplicity. The more complicated or cumbersome the experimental design or statistical analysis, the less economical the explanation. Thus, *simplicity of experimental design should be practiced whenever possible.* This is particularly true in the early stages of a research program. In later stages, when variables have been identified, more complicated schemes may be intelligently designed to provide productive information.

REFERENCES

ARNETT, B. and RIKLI, R. Effects of method of subject selection (volunteer vs random) and treatment variable on motor performance. *Research Quarterly for Exercise and Sport*, 1981, *52:4*, 433–440.

COX, D. R. *Planning of experiments.* New York: Wiley, 1958.

CHAPTER SIX
RESEARCH DESIGN I:
CONTROL

A research study is a performance; each aspect is carefully planned and staged by the experimenter; the subjects are the players. It may be helpful to think of planning and staging a research study in much the same way as a playwright and director think of planning and staging a play or a choreographer thinks of planning and staging a dance performance. The techniques used by the experimenter in preparing the detailed *script* necessary for a flawless performance are called, collectively, *research design*. The overriding purpose or goal of the researcher is the approximation of "truth." While the researcher can never *know* the "truth," adherence to research design principles can eliminate sources of potential error in its approximation.

Principles of research design are intended to give the researcher *control* over the study at three stages: before, during, and after the experiment. The strategies the researcher employs prior to the study influence the overall plan, the subjects and how they are selected, and the way in which the data are collected. The strategies the researcher employs during the study influence the actual procedures involved in obtaining the data. Finally, the strategies employed after the collection of the data involve the statistical analysis. Even though the strategies are employed at three different stages—or, more properly, the strategies influence the three different stages—they are specified and evaluated prior to the initiation of the study.

The notion of *control* underlies all research and is especially important in the area of experimental research, where the researcher seeks to establish cause-and-effect relationships by manipulating events and then observing the effect on the subject. Ultimately, the researcher would like to predict and control behavior. In addition, these findings should be generalizable to a wider population then just those subjects who are in the experiment. For example, if a skill were presented in two different ways to two randomly assigned groups of individuals and one of the methods were shown to be statistically superior to the other, the researcher would like to suggest that the findings have some validity in the real world of teaching and learning. If the study had not been appropriately designed this might not be possible. A research design helps us "to answer research questions as validly, objectively, accurately, and economically as possible" (Kerlinger, 1973: 301).

WHAT IS CONTROLLED

When a researcher designs a research study, the goal is the control of *variance* (Kerlinger, 1973). In Chapter 3 on descriptive statistics we used the notion of variance as the mean squared deviation of the scores from the mean of the distribution. This is the same variance that is referred to here. This variance may be referred to more specifically as *error variance*. There are two other types of variance which, together with the error variance, comprise the *total variance* of the study. These are *experimental variance* and *extraneous variance*. The goal of research design is to facilitate the maximization of treatment variance, the control of extraneous variance, and the minimization of error variance (Kerlinger, 1973).

Maximizing Treatment Variance

The *treatment variance* represents the difference between or among the treatment conditions. A *treatment condition* (*T.C.*) is a particular value that the independent variable (I.V.) can take. An I.V. may be considered as a factor which can take on different values at the will of the experimenter. Each different value that it can take is referred to as a *level*. Where there is only a single I.V., each level of the I.V. is considered to be a treatment condition. Traditionally, each I.V. is designated by a sequential letter of the alphabet. By using this method, we can present designs and statistical procedures generically. Thus, Table 6.1 shows how treatment conditions are designated when we have one I.V. with two levels, and I.V. with three levels, and two I.V.'s with two levels each.

The experimenter's primary means of maximizing the treatment variance is to plan and design the treatment conditions so that they are as different as possible. Several examples are given below to enforce this notion. Each example presents a research question and suggests a means to maximize the treatment variance. Notice that only a single I.V. is used in each case to keep the examples as simple as possible—although, as will be shown later, in some cases a two-factor design, like design C in Table 6.1, would be more suitable.

TABLE 6.1   Designation of Treatment Conditions

A. One I.V., two levels	A_1 T.C. 1	A_2 T.C. 2	
B. One I.V., three levels	A_1 T.C. 1	A_2 T.C. 2	A_3 T.C. 3

C. Two I.V.'s, two levels each

	A_1	A_2
B_1	T.C. 1 (A_1B_1)	T.C. 2 (A_2B_1)
B_2	T.C. 3 (A_1B_2)	T.C. 4 (A_2B_2)

Example 1

Problem: What is the effect of frequency of exercise on cardiovascular fitness?

I.V.: Frequency of jogging a two-mile track.

    Level 1: Not at all (control group)
    Level 2: Once per week (experimental group)

Analysis: The treatment conditions (not at all and once per week) are apt to be so similar in their effect on the dependent variable (cardiovascular fitness) that a statistically significant difference is unlikely. It would be far better to use not at all versus three, four, or more times per week.

Example 2

Problem: What is the effect of teaching style on student skill acquisition?

I.V.: Teaching method.

    Level 1: Problem-solving
    Level 2: Guided discovery

Analysis: The teaching styles chosen are very close in their theoretical basis (cognitive learning theory) and both emphasize the responsibility of the learner in directing learning. It might be more productive to select teaching styles which are more dissimilar in their approach. (In addition, the researcher would want to consider the monitoring of teacher behavior using a Descriptive Analytic Scale to ascertain that the intended treatment was, in fact, being carried out.)

Example 3

Problem: What is the effect of age of subject on coincidence anticipation performance?

I.V.: Age of subject.

    Level 1: 7 years old
    Level 2: 8 years old
    Level 3: 9 years old

Analysis: As you might recognize on your own, the ages of the subjects are far too close to maximize treatment variance. The performance measures of the subjects are apt to overlap because of the lack of differentiation among the age groups. That is, there may be some 7-year-olds who are more mature and are like the 8-year-olds in their CA performance. The same is true for the other groups. Thus, it would be far better if you were to use, for example, students of ages 7, 9, 11 or 7, 10, 13. In addition, it is important that you delineate the age range of each group. Children of age 7, for instance, might range in age from 6 years, 6 months to 7 years, 6 months, so that the average age of the members of the group would, theoretically at least, be 7 years. You would also want to be aware of any unique characteristics of children of different ages with regard to your study (the review of literature should reveal these characteristics) so that you may take these into account in selecting the ages to be tested.

Controlling Extraneous Variance

Extraneous variance is the result of variables not accounted for in the design of the study which may influence the outcome of the dependent variable (D.V.). As an illustration consider Example 1 above, which proposes to study the effect of frequency of jogging on development of cardiovascular fitness. We have not considered the potential effect of variables such as sex, age, beginning fitness level, jogging pace, exercise heart rate, and the like on the outcome of the study. Since the statistical tests we use do not differentiate between error variance and extraneous variance, any extraneous variance which is not controlled is added together (by the statistical procedure) with the error variance. As such it becomes part of the denominator of the fraction (critical ratio) we use in determining the statistical significance. Thus, it is important to control whatever extraneous variance we can identify.

Several procedures can be used to minimize, nullify, and isolate extraneous variance. These include eliminating the variable; adding the variable as an additional I.V.; matching subjects on the variable; controlling the variance statistically; or using random assignment. Eliminating the variable, for example, using only low-fitness individuals in Example 1, may not be the most satisfactory method, since this also serves to limit the generalizability of the findings. (This is an important consideration in research design and will be considered more fully later.) If you limit the subjects to low-fitness individuals, you will not be able to apply your findings to all individuals but only to those of similar fitness levels.

Adding a variable   The method of adding the variable as another I.V. is useful, since this not only controls the extraneous variable but also allows you the chance to observe its effect separately and in combination with other I.V.'s on the D.V. Again consider Example 1. The problem was the effect of frequency of exercise on cardiovascular fitness. In order to increase the generalizability of the findings, while maintaining control of extraneous variance, we can add fitness level as an I.V. The added factor, then, is cardiovascular fitness, and it can have two or more levels: high and low; high, medium, and low. In determining these variables, the principles considered previously regarding maximized treatment variance apply. A researcher may also wish to control other variables by including them as I.V.'s. In Example 2, gender and age might be considered. The inclusion of these factors as variables might not be worthwhile when we consider the increase in complexity and the potential difficulties regarding interpretation. Further, any increase in I.V.'s also increases the number of subjects needed to insure adequate numbers in each treatment condition. The researcher should identify those variables related to the topic of interest and should rank them in order of relevance to the problem under study. To avoid the danger of overspecification of treatment conditions, only the one or two most relevant variables should be considered as additional I.V.'s. This is particularly so where interactions are observed. A single extreme example should suffice to illustrate the point.

Williams (1968) was interested in the effect of speed and direction of object flight and skill and age classifications on visuo-perceptual judgments of moving objects. Her I.V.'s were: skill level—skilled versus nonskilled; age—junior high school, high school, and college age; speed—fast and slow; horizontal angle—right, center, and left; and vertical angle—high and low. She noted significant interactions between or among a number of factor combinations: speed of object by horizontal angle; speed of object by vertical angle; age by speed by vertical angle; skill by speed by vertical angle; and horizontal angle by vertical angle. These interactions indicate that particular combinations of I.V. factor levels differentially affect the D.V. When these interactions occur, discernment and interpretation of their meaning is virtually impossible. Thus it is preferable to avoid complex interactions by choosing a limited number of I.V.'s that are nevertheless critical and relevant to the problem under consideration. Interactions will be treated further in Chapters 16 and 17 on analysis of variance.

Matching subjects   A third option is to match the subjects with respect to some extraneous variable that you think important to control. The subjects are matched—grouped into blocks—because the researcher has reason to believe that the subjects in each block will be more alike, in their response on the D.V., than subjects assigned completely at random. This design can be termed a *matched-group* or *randomized block* design. The ultimate matching is achieved via the *repeated-measures* design, in which each subject is exposed to all treatments. This is the highest form of control of individual differences that can be achieved. Unfortunately, there may be carry-over effects from one treatment to the next, and it is difficult to determine their presence or absence. Thus, the researcher often employs techniques of experimental matching, by which group equivalency is forced through equating subjects on a selected characteristic or measure. Procedures for matching are presented in Table 6.2

If matching is used, it is critical that the variable used for matching be fairly highly correlated with the dependent variable. In addition, the number and type of variables used for matching should be carefully evaluated, since matching on an inappropriate variable can be misleading, and attempting to match on more than two variables may seriously delimit the available subject sets.

Suppose that we wished to assess the effectiveness of a diet and exercise program on weight loss. Our available subject population might vary widely in weights, but we might not wish to use starting weight as a variable. However, if we realize that starting weight can have an effect on the rapidity of weight loss and on the total weight loss, we may wish to match subjects on weight or on body-fat percentage. In addition, since males appear to lose weight more rapidly than females, we may wish to match on gender or use it as an additional I.V. Further, since height of the subject is important with regard to weight, the subjects may be restricted as to height so that males range in height from 5'7" to 5'9" and females from 5'4" to 5'6". (This is not the only way to conduct this experiment, but it is a possible way.) Thus, in choosing to use gender as an additional I.V., we have a 2 × 4 factorial design, where gender has two levels: male and female, and diet-exercise program has four levels: diet only, exercise only, diet and exercise, and control. The initial weights of the subjects will be used in matching them. In Tables 6.3 to 6.5 please notice that after subjects are matched on the selected characteristic, they are assigned (within the weight sets) to the diet-exercise groups at random. It is critical to use random assignment to the experimental treatment groups after matching on weight, because a systematic assignment procedure would result in the groups' being unequal at the start; random assignment may produce unequal groups, but it is unlikely. (The flaw of systematic assignment after matching will be illustrated in Tables 6.6 and 6.7.)

As can be seen in the totals for each gender group and for the grand total, the average weights of each of the groups are quite similar. Suppose, however,

TABLE 6.2   Procedure for Using Matching to Control Extraneous Variance

1. Ascertain the value of the matching characteristic for each subject.

2. Rank the subjects on this characteristic. (If an additional variable, such as gender, is involved, rank the subjects independently within each of the groups.)

3. Mark off sets of subjects equal to the number of experimental conditions to be accommodated. (The number of subjects must be a multiple of the number of experimental groups.)

4. Use random procedures to assign the first subject in a set to a treatment, then randomly assign the second subject in the set, and so on until all subjects in the set have been assigned.

5. Repeat step 4 for each set until all sets have been assigned.

TABLE 6.3 Example of Using Matching: Initial Subject Weights Ranked by Gender Groups and Blocked into Sets of 4

MALES			FEMALES		
S101	270		S201	210	
S102	268	Block 1	S202	209	Block 1
S103	265		S203	207	
S104	260		S204	205	
S105	259		S205	197	
S106	257	Block 2	S206	196	Block 2
S107	254		S207	195	
S108	250		S208	190	
S109	245		S209	188	
S110	240	Block 3	S210	185	Block 3
S111	235		S211	180	
S112	232		S212	173	
S113	230		S213	170	
S114	225	Block 4	S214	169	Block 4
S115	220		S215	165	
S116	210		S216	160	

that we had used a systematic assignment procedure in which we assigned the subjects in 1, 2, 3, 4 order. This is illustrated by Tables 6.6 and 6.7.

It is clear that even without any treatment having occurred, the control group of males averages 13 lb lighter than the diet group, while the female control group averages 9 lb lighter than the diet group. This is an unfair advantage, and the difference is obvious when the results of this systematic procedure are compared to those of the random procedure. The same procedure could have been used with any characteristic chosen. Had we selected percent body fat as the characteristic on which subjects were matched and then used this measure, rather than weight, as the dependent variable, we could have controlled for height and it would have been unnecessary to restrict our subjects by height.

TABLE 6.4 Matched Subjects Assigned to Diet-Weight Groups Using a Random Procedure

		DIET	EXERCISE	D & E	CONTROL
Males	Block 1	S103	S102	S101	S104
	Block 2	S106	S108	S107	S105
	Block 3	S111	S110	S112	S109
	Block 4	S114	S113	S115	S116
Females	Block 1	S202	S203	S201	S204
	Block 2	S207	S206	S208	S205
	Block 3	S212	S211	S210	S209
	Block 4	S214	S215	S216	S213

TABLE 6.5   Average Weights of Groups Using Random Assignment

		DIET	EXERCISE	D & E	CONTROL
Males	Block 1	265	268	270	260
	Block 2	257	250	254	259
	Block 3	235	240	232	245
	Block 4	225	230	220	210
	$\overline{X}_M$	245.5	247	244	243.5
Females	Block 1	209	207	210	205
	Block 2	195	196	190	197
	Block 3	173	180	185	188
	Block 4	169	165	160	170
	$\overline{X}_F$	186.5	187	186.25	190
	X_T	216	217	215.125	216.75

TABLE 6.6   Matched Subjects Assigned to Diet-Weight Groups Using Systematic Assignment

		DIET	EXERCISE	D & E	CONTROL
Males	Block 1	S101	S102	S103	S104
	Block 2	S105	S106	S107	S108
	Block 3	S109	S110	S111	S112
	Block 4	S113	S114	S115	S116
Females	Block 1	S201	S202	S203	S204
	Block 2	S205	S206	S207	S208
	Block 3	S209	S210	S212	S212
	Block 4	S213	S214	S215	S216

TABLE 6.7   Average Weights of Groups Using Systematic Assignment

		DIET	EXERCISE	D & E	CONTROL
Males	Block 1	270	268	265	260
	Block 2	259	257	254	250
	Block 3	245	240	235	232
	Block 4	230	225	220	210
	$\overline{X}_M$	251	247.5	243.5	238
Females	Block 1	210	209	207	205
	Block 2	197	196	195	190
	Block 3	188	185	180	173
	Block 4	170	169	165	160
	$\overline{X}_F$	191.25	189.75	186.75	182
	X_T	221.125	218.625	215.125	210

Although matching is an alternative in controlling extraneous variance, it is not the ideal procedure for doing so. If, for example, the researcher matches the subjects on a task or attribute different from that used in the study, then he/she must be concerned about the relationship (correlation) between the scores on the variable used for matching and the D.V. This necessitates using previous research findings or pilot testing to determine the correlative during the design phase of the study. Use of a different task is particularly important when exposure to the actual experimental task is contraindicated.

Use of initial trials of the actual experimental task for matching gives similar concern. How high is the correlation between initial performance on an experimental task and final performance? Work in psycho-motor skills by Fleishman and various colleagues (Fleishman, 1957, 1960; Fleishman and Hempel, 1954, 1955; Fleishman and Rich, 1963) has shown that, in many instances, the correlations between initial and final performance are very low. Thus, equating subjects on the basis of initial performance may be misleading.

Another problem relates to the notion that other variables, not used for matching, which may be unknown or unattended to by the experimenter, may introduce a systematic bias by virtue of their relationship to the treatment conditions or the matching variable or both. Random assignment is not associated with systematic differences, since the process is aimed at the creation of groups that are unbiased on both known and unknown variables.

Last, but not the least of the difficulties, researchers using matching procedures often find it necessary or prudent to match on more than one variable— for example, sex, I.Q., and socioeconomic status (SES). The biasing effect of unknown variables is still a problem but, in addition, the difficulty of finding a subject pair match increases as the number of matching dimensions increases. As a result, closeness of match may suffer as the available subjects are exhausted. Fortunately, as we shall see in the next section, initial subject differences on relevant dimensions can be accounted for statistically through use of analysis of covariance.

Statistical control   The fourth alternative is to control the extraneous variance statistically. Statistical methods exert control through isolation and quantification of variances. In effect, when you include a variable as a factor in your study you are enabling statistical control to operate. Each score obtained in a study can be thought of as the sum of many factors. Diamond (1959) illustrates this aspect of control in his proof of the variance law: "The sum of squares (and hence also the mean square, or variance) measures the aggregate strength of all the factors which are responsible for individual variations in scores" (p. 63). He presents two sets of scores *A* and *B*, termed the parent sets, the means of which are used to generate a third set, *C*. Consider a modification of his example, presented as Table 6.8. (Note that the assumption of additivity of effects is critical to this example.)

For simplicity we will use a total of subjects distributed across three fitness

TABLE 6.8   Interaction of Factors (A and B) to Produce Resultant Scores (C)

	FITNESS LEVEL			
	$A_1 = 20$	$A_2 = 15$	$A_3 = 10$	$\overline{A} = 15$
$B_1 = -0$	$C_{11} = 20 - 0 = 20$	$C_{12} = 15 - 0 = 15$	$C_{13} = 10 - 0 = 10$	
$B_2 = -5$	$C_{21} = 20 - 5 = 15$	$C_{22} = 15 - 5 = 10$	$C_{23} = 10 - 5 = 5$	
$B_3 = -10$	$C_{31} = 20 - 10 = 10$	$C_{32} = 15 - 10 = 5$	$C_{33} = 10 - 10 = 0$	
$\overline{B} = -5$				

levels: high, medium, and low doing sit-ups under three added-weight conditions: none, 5 lb, 10 lb. The questions we ask are: What is the number of sit-ups a high-, medium-, or low-fat individual can be expected to do? What is the decrement in sit-ups expected as a result of the weighted condition?

The resulting scores, shown as C_{11} through C_{33}, are the ones we would obtain in our experiment. The sum of the means of A and B yields the mean of C as

$$\overline{A} + \overline{B} = \overline{C} \tag{6.1}$$

where

$$\overline{A} = \frac{EA}{a} + \overline{B} = \frac{EB}{b} = \overline{C} = \frac{EC}{ab} \tag{6.2}$$

Thus

$$\overline{A} = \frac{45}{3} + \overline{B} = \frac{-15}{3} = \overline{C} = \frac{90}{9} \tag{6.3}$$

and

$$15 + (-5) = 10 \tag{6.4}$$

In a similar manner we can show the relationship among the variances. This is important, because the variance is the central focus in statistical procedures. Thus, if we have a study in which there are several variables, we can identify the amount of variance each contributes to the total variance. This can be important because variance not so partitioned becomes part of the error variance and serves to lower the resulting critical ratio in the generic formula:

$$\text{critical ratio} = \frac{\text{treatment variance}}{\text{error variance}} \tag{6.5}$$

As the error variance increases, owing in part to the contribution of extraneous variance, the critical ratio will decrease, and statistical significance will be more difficult to attain.

Random assignment   The final procedure to be discussed is random assignment. This is generally considered to be the best way to control extraneous variance, since proper and thorough randomization permits the researcher to assume that the experimental groups are statistically equal in all possible ways. The groups may not, in fact, be equal, but if randomization was properly accomplished, the probability of their being equal is greater than the probability of their not being equal.

Randomization is the assignment of members of a population so that every member of that population has an equal probability of being chosen. The principle of randomization may be illustrated by considering a single die. A die has six sides. If it is properly balanced, each side has an equal chance of occurring on each toss. This means that *in the long run* each side should appear an equal number of times. Table 6.9 illustrates this principle. A computer program was designed to simulate the toss of a single die and to record the frequency with which each side occurs. (You could do this experiment yourself but it would take too long; nevertheless you might wish to try it on your own.) You can see that as the number of tosses increases, the incidence of each face is more nearly equal.

The real plus of using randomization is in its action when each subject to be selected represents different levels of several factors. A good example is provided by Kerlinger (1973: 124–127). For population consisting of 98 senators, he recorded: political affiliation, Republican or Democratic; region, South or North; vote on issue 1, yea or nay; and vote on issue 2, yea or nay. He then

TABLE 6.9   Probability Using a Single Die with Increasing Tosses

		NUMBER OF TOSSES								
		36	72	144	288	576	1152	2304	4608	9216
1	N	6	10	32	36	86	223	400	792	1521
	%	16.67	13.89	22.2	12.5	14.7	19.3	17.4	17.2	16.5
2	N	8	11	26	53	100	186	374	856	1520
	%	22.2	15.28	18.1	11.4	17.1	16.1	16.2	18.6	16.5
3	N	7	15	25	43	106	218	349	762	1488
	%	19.4	20.8	17.4	14.9	18.1	18.9	15.1	16.5	16.1
4	N	7	10	29	60	98	151	370	753	1553
	%	19.4	13.89	20.1	20.8	16.7	13.1	16.0	16.3	16.9
5	N	4	7	18	53	103	185	404	721	1606
	%	11.1	9.7	12.5	18.4	117.6	16.1	17.5	15.6	17.4
6	N	4	19	14	43	83	189	407	724	1528
	%	11.1	26.4	9.7	14.9	14.2	16.4	17.7	15.7	16.6
	expected N	6	12	24	48	96	192	384	768	1536
	expected %	16.67	16.67	16.67	16.67	16.67	16.67	16.67	16.67	16.67

calculated the percentages for each of these four items for the total population ($N = 98$). He found 64 Democrats and 34 Republicans, or 65% and 35%, respectively. Further, he found 66% Northerners and 34% Southerners; 30% who voted yea and 70% nay on issue 1; and 51% who voted yea and 49% nay on issue 2. If we convert these findings into predicted frequencies for the samples of 20, we find that the observed frequencies are very close to what would be expected if the random samples reflected the population from which they were drawn. For ease of comparison, percentages are presented in Table 6.10.

TABLE 6.10   Votes by Party, Region, and Issue

	POLITICAL PARTY		REGION		ISSUE 1		ISSUE 2	
	DEMO.	REPUB.	N	S	Y	N	Y	N
Overall %	65%	35%	66%	34%	30%	70%	51%	49%
Group 1%	70%	30%	50%	50%	35%	65%	65%	35%
Group 2%	65%	35%	60%	40%	30%	70%	45%	55%
Group 3%	70%	30%	80%	20%	25%	75%	45%	55%
All groups	68%	32%	63%	37%	30%	70%	50%	50%

Two important points are illustrated here. First, although four factors were recorded, the random procedure resulted in samples which were reasonably related to the population from which they were drawn. Second, the approximations of the proportions in the original population were closer when the three samples of 20 were combined into one (see "All groups"). Thus, randomization does seem to randomize *all* factors; and as the sample size is increased, the proportions in the population are more closely approximated. This second point is illustrated in the die example, too. As the sample size was increased, the observed distribution of tosses more closely approximated the expected distribution.

Another reason for use of proper randomization procedures has been mentioned previously but deserves to be reiterated here. In conducting research, especially where treatment conditions are imposed on groups of subjects, the researcher wishes to insure, to the extent it is feasible, that the differences, if any, observed at the conclusion of the experimental treatment are the result of the treatment conditions imposed on the subjects rather than the expression of preexisting group differences resulting from the use of inadequate or inappropriate procedures.

Another important aspect of sample size concerns the assumption that the sample mean is an estimate of a population value. The larger the sample, the more accurate the estimate of those population values. In Chapter 9 on statistical inference we will see this principle illustrated using a computer program. For now, however, let us compare the means of the sample die tosses in Table 6.9. The theoretical mean of a perfectly distributed set of tosses of a single die is 3.5, the means for the sets of tosses in Table 6.9 are given in Table 6.11.

TABLE 6.11   Means for Sets of Die Tosses Presented in Table 6.9

N	$\overline{X}$	N	$\overline{X}$
36	3.19	1152	3.40
72	3.69	2304	3.53
144	3.12	4608	3.42
288	3.59	9216	3.52
576	3.49		

As the number of observations increases, the approximation of the "true" mean becomes more accurate. In Chapter 9 on statistical inference it is shown that with larger sample sizes the standard deviation and the standard error of the mean decrease. Estimates of the population mean based on large samples are far more dependable.

MINIMIZING ERROR VARIANCE

As indicated in equation (6.5), there is an inverse relationship between error variance and the critical ratio, expressed as t, F, or other statistic. As the error variance increases, the critical ratio decreases and statistical significance becomes less likely. Thus, it is important that error variance be minimized. In discussing extraneous variance we noted that uncontrolled extraneous variance is combined with error variance in the statistical analysis, since the tests cannot differentiate between the two.

Unfortunately, error variance is not easily identified or controlled, so the best we can do is to recognize its sources and act to minimize their effect. *Error variance* is defined as unpredictable variation in measurement. It may be due to individual differences among subjects, errors in the measurement of performance, fluctuations in subject performance from trial to trial or day to day, unintended differences in testing or instruction of subjects, and unplanned variation in the experimental setting: presence of spectators, change in experimenters, noise levels, lighting, or temperature.

Reduction of error variance can be accomplished by increasing experimental control and by increasing reliability of measurement. Experimental control can also be increased by moving from field-based research to laboratory research. It is more difficult to produce statistically significant findings in a field-based study than in a laboratory study. It is simply too difficult to minimize error and to control extraneous variance. This means that the maximizing of treatment variance is more critical in field studies.

Another method of minimizing error variance is through increasing the reliability of measures used to assess performance or behavior. Reliability is reflected by the consistency of measurement of performance. Simply, the relative position of individuals for one administration of a test will be similar to the relative positions on a second administration of the test. A totally unreliable test would give totally different rankings for the same group of individuals from one testing to another. The error variance will decrease as reliability of measurement increases.

Diamond (1959) contrasts information and error by indicating that the information is the message—in our case the treatment variance—and the error is the noise, or the error variance. There are many sources of noise in experiments, some of which were enumerated previously. Diamond indicates that "experimental technique and research design strive to reduce error; statistical technique measures the error which remains" (p. 8).

A final word about statistical significance is in order here. If the outcome of a statistical analysis reveals statistical significance, then the researcher correctly states that the groups are different with respect to the experimental treatments. If the outcome reveals no statistical significance, then the researcher can say only that the groups differed only by chance. A finding of "no difference" cannot be indicated. Analysis of equation (6.5) reveals why. If two groups (or any comparison of groups) are statistically different, then the treatment effect was sufficiently large to overcome the experimental error, or the experimental error was so small that even small experimental treatment differences would be statistically significant. If, on the other hand, the outcome was not significant, we do not know if the problem was in the lack of treatment differences or in the amount of error variance. We therefore do not know for certain whether there were no treatment differences, hence we cannot state that the groups were not different.

REFERENCES

DIAMOND, D. *Information and error*. New York: Basic Books, 1959.
FLEISHMAN, E. A. A comparative study of aptitude patterns in unskilled and skilled psychomotor performances. *Journal of Applied Psychology*, 1957, *41*, 263–272.
FLEISHMAN, E. A. Abilities at different stages of practice in rotary pursuit performance. *Journal of Experimental Psychology*, 1960, *60*, 162–171.
FLEISHMAN, E. A. and HEMPEL, W. E. Jr. A factor analysis of dexterity tests. *Personnel Psychology*, 1954, *7*, 15–32.
FLEISHMAN, E. A. and HEMPEL, W. E. Jr. The relationship between abilities and improvement with practice in a visual discrimination reaction task. *Journal of Experimental Psychology*, 1955, *49*, 301–312.
FLEISHMAN, E. A. and RICH, S. Role of kinesthetic and spatial-visual abilities in perceptual-rotor learning. *Journal of Experimental Psychology*, 1963, *66*, 6–11.
KERLINGER, F. N. *Foundations of behavioral research (2nd ed.)*. New York: Holt, Rinehart & Winston, 1973.
WILLIAMS, H. G. The effects of systematic variation of speed and direction of object flight and of skill and age classifications upon visuo-perceptual judgments of moving objects in three-dimensional space. Unpublished doctoral dissertation, University of Wisconsin-Madison, 1968.

CHAPTER SEVEN
RESEARCH DESIGN II: FACTORS AFFECTING VALIDITY

The purpose of research, experimental research in particular, is to ascertain the effect of one or more independent variables on one or more dependent variables. Thus, in designing the study, the researcher must be careful to avoid design pitfalls which may compromise the results and interpretations of the study. The study must provide adequate controls or account for factors which may threaten the internal and external validity of the study. Knowledge of these factors will enable the researcher to prevent or ameliorate their effect.

It is important to realize that a single study cannot be expected to contribute far-reaching conclusions. Rather, as suggested in Chapter 4, the researcher must think in terms of a program of research, in which each study focuses on a slightly different perspective. Drew (1980) has suggested that early in a research program the researcher may sacrifice the representativeness of the study (external validity) to gain more control and precision over specific variables; later on, however, the reverse may apply: the researcher may sacrifice control and precision in order to gain applicability. This chapter focuses on threats to precision and representativeness in order to increase awareness and appreciation of the nature of research.

Validity, when used in a statistical sense, indicates that a test or measuring instrument actually measures what it is intended to measure. Thus, a test of tennis skill would reflect an individual's skill in playing tennis; if you score higher on this test than another individual, you are likely to be a better tennis player. We determine statistical validity by calculating the correlation between the test we are using and a known measure of what we intend to test. In the tennis example, scores on our tennis test might be correlated with the final standings in a ladder tournament. In the case of *statistical validity* we obtain a numerical indication of the extent to which our test reflects what we say it does. This is not true in the case of *research design validity*.

Validity, used in connection with research design, is based on an assessment of the technical soundness of the study. This validity is of two types: internal validity and external validity. These concepts and their relationship to research design have been discussed at length by Campbell and Stanley in a classic and often-cited work (1963). This work provides the basis for much of this chapter.

Internal validity is an absolute necessity; it is to research design as reliability is to a test or other measure. It is the extent to which the results of an experiment reflect the effects of the independent variable or variables manipulated. Can the researcher be certain that the observed results are not influenced by: history, maturation, testing, instrumentation, statistical regression, differential selection, experimental mortality, or selection-maturation interaction (Campbell and Stanley, 1963)? A study that is not internally valid is worthless.

Once the internal validity has been established or planned for, the researcher must consider the extent to which the study has *external validity*. Are the results of the study generalizable to other settings, other populations, other treatment and measurement variables? Are the findings representative (generic) or are they unique to the particular conditions of this study? If a particular treatment produces particular results in this study, can it be expected to have a similar effect under other conditions? The factors which threaten external validity are: effects of testing or instrumentation, Hawthorne effect, interaction between selection bias and the experimental variable, and multiple-treatment interference.

FACTORS AFFECTING INTERNAL VALIDITY

The factors to be considered in this section threaten the internal validity of a study because they offer rival hypotheses to the one posed by the experimenter: that is, if (treatment variable) is manipulated, then (dependent variable) will be affected. If controls and safeguards are not adequate, the results may be a consequence of any number of factors the researcher's design does not control and thus may limit or confound the extent to which the researcher can ascertain if, in fact, the experimental treatment or treatments used in the study actually made a difference. The possible effect of these factors may not have been considered by the researcher. Although a number of these threats to internal validity can be evaluated through the use of a control group, others may require the use of more sophisticated designs.

History

Evaluating the role of *history* involves answering the question: Did events that were unplanned (that is, not treatment-related) occur between measurements in the study, and if so, what effect did these events have on the outcome of the study? As an example consider a study in which there is a single treated group and performance measures are taken before and after the administration of a treatment: *one-group pre-post design*. This might occur in a situation in which an instructor has planned pre- and posttesting of students to ascertain skill improvement in a particular activity as a consequence of a new method of organizing practice. All students in the class are exposed to the new practice organization; thus there is no control group to use for comparison. The pretest is administered on one day, practice takes place over a period of several weeks, and on the final day of the study a posttest is administered. A matched pairs *t*-test is applied to the data and reveals a significant change in the performance scores. The instructor concludes that the practice method was effective and decides to use that method in the future.

Since the study uses only a single group, the instructor has no way of knowing for certain that the treatment caused the improvement. All that is evident is that there were differences in performance. It is difficult to generate any explanations as to *why* these results were observed so that further research might elucidate the findings. One of the problems might, in fact, be *history*. Any number of factors related to unplanned events may have affected the final performance scores. Suppose, for example, that the task used in the study was basketball foul shooting and that between the pre- and posttests the town recreation department had conducted several clinics on basketball which the students attended. Had there been a control group, it is possible that their performance might have increased from the pretest scores also, leading the instructor to investigate further. In addition, if performances of both groups were improved, a *t*-test might reveal a significant difference in favor of the experimental group— that is, in spite of the increase in the performances of both groups, the experimental group maintained a statistically significant advantage over the control group.

As another example consider a study to assess the attitude of nonhandicapped students toward handicapped students who have been mainstreamed into physical education classes. A researcher administers Form A of an attitude-toward-the-handicapped scale to students in a school district in September. In June, Form B is administered. The researcher finds that there have been significant changes, in a positive direction, in the attitudes of the students toward their handicapped peers. On the basis of the findings the researcher concludes that the practice of mainstreaming has a positive effect on attitudes of students toward their handicapped peers in physical education.

Since there was no control group of students who were not mainstreamed, the researcher cannot be certain that the observed results were not the result of some unplanned event (history). Suppose, for example, that one of the units in the social studies curriculum for that year was planned to coincide with the International Year of the Handicapped and that a unit was similarly planned for the science curriculum. It is possible that these units of study, alone or in combination with the mainstreaming, were the critical factor in the change in attitude. The use of one or more control groups in combination with one or more experimental groups would enable the researcher to more readily ascertain the role of mainstreaming in attitude change.

While a control group cannot indicate that a historical event occurred compromised the internal validity of the study, its conclusion can serve to attune the researcher to these events should they occur by virtue of their potential unexpected effect on the performance of the control group. This is true whether the design is a *two-group pre-post design* or a *two-group post-test-only design*. It is a good idea in any case to entertain the idea that events you are unaware of may influence your results.

Maturation

Evaluating the role of maturation involves answering the question: Did changes in the individual(s), occurring over time, affect the outcome of the study? The subjects may perform differently on a posttest because they are older, in better physiological condition, more or less fatigued, or more or less interested than at the time of the pretest. This factor is particularly important to consider in studies involving children, or studies involving tasks which are fatiguing or boring and repetitive, or studies where the subjects are athletes in the midst of a competitive season. It is known, for example, that as children mature, their reaction time improves (decreases). Thus, if a study utilizes a task which relies to some extent on reaction time, children's task performance may improve as they mature simply because of the decrease in reaction time. A study conducted by Stadulis (1971) will serve as the basis for the example to be presented here.

The purpose of Stadulis' study was to evaluate coincidence-anticipation behavior in children of ages 7, 9, and 11. His task required subjects to press a key as a ball, propelled down a 6-foot inclined track, passed a designated intercept point. The ball was propelled at four different speeds, designated as slow, medium slow, medium fast, and fast. Owing to the nature of the mechanism used to propel the ball down the trackway, the medium fast ball was projected as a backup ball, and the ball slowed markedly after it had traveled approximately 4 feet. This occurrence will serve as the basis for an example.

Imagine that a researcher is able to create a backup ball, as in Stadulis' study, and is interested in testing the effect of information feedback on children's performance of a complex coincidence task (the backup ball). The researcher decides that previous research has shown that feedback is useful in improving performance and so decides not to use a control group in favor of comparing two different types of feedback, specific and directional. If the researcher decides to use 8-, 10-, and 12-year old children, and if the study extends over a lengthy period of time, then maturation, in the form of improved reaction time, may result in better performance even if the feedback treatment and practice are ineffective. How so? Accuracy in coincidence-anticipation performance depends upon a subject's initiating a response one reaction time and one movement time (if applicable) before the moving object arrives at the intercept point. If a subject's reaction time is short, then that subject can delay initiation of a response for a longer period than a subject whose reaction time is shorter. This means that the subject with the shorter reaction time can watch the ball longer before making a move. It is entirely likely that the subject with the shorter reaction time will see the ball decelerate and will adjust initiation accordingly, thus responding to a slower ball, and completing the response with a smaller error, while the subject with a longer reaction time will respond to the faster ball (before deceleration) and will likely have a large negative error (be very early in the response).

Thus, improved coincidence-anticipation performance may be the result of maturation (with improvements that occur in reaction time enabling the child to wait longer to initiate the response and therefore respond to the actual speed, after deceleration, rather than to the initial speed, before deceleration) rather than of learning based on the feedback. This same situation can be true in studies in which special methods of teaching children to throw, jump, run, and so on are used to improve performance. As the children mature, physiological changes enable them to throw further, jump higher, and run faster, and the changes observed may have nothing whatever to do with the treatment administered. The use of control groups is critical, and proper planning for their role in the experimental design is of the utmost importance.

Maturation should be interpreted as *all changes that can take place in an individual over time*, not just those changes due to growth and aging (Drew, 1980). These changes can take place between sessions of an experiment, between pre- and posttests, or within the testing session. They include changes in level of hunger, fatigue, attention, boredom, as well as age.

If subjects get bored by tedious experimental procedures, they may do worse on a posttest than a control group which did not have the opportunity to become stale from too much repetitive practice. If societal changes occur over a period of time covered by a research study (for example, changes in acceptance of women in heretofore nontraditional occupations), then subjects may reflect these changes, rather than any experimental treatments which may be administered. During the course of a long experimental session subjects may become hungry, and their performance may decrease as a result. Fatigue and waning of attention may have similar effects which are unrelated to the experimental treatment conditions.

The interpretation of maturation as growth and aging is more widely accepted than that of hunger, boredom, fatigue, etc. However, these other factors may affect the internal validity of the study and should be considered as potential threats during the development of the research plan.

Drew (1980) has further suggested that maturation, in the general sense, can also act to invalidate or confound a study by introducing systematic differences between groups in a comparative study. For example, if a researcher were to administer a fitness test to all of one experimental group in the morning and to another in the afternoon (a common occurrence in intact class experiments), fatigue may affect the performance of the afternoon group. To avoid this systematic difference the researcher would want to randomize the groups so that some members of each are tested at each time. In some cases this may not be possible because of class schedules, so the researcher might plan to use a common time for both groups.

Pretesting

Evaluating the effect of pretesting involves answering the question: Did the pretest serve as a learning experience for the subjects or otherwise sensitize them to the experimental conditions of the study? This is an important consideration in internal validity, because the pretest is not part of the experimental method but rather a way of assessing the effect of the treatment. If, for example, a health educator were interested in whether seeing a movie on lung cancer changed the attitude of high school students toward smoking as measured by a smoking attitude survey, it would be important to ascertain whether taking a pretest on attitude toward smoking induced an attentional set or any type of preset so that the students responded differently to the movie if they took the pretest than if they did not. Thus, the design would necessarily include a group that had the pretest and saw the movie, then took the posttest; a group that did not take the pretest, saw the movie, then took the posttest; and two additional groups that completed the testing as described above but did not see the movie. The design is illustrated in Table 7.1.

TABLE 7.1   Design to Evaluate the Effects of Pretesting

GROUP NO.	PRETEST	MOVIE	POSTTEST
1	Yes	Yes	Yes
2	No	Yes	Yes
3	Yes	No	Yes
4	No	No	Yes

A comparison of Groups 3 and 4 would indicate whether the pretest was a learning experience. If these groups had different scores on the posttest, then we might assume that the pretest did have an effect. If these groups were not statistically different, then we can turn to groups 1 and 2. This will indicate whether the pretest had an effect in conjunction with the movie. If the answer is no, then we can compare 1 and 3 to determine whether the group who viewed the movie changed their attitude toward smoking as measured by the difference in the scores from the pretest to the posttest.

Hawthorne Effect

The *Hawthorne effect* refers to the notion that subjects change in sensitivity to treatment or in performance simply because they are in an experiment or investigation. The name arose from an observation made at the Hawthorne Plant of the Western Electric Company (Homans, 1965). Researchers in the original experiment (Roethlisberger and Dickson, 1939) were attempting to study the effects of different conditions, such as rest periods, lighting levels, and methods of pay, on worker productivity. The changes were applied to a small group of workers in the plant over a period of a year. The experimenters noted that the production rate rose steadily over the course of the year, regardless of whether the work hours were lengthened or shortened, the lighting was brighter or dimmer, or the rest periods more or less frequent. They concluded that the most influential factor was the motivation engendered by the subjects' awareness that they were in an experiment and so were "special."

The Hawthorne effect must be suspected in any study in which the experimental conditions are known to the subjects. For example, in early studies on the use of videotape replay (VTR) in teaching motor skills, experimenters often used two conditions: one group participated in a traditional (control group) learning situation, and a second, experimental group, was treated exactly like the control group except for the addition of VTR as a means of administering feedback. In some of these early experiments VTR was found to be effective in contrast to the "traditional" method. The question arose, however, as to whether the traditional method was a reasonable control for the VTR condition. It was reasoned that merely seeing oneself on TV might be sufficient to enhance performance even if the feedback presented in this way had no effect. Thus, rather than using control groups that had no exposure to VTR whatsoever, researchers used control groups that merely viewed themselves on TV but did not see themselves performing the task. When this was done, many of the studies reported no significant differences between the control and experimental groups.

Thus, any conditions which may be motivational to the subject or which can be viewed as "attention" may serve to increase performance, even in the absence of a treatment effect. If the experimenter suspects that this might be the case, then these conditions must be applied to the control group as well as to the experimental group or, if this is contraindicated, must be controlled or eliminated. The effect of this special attention may be positive or negative for the subject, depending upon the stage of learning. The interested reader might consult some of the research on arousal in ascertaining the potential effect that perceived attention might have on experimental subjects.

Instrumentation

Instrumentation constitutes a potential threat to internal validity through changes in the devices used to measure performance or through differences in the individuals who serve as observers or scorers. Devices used in measuring and recording data in experiments or those used in producing experimental conditions must be initially calibrated and then checked and recalibrated as necessary throughout the experiment. Bicycle ergometers, treadmills, tethering devices, muscle stimulators, decade timers, high-speed cameras, different forms of written tests, and so on must consistently record or control performance for all subjects during all testing periods.

Suppose, for example, that a researcher wished to ascertain the effect of different exercise prescriptions on the cardiovascular efficiency of subjects. A test that might be used to evaluate cardiovascular efficiency is a submaximal stress test on a treadmill. The researcher might proceed as follows: administer a pretest to potential subjects and eliminate those subjects whose cardiovascular efficiency was better than a predetermined level; randomly assign subjects who meet the criterion to a number of treatment and control groups; conduct the study using proper procedures to control and monitor exercise levels (such as monitoring exercise heart rates and adjusting loads to maintain assigned levels); administer a posttest; and analyze the data using an appropriate statistical test (analysis of variance or covariance depending on the variance of the pretest scores). Instrumentation might affect the results of the experiment if, by chance, scheduled maintenance, including calibration of the treadmill or of any equipment used to monitor cardiovascular efficiency, were done during the pre- or posttesting phases of the experiment. Either way, the scores of some subjects would be systematically different from those of other subjects, invalidating the results of the study. If by chance this occurred during the pretesting phase of the experiment, the researcher could salvage the study by eliminating the subjects tested prior to the maintenance and/or calibration and testing additional subjects to obtain the number required. If this occurred during the posttesting phase of the study, the experimenter might, if enough subjects had been posttested prior to the maintenance, and, most important, testing had not been proceeding in any systematic fashion, eliminate subjects tested postmaintenance and analyze the data of the remaining subjects. Properly, however, the data for all subjects should be considered as pilot data and the study repeated with new subjects.

The second aspect of instrumentation noted relates to differences in observers or scorers used in obtaining data for the study. Concerns, problems, and solutions to some difficulties related to the role of the experimenter in research have been considered at length by Rosenthal (1976). In fact, in a recent application of meta-analysis procedures to 345 experiments Rosenthal and Rubin (1978) found that interpersonal expectancy effects were alive and well in both laboratory and everyday situations. A related but somewhat dissimilar problem concerns the effect that an observer has on the subjects in the study. In studies on descriptive analysis of teaching, for example, the presence of an observer, or of video recording equipment, in the classroom may serve to change the student's behavior so that the observed behavior is not typical. Another problem in this same vein concerns the gender of the experimenter and the possible effect this might have on the outcome of the study. In a study which included psychological testing of male college athletes (Berger, 1972), a male test administrator was employed because of the possibility that the athletes might respond differently to the test items in the presence of a female test administrator. Finally, various temporary and permanent characteristics of the observer or recorder may have an effect on the observations. Characteristics such as fatigue, location, eyesight, perception, memory, prejudice, illness, and emotional state can produce inconsistent, inaccurate, and consequently worthless data. Differences in observations may also result from learning; i.e., the judgment of the observers improves with practice in observing: they become more sensitive to changes, more discriminating in their observations, more demanding in their expectations.

In many experiments the use of observers is unavoidable. It is important that these observers be thoroughly trained and practiced to minimize errors and inconsistencies. This is particularly true when more than one observer is used to record data in the same experiment. (Use of different observers should be avoided if at all feasible because of the possibility that subject-experimenter interaction might influence the results.) If it is absolutely necessary to use more than one observer/recorder, then the results of the different observers should be compared in a pilot study after they have been trained, and in designing the experiment subjects should be assigned at random to the different observers.

Statistical Regression

In certain studies in physical education subject characteristics may be used to assign individuals to groups. For example, a researcher may be interested in the effect of method of teaching on individuals of high skill and low skill, or the effect of various training programs on individuals of high, medium, or low fitness levels. There are a number of possible research studies in which individuals at the extremes of some characteristic are used. Also recall that the use of extreme groups was recommended earlier as a way of maximizing the treatment variance. This is still an appropriate suggestion, but it is important to consider statistical regression as a potential threat to internal validity. In fact, consideration of the effects of statistical regression supports the need for using extreme groups in research design.

Statistical regression refers to the tendency for individual and group scores to move toward the mean. Thus, individuals whose scores are extremely high can be expected to score lower in the future, while individuals whose scores are extremely low can be expected to score higher in the future. This change will occur regardless of whether the treatment actually makes a difference.

An interesting discussion and application of statistical regression is provided by Efron and Morris (1977) in a presentation of what has come to be called *Stein's paradox*. Stein's discovery is paradoxical because it sometimes contradicts what is an elementary law of statistical theory. Until 1955, when Stein discovered the paradox, the mean was considered to be the best estimate of future performance. If a baseball batter had a batting average of .250, we would consider this a "true" estimate of batting ability, the average rate of success. If we wanted to estimate how many hits the player would get in the next 100 times at bat, we would, logically, report 25. Efron and Morris (1977) report that "In traditional statistical theory no other estimation rule is uniformly better than the observed average" (p. 119). Stein's theory is a paradox because it sometimes contradicts this elementary law. Stein's method, which calculates estimators based on regression toward the grand mean of a group of batters, for example, tends to predict future averages more accurately. If a batter is doing better than the grand mean, the method will decrease the average; if a batter is doing worse, the method will predict an increase in the average.

In an illustration of Stein's method, using the James-Stein estimator (a simplified version of the method), Efron and Morris use batting averages from the first half of a season to estimate averages for the second half of a season. They indicate that

> The statistician who employs Stein's methods can expect to predict the future averages more accurately no matter what the true batting abilities of the players may be. (p. 119)

In illustrating Stein's paradox they used the batting averages of all major-league players as recorded after their first 45 times at bat in the 1970 season. The subjects were all batters who had been at bat 45 times prior to the day the data were collected. There were 18 players who met the criteria. Each player's average was determined by the number of hits divided by the at-bats. Each player's average was denoted by y. Next they obtained the average of the averages (called the grand average), denoted by $\bar{y}$. If a player's batting average was above the grand mean, then it had to be reduced; if below, then it had to be increased. The resulting value for each player was designated z. The z value for each player was determined by the formula:

$$z = \bar{y} + c(y - \bar{y}) \tag{7.1}$$

The value c is the shrinking factor. In the case of the baseball data which Efron and Morris report, the $\bar{y} = .265$ and the $c = .212$. The value c is obtained by:

$$c = 1 - \frac{(k - 3)\sigma^2}{\Sigma\,(y - \bar{y})^2} \tag{7.2}$$

In this equation k is the number of unknown means.

In the application of this procedure to the batting-average example, Efron and Morris found that

> for 16 of the players the initial average is inferior to [z] . . . as a predictor of batting ability. The . . . estimators, considered as a group, also have the smaller total squared error. (p. 120)

Differential Selection
of Subjects

Evaluating the role of differential selection of subjects requires answering the question: Was there bias in group composition or in the way subjects were assigned to groups? The term "bias" relates to any *systematic* difference between or among treatment groups. Bias in group composition has always been a problem when intact classes or groups are used and assigned, as a group, to an experimental treatment.

Suppose, for example, that a researcher was interested in determining the effect of knowledge of movement principles on skill acquisition and performance or the effect of knowledge of physiological principles on adherence to an exercise program. Assume the subjects are high school students and, for convenience in administering the treatment, the researcher randomly assigns one physical education class to the treatment and another physical education class to the control condition. At the conclusion of the experiment it appears that the treated group performed far better than the control group. It is possible that the groups were different to begin with in a way that made the treated group more susceptible to the treatment.

Suppose, for instance, in the case of the movement-principles experiment, that the only physics class given was scheduled during the time that the control-group physical education class met. Students in the physics class, therefore, could be in the treatment group but could not be in the control group because of the schedule. A physics student might be in a better position to benefit from the presentation of movement principles than a nonphysics student, biasing the groups. A similar scenario could be developed for the physiological-principles group. For this reason intact, preformed classes should not be used if at all possible. If it is necessary to use classroom units, these individual units should be structured, using random procedures, from a pool of subjects who are available at both times.

Another example of bias is in fitness studies done in industrial settings. Often groups are constituted by using individuals who volunteer to participate in an aerobic fitness program as the experimental group while a group of matched nonvolunteers are used as the control group. The very fact that individuals volunteer to participate may indicate an underlying difference between the two groups which may be related to the treatment variable being manipulated and thus may constitute a systematic difference which may influence the outcome of the study. It would be far better to avoid the possibility of bias by using the volunteers only and assigning them, using random procedures, to an experimental group or a control group. Bias is more prevalent in studies in which preformed groups are utilized.

It has been suggested (Drew, 1980) that the researcher ascertain whether, in fact, random assignment procedures have yielded groups which are statistically equal on antecedent factors. It is suggested that "chance variation will, in a certain number of instances, result in significantly unequal groups before treatment. When this occurs, the groups should be placed back in the subject pool and reconstituted" (p. 168).

Experimental Mortality

Evaluating the role of experimental mortality involves answering the questions: Was there a differential loss of subjects from the different treatment groups? What effect is this likely to have on the outcome of the study? Is the composition of the groups different at the end than at the beginning of the study? As an example, consider a study on the effect of a weight-loss program on change in body weight. The researcher randomly assigns a group of overweight volunteers to an experimental and a control group. An initial weigh-in reveals that the groups are not statistically different. The treatment group follows a specific weight-loss program; the control group is untreated. Over the course of the study a number of subjects drop out: some move away; others lose interest; still others drop out for other reasons. Experimental mortality would negatively affect the internal validity of the study if subjects who dropped out of the experimental groups tended to be those who were unsuccessful in losing weight. If this were the case, then the average weight loss of the experimental group would appear greater than if all subjects were to remain in the study until the end.

Experimental mortality can occur in any study. In the study on industrial fitness described in the previous section, differential loss of subjects who found exercising an imposition, or painful, or boring, or who lacked the motivation to continue, might artificially inflate the changes over time. In a motor learning experiment using a complex coordination task, individuals who are frustrated in a no-feedback condition might drop out and thus affect the outcome in contrast to a group which received feedback.

One means of evaluating the potential threat of experimental mortality is to compare the scores of those who drop out to those of individuals who continue. If, up to the point of dropping out, there is little difference, then it may be safe to assume that performance differences did not play a role. If, by contrast, significant differences are noted, then the study has been compromised. Differences in averages may reflect differences in group composition as much as differences in treatment.

FACTORS AFFECTING
EXTERNAL VALIDITY

The factors to be considered in this section affect the extent to which the results of a study can be generalized to other situations, other populations, other tasks, other measures. Evaluation of external validity answers the question: "Are the results of this study representative, generic, typical, or are they unusual or unique to the particular conditions of the study?" The contrast between internal and external validity may be likened to the contrast between "pure" and "applied" research. The focus of pure research is on how a given factor, such as feedback, operates. Thus, the researcher is interested in maintaining as uncontaminated an experimental setting as possible and chooses control of the experimental setting over the potential for application of the findings to the real world. In applied research, by contrast, the researcher is concerned with the application of the findings to events of the real world. In order to accomplish this the researcher must, of necessity, give up some fine experimental controls. In a similar fashion the researcher who wishes to gain external validity—application of the results in the real world—must be prepared to sacrifice some internal validity to accomplish this goal.

Commonly, in the initial stages of exploring a topic the researcher will pay close attention to control of the factors which bear upon the question of internal validity. In subsequent stages of investigation attention may shift to applicability or transferability of the findings to other forms of the variable, different tasks, different subject populations, different settings, and different measures.

Representativeness

A critical consideration in assessing external validity is the degree to which the sample is representative of the population to which the results of the study are to be applied. If, for example, an administrator wished to determine the physical fitness levels of incoming college freshman at an urban university, testing would be done on a sample selected at random from all those students in the freshman class. If the incoming class contained disproportionate numbers of males and females, the investigator might wish to use a proportional random sample to insure that the elements in the sample were proportional to the population. (If the researcher wished to determine the fitness levels of the males and the females independently and was not concerned with overall figures, then proportional sampling would not be necessary.)

Suppose that an experimenter wishes to assess the effect of different types of feedback on motor skill acquisition of elementary school children. If the researcher uses an artificial laboratory task and uses elaborate mechanical procedures in administering the different types of feedback, then the likelihood of application to the real world of the gymnasium and sport is poor. In addition, if the population used is a unique one, from a private school with particular socioeconomic characteristics or from a school for special populations, the results may not be generalizable.

As a final example, assume that an experimenter is interested in evaluating the effectiveness of a new method of teaching biomechanics and uses unique testing procedures to evaluate the outcome. The findings may not be representative of what would occur with the new method if traditional types of testing were employed. The researcher has confounded the results and compromised the external validity.

The factors identified in these examples are considered more specifically in the sections that follow, together with some other aspects of external validity. It is clear, however, that the evaluation of external validity centers on whether the experimental conditions imposed compromise the findings' representativeness and thus their generalizability.

Interaction of Treatment and Subjects

Characteristics of the particular subjects treated in the study may interact with the experimental conditions in a way that precludes generalizing the results to other populations. For example, suppose a researcher was concerned with the effectiveness of videotape replay on the learning of the tennis serve and, because of availability, chose an intermediate tennis class. One group was used as a control group and, because the researcher wished to avoid the "Hawthorne effect," they saw themselves standing at the baseline preparing to serve but did not see themselves serving. The other group saw themselves serving repeatedly over a period of days. Both groups saw themselves for the same amount of time over the days of the experiment. The results showed that the videotape feedback was effective and significantly enhanced the learning of the serve. The researcher therefore recommended its use to colleagues. One of the instructors decided to replicate the study with another tennis class, but one of beginning students. The procedures employed were precisely as in the initial study, but the results were different; this time there was no significant difference in learning of the serve. Based on research published by Rothstein and Arnold (1976) it is likely that the treatment, videotape replay, interacted with the level of the subjects, intermediate players, so that they benefited from the treatment while players of different skill levels might not so benefit.

Effect of Pretesting

It is not uncommon to read studies in which the experimenter used a pretest or warm-up task prior to the administration of the experimental treatment. This is done to provide baseline information, data on which to block subjects, to give the subject an idea of what is expected in the task, or, in some physical activities, to prevent injury. Rarely are pretest procedures, practice, or formal warm-up tasks used in the real world prior to the teaching of a new skill. Thus, the use of these procedures in the experiment may sensitize the subjects so that they benefit from the treatment in a way in which students in classes might not.

The most used examples of this threat to external validity are attitude scales. A researcher interested in the effect of violence in sport on spectator aggressiveness would typically administer an aggressiveness scale prior to the viewing of a sport contest in which violence occurred. Half of the subjects would watch a violent sport contest, half would watch a neutral contest, and then a second form of the scale would be administered following the game. It is possible that the pretesting sensitized the subjects and thus compromised the results of the study.

As a rule a design called a Solomon four-group design is used to ascertain the effect of the pretest on the outcome while at the same time enabling the researcher to have a tight, internally valid design. The experimental design is:

Group 1	Pretest	Treatment	Posttest
Group 2	Pretest	Nothing	Posttest
Group 3	Nothing	Treatment	Posttest
Group 4	Nothing	Nothing	Posttest

Comparison of the various groups enables the effect of the pretest to be ascertained.

Hawthorne Effect

The Hawthorne effect is sometimes called "reactive effects of experimental procedures," and is something like a student in a tennis class saying to the instructor, "I never do well when you are watching but I am terrific when you aren't here." This factor was discussed at length under internal validity; the explanation and discussion are the same here. Its relevance to external validity should be clear; since the situation is perceived as special to the subjects, they behave uniquely; this may not be true in the real world.

Multiple-Treatment Interference

In some studies it is necessary or convenient to have the same subject undergo more than one, or all, of the treatments used in a study. A researcher, for example, was interested in comparing coincidence-anticipation performance under central-vision and peripheral-vision conditions. In order to obtain comparable data, it was necessary to test all subjects under both conditions. A counterbalanced design was used so that half of the subjects were tested first under the central-vision condition and second under the peripheral condition; the other subjects were tested first under peripheral, then under central conditions. The analysis revealed that the effect of order of testing was significant. Thus, the researcher was unable to reach a conclusion regarding the factor of interest. In this case another means would have to be found to account for differences in coincidence-anticipation performance between subjects. A possible solution would be to pretest the subjects and use their performance scores as a covariate. In this way half the subjects could be randomly assigned to the central-vision group and half to the peripheral vision group. In order to ameliorate the effect of pretesting, the experimental treatment could take place several days after the baseline performance had been established.

SUMMARY

The factors presented in this chapter represent threats to the internal and external validity of experiments. Failure to acknowledge and control the potential confounding which these factors can produce may lead to studies which lack precision and representativeness. These factors may be applied in the analysis of research designs to determine the adequacy of a particular design for producing accurate and generalizable results. Designs which score poorly on internal validity are the one-shot case study, the one-group pretest-posttest design, and the intact-group design. Designs of this type should not be used unless there is absolutely no other possible means of designing the study. The critical difference between these designs and other, more appropriate designs is randomization of subjects. Thus, if intact classes must be used, the treatments can be randomly assigned to the groups, and if different instructors are used, they should be randomly assigned as well. An alternative is to schedule a large group of students for the same period, randomly divide these into two groups (classes), and then randomly assign both the treatments and the teachers. In field-based physical education studies this may in fact be a possible solution to the use of static groups.

Accurate research is internally valid and enables the researcher to report with some certainty that the experimental treatment did, in fact, produce the observed effects. *Representative* research is externally valid and enables the researcher to apply the results to other samples from the same population to indicate that the findings would be similar for other, comparable students. One of the most universally accepted methods for dealing with threats to the internal validity of research is the use of a control group. Sampling and random assignment are two methods for dealing with threats to external validity.

REFERENCES

BERGER, B. Relationships between environmental factors of temporal-spatial uncertainty, probability of physical harm, and nature of competition and selected personality characteristics of athletes. Unpublished doctoral dissertation, Teachers College, Columbia University, 1972.

CAMPBELL, D. T. and STANLEY, J. C. Experimental and quasi-experimental designs for research on teaching. In N. L. GAGE (Ed.), *Handbook of research on teaching.* Chicago: Rand McNally, 1963.

DREW, C. J. *Introduction to designing and conducting research.* St. Louis: C. V. Mosby, 1980.

EFRON, B. and MORRIS, C. Stein's paradox in statistics. *Scientific American,* 1977, *236:5,* 119–127.

HOMANS, G. Group factors in worker productivity. In H. PROSHANSKY and B. SEIDENBERG (Eds.), *Basic studies in social psychology.* New York: Holt, Rinehart & Winston, 1965, 592–604.

ROETHLISBERGER, F. J. and DICKSON, W. J. *Management and the worker.* Cambridge, Mass.: Harvard University Press, 1939.

ROSENTHAL, R. *Experimenter effects in behavioral research (rev. ed.).* New York: Irvington, 1976.

ROSENTHAL, R. and RUBIN, D. B. Interpersonal expectancy effects: The first 345 studies. *The Behavioral and Brain Sciences,* 1978, *1,* 377–416.

ROTHSTEIN, A. L. and ARNOLD, R. K. Bridging the gap: Application of research on videotape replay and bowling. *Motor Skills: Theory into Practice,* 1976, *1,* 35–62.

STADULIS, R. E. Coincidence-anticipation behavior of children. Unpublished doctoral dissertation, Teachers College, Columbia University, 1971.

CHAPTER EIGHT
RESEARCH DESIGN III: SAMPLING

An important consideration in the last chapter was the external validity of a study—the extent to which the results of a particular study have meaning beyond the particular settings, the particular conditions, and the particular subjects. Are the results representative of other settings, other procedures, and other populations? Do the principles discovered have universal application?

While the generic nature of the results is important, a far more critical question is whether the results are applicable to the population the researcher *intended* to study. If, for example, a researcher intends to study the effects of two different training programs on the aerobic fitness of high school women, then the subjects selected for the study must be representative of high school women. That is, they should be similar in age, weight, fitness level, academic standing, and so on to a population of typical high school women. (The obvious difficulty that individuals of different beginning fitness levels may respond differently to the training program may be accounted for by employing fitness level as a second I.V., by using a pretest-posttest design, or by using an analysis-of-covariance procedure with incoming fitness level as a covariant.) The extent to which the results of a study are representative of the *intended* population depends on sampling techniques. Although sampling techniques are usually considered in connection with descriptive research, they are important to the design of any type of research, and their study will serve to add to the repertoire of skills and tools you are developing.

SAMPLING

With the exception of the Census, research is based on samples. These samples are considered in relation to the population.

Population   A population consists of all units possessing certain characteristics which have been specified by the researcher. It is the complete set of subjects which might be tested—for example:

All college women

All college women in a particular city

All college women in a specific section of a city

All college women at a certain college

All college women at a certain college majoring in physical education

All college women at a certain college majoring in physical education who are juniors

All college women . . .

The examples above represent increasingly smaller populations, owing to the delimitations that have been set by the specific characteristics. At some point it will be possible to define the population so specifically that all generalizability is lost.

Sample   A sample represents that portion of the population from which measurements are actually obtained. In order to generalize findings to the total population, the sample must be selected in a way that assures its representativeness.

Sampling is concerned with the ways in which representativeness can be assured; otherwise the results you obtain will give a false impression of the population you wish to characterize. Sampling techniques which may be used are simple random sampling, systematic sampling, stratified sampling, cluster sampling, and proportional sampling.

A *simple random sample* insures that each element in the population has an equal chance of being selected. Usually each element (a person) is assigned a number. Then a table of random numbers is used to select a sample of size 20. In practice you would begin at some random point in the table and then, using two columns, if you have a total of 80 elements, you would select the units having the numbers appearing in the table until a total of 20 units had been selected. (Numbers which repeat or which are not in your population would be skipped.) To illustrate, a portion of a random-number table is reproduced below and an example follows.

55216	20770	32281
04336	22031	66210
06546	76265	31767
38571	78215	43330
54715	08616	27856
14824	22626	76461
60740	42466	08314
52300	17483	66716
47318	47125	82854
28165	27747	60583

We enter the table at random. The randomly chosen point is indicated by the bar over the digits 16. (This point could be chosen by closing your eyes and pointing.) Proceeding down the column of two-digit numbers, we would choose elements 16, 36, 46, 71, 15, 24, 40, (skip 00, no element), 18, 65, (go to next full column, last two digits), 70, 31, (skip 65, we have already chosen that one), (skip 15, we have already selected that one), 26, 66, (skip 83, no unit), 25, 47, (go to next full column, last two digits), (skip 81, no element), 10, 67, 30, 56, 61. We have selected 20 elements for our sample. (If we had 100 or more units, we would have had to use three columns for selection of our sample.)

Choose a sample of 10 units from a population of 50, beginning at the same place. Which units would constitute your sample? Tables of random numbers may be found in any statistics textbook in the library, if you should have need to use them in the future. Random numbers can also be generated by computer.

Systematic samples are selected by using a list of all the elements, determining how many elements you require, and then sampling at intervals that will provide the number of elements you want. For example, if you have 1000 elements and you require 100 in your sample, you will need to select every tenth element. In this procedure the first unit is selected at random by selecting a number between 1 and 10 from the table of random numbers (close your eyes and point, then follow the two-digit numbers until you come to one that is between 1 and 10). You start with that element and select every tenth element after it.

The only problem that may arise in systematic sampling is related to the arrangement of the elements in the list. If, for example, we required a sample of schools in the Bronx for some study and we took an alphabetical list, we might find the Catholic parochial schools underrepresented because they were all grouped together in the list under St. _____ . If you anticipate this, you might change the list so that these schools are arranged by order of the saint's name. To avoid such problems, the list should be examined carefully and then steps taken to avoid the bias which might be created.

Stratified sampling may be regarded as a modification of the previous methods. It is used to insure that all subsets of the population are represented in appropriate numbers. Suppose, for example, that you wish to survey students at a certain college to ascertain their opinion about intercollegiate athletics. You might wish to be assured that you have sufficient numbers of seniors, juniors, sophomores, and freshmen to obtain a representative opinion. You therefore decide ahead of time to obtain your sample equally from all segments of the student body. You can use more complex methods by increasing the number of characteristics you include in your sampling plan. You might add sex to the plan to assure that you obtain sufficient males and females.

Cluster sampling is used when sampling by element would be cumbersome or impossible. If, for instance, a researcher wants to study the impact of physical activity on elementary school children in a certain city, it might be impossible to generate a list of all elementary school children. Therefore, the researcher might generate a list of elementary schools which provide a physical activity program and one of those that do not. The next step would be to randomly sample schools from the two groups. Each school would be considered to be a cluster. The next procedure would involve sampling within the cluster to obtain the actual children who would be studied. (It is possible to cluster-sample at the second stage and choose classrooms within the schools, then randomly select the children from the classrooms which were randomly chosen.)

Proportional sampling can be used with any method previously discussed. It involves determining the percentage representation of particular groups within the population and then sampling so that proportionate representation in the sample is the same as in the population at large. If we are sampling college students and we know that the proportions are

Seniors	20%
Juniors	35%
Sophomores	25%
Freshmen	20%

then in our sample of 1000 students we would want to have numbers that are equivalent to the percentages represented on campus. Thus, we would calculate how many of each class we require by the following:

$$
\begin{aligned}
\text{Seniors} &= 1000(.20) = 200 \\
\text{Juniors} &= 1000(.35) = 350 \\
\text{Sophomores} &= 1000(.25) = 250 \\
\text{Freshmen} &= 1000(.20) = \underline{200} \\
&\quad\quad\quad\quad\quad\; 1000 = \text{total sample}
\end{aligned}
$$

POTENTIAL PROBLEMS

Even a carefully planned sampling plan may go awry. A principal reason for failure to obtain a *representative* sample is to define t . *population* in a biased fashion. Two examples will serve to illustrate this point. The first is an old one, often cited. In the presidential election of 1948 the candidates were Thomas Dewey and Harry Truman. In a precursor of the Gallup poll, prediction of the outcome was attempted via a telephone survey of individuals chosen *at random* from the phone book. Based on this survey the pollsters predicted that Dewey would win by a wide margin. As we know, they were wrong. Why? Well, in 1948 not all families had phone service, and those that did shared many common characteristics. Thus, the population from which the sample was selected was a biased one. Hence, the sample was similarly biased. The prediction was not based on a representative sample of voters but rather on a representative sample of those with telephone service, and the two sets were clearly different in terms of their presidential preference.

A second example concerns a question considered earlier—that of student opinion about intercollegiate athletics. Suppose the student government was planning a referendum to raise the student activity fee, intending to allocate more funds to athletics. Prior to the actual vote they wished to ascertain student opinion about intercollegiate athletics. This was done partly to determine how the referendum should be presented. Since the college is in an urban setting, the researchers decided to conduct the survey in the college cafeteria. They sent interviewers to the cafeteria from Monday to Friday during the hours of 7 A.M. to 9 P.M. It was reasoned that they would obtain a cross section of student opinion. They were very careful not to question the same individual more than once. The results of the survey revealed that the referendum would be passed by an overwhelming majority of students. Thus, the student government officers were confident that the vote would go in their favor, and they proceeded to plan for the extra funds that the increase would provide. The referendum was included on the student government ballot. The final vote was overwhelmingly against any increase in student fees. What happened?

The individuals who planned the survey failed to take into account the large number of students who attend classes and work or raise families. These students tend not to frequent the cafeteria but attend classes and then leave for work or home. It turned out that this group of individuals, who rarely avail themselves of extracurricular activities, resent the fact that they pay student fees and then cannot utilize the benefits these payments provide. Thus, they turned out in large numbers to vote against the referendum. The student leaders, thinking that the overwhelming majority obtained in the survey assured victory, were not as attentive to organizing the students who favored the increase.

Another problem concerns the type of subjects used. If you survey studies published in a variety of journals in the field of physical education and categorize them according to type of subject studied, you will note that in most the subjects are *college students* and that most of the college students are *male*. Unfortunately, this is also true in a majority of psychology studies. We may consider these as *accidental samples*. The students are available and so researchers—who are, more than likely, college professors—use them. This problem reflects, of course, on the representativeness and generalizability of the results obtained, as discussed earlier in connection with external validity.

The size of the sample is also an important consideration—particularly when the expected mean differences for the treatments employed are apt to be quite close. The truth is that any treatment difference, no matter how miniscule, can be significant if sufficient subjects are used. This is principally a function of the method by which the statistical test is calculated. In some procedures, particularly multivariate tests, the accuracy of the results depends on the use of a minimum number of subjects per individual variable. If, for example, a research study were to employ a finite population—for example, women at a service academy, such as West Point—then the number of measures which could be handled in a multiple-correlation procedure would be limited by the total subjects available. This is true of other tests as well. Chi-square is another good example. In order for the obtained statistic to be accurate, there must be a minimum of five observations per cell. If this is not the case, then the procedures suggest that categories be collapsed in order to correct for this lack.

Another factor which can influence the results is the method by which the subjects were obtained. Did they volunteer for the study? Were they coerced into participating, as where participation was a requirement of a course? Were subjects paid to participate? Were rewards provided for subjects who completed all sessions of the study? (Think, for example, what this last might mean for the notion of experimental mortality.) Were rewards given to subjects who achieved high scores? These are interesting and important considerations which might serve as topics for future research.

Although these sampling pitfalls cannot always be avoided, recognition of their potential effect on the results of research can alert the researcher to watch for their presence. In Chapter 20, on meta-analysis, the notion of sampling will be further discussed, but the unit to be sampled will be the research study rather than the individual subject. In that instance we will see that the larger the number of studies, the less likely it is that design pitfalls, including sampling errors and such, will affect the overall conclusions. In our case, however, we can work to eliminate design and sampling errors beforehand. In the case of meta-analysis we use studies which have already been completed, and we must do the best we can with what is available.

POWER, SAMPLE SIZE, AND RELIABILITY

Another problem related to sampling concerns the number of subjects needed for a particular experiment. Too few subjects are as wasteful of the experimenter's time as too many. In the latter case subjects are wasted who might be used in other studies in the research program; they are now contaminated by the testing procedure and may not be used in future studies in the same area. In the former case, too few subjects limit the reliability of the results, and the time taken to conduct the study is wasted.

The methods of estimating appropriate sample size to achieve adequate power and reliability of results can help us to avoid the problems of too few or too many. Before considering this, however, we need to consider what are termed Type I and Type II errors. To facilitate our understanding these concepts, we will consider them in relation to a two group design.

Type I and Type II Error

The independent variable in our study is feedback and the dependent variable is performance. Group A receives feedback after every attempt at performing a skill, while group B receives no feedback at all (control group). The object of conducting this study is to make a decision, hopefully the correct one, about the effect of feedback on performance. We designate two statistical hypotheses: the null hypothesis, H_0, which states that $A = B$; and the alternate hypothesis, H_1, which indicates that $A \neq B$. A *Type I error* occurs if H_0 is true and we reject it, finding that $A \neq B$. A *Type II error* occurs if H_0 is false and we accept it, finding that $A = B$. The risk of making a Type I error is indicated by the level of significance you choose. A .05 level of significance indicates that there are 5 chances out of 100 that you will reject the null when, in fact, it is true. It is the chance of a false positive.

A Type II error relates to the power of a test. How often will the test identify the presence of a hypothesized difference when it actually exists? The reciprocal indicates how often researchers will fail to reject the null when a difference actually exists. A summary of Type I and Type II errors is presented in Table 8.1.

TABLE 8.1   Comparision of Type I and Type II Errors

TRUE CONDITION	REJECT H_0	ACCEPT H_0
H_0 is true	Type I error	No error
H_0 is false	No error	Type II error

In attempting to insure that the results of a statistical test are accurate, you must consider these two factors—level of significance and power of the statistical test—as well as sample size and effect size. Effect size will be discussed at length in Chapter 20. For our purposes here we need only understand that it is an expression of the magnitude of the difference between the groups. The sample size is the number of subjects in each group.

Although we directly control the Type I error through selection of the level of significance, Type II error is less easily controlled. The probability of a Type II error increases as the level of significance is made more stringent, as it changes from .05 to .01; it also increases as sample size decreases and as effect size decreases. Generally, the simplest way for a researcher to increase the power of a test—decrease the probability of a Type II error—is to increase sample size. Another approach is to use a homogeneous population to minimize variability.

It is possible to formally determine the sample size necessary to achieve a predetermined test power (Cohen, 1977). This may be done in two ways. First, set a significance level, the desired power level, and an expected effect size (based on prior research or on a meta-analysis of research findings). Then statistical power tables can be used to determine the number of subjects needed to reduce the probability of a Type II error. A second approach is to set the significance, determine the effect size, decide on the number of subjects, and use the table to ascertain the power. If the power is unacceptably low, then the number of subjects should be increased. By manipulating two of the factors reviewed here—sample size and effect size (which may be increased by maximizing treatment differences)—it is possible to design a study so that you make the right decision most of the time.

REFERENCES

COHEN, J. *Statistical power analysis for the behavioral sciences, rev. ed.* New York: Academic Press, 1977.

CHAPTER NINE
STATISTICAL
INFERENCE

Chapters 1 to 3 dealt with using statistics to describe or characterize a group of scores. Chapters 4 to 8 dealt with research methods and with doing research. There is another aspect of statistics which is critical as a tool for doing research: *inferential statistics.*

Through the use of inferential statistics we can generalize from a sample of scores selected from a population back to that population from which those scores were randomly sampled. Through the use of inferential statistics we can compare the mean score of one group to the mean score of another group. The techniques used in inferential statistics are based on *parameters*—population statistics. These population values are derived with reference to the normal curve, discussed in Chapter 10.

There are also a number of techniques which are termed *nonparametric.* That is, the measurements we observe are not normally distributed in the population from which the sample was selected. Therefore, different techniques must be used to make inferences about the obtained scores. The general techniques of hypothesis testing are, however, the same.

In statistical inference we are concerned with the precision of measurement. In order to estimate this, we need to discover the probable limits of error. In other words, if we use the statistics of the sample to estimate the mean of the population from which the sample was drawn, we need to calculate the error of this estimate. In order to understand this concept of error in estimation of the mean of the population you would do well to conduct the experiment illustrated in Tables 9.1 and 9.2.

Using a pair of dice, toss and record the results of 36 throws. Calculate the

TABLE 9.1   Paradigm for a Dice-Throw Experiment

NUMBER OF THROWS	$\overline{X}$	s
1		
2		
3		
4		
5		
6		
7		
8		
9		
10		

mean and standard deviation of these throws. Now repeat the same experiment. It would help to illustrate the point if you could get several other individuals to carry out the same procedure. Record your observations and those of the other individuals in Table 9.1.

If you carried out this small experiment, you might get the results illustrated in Table 9.2.

What you have done is similar to the concept we referred to at the beginning of this chapter. You have, in effect, selected 36 throws, at random, from the total population of possible throws. (Dice throws are normally distributed, and if the dice are fair, they will distribute in an approximately normal manner.) In statistical inference we know that the larger the sample, the more likely you are to get a *precise* estimate of the population mean. What happens if we increase the number of throws? Let us see how this would affect the mean and *s* that we obtain. Look at Table 9.3. (This table was created with the help of a minicomputer, which was programmed to throw the requested number of dice and calculate the mean and standard deviation of each set of throws.)

The column labeled SEM is a measure that is unfamiliar to you at this point. The SEM is a measure of the precision of the estimate of the mean. It is called the standard error of the mean. As you can see, the SEM in the first table is fairly constant at about .39 or so. (The range is .31 to .45.) In the second table SEM starts at .39 and decreases steadily as the number of throws increases. This indicates that as the number of throws increases, the precision of our estimate increases. We can be fairly certain that the actual population mean is very close

TABLE 9.2   Sample Results for a Dice-Throw Experiment

	NUMBER OF THROWS	$\overline{X}$	s	SEM
1	36	6.5	2.10	.35
2	36	6.7	2.21	.37
3	36	7.44	2.37	.40
4	36	7.33	1.87	.31
5	36	7.02	2.39	.40
6	36	6.86	1.94	.32
7	36	6.97	2.49	.41
8	36	7.11	2.72	.45
9	36	6.53	1.91	.32
10	36	6.56	2.19	.36

to 7.00. Thus, we also see that the larger the sample, the more likely we are to get an accurate estimate; the last three samples, with throws of 4608, 9216, and 18,432, yielded means of 7.03, 7.01, and 7.02 respectively.

The standard error of the mean, SEM, is a measure used to make statistical inferences. We will see, in Chapter 10, how this statistic is used to write a confidence interval to estimate the population mean. The SEM is to a distribu-

TABLE 9.3   Results of Increasing Numbers of Dice Throws

	NUMBER OF THROWS	$\overline{X}$	s	SEM
1	36	7.39	2.34	.39
2	72	7.21	2.09	.25
3	144	6.85	2.18	.18
4	288	6.72	2.43	.14
5	576	7.03	2.53	.11
6	1,152	6.94	2.45	.07
7	2,304	6.89	2.38	.05
8	4,608	7.03	2.39	.04
9	9,216	7.01	2.45	.02
10	18,432	7.02	2.44	.02

tion of means as the standard deviation is to a distribution of scores. The standard deviation is a measure of variability of scores; the SEM is a measure of the variability of means.

If you are clear on the concepts that have been presented thus far, then you should read on to the next level of the presentation, which illustrates the notion of inference as comparison of two means. These means represent two groups of individuals, each drawn at random from the same population. (If you are not clear about the SEM concept and its relation to standard deviation, then you should reread the first section of the chapter, ask questions of your instructor, *and* try the experiment before proceeding further.)

USING STATISTICAL INFERENCE TO COMPARE TWO SAMPLES

Let us suppose that we have infinite time to do the following experiment.

Using the same pair of dice, toss and record the results of 36 throws. Calculate the mean and standard deviation. Throw another 36 times, record, calculate the mean and standard deviation. Now create a new column called the mean difference column. In it put the difference between the mean of the first set of throws and the mean of the second set of throws, as illustrated in Table 9.4.

TABLE 9.4   Dice-Throw Experiment to Illustrate Mean Difference

	NUMBER OF THROWS	$\bar{X}_1$	s_1	SEM$_1$	$\bar{X}_2$	s_2	SEM$_2$	$\bar{X}_1 - \bar{X}_2$
1	36	6.69	2.63	.44	6.67	2.60	.43	.02
2	36	6.69	2.89	.48	6.75	2.88	.48	−.06
3	36	6.56	2.48	.41	6.25	2.44	.41	.31
4	36	7.33	2.11	.35	6.53	2.44	.41	.80
5	36	6.33	2.18	.36	6.56	2.41	.40	−.23
6	36	6.89	2.64	.44	6.61	1.92	.32	.28
7	36	7.17	2.28	.38	6.72	2.41	.40	.45
8	36	6.58	2.22	.37	6.42	2.41	.40	.16
9	36	5.72	2.19	.36	6.80	2.72	.45	−1.08
10	36	6.47	2.61	.43	7.28	2.63	.44	−.81

The idea is to plot the mean differences. If there were enough of them, say 1000, we would obtain a normal distribution with a mean-mean difference of 0. If we average the mean differences in this sample of differences, we find that the total is −.16 (+2.02 − 2.18) and the average is −.16/10 or −.016. This is a fairly good approximation. As you might guess, there is a statistic that is comparable to the *standard deviation* and to the *standard error of the mean* that applies to the distribution of mean differences. This is the *standard error of the difference between the means.* We will be dealing further with this statistic when we consider the *t*-test of the difference between the means.

Using the means for the two groups in line 1 of the table, we can determine the likelihood that the samples which yielded these two means were drawn from the same population. This is essentially what is done in the t-test. The only difference is that in the t-test we hope that the two groups will appear as if they have come from different original populations (especially if each group has been subjected to a different treatment) rather than the same population, as is true here. We will see in Chapter 11 on the t-test that the mean difference is divided by the standard error of the difference between the means, yielding the critical ratio, to determine the likelihood of both samples' having been drawn from the same population. The greater the ratio between these two, the greater the likelihood that the two samples were drawn from different populations.

RELATIONSHIP AMONG s, SEM, AND $s_{\bar{X}_1 - \bar{X}_2}$

Thus far in this chapter we have conducted small experiments to demonstrate several notions related to statistical inference. One of the most important notions concerns the relationship between the standard deviation, the standard error of the mean, and the standard error of the difference between the means. The population of dice throws that we are using for the example can be thought of as normally distributed. That is, there are known probabilities for obtaining different combinations of throws. This probability distribution is illustrated in Chapter 10 on the normal curve. Samples drawn from the population of dice throws can be characterized using the mean and standard deviation.

In statistical inference, however, it is not sufficient to simply calculate the mean and standard deviation of a sample of scores (dice throws) drawn from a population. Often we will want to be able to estimate the accuracy of the mean we have obtained. How good an estimate of the population mean is the one we have obtained? The SEM is to the mean as the standard deviation is to a score. Imagine if you will that we select scores 36 at a time and calculate the mean for each set of scores. We can do this 1000 or more times (with the assistance of a computer, of course). If we do this, we can then use these means in the formula presented in Chapter 3 to calculate a standard deviation of the means. This value, called the standard error of the mean, has the same relationship to the distribution of means as the standard deviation has to the distribution of scores. Notice that this distribution will have the same mean as the distribution of scores but the estimate of variability (SEM) will be much less, as indicated by the values in the charts.

Often we do not simply want to know the accuracy of our estimate of the mean. Rather we want to compare the means of two or more samples in order to determine whether the difference between or among the means is within the difference we might expect if the two or more samples were drawn from the same population. As you might predict from the foregoing, we can do this by creating a distribution of mean differences. To do so, we again calculate a mean based on a particular sample size (we have used 36, but this is not a magic number—simply convenient). We do this for two random samples and then take the difference between the two means, the mean difference. If we do this 1000 times, we can, as in the previously calculated SEM, use the formula in Chapter 3 to calculate the standard deviation of the mean differences. This value is called the *standard error of the difference between the means.* In contrast to the mean of the distribution of means, this mean is 0 (zero), reflecting the balance of positive and negative mean differences usually obtained from a normal distribution of scores.

Estimating s, SEM, and $s_{\bar{x}_1-\bar{x}_2}$

Since it is cumbersome to calculate the values of the SEM and the $s_{\bar{x}-\bar{x}}$ from the means and mean differences, respectively, these values can be estimated from the standard deviation. The SEM is estimated by the formula

$$\text{SEM} = \frac{s}{\sqrt{N}} \tag{9.1}$$

The $s_{\bar{x}_1-\bar{x}_2}$ is estimated by the formula

$$s_{\bar{x}_1-\bar{x}_2} = \sqrt{\text{SEM}_1^2 + \text{SEM}_2^2} \tag{9.2}$$

The values calculated by using the means and the mean differences given in the various tables in this chapter are reasonably close to the values estimated by the formulas above. Interested students should use the formula presented for calculating the standard deviation to calculate SEM and $s_{\bar{x}_1-\bar{x}_2}$ to demonstrate this for themselves.

TESTING HYPOTHESES

The hypothesis, you may remember, is an educated guess about the relationship between two or more variables or about the cause-and-effect relationship between two or more variables. We shall be concerned with two types of hypotheses: statistical hypotheses and research hypotheses. The *research hypothesis* is the actual prediction that you wish to test. Thus, if you indicated that jogging around the reservoir every day for 5 days is better for development of cardiovascular/respiratory fitness than jogging around the reservoir 2 days per week over a period of 6 months, this would be a research hypothesis. It is what you expect will happen as a result of the treatments you impose.

A *statistical hypothesis,* on the other hand, is a statement that is evaluated in terms of probabilities. Statistical hypotheses are classified as *null hypotheses* (statements of no difference) or *alternative hypotheses* (statements that there is a difference or that there is a directional difference). For the above example the null hypothesis would indicate that the mean cardiovascular/respiratory fitness for the subjects in group 1 (running 5 times per week) is not different from that for the subjects who ran 2 times per week. The alternative hypothesis would indicate that there will be a difference between the groups. In shorthand we would write:

$$\text{(Null hypothesis)} \qquad H_0: \quad \overline{X}_1 = \overline{X}_2 \qquad\qquad (9.3)$$

$$\text{(Alternative hypothesis)} \qquad H_1: \quad \overline{X}_1 \neq \overline{X}_2 \qquad\qquad (9.4)$$

The alternative hypothesis is used for what is called a *two-tailed test.* This means that the difference can be in either direction. The mean for group 1 can be larger or smaller than the mean for group 2, and you will be able to reject the null. It is possible to use an alternative hypothesis that is *directional.* That is, you can write

$$H_1: \quad \overline{X}_1 < \overline{X}_2 \quad \text{or} \quad H_1: \quad \overline{X}_1 > \overline{X}_2 \qquad\qquad (9.5)$$

If you are wrong in your prediction, however, you cannot change your mind after the fact. For most studies the use of the nondirectional alternative hypothesis is sufficient.

In testing hypotheses, it is helpful to have a standard procedure for systematizing your consideration. This procedure will be individualized for each different test to be considered, but it is wise to become familiar with it now.

1. Indicate the problem under consideration.
2. State the research hypothesis.
3. State the statistical hypothesis (in shorthand):
   a. H_0:
   b. H_1:
4. Indicate the level of significance you are using.
5. What is the decision rule?
6. What is the result?
7. What is your decision?

Using the problem stated above about jogging around the reservoir 5 times per week versus 2 times per week, let us go through the steps. (Remember that the *t*-test is appropriate for comparing the means of two groups, so we will use that test.)

Description of study: An instructor wishes to determine whether it is better to jog a certain distance 5 times per week or whether 2 times per week is sufficient to develop cardiovascular/respiratory fitness.

1. *The problem:* Is there a difference in the level of cardiovascular fitness achieved by a group jogging 5 times per week as compared to a group that jogs 2 times a week?
2. *Research hypothesis:* If one group jogs 5 times per week and another group jogs 2 times per week, there will be a difference in their cardiovascular fitness.
3. *Statistical hypothesis:*

$$H_0: \quad \overline{X}_{5/wk} = \overline{X}_{2/wk}$$

$$H_1: \quad \overline{X}_{5/wk} \neq \overline{X}_{2/wk}$$

4. Use the .05 level of significance.
5. Reject H_0 if t with number of degrees of freedom (value from t-table) is equal to or greater than value obtained.
6. Value obtained $>$ than value in table, $\overline{X}_{5/wk}$ $\overline{X}_{2/wk}$
7. Reject null, 5 times per week better. (look at $\overline{X}$'s)

In the example given above there are two concepts that you have not been introduced to as yet. They are important in statistical inference. These are *level of significance* and *degrees of freedom.* The information on the value from the table is unique to each test and so will be detailed in the individual chapters.

Level of Significance

The level of significance is a statement about the probability that we will reject the null hypothesis when, in fact, it is true. In reality, which we do not know and can never know, there *may* actually be *no difference* between the treatments we administered: jogging 5 times per week and jogging 2 times per week. In our study we happen to find that there is a difference, a statistically significant difference, between the means of the groups. If, in fact, the reality is that there is *no difference,* then we have made an error in concluding that there is a difference. The level of significance is a statement of the likelihood that we were wrong in rejecting the null. In the case of the example we chose the .05 level. This indicates that 5 times out of every hundred times this same comparison is made, we might be in error in rejecting the null. Conversely, then, 95 times out of 100 we are *correct* in saying that there is a difference between the 5-times-per-week treatment group and the 2-times-per-week treatment group.

The levels of significance most often used are .05 and .01. These levels specify the amount of error the researcher is willing to tolerate. The significance level we set, in combination with the degrees of freedom, determines the value that our statistical test must yield for us to reject the null. This level is used in conjunction with the degrees of freedom to give us the required value.

Degrees of Freedom

The concept of degrees of freedom is generally thought of in terms of the number of scores that are free to vary—that is, free to take on any value. If you remember the raw-score method for calculating the standard deviation (Chapter

3), you may recall that the sum of the deviations from the mean always totals 0 (zero). You used this as a check on your calculations. The concept of degrees of freedom implies that, in the case of a distribution of 10 scores, each of 9 scores can vary infinitely. The tenth score, however, must be such that the deviation from the mean, when added to the other deviations, results in a sum of 0. In any set of scores the degrees of freedom will be $N - 1$. In the case of a t-test where there are two groups of scores the degrees of freedom is the $N - 1$ for the first group plus the $N - 1$ for the second group. The degrees of freedom (df) concept is employed in every statistical test to be used. In some cases df is figured based on the number of groups (ANOVA) or the number of cells (chi-square). The stable fact is that it is the number of elements or units minus one.

These concepts and the decision procedure outlined will be considered for each statistical test. This presentation has been a cursory overview of the concepts to be considered.

Before we consider specific aspects of inferential statistics, a summary of the descriptive statistics we have used and of the inferential statistics we will use is in order. Table 9.5 indicates the type of data (nominal, ordinal, interval, and ratio) and the type of statistic or test appropriate to particular comparisons. This table will serve as a handy reference. The section on inferential statistics is further divided into parametric and nonparametric tests. *Parametric statistics* is based upon certain assumptions concerning the population from which the data are drawn and requires interval or ratio measurement. *Nonparametric statistics* is typically used with nominal and ordinal data, though higher levels of data may be downgraded for use with these procedures.

Relationship questions, which use correlational procedures, are included in a section of the table separate from procedures which are used to answer difference questions. The majority of the parametric tests are considered in this book, but most of the nonparametric tests are not. Note that ordinal data, when not in the form of ranks, can be analyzed using parametric statistics if the distribution approaches normality. Nominal data, however, require nonparametric statistical analysis.

TABLE 9.5   Statistical Tools

Descriptive Statistics: Used to compile, summarize, and describe data

PURPOSE	TYPE OF DATA	STATISTIC
I *Measures of Central Tendency*	Ratio and interval	Mean
	Ordinal	Median
	Nominal	Mode
II *Measures of Dispersion*	Ratio and interval	Standard deviation
	Ordinal	Interquartile range
	Nominal	Range

Inferential Statistics: Used to draw implications (inferences) from data; to determine whether results differ significantly from chance findings

I *Comparison Statistics* (difference questions)

   A *Parametric Statistics:* Based upon certain assumptions concerning the nature of parameters of the populations from which data are drawn (e.g., normally distributed, equal variances), require at least interval data and relatively large sample size

PURPOSE	TYPE OF DATA	STATISTIC
1 Comparison of two independent data points (e.g., means of two sample groups)	Interval, ratio, and some ordinal data[a]	*t*-test (independent)
2 Comparison of two nonindependent data points (e.g., test-retest means for one sample)	Interval, ratio, and some ordinal data[a]	*t*-test (correlated)
3 Comparison of more than two independent data points for one experimental variable (e.g., means of three sample groups)	Interval, ratio, and some ordinal data[a]	One-way analysis of variance (ANOVA)
4 Comparison of more than two nonindependent data points for one experimental variable (e.g., means for same subject tested three times)	Interval, ratio, and some ordinal data[a]	One-way ANOVA with repeated measures
5 Comparison of two or more independent data points for two experimental variables (factorial design)	Interval, ratio, and some ordinal data[a]	Two-way ANOVA
6 Comparison of two or more independent data points for one variable and two or more nonindependent data points for a second variable (mixed design)	Interval, ratio, and some ordinal data[a]	Two-way mixed ANOVA

TABLE 9.5   (Continued)

A *Parametric Statistics* (continued):

PURPOSE	TYPE OF DATA	STATISTIC
7 Comparison of two or more data points (independent and/or nonindependent) for three or more experimental variables	Interval, ratio, and some ordinal data[a]	Three-way (four-way, etc.) ANOVA

B *Nonparametric Statistics:* Based upon fewer assumptions concerning the populations from which data are drawn; may be used with ordinal and nominal data; require smaller sample size

PURPOSE	TYPE OF DATA	STATISTIC
1 Comparison of two independent data points (e.g., two sample groups)	Nominal Ordinal[a]	Chi-square Median test Mann-Whitney *U*
2 Comparison of two nonindependent data points (e.g., pretest–past test design)	Nominal Ordinal[a]	McNemar test Wilcoxin test Sign test
3 Comparison of more than two independent data points for one experimental variable	Nominal Ordinal[a]	Chi-square Median test Kruskal-Wallis
4 Comparison of more than two nonindependent data points for one experimental variable	Nominal Ordinal[a]	Cochran *Q* test Friedman analysis of variance

II *Correlation Coefficients* (relationship questions)

PURPOSE	TYPE OF DATA	STATISTIC
Determine relationship between two variables	Interval or ratio data for both variables	Pearson product-moment correlation
	Ordinal data for both variables[a]	Spearman rank-order correlation Kendall's tau
	Nominal: two artificial dichotomies	Tetrachoric correlation
	Nominal: two true dichotomies	Phi coefficient
	Artificial dichotomy on one variable; interval or ratio data on one variable	Biserial correlation
	True dichotomy on one variable; interval or ratio data on one variable	Point biserial correlation

[a]Ordinal data, when not in the form of actual ranks, can be analyzed using parametric statistics as long as the distribution approaches normality.

Prepared by R. K. Arnold and A. L. Rothstein for use in a conference program on *Preparing Research Proposals.*

CHAPTER TEN
PROBABILITY AND
THE NORMAL CURVE

The topic of probability is central to an understanding of statistical inference. The normal curve provides an easily understood and useful application of this concept. This chapter will consider both probability and the normal curve in relation to the notions of sampling, descriptive statistics, and statistical inference.

PROBABILITY

Although the notion of probability often seems formidable, we use it daily. This morning's weather report provided you with the probability that it might rain: "a 25 percent chance of rain." The basketball announcer indicated the probability that the player at the foul line would sink the shot: "This player's foul-shot percentage is 80 percent." A deck of cards could further illustrate the notion of probability. If you shuffle the deck and turn over the first card, you have a 50 percent probability of its being red, a 25 percent probability of its being a heart, an 8 percent chance of an ace, and a 2 percent chance of drawing a king of hearts. These probabilities are figured by taking the number of opportunities for an event to occur and dividing by the total number of opportunities in the universe or sample you are considering. The card example is illustrated in Table 10.1.

In the sport examples it works the same way. If a hockey goalie had 50 opportunities to block shots on goal in a game and missed only 4, then the percentage of shots scored on that goalie would be 8 percent, or the success rate (blocked shots) would be 92 percent. That is, we can expect the goalie to block 92 percent of the shots on goal. Thus, if 25 shots were taken in a game under similar conditions, we would expect that 2 would score.

TABLE 10.1   Percentage of Occurrences of Events

	RED	HEART	ACE	KING OF HEARTS
No. of possibilities	26	13	4	1
Total possible	52	52	52	52
Percent	50%	25%	7.6%	1.9%

If you recall our dice experiment in the last chapter, we were really asking: What is the percentage of 2, 3, 4, 5, 6, 7, 8, 9, 10, 11, and 12 we can expect when we roll a pair of dice 36 times? The computer in that experiment kept track of how many of each possible throw occurred, but then it summed all the throws and calculated the average. If we wished to determine the probability of each combination of the dice, we would have to determine all the ways you could get 2, 3, 4, and so on and then work the formula above. If we did this, it would look something like Table 10.2.

TABLE 10.2   Probabilities of Rolling 2–12 in Dice

EVENT	PROBABILITY	NUMBER EXPECTED
2	.028	38
3	.056	75
4	.083	112
5	.111	149
6	.139	187
7	.167	224
8	.139	187
9	.111	149
10	.083	112
11	.056	75
12	.028	38
Total passes	1.001	1342

In each of the instances in the table the probability of the particular event was calculated by determining how many combinations of the two dice would give the desired outcome. What was used was the multiplication rule of probability. In the case of the 2, for example, you needed a 1 on the first die and a 1 on the second die. Each event had a probability of $\frac{1}{6}$. You would therefore multiply the $\frac{1}{6}$ for the first event by the $\frac{1}{6}$ for the second event, and the probability of the combination would be $\frac{1}{36}$ or .028.

In a more difficult example, there are 6 possible throws of the first die that would give a 7 in combination with throws of the second die: 1, 2, 3, 4, 5, and 6. Once the first die is thrown, however, only 1 particular throw on the second die will yield a total of 7. Hence, for the first die the probability is $\frac{6}{6}$. But once it is thrown, the probability of obtaining the particular throw needed (only one will suffice) is $\frac{1}{6}$. Thus, $\frac{6}{6} \times \frac{1}{6} = \frac{6}{36}$ or .167. The expected number of throws was then obtained by multiplying the probability times the total throws to be completed.

Just for fun, let us see how many of each roll would be obtained if we simulated 1344 passes by using the same minicomputer program which yielded the information used in the last chapter. The difference here is that the computer will keep track of, and print out, the number of each type of pass. Then we can compare the expected yield with what was actually obtained. Let us do it twice. This is presented in Table 10.3.

Notice that the more passes you were to throw, the greater the likelihood that you would be correct in your estimates, using the probabilities provided. Over the long run, then, probabilities can be used to estimate the likelihood that a batter will get a hit, a goalie will prevent a score, a basketball player will sink a foul shot. Gambling is based on probabilities. If you knew that there was an 80 percent chance of a particular event occurring, you would be more likely to bet a considerable sum than if the probability was 50 percent.

Researchers use this concept of probability in making statistical inferences. Recall that the level of significance the researcher chooses represents the probability that he or she is *wrong* in rejecting the null. The level of significance is .05 or .01. The converse for each of these levels is that there is a 95 or 99 percent chance that he or she is *correct* in rejecting the null because there really is a difference. These levels of significance are based on the concept of the normal distribution and on the principles of statistical inference reviewed in Chapter 9.

The difference between the normal distribution, which we will now consider, and the dice-throw examples used previously, is that the dice-throw examples represented *discrete points*. We could throw a 2, a 3, a 4, and so on. We cannot obtain a dice throw of 5.7, for example. So even though we could obtain a mean of throws of 6.87, for instance, that value is not meaningful in real life. In many instances in physical education we will find that our averages are not meaningful because they do not exist. Sit-ups, pull-ups, baskets made, number of strikeouts, are all discrete variables. Height, weight, running time, max V_{O_2}, on the other hand, are all *continuous variables*. Continuous variables can change continuously over their limits. You can weigh 135.79 pounds. You can be 67.43 inches tall. You can run a mile in 4:32.134 minutes. The only limitation

TABLE 10.3   Computer-Simulated Dice Throws ($N = 1344$)

EVENT	PROBABILITY	EXPECTED	OBSERVED$_1$	OBSERVED$_2$
2	.028	38	39	42
3	.056	75	66	93
4	.083	112	110	119
5	.111	149	164	140
6	.139	187	215	171
7	.167	224	223	216
8	.139	187	181	175
9	.111	149	135	155
10	.083	112	113	107
11	.056	75	71	87
12	.028	38	27	39

we have in assessing continuous variables is in the sensitivity of the measuring instrument or technique. (These considerations are dealt with extensively in courses on tests and measurements.)

NORMAL CURVE

The normal distribution and the normal curve are one and the same. The difference is that the *normal distribution* refers to the set of scores and the *normal curve* is the pictorial representation of the distribution. As indicated previously, the normal curve undergirds all parametric statistics, and the concepts inherent in our discussion undergrid all of statistical inference. You may be more familiar with references to the "bell-shaped curve." This is the shape of the graph of a normal distribution. It resembles, more or less, the picture presented in Figure 10.1.

As with all graphic representations of frequency distributions, the score values are given on the horizontal axis while the frequency of each score is plotted with reference to the vertical axis. In a perfect normal distribution the mean, the median, and the mode split the distribution exactly. This means that 50 percent of the scores are above the mean, median, and mode (which are all the same) and 50 percent of the scores are below. Thus, the normal distribution accounts for 100 percent of the scores 50 percent above + 50 percent below = 100 percent.

A second property of the normal curve is that other percentages of area under the curve, in addition to the 50–50, can be determined by using the standard deviation of the distribution. Thus, it is given that 34.13 percent of the total area under the curve falls between the mean and one standard deviation from the mean. Then, 47.72 percent of the total area falls between the mean and two standard deviations from the mean. Finally, 49.86 percent of the scores fall be-

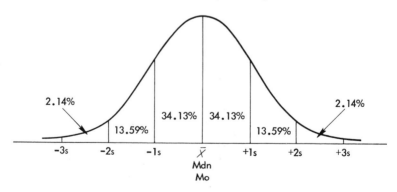

FIGURE 10.1   Percentages Under Normal Curve at ±1, ±2, and ±3 Standard Deviations from the Mean.

tween the mean and three standard deviations from the mean. The remaining .14 percent of the scores fall beyond the three-standard-deviation point.

A third property of the normal curve is that it is symmetrical; that is, whatever happens on one side of the curve is mirrored on the other. Therefore, we can speak of one standard deviation above the mean or one standard deviation below the mean. The areas between both these points and the mean are 34.13 percent. If we were to indicate the percentages of area between specific points on the curve, we would obtain those shown in Figure 10.1.

Typically, we express the area under the normal curve as a proportion. Table 1 in Appendix A uses this format. Thus, the area between the mean and +1s is .3413. To convert from a proportion to a percent you multiply by 100. Thus .3413 × 100 = 34.13. To convert from a percent to a proportion divide by 100. Thus, 34.13/100 = .3413.

Since the mean and the standard deviation of a distribution can vary widely, it would be helpful to be able to convert into a standardized system that would be applicable in all distributions that are assumed to be normally distributed. The numbers below the curve, +3s, +2s, −2s, and so on, represent standard score equivalents of the relationship between the mean and the standard deviation of the distribution. Thus, +3s represents a point that is 3 standard deviations above the mean. Likewise, −2s represents a point that is 2 standard deviations below the mean. These scores are called Z-scores. They can be defined by Equation (10.1):

$$Z = \frac{X - \overline{X}}{s} \qquad (10.1)$$

You should recognize the numerator (top of the fraction) as the same deviation score we used in computing the standard deviation by the raw-score method. A few examples are presented in Table 10.4 to illustrate how this works.

As you can see, it doesn't matter what the mean and standard deviation are; the Z-score yields its result in terms of the relationship among the components. Thus, we can compare individuals on very diverse tests. The Z-scores we obtain can be added and subtracted, and the mean Z-score can be obtained. We can obtain the Z-score on one test and then find the score that would be comparable to that on another test.

TABLE 10.4   Computing Z-Scores

$\overline{X}$	s	X	$Z = \dfrac{X - \overline{X}}{s}$	Z
10	2	6	(6 − 10)/2 = −4/2 =	−2
25	5	30	(30 − 25)/5 = 5/5 =	1
40	10	50	(50 − 40)/10 = 10/10 =	1
100	15	80	(80 − 100)/15 = −20/15 =	−1.33

If, for example, you had a distribution with a $\overline{X} = 25$ and $s = 3$ and you wished to convert a score of 20 into a score compatible with another score from a distribution with a $\overline{X} = 50$ and $s = 10$, you would obtain the Z-score for the score of 20 and then convert it by using the *new* $\overline{X}$ and s. The equation is presented in (10.2) and (10.3). Equations (10.4) to (10.6) illustrate the process of converting a score from one scale to another.

$$X \text{ (new)} = X \text{ (new)} + Z(s \text{ (new)}) \tag{10.2}$$

or

$$X = \overline{X} + Z(s) \tag{10.3}$$

old distribution (scale)	new distribution (scale)	
$\overline{X} = 25, \quad s = 3, \quad X = 20$	$\overline{X} = 50, \quad s = 10, \quad X = ?$	(10.4)

$$Z = \frac{X - \overline{X}}{s} = \frac{20 - 25}{3} = \frac{-5}{3} = \underline{-1.67} \tag{10.5}$$

$$X = \overline{X} + Z(s) = 50 + -1.67(10) = 50 + -16.70 = \underline{33.30} \tag{10.6}$$

As a final example let us get the average Z-score for the scores in Table 10.5.

TABLE 10.5   Averaging Z-Scores

$\overline{X}$	s	X	Z
100	25	125	$(125 - 100)/25 = 1$
75	6	88	$(88 - 75)/6 = 2.17$
24	3	20	$(20 - 24)/3 = -1.33$
44	4	36	$(36 - 44)/4 = -2.00$
			Sum of Z-scores $= -.16$
			Average $= -.16/4 = -.04$

Assuming that we know the mean and standard deviation of a distribution, we can obtain the Z-score for any score by

$$Z = \frac{X - \overline{X}}{s} \tag{10.7}$$

or the score equivalent for any Z by

$$X = \overline{X} + Z(s) \tag{10.8}$$

Therefore, we can go back and forth between the X and the Z

Score $\longleftrightarrow$ Z

by using the appropriate formula.

FURTHER USE OF THE
NORMAL CURVE

We have seen that we can use the properties of the normal curve to find equivalences among varied distributions. In doing so, we have noted also that we can estimate the area of the normal curve between the mean and specific scores (by obtaining Z and looking at the percentage in the curve in Figure 10.1), or between two scores, or above a certain score, or below a certain score. Let us see how this works in the curve drawn in Figure 10.2. (This is the same curve as in Figure 10.1, but score values have been added.) The mean of the distribution is 70 and the standard deviation is 5.

Some simple examples should give you the idea of how we will use the normal curve to estimate the area under different portions of the curve and how we will use it to estimate the number of cases under different portions.

Example 1
What is the area between the mean and a score of 75? (Looking on the curve, we find the mean and then find 75; i.e., Z = 1. The area between 70 and 75 is .3413, so that is our answer.)

Example 2
What is the area between a score of 65 and a score of 75? (The area between 65 and the mean is .3413; the area between 75 and the mean is .3413. We add these, because they cross the mean, and obtain .6826. The Z-scores are −1 and +1, respectively.)

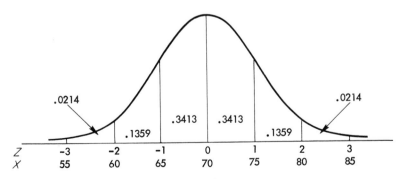

FIGURE 10.2   Score Values and the Normal Curve.

Example 3

What is the area above a score of 75? (We add together all the proportions above $Z = +1$ and obtain $.1359 + .0214 + .0014 = .1587$.)

Example 4

What is the area below a score of 80? (We add together all the proportions below $Z = 2$ and obtain $.1359 + .3413 + .3413 + .1359 + .0214 + .0014$, which $= .9772$.) We could have obtained the same value by calculating 1.00 (the total area under the curve) $-$ the proportions above $Z = 2$. Thus $1.00 - .0214 + .0014 = .9772$.

We see that by using the diagram that specifies the proportion of areas under different portions of the normal curve, we can find proportions that are not specifically indicated. However, we are limited to gross estimates (1, 2, 3, and so on standard deviations). Unfortunately, the area under the curve is not equally distributed within areas, as you might guess from the shape of the curve. Thus, the area between the mean and $.5 Z$ is not half of $.3413$ (which would be $.1707$) but is more than half or $.1915$. In order to obtain precise estimates, then, of the area under the normal curve it is necessary to use Table 1 provided in Appendix A (Table A1).

Table A1 provides information about the area under the normal curve:

1. Between the mean and any Z-score.
2. In the larger portion of the curve in relation to Z.
3. In the smaller portion of the curve in relation to Z.

In Examples 5 through 10 it is assumed that you already know how to calculate Z, given a particular score and the X and s of the distribution. It is recommended that you use diagrams of the type shown in these examples to do Exercises 6 and 7 at the end of the chapter. (*Note:* Since the curve is symmetrical, Table A1 is written for $+Z$; the $-Z$ values are the same.)

Example 5

In Figure 10.3, what is the area between the mean and $Z = .54$? (Look for $Z = .54$ in column 1. Read the answer in column 2, "Area from mean to Z.")

Example 6

In Figure 10.4, what is the area between the mean and $Z = -.32$? (Look for $Z = .32$ in column 1. Read the answer in column 2, "Area from mean to Z.")

Example 7

In Figure 10.5, what is the area below $Z = .47$? (Look for $Z = .47$ in

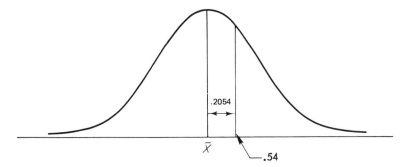

FIGURE 10.3

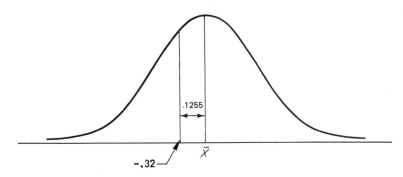

FIGURE 10.4

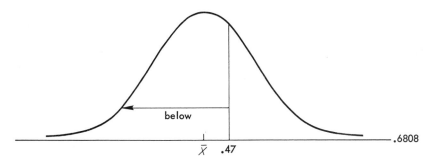

FIGURE 10.5

column 1. Since the area below is larger than that above, look in column 3, "Area in larger portion.")

Example 8

In Figure 10.6, what is the area above $Z = .47$? (Look for $Z = .47$ as in Example 7. Since the area above is the smaller area, read the answer from column 4, "Area in smaller portion.")

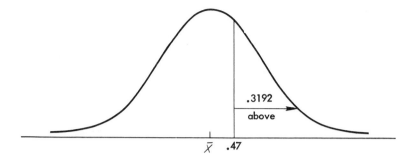

FIGURE 10.6

It is also possible to calculate the area between any two scores on the curve by adding and subtracting appropriately.

Example 9
In Figure 10.7, what is the area between $Z = 1.04$ and $Z = 1.98$? (Look for both Z-scores in the table and write down the area from the mean to Z in both cases. Then to obtain the area between the two scores, *subtract*.)

Example 10
In Figure 10.8, what is the area between $Z = -2.10$ and $Z = .60$? (Look for both Z-scores in the table and write down the area from the mean to Z for both. *Then add* these areas together.)

When scores or Z-scores are on opposite sides of the mean, then the area between will be obtained by *addition*; when they are on the same side of the mean, the area will be obtained by *subtraction*. In the latter case it is appropriate to look at the area between the mean and Z to obtain initial values.

Once we know the proportion of area between any two points under the normal curve, it becomes a simple matter to estimate the number of elements

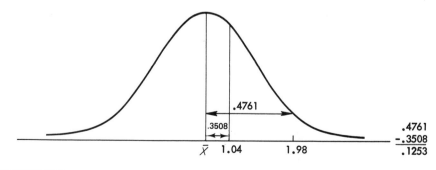

FIGURE 10.7

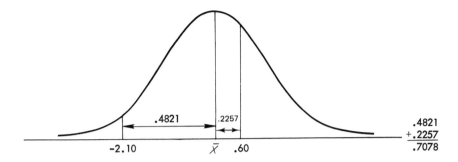

FIGURE 10.8

(people or cases) in that area. We obtain this by multiplying the total number of elements in the population by the proportion:

$$\text{number of elements represented} = N(\text{proportion}) \qquad (10.9)$$

In Example 10 the total area represented was .7078. If the total number of cases was 500,

$$\text{number of elements represented} = 500(.7078) = 353.9 \qquad (10.10)$$

In Example 9 the total area was .1253. If the total elements were 150,

$$\text{number of elements represented} = 150(.1253) = 18.795 \qquad (10.11)$$

Thus, we can proceed as follows:

$$\text{Score} \xrightarrow[\text{(Formula)}]{} Z \xrightarrow[\text{(Table)}]{} \text{Proportion} \xrightarrow[\text{(Formula)}]{} \text{Number Cases}$$

Let us calculate two examples.

Example 11
$\overline{X} = 90$, $s = 10$, $N = 300$, $X = 78$; what is N between 78 and mean?

$$\text{Score} \xrightarrow{\hspace{1.5cm}} Z \xrightarrow{\hspace{1.5cm}} \text{Proportion} \xrightarrow{\hspace{1.5cm}} \text{Number Cases}$$

$$Z = \frac{78 - 90}{10} \qquad\qquad (300).3849 \quad (10.13)$$

$$= \frac{-12}{10} \qquad (10.12)$$

78	-1.2	.3849	115.47

Example 12
$\overline{X} = 90$, $s = 10$, $N = 300$, N of interest $= 100$ above score.

Score $\longleftarrow$ Z $\longleftarrow$ Proportion $\longleftarrow$ Number Cases

$$X = \overline{X} + Z(s)$$
$$= 90 + .44(10) \quad (10.14)$$
$$= 90 + 4.4$$

$$\text{prop} = \frac{100}{300} \quad (10.15)$$

94.4   .44   .33   100

The procedure used in Example 12 may not be as straightforward or clear as those used in Example 11, so let us go through the process. Given that we want to know the score that 100 cases are above, we know that we are working with the upper (+) portion of the curve. (See Figure 10.9.) First we find the proportion that this represents. It is evident from the diagram that the area .3300 is the smaller area of the curve. Hence, we must find a number in column 4 of Table A1 that yields .3300. We look in Table A1 and find that .3300 appears in column 4 in conjunction with a Z of .44. Substituting in the formula for obtaining the score given Z, we find that the score which separates the top 100 cases from the rest is 94.4.

prop $= .33$ 100 cases   (10.16)

$Z = .44$ (10.17)

$X = \overline{X} + Z(s)$

    $= 90 + .44(10)$

    $= 90 + 4.4$

    $= 94.4$ (10.18)

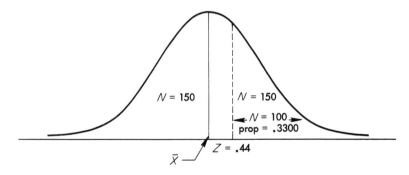

FIGURE 10.9   Illustration for Example 12.

CONFIDENCE INTERVALS

Another reason for being knowledgeable about the normal distribution is that we can use the concepts for estimating the range within the population mean might fall, given the mean and standard deviation of a sample drawn from that population. For this you need to recall that in Chapter 9 on statistical inference we demonstrated that we could generate a distribution of means and its accompanying variability estimate, the standard error of the mean. We also noted that we could estimate what the variability of this population would be by using the standard deviation of the sample to estimate the standard error of the mean. (The mean of the sample is the estimate of the mean of the population.)

$$\text{SEM} = \frac{s}{\sqrt{N}} \qquad\qquad (10.19)$$

By using the mean of the sample and the standard deviation of the sample (for calculating the SEM), we can identify a range within which the mean of the population that yielded the sample can be expected to fall 95 percent or 99 percent of the time. (As a rule we are interested only in these percentages.)

The way we do this is by estimating the variability of the normal curve of means through the SEM. We then consider this normal distribution as an extension of the Z-scores we have just been considering. (This is true only when the number of cases in our sample is 100 or more. When there are less than 100 scorces, we use a different distribution, the t-distribution.) We are therefore asking, "What Z-score would encompass 95 percent or 99 percent of all the possible means?" In fact, we are looking for a Z-score on each end (see Figure 10.10). The calculation for the left end is shown in equation (10.20) and for the right end in equation (10.21).

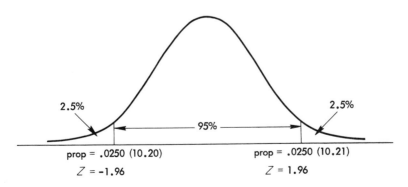

FIGURE 10.10

prop = .0250

$$Z = -1.96 \tag{10.20}$$

prop = .0250

$$Z = 1.96 \tag{10.21}$$

Once we have obtained the Z-score, in this case 1.96, the means corresponding to those Z-scores are calculated as in Equation (10.22):

$$\text{means} = \overline{X} \pm Z(\text{SEM}) \tag{10.22}$$

Thus if the mean and standard deviation of the sample are 40 and 3, respectively, and there are 144 in the sample, we would calculate as in equations (10.23) and (10.24):

$$\text{SEM} = \frac{3}{\sqrt{144}} = \frac{3}{12} = .25 \tag{10.23}$$

Then:

$$\text{means} = 40 \pm 1.96(.25) \tag{10.24}$$

$$= 40 \pm .49$$

$$= 39.51, \ 40.49$$

The solution to (10.24) identifies the means that encompass 95 percent of the distribution of means. That is to say, 95 times out of 100 the population mean will fall between 39.51 and 40.49 when samples of size 144 are used.

In the event that a 99 percent confidence interval is desired, the Z-scores that will cut off 99 percent of the normal curve are +2.58 and −2.58. This can be figured, if you wish, in the same way as the 95 percent was obtained.

If the N of the sample is less than 100, the normal distribution will not give an accurate estimate of the means that may be obtained 95 percent and 99 percent of the time. The estimate for small sample sizes is best obtained by using the t-distribution. This distribution is found in Appendix A, Table 2 (5 percent in this table corresponds to 95 percent and 1 percent to 99 percent). The t-value to be used in place of the Z-score is obtained by using the df for the sample. Thus if the sample consisted of 81 individuals, the df would be 80, $N - 1$. Looking in the df column in Table A2, we would find 80 df. The 5 percent (95 percent confidence interval) value is 1.99; the 1 percent value, 2.638. Thus, if $\overline{X} = 50$, $s = 9$, $N = 81$:

$$\text{means} = \overline{X} \pm t(\text{SEM}) \tag{10.25}$$

where

$$\text{SEM} = \frac{s}{\sqrt{N}} = \frac{9}{\sqrt{81}} = \frac{9}{9} = 1 \qquad\qquad (10.26)$$

and

$$\text{means} = 50 \pm 1.99(1) \qquad\qquad (10.27)$$
$$= 50 \pm 1.99$$
$$= 48.01, 51.99$$

Thus, 95 percent of the time the population mean can be expected to fall between 48.01 and 51.99.

EXERCISES

1. Given $\overline{X} = 65$, $s = 5$, find the Z-score for the following:
   a. 60   b. 70   c. 62   d. 75   e. 57   f. 65
2. Convert the Z-scores obtained in Exercise 1 to scores given $X = 25$, $s = 3$.
3. What is the average of the scores given in Exercise 1?
4. What is the average of the Z-scores obtained in Exercise 1?
5. What is the average of the scores obtained in Exercise 2?
6. What is the area between $Z = -1.36$ and $Z = .97$?
7. Given $\overline{X} = 66$, $s = 4$, $N = 600$:
   a. What is the area above a score of 70?
   b. What is the area between scores of 60 and 64?
   c. What is the area between scores of 65 and 75?
   d. What is the area above a score of 69?
   e. What is the area below a score of 73?
   f. What is the area below a score of 58?
   g. How many cases are represented in part (e) above?
   h. How many cases are represented in part (c) above?
   i. What is the score that marks off the lower 100 cases?
   j. What is the score that marks off the lower 350 cases?
8. Given $\overline{X} = 40$, $s = 7$, $N = 49$, calculate a 95 percent *and* a 99 percent confidence interval.
9. Given $\overline{X} = 95$, $s = 6.5$, $N = 169$, calculate a 95 percent and a 99 percent confidence interval.

CHAPTER ELEVEN
TESTING THE DIFFERENCES BETWEEN TWO MEANS

The simplest research situation you might imagine, which still has an element of control, is one in which there are two groups. One group is experimentally treated and a second group is not. Subjects are typically assigned to the two groups at random, and it is assumed that the individuals do not differ on the variable to be measured at the outset of the study but that they *may* differ at its conclusion.

Typically, you impose the experimental treatment on one group for a certain period of time. At the end of this time, or number of practice sessions, you test both the experimental or treated group and the control or untreated group. You organize the test scores by group and then calculate the mean and standard deviation of each group. You then compare the mean of the experimental group with the mean of the control group to ascertain whether there is an observable difference. If the mean for the experimental group is higher than that for the control group, you might conclude, subjectively, that the experimental group did better.

Your conclusion is based on descriptive statistics, the mean and perhaps the standard deviation. These procedures cannot be used to make statistical inferences regarding samples of a larger population. In order to use the decision-making procedure outlined in the chapter on statistical inference, we must have some way of statistically comparing the means of the two groups to the population of means and mean differences we would expect to obtain from a set of scores that included the values measured in this study.

The following assumptions are made in comparing the means of the two samples:

1. Initially, at least, these two samples of individuals came from the same population of scores.
2. The population was normally distributed.
3. The two groups of individuals are representative samples.

When we compare the mean of one group to the mean of another group, we are, in effect, calculating a Z-score in which the numerator is the mean difference and the denominator is the standard error of the difference between the means. In Chapter 9 we demonstrated, using a pair of dice, how the distribution of means is derived from the distribution of scores and how the distribution of mean differences is derived from the distribution of means. Each distribution has its own variability estimate, as shown in Table 11.1.

TABLE 11.1   Distributions and Their Variability Estimates

TYPE OF DISTRIBUTION	VARIABILITY ESTIMATE
Scores	Standard deviation (s)
Means	Standard error of the mean (SEM)
Mean differences	Standard error of the difference between the means ($s_{\overline{X}_1 - \overline{X}_2}$)

For the distribution of scores you have seen that we can calculate a Z-score, for the distribution of means we calculate a confidence interval, and for the distribution of mean differences we calculate a *t*-ratio. The *t*-ratio we obtain is based on the difference between the means of the two groups divided by the standard error of the difference between the means. If the *t*-ratio obtained is large enough, we can say, for example, that we would expect a mean difference of this size to come from the same population only 5 times in 100, or only 1 time in 100, for the .05 and .01 levels of significance, respectively. The larger the *t*-ratio, the less likely it is that the two groups (which have been created through your experimental treatment) now come from the same population.

In order to fully understand the importance of this statement, you must recall the assumption that the two groups initially came from the same population, which was normally distributed, and that they were both representative samples of the population. In effect, your treatment changed one of the groups so that it now no longer appears to be a member of the same population as the other group.

CALCULATING THE
T-RATIO

The *t*-ratio as we have described it above is

$$t = \frac{\overline{X}_1 - \overline{X}_2}{s_{\overline{X}_1 - \overline{X}_2}} \tag{11.1}$$

The standard error of the difference between the means, the denominator, can be calculated by using the SEM's for each group:

$$s_{\bar{X}_1 - \bar{X}_2} = \sqrt{SEM_1^2 + SEM_2^2}$$ (11.2)

To calculate SEM, which was reviewed in Chapter 10 on confidence intervals:

$$SEM_1 = \frac{s_1}{\sqrt{N_1}}, \qquad SEM_2 = \frac{s_2}{\sqrt{N_2}}$$ (11.3)

You should know how to calculate the mean and standard deviation. If not, review the material on descriptive statistics presented in Chapter 3. Let us review and calculate a simple problem.

PROBLEM: A physical educator teaching exercise classes for adult women wishes to determine whether individuals in the class who have been consistently involved in vigorous physical activity over many years differ in physiological fitness from a group of women who have been sedentary.

DEFINITIONS: *Adult women:* Women over 30.
Consistently involved: Participation in classes or in jogging or other aerobic activity program on a regular basis (minimum 3 times per week) over a period of 5 years.
Sedentary: No regular participation in an aerobic exercise program over the past 5 years.
Physiological fitness: Measured by percent body fat, resting heart rate, and heart rate after exercise.

PROCEDURES: The sedentary ($N = 10$) and active women ($N = 10$) who met the criteria were asked to participate in the study. All subjects were tested on the same day. Each subject's height, weight, and age were recorded. Percent body fat was determined using the Sloan-Weir formula. Resting heart rate was obtained by taking the subject's pulse. Heart rate after exercise was measured using the progressive pulse-rate test (the data for the total two-minute count after 24 steps/min were used in the analysis, since all subjects completed this phase).

RESULTS: The scores are presented in Table 11.2(a). (Only the data for the percent body fat will be analyzed for the example. You should analyze the other data as practice.)

STATISTICS: The calculation of the t-test for percent body fat is presented in Table 11.2(b). The calculation of each of the intermediate steps is illustrated in Table 11.3.

In order to determine whether the t-ratio obtained, 6.29, is large enough to yield a statistically significant difference, we must use the t-table, Table 2 in Appendix A, to determine the t-ratio required for significance. First, how-

TABLE 11.2(a)   Scores for Sedentary and Active Women on Three Fitness Measures

PERCENT BODY FAT		RESTING HR		POST-EX HR	
SED.	ACT.	SED.	ACT.	SED.	ACT.
28	15	78	55	150	94
32	20	84	50	160	90
40	10	90	60	170	100
35	23	70	45	155	120
18	9	95	65	175	110
25	17	88	52	140	140
33	12	72	51	145	135
30	16	74	58	151	99
37	15	80	50	135	130
28	21	72	46	160	105

TABLE 11.2(b)   Statistical Calculations for *t*-test of Difference Between Sedentary and Active Women on Percent Body Fat

	SEDENTARY		ACTIVE
ΣX	306		158
N	10		10
$\overline{X}$	30.6		15.8
ΣX^2	9724		2690
s	6.0		4.4
SEM	1.9		1.4
$s_{\overline{X}_1 - \overline{X}_2}$		2.36	
t		6.27	

ever, we must determine the *df* (degrees of freedom). The *df* for the sedentary group is $N - 1$ or $10 - 1$ or 9. The *df* for the active group is $N - 1$ or $10 - 1$ or 9. Therefore, the total *df* are 18. We go to Table A2 and find that the critical value, the *t* which we must equal or exceed, is 2.101 if we have chosen the .05 level of significance and 2.861 if we have chosen the .01 level of significance. Knowing this information, we can follow the decision steps outlined in Chapter 9. These steps are illustrated in Table 11.4.

THE *T*-TEST FOR DEPENDENT GROUPS

The *t*-test that we have just considered is generally known as the *t*-test for *independent groups*. That is, the groups are made up of individuals who have been assigned randomly or because they have some characteristic (personality,

TABLE 11.3 Calculation of t-Test

---

a. STANDARD DEVIATION

SEDENTARY   ACTIVE

$$s = \sqrt{\frac{\Sigma X_1^2 - N(\overline{X}_1^2)}{N_1}} \qquad s = \sqrt{\frac{\Sigma X_2^2 = N(\overline{X}_2^2)}{N_2}} \qquad (11.4)$$

$$= \sqrt{\frac{9724 - 10(30.6)^2}{10}} \qquad = \sqrt{\frac{2690 - 10(15.8)^2}{10}}$$

$$= \sqrt{\frac{9724 - 10(936.36)}{10}} \qquad = \sqrt{\frac{2690 - 10(249.64)}{10}}$$

$$= \sqrt{\frac{9724 - 9363.6}{10}} \qquad = \sqrt{\frac{2690 - 2496.4}{10}}$$

$$= \sqrt{\frac{360.4}{10}} \qquad = \sqrt{\frac{193.6}{10}}$$

$$= \sqrt{36.04} \qquad = \sqrt{19.36}$$

$$= 6.00 \qquad = 4.4$$

b. STANDARD ERROR OF THE MEAN

SEDENTARY   ACTIVE

$$\text{SEM}_1 = \frac{s_1}{\sqrt{N_1}} \qquad \text{SEM}_2 = \frac{s_2}{\sqrt{N_2}} \qquad (11.5)$$

$$= \frac{6.00}{\sqrt{10}} \qquad = \frac{4.4}{\sqrt{10}}$$

$$= \frac{6.00}{3.16} \qquad = \frac{4.4}{3.16}$$

$$= 1.9 \qquad = 1.4$$

c. STANDARD ERROR OF THE DIFFERENCE BETWEEN THE MEANS

$$s_{\overline{x}_1 - \overline{x}_2} = \sqrt{\text{SEM}_1^2 + \text{SEM}_2^2} \qquad (11.6)$$

$$= \sqrt{(1.9)^2 + (1.4)^2}$$

$$= \sqrt{3.61 + 1.96}$$

$$= \sqrt{5.57}$$

$$= 2.36$$

TABLE 11.3   (Continued)

d.   *t*-RATIO

$$t = \frac{\bar{X}_1 - \bar{X}_2}{s_{\bar{X}_1 - \bar{X}_2}} \tag{11.7}$$

$$= \frac{30.6 - 15.8}{2.36}$$

$$= \frac{14.8}{2.36}$$

$$= 6.27$$

TABLE 11.4   Decision-Making Steps for Sedentary versus Active Women

1.   THE PROBLEM

Is there a difference in physiological fitness, as measured by percent body fat, between sedentary and active women? (The problem would be stated similarly for the other measures.)

2.   RESEARCH HYPOTHESIS

If one group of individuals is sedentary and the other group is active, then there will be a difference in percent body fat.

3.   STATISTICAL HYPOTHESES

H_0: $\bar{X}_{sed} = \bar{X}_{act}$
H_1: $\bar{X}_{sed} \neq \bar{X}_{act}$

4.   LEVEL OF SIGNIFICANCE

.01

5.   DECISION RULE

Reject H_0 if *t* with 18 *df* equals or exceeds 2.861.

6.   RESULTS

The value obtained is $t = 6.27$ (if negative value obtained, use absolute value for comparison).
Mean percent body fat for sedentary = 30.6.
Mean percent body fat for active = 15.8.

7.   CONCLUSION

Reject null; sedentary individuals have higher percentage of body fat than active individuals.

fitness level) which differentiates them from individuals assigned to the other group. You will have occasion in doing research to test the same individual under different conditions (the person is the best control for some of the factors that may influence results) or to test individuals who are matched for some characteristic which may influence the outcome. In these cases we cannot use the independent-groups t-test but must use the *dependent-groups* t-test. The decision-making procedure is the same, but the method of obtaining the t-ratio is different. Instead of working with the scores of the two different groups, you work with the differences between the first set of scores and the second set. Rather than using the difference between the means of the two groups, you use a mean difference score. The first step in calculating the matched-pairs or dependent-groups t-test is to align the matching scores (unlike the independent t-test, the number of scores must be the same for both groups) and take the difference, always in the same direction, algebraically.

CALCULATING THE t-RATIO FOR DEPENDENT GROUPS

The t-ratio for dependent groups is

$$t = \frac{\bar{D}}{s_{\bar{D}}} \tag{11.8}$$

Verbally, t equals the mean difference divided by the standard error of the difference. As you might imagine, the standard error of the difference is related to the standard deviation and the SEM. In fact, it is equivalent to the SEM and is obtained in a similar manner. The standard deviation is the first step, and we calculate it in the same way as when we considered X, but instead we use D wherever X appeared:

$$\bar{s}_D = \sqrt{\frac{\Sigma D^2 - \frac{(\Sigma D)^2}{N}}{N}} \quad \text{or} \quad s_D = \sqrt{\frac{\Sigma D^2 - N(\bar{D}^2)}{N}} \tag{11.9}$$

It should be noted that in this formula, as well as in the formula for the t-test, some individuals use $N - 1$ in the denominator. That formula tends to give a more conservative test, but the formula used here is acceptable.

Once s_D is obtained, $s_{\bar{D}}$ can be obtained by

$$s_{\bar{D}} = \frac{s_D}{\sqrt{N}} \tag{11.10}$$

As before, let us proceed through an example.

PROBLEM: A fitness instructor wished to determine whether individuals could perform more bent-leg sit-ups with the legs held than without.

PROCEDURES: An instructor asked a group of 9 individuals to participate in the study. The individuals were randomly assigned to two groups. One group did the held-leg sit-ups the first week and the nonheld-bent-leg sit-ups the second week. The other group did the two types of sit-ups in reverse order. The subjects were asked to perform as many sit-ups as they could each time. *Did the individuals do more sit-ups with legs held than without?* (*Note:* Before using the matched-pairs *t*-test, the instructor determined that the order of testing did not make a difference in the outcome and therefore the test would be appropriate.)

RESULTS: The results of the testing and the preliminary calculations are presented in Tables 11.5 and 11.6. The decision-making steps are presented in Table 11.7.

TABLE 11.5   Number of Sit-ups Done by Subjects with Held and Nonheld Legs

SUBJECT	HELD BENT LEG	BENT LEG	D	D²
a	35	30	5	25
b	40	30	10	100
c	25	25	0	0
d	36	38	−2	4
e	44	35	9	81
f	56	50	6	36
g	24	23	1	1
h	22	18	4	16
i	18	14	4	16
			ΣD: 37	
			ΣD^2:	279

TABLE 11.6   Calculation of Matched-Pairs *t*-test

To find s_D using equation (11.9):

$$s_D = \sqrt{\dfrac{279 - \dfrac{(37)^2}{9}}{9}} = 3.75 \qquad (11.11)$$

To find $s_{\bar{D}}$:

$$s_{\bar{D}} = \frac{s_D}{\sqrt{N}} = \frac{3.75}{\sqrt{9}} = \frac{3.73}{3} = 1.25 \qquad (11.12)$$

Then $\bar{D}$ is

$$\bar{D} = \frac{37}{9} = 4.11 \qquad (11.13)$$

Finally, *t* is calculated by

$$t = \frac{\bar{D}}{s_{\bar{D}}} = \frac{4.11}{1.25} = 3.29 \qquad (11.14)$$

TABLE 11.7   Decision-Making Steps for Held and Nonheld Sit-ups

---

1. THE PROBLEM

Is there a difference between the number of held-bent-leg sit-ups and nonheld-bent-leg sit-ups a subject can do?

2. RESEARCH HYPOTHESIS

If the same individuals do held-bent-leg sit-ups and nonheld-bent-leg sit-ups, then the number of sit-ups will differ.

3. STATISTICAL HYPOTHESES

H_0: $\bar{X}_1 = \bar{X}_2$ or $\bar{D} = 0$
H_1: $\bar{X}_1 \neq \bar{X}_2$ or $\bar{D} \neq 0$

4. LEVEL OF SIGNIFICANCE

.05

5. DECISION RULE

Reject H_0 if t with 8 df is equal to or greater than 2.306.

6. RESULTS

The value obtained is 3.29.
Mean difference is 4.11.
Average bent-leg sit-ups legs held is 33.33
Average bent-leg sit-ups legs free is 29.22

7. CONCLUSION

Reject null. Individuals do more bent-leg sit-ups if legs are held.

EXERCISES

Exercises 1–5 relate to the independent t*-test presented in the first part of the chapter and Exercises 6–9 to the matched-pairs* t*-test presented in the second part.*

1. Complete the statistical analysis for the resting-heart-rate scores presented in the example in the chapter.
2. Complete the statistical analysis for the heart-rate-after-exercise scores presented in the example in the chapter.
3. A physical education teacher wished to determine whether mental practice would lead to skill acquisition when compared to no prac-

tice at all. She therefore divided the group of students into an experimental and a control group. There were 10 students in the experimental group (mental practice) and 8 students in the control (no-practice) group. The scores are given below. *Did mental practice enhance learning?* (Use decision-making steps.)

Mental practice: 10, 9, 8, 11, 12, 11, 8, 7, 9, 12
Control group: 3, 4, 5, 7, 2, 5, 4, 7

4. A researcher wished to determine the effect of perceptual style on the learning of a skill. A group of 50 students were tested and the 10 extremely field-dependent and 10 extremely field-independent were then tested on a task. The scores they obtained on the task are presented below. *Did the field-dependent individuals score differently than the field-independent individuals?*

Field dependent: 2, 3, 5, 6, 7, 3, 4, 5, 4, 3
Field independent: 6, 7, 5, 8, 9, 4, 6, 5, 6, 9

5. A bowling instructor wished to determine whether it would be better to start a class off with a hook ball immediately or whether it would be better to begin by teaching a straight ball. A class of beginning bowlers were randomly assigned to either the hook-ball group ($N = 9$) or the straight-ball group ($N = 16$). The unequal N's are the result of individuals' dropping out over the semester or missing too many classes to be continued in the experiment. At the end of the sixth week of class the instructor recorded the score. *Was there a difference in the performance of the two groups?*

Hook-ball group: 90, 95, 100, 120, 80, 95, 80, 100, 120
Straight-ball group: 80, 90, 110, 100, 95, 80, 95, 100, 90, 85, 110, 120, 80, 90, 85, 100

[Hint: To make the numbers easier to deal with you can divide each by 10 and use the adjusted scores.]

6. A teacher of young children wanted to find out whether they would do better at catching a large playground ball or a small playground ball. To test the difference the teacher used the 16 children in the class and two playground balls—a 12-inch (large) and an 8-inch (small). *Did the children do better with the large or the small ball?*

Child:	a	b	c	d	e	f	g	h	i	j	k	l	m	n	o	p
Large:	5	4	6	7	8	4	9	3	6	8	9	10	13	14	7	8
Small:	7	8	4	8	8	4	7	9	8	9	11	13	14	10	5	6

7. A basketball coach wished to determine the effect of fatigue on accuracy in foul shooting. A total of 9 players were selected. These players shot 25 shots at the beginning of practice, and then after practice they shot 25 more shots. The practice was strenuous, and these players were on the go constantly. *Was there a difference in accuracy due to fatigue?*

Player:	a	b	c	d	e	f	g	h	i
Before:	20	18	16	24	22	19	18	22	21
After:	18	16	17	22	23	17	16	20	17

8. A recreation supervisor wanted to determine whether the environment affected the play behavior of children. Two environments were used, and the same 12 children played on both. The score was the amount of time they paid attention to the task. *Was there a difference in task-centered behavior in the two environments?*

Child:	a	b	c	d	e	f	g	h	i	j	k	l
Env. 1:	30	35	20	35	25	20	21	23	18	29	40	30
Env. 2:	40	30	18	34	22	19	20	26	16	34	38	38

9. A motor-learning teacher wished to demonstrate the effect of the number of stimulus choices on the time to complete a task. Therefore the members of the class were asked to sort a deck of cards into 2 piles by color (black and red) and then into 4 piles by suit (hearts, diamonds, spades, clubs). Each of the 14 members of the class completed the two tasks. The scores, in time to complete the sort, are given below. *Was there a difference in the time to complete the sorts?*

Student:	a	b	c	d	e	f	g	h	i	j	k	l	m	n
Color:	30	28	34	26	24	29	30	27	26	34	21	27	29	30
Suit:	45	40	44	35	30	40	44	45	40	46	39	38	41	45

CHAPTER TWELVE
DETERMINING THE RELATIONSHIP BETWEEN TWO MEANS

Often researchers, teachers, employers, and college admissions officers wish to describe the relationship between two sets of scores. Is there a tendency, for example, for individuals who do well on a test of sit-ups to also do well on a test of leg lifts? What is the relationship between the bowling scores of students on the first day of class and their scores on the last day? If I know the SAT scores of a group of college admissions applicants, can I predict their college GPA, or their class standing?

Basically, people who are interested in researching relationships between and among variables are attempting to discover whether, knowing one fact about an individual (say, his or her height), they can predict another variable (such as weight). Sometimes the relationship between two variables is so strong that you can ascertain it merely by scanning the two sets of scores. This occurs rarely in practice, however, and so we must turn to a statistical method for estimating the relationship between the variables.

In this chapter we will discuss two methods of determining the strength of a relationship. The first method, the Pearson product-moment correlation (PPM), is used with interval or ratio data. It is therefore a parametric test and assumes that the population from which the sample was drawn is normal. The second method, the Spearman rank-order correlation (ROC), is used with ordinal data and, as you might guess, does not assume a normal distribution but is a nonparametric test.

Before considering the statistical measurement of the strength of a correlation, let us review the concept of correlation by discussing the scattergram. This, you will see, is a method of graphing the relationship between two variables. The picture we derive from this graph can provide a hint about the relationship we will find, and it provides an opportunity to discuss the types of relationships and their interpretation.

SCATTERGRAM

A *scattergram* is a graph. One of the variables under consideration is scaled along the horizontal axis, the other along the vertical axis. Let us assume that we are interested in the relationship between individuals' performances on a 3-minute step test and a 1-minute step test. The reason for this interest is obvious. If we could obtain *comparable* predictions of cardiovascular efficiency by administering a 1-minute step test and a 3-minute test, we might for a variety of reasons choose the 1-minute test.

Thus, we administer the two tests to a group of subjects, each subject taking both tests on different days. We record the pulse rate of the subjects after 30 seconds, 1 minute, and 1:30 minutes following exercise on each test. For purposes of illustration we will use only the 1:30-minute score on each of the tests. These scores are listed in Table 12.1.

To create a scattergram, we first find the highest and lowest scores (the range) for each variable. We then draw and label the axes. Finally we plot each

TABLE 12.1   Scores Obtained on the 3-Minute and 1-Minute Step Tests (Pulse Rate after 1:30 Minutes)

SUBJECT	3-MINUTE	1-MINUTE
a	110	90
b	105	88
c	100	89
d	115	95
e	118	100
f	100	90
g	100	80
h	120	102
i	98	80
j	102	95
k	108	84
l	113	97
m	112	92
n	120	104
o	110	100
p	108	96
q	101	90
r	120	99
s	100	87
t	95	79

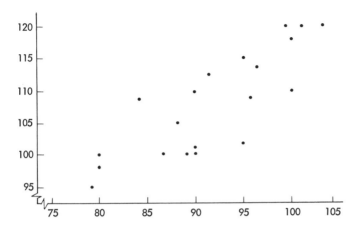

FIGURE 12.1   Scattergram of the relationship between a 1- and a 3-minute step test.

pair of scores on the graph by placing a point at the intersection of the two scores in the pair. Thus in the scores for subject a, we plot a point at the intersection of 110, 90; for b, at the intersection of 105, 88. Thus, we obtain a scattergram as illustrated in Figure 12.1.

The scattergram provides a picture of the relationship of the two sets of scores. In Figure 12.1 we can discern a positive relationship between the scores obtained on the 1-minute and 3-minute step tests. Even though the scores on the 1-minute tests were generally lower than those on the 3-minute test, individuals who had the higher pulse rates after 1:30 minutes on one test had the higher pulse rates after 1:30 minutes on the other test. This is generally true, even though there were some exceptions. Correlation is used to indicate an average relationship.

The scattergram can indicate:

1. A positive relationship—both sets of scores increase.
2. A negative relationship—as one set of scores increases, the other set decreases.
3. No relationship—there is no discernible pattern common to both sets of scores.

The general pattern of scores for these relationships is shown in Figure 12.2. The general pattern can be discerned by drawing a figure which includes all the points.

While the scattergram provides an approximation of the relationship between two variables or sets of scores, we often require a precise indication of the relationship. This precision is obtained through the Pearson product-moment correlation (used with interval and ratio data) or the Spearman rank-order correlation (used with ordinal data). Each of these statistical techniques will be reviewed, and then we shall look at a problem that illustrates the use of the decision-making process in these tests.

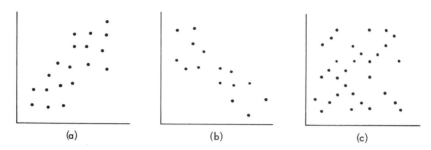

FIGURE 12.2   Illustration of (a) positive, (b) negative, and (c) zero relationships between two variables.

PEARSON PRODUCT-MOMENT CORRELATION

The *Pearson product-moment correlation* compares the *joint variance* (called *covariance*) of the variables X and Y with the variance of X and Y calculated individually and then combined. Thus, to calculate the *correlation coefficient* (r), the estimate of the relationship, you need to calculate the standard deviation of X, of Y, and of the created variable XY. The variable XY is obtained by multiplying each X by its associated Y. The standard deviation is then calculated on the resulting set of cross products. (It is immaterial which of the existing variables is labeled X and which Y.)

The steps in calculating the correlation coefficient are presented in Table 12.2. Thus, the relationship between the variables X and Y is estimated at .92. The correlation coefficient can vary between -1 and $+1$. The closer the correlation is to $+1$ or -1, the more predictable the relationship between X and Y. Therefore a relationship of .92 is very good and tells us that the two sets of scores have a high relationship to one another. The two sets of scores share very strong common variance. We could predict the score on Y given the score on X. (In more advanced courses in statistics the point is to write an equation based on the relationship between X and Y that will enable you to predict Y if you know X. This is called linear regression, and you may study it in the future.)

As with other statistical tests we want to know the stability of the correlation coefficient we have obtained. We use Table 3 in Appendix A. The *df* for the correlation is $N - 2$, where N is the number of pairs. Thus, for this problem $df = 8$. Our r must be greater than or equal to .632 to be significant at the .05 level and .765 to be significant at the .01 level. The value we obtained, .92, was sufficient for either significance level. Therefore the relationship is a significant one, and we could predict Y given X if we had calculated the linear regression equation.

In conducting research using the Pearson product-moment correlation we follow the decision-making steps outlined in Chapter 9. Let us carry

TABLE 12.2   Calculating the Correlation Coefficient (r)

1. Obtain $\Sigma\ X$, $\Sigma\ X^2$, $\Sigma\ Y$, ΣY^2, and $\Sigma\ XY$.

X^2	X	XY	Y	Y^2
1	1	4	4	16
9	3	6	2	4
25	5	40	8	64
49	7	42	6	36
81	9	90	10	100
121	11	176	16	256
169	13	182	14	196
225	15	180	12	144
289	17	340	20	400
361	19	342	18	324
1330	100	1402	110	1540

2. Obtain the standard deviation of X and of Y, using the formula presented in Chapter 3. (*Note:* You will need to calculate s_{XY} as indicated in step 3.)

$$s_X = 5.74, \qquad s_Y = 5.74$$

3. To calculate s_{XY}, use

$$s_{XY} = \frac{\Sigma\ XY - \dfrac{(\Sigma\ X)(\Sigma\ Y)}{N}}{N} \quad \text{or} \quad \frac{\Sigma\ XY - N(\overline{X})(\overline{Y})}{N} \quad (12.1)$$

$$= \frac{1402 - \dfrac{(100)(110)}{10}}{10} \qquad \frac{1402 - 10(10)(11)}{10}$$

$$= \frac{1402 - 1100}{10} \qquad\qquad \frac{1402 - 1100}{10}$$

$$= \frac{302}{10} \qquad\qquad\qquad \frac{302}{10}$$

$$= 30.2 \qquad\qquad\qquad 30.2$$

4. Find r_{XY} by substituting in the formula:

$$r_{XY} = \frac{s_{XY}}{(s_X)(s_Y)} \qquad\qquad (12.2)$$

$$= \frac{30.2}{(5.74)(5.74)}$$

$$= \frac{30.2}{32.95}$$

$$= .92$$

through a sample problem which would employ the correlation coefficient just explained.

PROBLEM: In the February 1980 issue of *JOPER* an article discussed the use of the curl-up as an alternative to the bent-leg sit-up. A physical educator wished to test whether the results obtained for curl-ups would be comparable to those obtained for bent-leg sit-ups.

PROCEDURES: The instructor asked students in a fitness class to serve as the subjects. She asked them to perform as many curl-ups as they could in 30 seconds. One week later she asked the same students to perform as many bent-leg sit-ups as they could. She was interested in determining whether the number of curl-ups the students could perform was comparable to the number of bent-leg sit-ups. *Is there a relationship between the number of bent-leg sit-ups and the number of curl-ups that students can perform?*

RESULTS: The numbers of sit-ups and curl-ups recorded for each student are presented in Table 12.3. The statistical analysis is presented in Table 12.4, and the decision-making steps are summarized in Table 12.5.

SPEARMAN RANK-ORDER CORRELATION

Ordinal data do not permit the use of the Pearson product-moment correlation (PPM). The Spearman rank-order correlation (ROC) is designed for use in these situations. It, like the PPM, provides a measure of the relationship between two variables, X and Y, either or both of which are ordinal or ranked

TABLE 12.3   Number of Sit-ups and Curl-ups Performed

STUDENT	X^2	NUMBER OF SIT-UPS X	XY	NUMBER OF CURL-UPS Y	Y^2
a	225	15	285	19	361
b	144	12	156	13	169
c	256	16	224	14	196
d	196	14	168	12	144
e	324	18	360	20	400
f	121	11	154	14	196
g	100	10	150	15	225
h	196	14	224	16	256
i	289	17	323	19	361
j	256	16	320	20	400
k	100	10	140	14	196
l	81	9	81	9	81
	2288	162	2585	185	2985

TABLE 12.4   Statistical Analysis of Curl-up and Sit-up Scores

a. Standard Deviation of X and Y

$$s_x = \sqrt{\dfrac{\Sigma X^2 - \dfrac{(\Sigma X)^2}{N}}{N}} \qquad\qquad s_Y = \sqrt{\dfrac{\Sigma Y^2 - \dfrac{(\Sigma Y)^2}{N}}{N}}$$

$$= \sqrt{\dfrac{2288 - \dfrac{(162)^2}{12}}{12}} \qquad\qquad = \sqrt{\dfrac{2985 - \dfrac{(185)^2}{12}}{12}}$$

$$= \sqrt{\dfrac{2288 - 2187}{12}} \qquad\qquad = \sqrt{\dfrac{2985 - 2852.1}{12}}$$

$$= \sqrt{\dfrac{101}{12}} \qquad\qquad = \sqrt{\dfrac{132.9}{12}}$$

$$= \sqrt{8.42} \qquad\qquad = \sqrt{11.07}$$

$$= 2.9 \qquad\qquad = 3.33$$

b. Standard deviation of XY

$$s_{XY} = \dfrac{\Sigma XY - \dfrac{(\Sigma X)(\Sigma Y)}{N}}{N}$$

$$= \dfrac{2585 - \dfrac{(162)(185)}{12}}{12}$$

$$= \dfrac{2585 - 2497.5}{12}$$

$$= \dfrac{87.5}{12}$$

$$= 7.29$$

c. Correlation Coefficient

$$r_{XY} = \dfrac{s_{XY}}{(s_x)(s_Y)}$$

$$= \dfrac{7.29}{(2.9)(3.33)}$$

$$= \dfrac{7.29}{9.66}$$

$$= .75$$

TABLE 12.5   Decision-Making Steps for Correlation

1.   THE PROBLEM

Is there a relationship between the number of sit-ups a student can do in 30 seconds
and the number of curl-ups a student can do in 30 seconds?

2.   RESEARCH HYPOTHESIS

If an individual does both bent-leg sit-ups and curl-ups, then there will be a relationship between the number of each he or she can do.

3.   STATISTICAL HYPOTHESES

   H_0: $r_{XY} = 0$
   H_1: $r_{XY} \neq 0$

4.   LEVEL OF SIGNIFICANCE

   .05

5.   DECISION RULE

Reject null if r with 10 df (number of paired scores −2) ≥ .576.

6.   RESULT

The r value obtained is .75.

7.   CONCLUSION

Reject null; curl-ups and sit-ups are related; as the number of curl-ups performed
increases, the number of sit-ups performed increases.

variables. The ROC uses the difference (D) between the ranks of the two sets of
scores in determining the correlation coefficient (rho).

The first step in calculating rho is to obtain D (the difference between the
rankings for each case). Always take the difference in the same direction (that
is, $X - Y$). This step is illustrated in Table 12.6.

The second step is to obtain D^2 by squaring each D, also shown in Table
12.6.

The third step is to obtain the $\Sigma\ D$ and the $\Sigma\ D^2$. These are included in
Table 12.6.

The fourth step is to calculate rho. This is shown in Table 12.7.

Finally the value obtained is compared to the value, from Table 4 in
Appendix A, required for significance. This is presented in Table 12.8, which
illustrates the decision-making steps.

This was a simple problem because there were no duplicate ranks and
because both sets of scores were ranked to start. More generally you will have
to rank at least one set of scores and will have to deal with duplicate scores.

TABLE 12.6   Scores and Initial Calculations for Rank-Order Correlation

SUBJECT	RANK ON X	RANK ON Y	D	D²
1	1	2	−1	1
2	2	10	−8	64
3	3	1	2	4
4	4	8	−4	16
5	5	6	−1	1
6	6	3	3	9
7	7	4	3	9
8	8	5	−3	9
9	9	9	0	0
10	10	7	3	9
			D: −6	
			D²:	122

TABLE 12.7   Calculation of Rho

$$rho = 1 - \frac{6 \, \Sigma \, D^2}{n(n^2 - 1)}$$

$$= 1 - \frac{6(122)}{10(10^2 - 1)}$$

$$= 1 - \frac{732}{990}$$

$$= 1 - [.74]$$

$$= .36$$

The original scores before ranking are called *raw scores*. The important thing to remember is that the rankings of one individual are considered as a pair and are to be considered as a unit for obtaining D and D^2.

In ranking a set of raw scores, follow the procedures given below.

1. Find the *best* score.
2. Label that score 1.
3. Find the next *best* score.
4. Label that 2.
5. Continue labeling each score in turn until all scores have been labeled.

In the event that two or more scores are the same, assign the ranks to those scores from top of column to bottom of column. When all rankings are assigned, go back and find the scores which are the same. Average the ranks you have assigned to these scores and then use the average rank to calculate D and D^2. (See the examples in Table 12.9.) After both sets of scores have been ranked, follow the procedures in the example to calculate rho. In instances in

TABLE 12.8   Decision-Making Steps for Rank-Order Correlation

1. THE PROBLEM

Is there a relationship between the rankings of a group of individuals on variables X and Y?

2. RESEARCH HYPOTHESIS

If the ranks of a group of individuals on X and Y are compared, there will be a relationship.

3. STATISTICAL HYPOTHESES

H_0:   rho $= 0$
H_1:   rho $\neq 0$

4. LEVEL OF SIGNIFICANCE

.05

5. DECISION RULE

Reject null if rho with $N = 10$ is equal to or greater than .648.

6. RESULTS

rho $= .36$

7. CONCLUSION

Do not reject null; rankings on X and Y are not related.

which there are scores which are equal, decimal ranks may be obtained. Be especially careful in working through the problems when decimals are present.

FURTHER USES OF CORRELATION

In addition to its use in research studies involving questions about the relationship between or among variables, correlation is used extensively in measurement, in test construction, and in research to determine validity and reliability. Correlation is certainly one of the most important tools a researcher uses in designing and executing studies. In the initial design stage the researcher must choose independent and dependent variables which are appropriate to the concepts under study and to the purpose of the research. Often this involves using correlational techniques to determine relationships between selected measures and research constructs. The researcher also needs to establish the objectivity of the measures used. This may involve correlations

TABLE 12.9   Examples of Ranking Sets of Scores

EXAMPLE 1   (RAW SCORES, NO DUPLICATES)

STUDENT	RANK ON X	RAW SCORE ON Y	RANK ON Y
1	1	87	4
2	2	90	3
3	3	85	6
4	4	84	7
5	5	86	5
6	6	92	2
7	7	80	8
8	8	93	1
9	9	79	9
10	10	75	10
11	11	70	12
12	12	73	11
13	13	65	14
14	14	69	13
15	15	50	15

EXAMPLE 2   (RAW SCORES, DUPLICATES)

STUDENT	RANK ON X	RAW SCORE ON Y	POSITION	RANK ON Y	
1	1	90*	(1)	$(1 + 2)/2 =$	1.5
2	2	87	(3)		3
3	3	90*	(2)		1.5
4	4	86	(4)		4
5	5	80*	(6)	$(6 + 7 + 8)/3 =$	7
6	6	85	(5)		5
7	7	80*	(7)		7
8	8	80*	(8)		7
9	9	75*	(9)	$(9 + 10)/2 =$	9.5
10	10	75*	(10)		9.5
11	11	70	(11)		11
12	12	65	(12)		12

to determine interobserver, intraobserver, equipment, instrument, or test reliability.

In Chapter 3 we discussed the *score* and indicated that for the purpose of understanding variance we could partition a score into two parts—one part representative (this was the mean of the group) and one part individual (this was the part which was unique to each individual and was the indicator of individual differences). This view is helpful when we consider scores in a group and want to understand variance. For the purpose of understanding problems of measurement and reliability and validity, however, it is useful to consider the score of an individual subject. Each person's observed score has two components: a true score and an error score. Since we can never know what a person's true score really is, this is hypothetical. We do know, however, that the error scores are random. Sometimes the observed score will be higher than the true score and sometimes lower, but the sum of the differences between the true score and the observed scores should be zero over the long run. Thus, correlation techniques can be used to estimate the stability of the observed score. By doing so we can determine the reliability or validity of the observed scores and the test, equipment, instrument, or measure.

Reliability

When measurement is reliable, it is dependable; it provides an accurate estimate of the characteristic being measured and it is precise. In short, the measure is internally consistent. Reliability is determined through correlation: the higher the correlation coefficient, the more stable and consistent the test and the more dependable its results. It is important to establish the reliability of performance tests, written tests, equipment, observation scales, and instruments before they are used in research and testing. There are several methods for establishing reliability: test-retest, equivalence, and internal consistency.

Test-retest reliability is established by testing the same subjects on the same test at two different times, preferably a week or more apart. The scores achieved on the first administration are correlated with those achieved on the second. This form of reliability should be established if the study or testing necessitates assessment of performance or behavior over long time intervals.

Equivalence reliability is established by designing equivalent forms of the same test and administering them to the same group of individuals within a short time. Stability can also be established by lengthening the time between administrations of the equivalent forms. This might be important in cases where the students could recall the answers given on a particular test or pre- and posttesting might occur after a short interval.

Internal-consistency reliability is used to determine whether a test is homogeneous and is useful if a test is timed and some subjects may not finish. It is generally determined by correlating the scores obtained on the first and second halves of the test or on the odd- and even-numbered questions.

Reliability of testing instruments or performance measures may be low for a number of reasons, most of which are under the control of the researcher. The measuring instrument may not be accurate or sensitive and may need checking and calibration prior to each testing session. Bicycle ergometers, object projection devices, computers, and other mechanical devices are subject to the effects of humidity, heat, dust, and other environmental changes and should be tested frequently. Certainly they should be tested prior to each day's testing but sometimes between or within subjects. Your research is only as good as your data.

The instructions for scoring a particular behavior or for reading an instrument scale may be ambiguous. Often research assistants are given cursory instruction, tested briefly on the procedures and equipment, and then turned loose to test subjects. As the testing proceeds, they will get better; practice makes perfect, and the quality and consistency of their work will improve. Research assistants should practice until they become consistent in their measurements or manipulations, or mechanical measuring and recording devices should be used as much as possible.

If different researchers test different subjects, they may score the test differently. We can test an instrument, observation form, or procedure for inter- and intrarater reliability. For interrater reliability, different raters rate the same subject and their ratings are correlated; for intrarater reliability, the same rater rates the same subject more than once and the ratings are correlated. The growing use of descriptive scales for observing teacher behavior demands that this type of assessment be extensive, since individuals other than trained observers are beginning to utilize scales.

Other factors which can affect the reliability of a test are: number of trials, length of testing, instructions, distractions, task difficulty, and intertrial interval. In designing and evaluating an experimental design and procedure, the researcher must pay careful attention to establishing the reliability and must be aware of the factors that can affect the outcome of the testing by undermining attempts to minimize the error variance.

The researcher also can use some less-than-adequate methods for maximizing reliability estimates. One method is to insure that your group is heterogeneous; that is, maximize individual differences. That way, the individuals who test poorly will continue to do so and those who test well will continue to do so. It is far better, and more honest, to try to control the factors that underlie error variance.

Validity

Establishing the validity of a test, performance measure, or instrument involves assessing the relationship (correlation) between the variable observed and the behavior you want to measure. "Does the test measure what I say it measures?" In order for a test to be valid, it must be reliable; it must measure whatever it measures consistently. A test may be reliable and not valid, but a test that is not reliable cannot be valid. For research both reliability and validity are desirable; often, however, validity is difficult or impossible to establish, and for a particular measure it may not exist.

In motor-behavior research, for example, two major schools of thought are emerging. One group uses information-processing paradigms in designing and interpreting research; another uses an ecological perception approach. The latter group asserts that information-processing paradigms are not *valid* because they ignore the total system in which behavior takes place by constraining the subject in artificial laboratory settings. In some cases it is difficult to establish validity. Doing so is often a three-stage process: (!) establishing the existence of a construct, (2) operationally defining it, and (3) finding a behavior which is accepted as a valid operational definition of the construct to use in establishing validity. This third step is not always possible to accomplish. Fortunately, there are other means by which validity can be established.

The three types of validity are content validity, criterion-related validity, and construct validity. If we wanted to design a test which would screen individuals who try out for a baseball team, we could evaluate the *content validity* of the test by asking baseball experts to review the test items and comment on the content. If our test contains items which assess performance in hitting, catching, running, fielding, and throwing, some individuals might say that the test is valid. Others might indicate that baseball is more than just the items mentioned and that a valid test should measure perseverance, teamwork, motivation, knowledge of rules, and the like. The idea, however, is that individuals who are knowledgeable in a particular area would review the items on your test and would indicate whether, in their opinion, the test was a valid measure of baseball performance: "Does the test contain items and content which sample the area being measured?"

Criterion-related validity is established by correlating the test scores with other measures known to measure the characteristic you want to assess. Continuing with the baseball example: "How well does the test predict performance over the baseball season?" "Will players who score high on the test also have higher batting averages, fewer errors, more stolen bases, more runs batted in than players who score low on the test?" This is predictive validity. We can also assess concurrent validity. Our example in the text related to the 3-minute versus the 1-minute step test as an example of concurrent validity. If the scores on the 1-minute step test correlate highly with those on the 3-minute step test, assuming that the 3-minute test is a good measure of cardiovascular endurance, then the 1-minute test has concurrent validity. It might be a good idea, however, to correlate the 1-minute test with a 12-minute run test or a bicycle ergometer test. That is, the test to be validated should be correlated with the best available test of that characteristic which it is feasible for the researcher to administer.

Construct validity establishes the degree to which a test measures the underlying concept it was designed to assess. If we return to the baseball example, we could establish construct validity of the test if we tested groups differing in baseball-playing ability and found that they differed in their performance on the test. It is also possible to test the construct validity by assessing individuals as they improve over time and establishing whether the test reflects this improvement. Establishing construct validity requires that the researcher engage in a theory-based research program.

EXERCISES

Problems 1–3 relate to the Pearson product-moment correlation and 4–8 relate to the Spearman rank-order correlation.

1. A statistics professor wishes to determine whether a student's semester average can be predicted from the results of a diagnostic math test taken at the beginning of the semester. The professor gathers data on 15 students in class. *Is there a relationship between the grade on a diagnostic test and the grade in statistics?*

Student:	1	2	3	4	5	6	7	8	9	10	11	12	13	14	15
Math (X):	85	90	75	65	78	92	84	79	83	71	68	65	87	92	81
Stat (Y):	90	87	79	75	86	75	76	85	90	76	75	68	90	81	94

2. A physical education major was interested in determining whether height was related to weight. The major asked 16 friends to write their height in inches and weight in pounds on a chart. *Are height and weight related?*

Person:	1	2	3	4	5	6	7	8	9	10	11	12	13	14	15	16
Height:	61	72	65	68	67	63	65	64	68	58	72	63	62	68	70	64
Weight:	115	160	140	158	125	120	130	127	148	94	163	147	130	165	200	112

3. Using the data provided previously regarding the 1- and 3-minute step test, determine the correlation coefficient. *Can the 1-minute step test be substituted for the 3-minute step test?*

SUBJECT	3 MINUTES (X)	1 MINUTE (Y)
a	110	90
b	105	88
c	100	89
d	115	95
e	118	100
f	100	90
g	100	80
h	120	102
i	98	80
j	102	95
k	108	84
l	113	97
m	112	92
n	120	104
o	110	100
p	108	96
q	101	90
r	120	99
s	100	87
t	95	79

4. A tennis coach wishes to determine whether a screening test for selecting players is a good measure of tennis ability. Therefore the players are tested on the tennis test and then asked to participate in a ladder tournament. *Is there a significant relationship between the score on the tennis test and final position in the ladder tournament?*

Player:	a	b	c	d	e	f	g	h	i	j	k	l	m	n
Rank in lad.:	1	2	3	4	5	6	7	8	9	10	11	12	13	14
Test score:	90	95	88	87	88	88	85	84	83	84	70	65	74	60

5. A sport sociologist seeks to determine whether there is a relationship between leadership ability as perceived by others and an individual's score on a test of democratic style. A group of individuals are asked to rate their supervisor on leadership ability using a questionnaire format. The supervisors are then given a democratic–authoritarian scale. *Is there a relationship between leadership ability and democratic–authoritarian style?*

Supervisor:	a	b	c	d	e	f	g	h	i	j	k	l
Leadership rank:	1	2	3	4	5	6	7	8	9	10	11	12
A-D Score:	98	96	94	94	93	94	85	88	90	75	80	75

6. A researcher was interested in whether the final ranking of softball teams was related to the number of years of experience of the players. *Is there a relationship?*

Team:	a	b	c	d	e	f	g	h	i
Rank:	1	2	3	4	5	6	7	8	9
Years of Exper.:	26	27	22	30	20	15	24	20	18

7. Calculate rho for Example 1 in Table 12.9.

8. Calculate rho for Example 2 in Table 12.9.

CHAPTER THIRTEEN
ANALYZING
CATEGORIZED
DATA

Often researchers work with data that represent classification of events rather than measurement of the level of a particular characteristic. This qualitative or nominal approach involves only crude levels of measurement rather than sensitive estimation of the quantity of a trait. Some research questions can be answered only by categorizing observations. If, for example, you were to obtain a sample of students from your college and wished to determine whether the sample was representative in terms of class membership (i.e., freshman, sophomore, junior, senior), you would use chi-square to determine whether the frequencies of freshman, sophomore, junior, senior were different from those expected. The expected levels are based on the proportions of those class members in the college population. An example will be helpful here.

ONE-WAY CHI-SQUARE

We have surveyed a sample of college students regarding their opinion about intercollegiate athletics and wish to determine whether the sample is representative of the college population as a whole. We obtain the numbers of different class members shown in Table 13.1.

We consult the registrar and obtain the actual percentage of different classes at the college. These are shown in Table 13.2.

We convert the expected percentages into the numbers expected for each class in our sample by determining the percentage of 400 each represents. Then

TABLE 13.1   Distribution by Class of College Sample

	FRESHMEN	SOPHOMORES	JUNIORS	SENIORS	TOTAL SAMPLE
Observed	50	100	150	100	400

TABLE 13.2   Actual Class Distribution in Percent of College Students

	FRESHMEN	SOPHOMORES	JUNIORS	SENIORS	TOTAL SAMPLE
Expected %	30%	20%	25%	25%	100%

TABLE 13.3   Comparison of Observed and Expected Samples

	FRESHMEN	SOPHOMORES	JUNIORS	SENIORS	TOTAL SAMPLE
Observed	50	100	150	100	400
Expected	120	80	100	100	400

we compare the expected numbers (based on the percentages in the total population) with the observed numbers in our sample by creating Table 13.3

The chi-square test enables us to determine, statistically, whether the observed frequency of class members is different from what we would expect by chance alone. That is, the probability of obtaining the expected values is high if we have a true random sample. If the sample is not random, we might expect deviations from the expected frequencies. The chi-square test and distribution enable us to test this statistically. For problems in which there is only one variable, e.g., class in college, we use a one-way chi-square test. For each cell, each classification, we determine the chi-square value by equation (13.1):

$$\text{chi-square} = \frac{(\text{observed} - \text{expected})^2}{\text{expected}} \quad \text{or} \quad \frac{(O - E)^2}{E} \qquad (13.1)$$

Thus, for each of the cells in Table 13.3 we solve equation (13.1) as shown in equations (13.2) through (13.5):

$$\text{Freshmen} \quad = \frac{(50 - 120)^2}{120} = \frac{(-70)^2}{120} = \frac{4900}{120} = 40.8 \qquad (13.2)$$

$$\text{Sophomores} = \frac{(100 - 80)^2}{80} = \frac{(20)^2}{80} = \frac{400}{80} = 5.00 \qquad (13.3)$$

$$\text{Juniors} \quad = \frac{(150 - 100)^2}{100} = \frac{(50)^2}{100} = \frac{2500}{100} = 25.00 \qquad (13.4)$$

$$\text{Seniors} \quad = \frac{(100 - 100)^2}{100} = 0 \qquad (13.5)$$

We then add all the individual chi-squares together to obtain the total chi-square value as shown in equation (13.6):

Freshmen	40.8
Sophomores	5.0
Juniors	25.0
Seniors	0
Total	70.8

(13.6)

The df for a one-way chi-square is the number of cells minus 1. For this problem, then, the df is 4–1 or 3. Using Table 5 in Appendix A, we see that to achieve significance our obtained chi-square must equal or exceed 7.82 (.05 level). It clearly does. In attempting to explain why the observed numbers are significant we conclude that the proportions of freshmen and juniors are too low and too high, respectively, in comparison to what we would expect to obtain by chance alone.

The chi-square statistic is especially useful for survey studies in which data can only be organized by categories. We might ask, for example, whether there is a significant difference in the psychological sex-role classifications of individuals engaged in team sports. We might administer a personality test and categorize members of teams according to their tendency on the test. We would then evaluate the frequencies according to the expectation of equal probability (or of the known distribution of these types in the population at large). An interesting study related to sport performance might be done by taking a basketball shooting chart and, using assigned probabilities of sinking a shot from different areas of the court (or equal probability), determining whether the team's or an individual player's performance differs significantly from chance. In each instance the observed frequencies are recorded and then the expected frequencies are determined. The chi-square statistic is used to compare the observed to the expected. (An interesting and useful application of chi-square using game statistics is discussed in Chapter 20.)

The steps in calculating the chi-square statistic in a one-sample or single-variable test are presented in Table 13.4.

DECISION MAKING

The decision-making steps can be used with the chi-square test to facilitate your work. This is shown in Table 13.5.

TABLE 13.4   Steps in Calculating a One-Way Chi-Square

1. Record the observations in the established or existing categories.
2. Determine the expected frequencies.
3. Calculate the chi-square value for each cell by

$$\text{chi-square} = \frac{(\text{observed} - \text{expected})^2}{\text{expected}}$$

4. Sum the individual chi-square values.
5. Determine the *df* by number of cells minus 1 and obtain the required chi-square value from Table A5.
6. Compare the value obtained in step 4 with the required value. If the obtained value is equal to or greater than the required value, then the frequencies observed are different than those expected by chance.
7. To determine where the differences lie, inspect the individual chi-square values. Those which individually exceed the required value are the source of the significance.

TABLE 13.5   Decision-Making Steps for One-Way Chi-Square Analysis

1. PROBLEM AND PROCEDURE

A physical education instructor who runs a local recreation program wishes to determine the number of assistants to hire for the program. In order to determine the pattern of use of the center, the number of individuals using it each time block is tallied. The instructor wishes to determine if the pattern is significantly different from chance.

2. RESEARCH HYPOTHESIS

If the tallies of the use per time block of a recreational center are recorded, then the usage per time block will differ.

3. STATISTICAL HYPOTHESES

   H_0: observed = expected
   H_1: observed ≠ expected

4. SIGNIFICANCE LEVEL

Use .05 level of significance.

5. DECISION RULE

Reject null if chi-square with 4 *df* (5 time blocks − 1) ≥ 9.49.

6. RESULT

The value obtained is:

TABLE 13.5   (cont.)

TIME BLOCK

	8–10	10–12	12–2	2–4	4–6	TOTAL
Obs.	15	30	35	40	20	140
Exp.	28	28	28	28	28	140

$$\frac{(O-E)^2}{E}$$

8–10: $\dfrac{(15-28)^2}{28} = 6.04$

10–12: $\dfrac{(30-28)^2}{28} = .14$

12–2: $\dfrac{(35-28)^2}{28} = 1.75$

2–4: $\dfrac{(40-28)^2}{28} = 5.14$

4–6: $\dfrac{(20-28)^2}{28} = \underline{2.28}$

Total = $\underline{15.35}$ chi-square

7. CONCLUSION

Reject null; the pattern of use changes as the day proceeds. Use appears to be below average from 8–10 and above average from 2–4.

CHI-SQUARE TEST FOR TWO VARIABLES

In many applications of the chi-square test there is no basis for generating expected frequencies. This is especially true when two independent variables are involved. In analyzing the results of research of this type the two-way chi-square test is used. In this test the cell frequencies are compared to the marginal totals, and what is tested is whether the two variables are independent or whether they interact to produce joint effects. An example will serve to clarify the point.

A researcher was interested in assessing the independence of the variables sex and sport participation. Thus, a survey of the intercollegiate athletes at a particular college was completed. The data were organized as shown in Table 13.6.

If we look at the row and column totals, we observe that they are all equal. A glance at the cell frequencies, however, reveals that when the two

TABLE 13.6   Sport Participation by Sex

	PARTICIPANT	NONPARTICIPANT	ROW TOTALS
Males	60	40	100
Females	40	60	100
Column totals	100	100	200 Grand total

variables are combined, there is a reversal in the frequencies. Thus, for the males the participants outnumber the nonparticipants 3:2, whereas for the females the relationship is reversed. The variables are not independent of each other; the combination leads to effects which are different from those seen in the marginal totals.

The major differences between the one-way chi-square test, which you are familiar with, and the two-way chi-square test, which we are considering now, are the way the df are calculated and the way the expected frequencies are obtained. The df are obtained by multiplying the number of rows minus 1 by the number of columns minus 1. In fact, we multiply the levels of one variable, e.g., sex minus 1, by the levels of the other variables, e.g., participation minus 1. Thus, for the present example the df are $(2 - 1)(2 - 1) = 1$.

In calculating the expected frequency for each cell we use equation (13.7):

$$\exp. = \frac{(\text{row sum})(\text{column sum})}{\text{grand sum}} \tag{13.7}$$

TABLE 13.7   Calculation of Expected Value and Chi-Square for Two-Factor Study

Cell name	$\dfrac{(\text{Row})(\text{Column})}{\text{Grand}}$	Expected	$\dfrac{(O - E)^2}{E}$
Male—Part.	$\dfrac{(100)(100)}{200}$	50	$\dfrac{(60 - 50)^2}{50} = 2$
Male—Non.	$\dfrac{(100)(100)}{200}$	50	$\dfrac{(40 - 50)^2}{50} = 2$
Female—Part.	$\dfrac{(100)(100)}{200}$	50	$\dfrac{(40 - 50)^2}{50} = 2$
Female—Non.	$\dfrac{(100)(100)}{200}$	50	$\dfrac{(60 - 50)^2}{50} = \underline{2}$

Total chi-square = 8
$df = 1$
Required value = 3.84
Reject null

In this way we obtain an expected frequency for each cell based upon the context of the marginal totals and the total frequency. We ask, "What proportion of the total should be in this cell if the variables were independent?" For each of the cells we calculate the expected and then the chi-square as illustrated in Table 13.7. We would conclude that sport participation appears to be related to gender.

This problem was unique in that the cells were an exact reversal of one another. Normally the expected value will be different for each cell, depending on the combination of marginal totals. As before, we can use the decision-making procedures to systematize our data analysis and conclusions. Since you should be familiar with this aspect, an example will not be presented here.

EXERCISES

1. A physical education professor at a small college complained that the library tended to favor the arts and sciences over physical education in their acquisition of new books. To demonstrate the point the professor gathered the following data. *Was there a significant difference in the numbers of books acquired in each subject area?*

PHYSICAL EDUCATION	CHEMISTRY	HISTORY	BIOLOGY	ECONOMICS
30	45	50	35	20

2. A swim coach wished to determine if the lane position at the start of a race had any effect on winning. Over a season the coach tallied the wins from each lane. (Swimmers were assigned on a random basis.) *Was there a significant difference in the frequency of wins from a particular lane?*

LANE 1	LANE 2	LANE 3	LANE 4	LANE 5	LANE 6
24	28	24	29	22	33

3. A physical education instructor interested in the psychosocial aspect of sports wished to determine whether the proportion of androgynous individuals required and elective programs. *Was there a difference in the proportion of androgynous individuals in the two programs?*

	MASCULINE	FEMININE	ANDROGYNOUS
Required program	7	16	16
Elective program	28	23	36

4. An athletic trainer wanted to determine whether taping was related to the incidence of ankle injuries in games. The trainer surveyed the local teams to determine which teams used taping and which did not use taping. The following data on injuries by taping and not taping were obtained. *Did taping affect the frequency of injuries?*

	INJURIES	NO INJURIES
Taping	13	37
No taping	27	48

5. An exercise physiologist wanted to determine whether the rate of failure on a physical education exemption test was related to gender. The following data were obtained. *Was there a difference?*

	PASS	FAIL
Females	30	50
Males	60	40

CHAPTER FOURTEEN
ANALYZING DIFFERENCES AMONG THREE GROUPS OR MORE

The type of statistical test to be considered in this chapter is crucial to research and to meaningful decision making. The alternative to conducting a single test of the three or more means of, for example, groups *a, b,* and *c* is to conduct three independent *t*-tests: *ab, bc,* and *ac.* This technique is unacceptable for a variety of reasons. The simplest example will be considered first.

Imagine that we have three groups of subjects and we are going to ask them to perform a task under varying levels of stress (our independent or treatment variable) and then measure their degree of success (our dependent variable or performance measure). We conduct the study and obtain the mean performances for the groups shown in Table 14.1.

Imagine for a moment that we only had a *t*-test available (this was true in the dark past). We would probably have approached the study quite differently and, instead of having three groups with three stress levels, we might have chosen only two groups. True to research techniques of maximizing the treatment differences we would probably have chosen only low and high stress. (This was, in fact, true in the past.) After conducting our experiment we would have ascertained, quite probably, that we could not reject the null and that low- and high-stress performance differed only by chance—a shocking discovery. The fact that we have analysis of variance available as a tool enables us to add intermediate conditions, such as the moderate-stress condition above. In this instance we observe that the effect of stress on performance is a U-shaped function. That is, performance is poor at low or high stress but seems to improve at moderate levels of stress.

This is only one example of effects that might not have been noted if

TABLE 14.1   Mean Performance Under Low, Moderate, or High Stress

LOW STRESS	MODERATE STRESS	HIGH STRESS
10	20	12

researchers had been constrained by primitive statistical techniques. In fact, the future of statistics holds highly complex multi-dependent-variable techniques which enable finer- and finer-grain analysis of observed effects. At this moment, however, we are concerned with a technique, one-way analysis of variance, which will enable us to evaluate the effect of a single variable which has more than two levels. We can, for example, evaluate multiple levels of the variables listed in Table 14.2.

TABLE 14.2   Examples of Levels of Variables

VARIABLE	LEVELS				
Fitness	High	Medium	Low		
Practice	None	1 day/wk	3 days/wk	5 days/wk	
Skill	High	Medium	Low		
Teaching meth.	Verbal	Demo	Combo	None	
Implement wgt.	30 oz	26 oz	22 oz	18 oz	14 oz
Reinforcer	Verbal	Money	Candy	None	

We can expand our horizons to the limits of our imaginations in exploring the variables of interest. We can explore the law of diminishing returns: when is practice too long? when is explanation too confusing? when is feedback too precise? how much should we tell students about the skill performance? how many miles should a runner jog a week? The analysis-of-variance technique permits the juxtaposing of a myriad of treatments. It is a useful technique to know. First let us consider the simplest case: one variable—stress; three levels—high, moderate, and low.

The final step in the calculation of the analysis of variance is the computation of the F-ratio. This is related to the t-ratio in that the treatment effect is divided by the error variance. (In ANOVA the term treatment variance is used.) The F-ratio is a slightly different distribution and is found in Table 6 in Appendix A. It is distributed according to the df for the treatment and the df for the error. The df for the treatment is obtained by calculating the number of treatment means minus 1; the df for the error is calculated by summing the df for each group. Thus, for the data presented in Table 14.3 the df for the treatment $= 3 - 1 = 2$ and the df for the error $= (7 - 1) + (7 - 1) + (7 - 1) = (6) + (6) + (6) = 18$. The total df should be one less than the total number of subjects, or $21 - 1 = 20$. $18 + 2 = 20$.

TABLE 14.3 Performance Scores Under Low, Moderate, and High Stress

LOW STRESS	MODERATE STRESS	HIGH STRESS
8	17	12
7	19	9
6	20	10
11	22	13
12	23	15
13	18	12
13	21	13

PARTITIONING THE VARIANCE

In analysis of variance we speak of partitioning the total variance into the component that represents the *between-group variance,* also called the *treatment variance,* and the component that represents the *within-group variance,* also called *error variance.* The relationship between these components is illustrated in equation (14.1):

total variance = between-group variance + within-group variance (14.1)

If one is known (of treatment and error), the other can be obtained by subtraction (if the total is known); however, it is best to compute both independently for a check. In analysis of variance we refer to the sum of squares (or sum of squared deviations from the mean), which you will remember from Chapter 3. The calculation of the SS is presented as equation (14.2):

$$SS = \Sigma \ X^2 - \frac{(\Sigma \ X)^2}{N} \tag{14.2}$$

By adding the appropriate subscripts, we can calculate this for each group independently or for the entire set of scores (ignoring the groups) or the group sums independently. We, in fact, do each of these three in completing an analysis of variance. Thus, we obtain SS_T, total sum of squares; SS_B, between-groups (treatment) sum of squares; and SS_W, within-group (error) sum of squares by similar means.

In calculating the SS_T, we consider all the scores in total. Thus, equation (14.3)

$$SS_T = \Sigma \ X^2 - \frac{(\Sigma \ X)^2}{N} \tag{14.3}$$

indicates that we square each of the 21 scores and sum them, then add the 21 scores, square the total, and divide by the number (21) of scores. We get the results illustrated in Table 14.4 and equation (14.4).

$$SS_T = (752 + 2828 + 1032) - \frac{(70 + 140 + 84)^2}{21}$$

$$= 4612 - \frac{(294)^2}{21} \tag{14.4}$$

$$= 4612 - 4116$$

$$= 496$$

TABLE 14.4 Sum of Scores and Sum of Squared Scores

LOW		MODERATE		HIGH	
X	X²	X	X²	X	X²
8	64	17	289	12	144
7	49	19	361	9	81
6	36	20	400	10	100
11	121	22	484	13	169
12	144	23	529	15	225
13	169	18	324	12	144
13	169	21	441	13	169
70	752	140	2828	84	1032

In calculating the SS_B, we obtain the average of the squared sums of the groups as in equations (14.5):

$$SS_B = \frac{(\Sigma\ X_1)^2 + (\Sigma\ X_2)^2 + (\Sigma\ X_3)^2}{\text{number in group}} - \frac{(\Sigma\ X)^2}{N} \tag{14.5}$$

In this instance the number of cases in each group is the same. If the numbers were different, then it would be necessary to calculate each group separately and then the total group effect, as shown in equation (14.6):

$$SS_B = \frac{(\Sigma\ X_1)^2}{n_1} + \frac{(\Sigma\ X_2)^2}{n_2} + \frac{(\Sigma\ X_3)^2}{n_3} - \frac{(\Sigma\ X)^2}{N} \tag{14.6}$$

Substituting in equation (14.5), because the n of each group is equal, we obtain the results of equation (14.7):

$$SS_B = \frac{(70)^2 + (140)^2 + (84)^2}{7} - \frac{(294)^2}{21}$$

$$= \frac{4900 + 19,600 + 7056}{7} - 4116 \qquad \text{(from previous work)} \qquad (14.7)$$

$$= \frac{31,556}{7} - 4116$$

$$= 4508 - 4116$$

$$= 392$$

Finally, we can obtain SS_W by subtraction as in equation (14.8):

$$SS_T = SS_B + SS_W$$

$$496 = 392 + SS_W \qquad\qquad (14.8)$$

$$SS_W = 496 - 392$$

$$= 104$$

Since it is always a good idea to check, let us determine the SS for each group independently, as illustrated in equation (14.9):

$$SS_{G1} = X_{G1}^2 - \frac{(\Sigma X)^2}{n_1}$$

$$= 752 - \frac{(70)^2}{7} \qquad\qquad (14.9)$$

$$= 752 - 700 = 52$$

Similarly, for groups 2 and 3 we obtain 28 and 24, respectively. The total is calculated by equation (14.10):

$$SS_W = SS_{G1} + SS_{G2} + SS_{G3} \qquad\qquad (14.10)$$

$$= 52 + 28 + 24 = 104$$

To present the results of the analysis of variance, we organize the information into tabular form as in Table 14.5.

TABLE 14.5   Summary of Analysis of Variance for Mean Scores

SOURCE OF VARIATION	SUM OF SQUARES	df	MEAN SQUARES	F-ratio
Total	496	20	—	—
Treatment	392	2	196	33.91
Error	104	18	5.78	

In Table 14.5 the heading "source of variation" refers to the factor that is being evaluated. The sum of squares is the sum of the squared deviations from the mean. The *df* is the number of scores or means free to vary. The mean square is the same as the variance. (It represents the same number as the squared standard deviation.) The *F*-ratio is the relationship between the treatment

TABLE 14.6   Decision-Making Steps in One-Way Analysis of Variance

1. THE PROBLEM

A researcher wishes to determine the effect of different levels of stress—low, moderate, and high—on performance. To do this a group of 21 subjects are randomly assigned to one of the three stress groups and tested.

2. RESEARCH HYPOTHESIS

If individuals perform under different levels of stress, then performance will differ.

3. STATISTICAL HYPOTHESES

H_0: $\bar{X}_1 = \bar{X}_2 = \bar{X}_3$
H_1: $\bar{X}_1 \neq \bar{X}_2 \neq \bar{X}_3$

4. SIGNIFICANCE LEVEL

.05

5. DECISION RULE

Reject null if *F*-ratio with 2, 18 *df* ≥ 3.68.

6. RESULT

The results are illustrated in Table 14.5. The observed *F*-ratio is 33.91.

$\bar{X}_{LOW} = 10;$ $\bar{X}_{MOD} = 20;$ $\bar{X}_{HIGH} = 12$

7. CONCLUSION

Reject null. Performance differs under different levels of stress. It appears that performance is better under moderate stress than under low or high stress. (This latter statement requires that a follow-up test be used. These tests are illustrated in Chapter 19.)

variance (MS) and the error variance, as in equation (14.11):

$$F = \frac{\text{treatment variance (treatment}_{MS})}{\text{error variance (error}_{MS})} \tag{14.11}$$

As in the other tests we have done, you must compare the obtained F-ratio to that required for significance, shown in Table A6. (Required to reject the null.) Thus, we obtain the required value by using the df for the treatment (2) and the df for error (18). The df for the treatment is found across the top row, that for the error down the side. Thus, the junction of 2, 18 yields a required value of 3.68 at the .05 level (5%). (We used 15 instead of 18 because it is the closest without going over.) Most tables will have more required values represented. Substituting in equation (14.11), we have the result of equation (14.12):

$$F = \frac{196}{5.78} = 33.91 \tag{14.12}$$

This result, 33.91, clearly exceeds the required value. Therefore we reject the null and conclude that stress has a significant effect upon performance.

The use of the decision-making steps in this one-way analysis of variance is illustrated in Table 14.6.

EXERCISES

1. A coach was interested in the effect of praise and punishment on the performance of a group of swimmers. Thus, three conditions were employed: praise, punishment, and a control group. *Which technique was more effective?* (Lower scores are better.) (*Note:* The N's are different for the different groups.)
   Praise group: 2, 3, 4, 2, 5, 3, 4, 2, 6, 5, 4, 5
   Punishment group: 7, 6, 5, 8, 9, 5, 4, 3, 6, 6
   Control group: 4, 5, 6, 7, 3, 8, 5

2. A gymnastics coach was interested in having team members increase abdominal strength as rapidly as possible. There were three methods that were used by various coaches in the area. It was decided to try all three to determine which was better. *Was one method more effective than another?*
   Method A: 9, 10, 11, 13, 15, 12, 10, 8
   Method B: 12, 14, 15, 16, 10, 8, 11, 15
   Method C: 20, 18, 12, 16, 17, 10, 13, 19

3. Having heard a great deal about special liquid supplements to be used to quench thirst and replace chemicals lost during exertion, an exercise physiologist decides to conduct a pilot project

comparing five different brands in their effect on performance during exertion. *Is there a difference?*

Brand A: 14, 12, 17, 13, 12, 16, 15
Brand B: 13, 11, 13, 10, 12, 11, 10
Brand C: 14, 14, 11, 12, 13, 13, 11
Brand D: 9, 8, 8, 12, 7, 9, 10
Brand E: 10, 11, 10, 9, 11, 12, 9

CHAPTER FIFTEEN
ANALYZING REPEATED MEASURES

In Chapter 14 we considered research designs in which different subjects were tested under different treatment conditions. This may be called a between-subjects design, because the focus is on the differences beween the subjects in each group. We do, however, use the within-subjects variation as our error term.

Very often researchers in physical education wish to evaluate changes in the same subject over time. These changes may occur as a result of factors identified as practice, testing, learning—in short, any factor or study in which one is concerned with changes in subjects over time. In order to incorporate these factors into our research, we must use a different design and a statistical analysis appropriate to that design. Recall that in discussing the difference between two means, we reviewed two t-tests: the independent t-test, used when the two groups were comprised of different subjects; and a matched-pairs t-test, used when the same subjects were tested twice as in a pretest/posttest design.

In this book we will review two types of repeated-measures designs—one in which all subjects are tested repeatedly over time, and one which combines a between-subjects factor, such as type of feedback, with a within-subjects factor (repeated measure), such as practice trials. This latter type of design is presented in Chapter 17 and is referred to as a mixed design, since it contains both a between-subjects factor (type of feedback) and a within-subjects factor (practice trials). As we shall see, both these designs are useful for physical education research, but the mixed design and its extensions in more complex factorial designs is critical.

In the repeated-measures design, subjects are used as their own controls.

Often subjects will differ markedly prior to an experiment. When subjects are used as their own controls, the error variability due to individual differences is removed completely, hence the likelihood of finding statistical differences among the treatments (if they exist) is greater. If individual variability is not extracted, it will be included, statistically, as part of the experimental error. This, then, is the primary purpose of a repeated-measures or totally within-subjects design. The treatment effects for each subject are measured in relation to the average response made by that subject on all treatments. In this way individual variability is effectively separated from the experimental error. Another gain, in addition to increased precision, is that fewer subjects can be used than in other designs. Thus, it should be considered in situations in which limited numbers of subjects are available over extended periods.

This design is not without problems, however, and must be carefully planned. First, systematic errors must be avoided. For example, where feasible, treatment or testing conditions should be randomized for each subject. Second, potential interference of treatments should be carefully considered. That is, will a particular treatment order, A–B–C, produce a different effect than another order, B–C–A? In testing different methods of strength training, for example, there is likely to be interference from one method to another, since the subject will get stronger as training progresses. In experiments involving performance testing under different conditions, subjects may "learn" from one condition to the next, and this may affect conclusions. Since skill acquisition appears to occur logarithmically (as skill increases, gains become progressively smaller), it is difficult to account for this effect. One solution may be to schedule testing so that the effects of previous practice will have dissipated. Another solution is to systematically vary the order of testing and use it as a between-subjects variable (making the design a two-factor design with repeated measures on the second factor) and then, if order of testing is not statistically significant, eliminate it. Alternately, as will be shown in the study to be considered, the treatments may be randomized throughout the testing for each subject.

Consider a study designed to test the effect of object speed on interception performance. All subjects are tested at all speeds: 10 feet per second (fps), 20 fps, and 30 fps. The presentation of speeds is randomized so that each speed occurs 10 times; thus subjects have 30 trials, and no speed presentation follows itself. The performance measure is distance error, defined as the distance in centimeters between the intercept point and the actual object position when the subject presses a response key. A distance error of zero indicates that the response was coincident with the arrival of the object at the intercept point; a positive error indicates that the subject was late in responding; and a negative error indicates that the subject was early. The design schematic is presented in Table 15.1.

In the last chapter we indicated that the total variance was partitioned as shown in Table 15.2a. In the repeated-measures design the partitioning of the variance changes as shown in Table 15.2b and c.

TABLE 15.1   Schematic for Repeated-Measures Design

	TREATMENTS		
	10 FPS	20 FPS	30 FPS
Subject 1			
Subject 2			
Subject 3			
$\vdots$			
Subject n			

TABLE 15.2   Partitioning of the Variance: Repeated-Measures Design

a. Partitioning of the variance in one-way ANOVA:

   Total variance = between-group variance + within-subjects variance

b. Partitioning of the variance in a repeated-measures ANOVA:

   Total variance = between-subjects variance + within-subjects variance

c. Partitioning of the within-subjects variance in a repeated-measure ANOVA:

   Within-subjects variance = between-treatments variance + residual variance

NUMERICAL EXAMPLE

In order to clarify the calculations for the repeated-measures analysis of variance, sample data are presented in Table 15.3. The decision-making steps are presented in Table 15.4. The steps of the analysis are shown in equations (15.1) to (15.5). Finally the summary of the analysis of variance is presented as Table 15.5.

The calculation of the total sum of squares, SS_T, is shown in equation (15.1), where k = number of treatments, n = number of subjects:

$$SS_T = \Sigma\ X^2 - \frac{(\Sigma X)^2}{kn}$$

$$= 2833 - \frac{(269)^2}{(3)(10)}$$

$$= 2833 - \frac{72,361}{30}$$ (15.1)

$$= 2833 - 2412.03$$

$$= 420.97$$

TABLE 15.3 Distance Error Scores (in inches)
for Three Object-Speed Conditions

| SUBJECT | OBJECT SPEED (FPS) | | | |
	10	20	30	(P)
S_1	4	6	12	22
S_2	5	7	14	26
S_3	6	8	15	29
S_4	5	9	11	25
S_5	7	8	16	31
S_6	3	9	12	24
S_7	4	10	13	27
S_8	5	12	15	32
S_9	6	11	14	31
S_{10}	4	8	10	22
(T)	49	88	132	269
ΣX^2:	253	804	1777	ΣP^2: 7361

TABLE 15.4 Decision-Making Steps for Repeated-Measures ANOVA

1. THE PROBLEM

A researcher wishes to determine whether prediction of a moving object, as measured by distance error (in centimeters), differs for different object speeds.

2. RESEARCH HYPOTHESIS

If subjects are tested under three different object speeds, then distance error will differ.

3. STATISTICAL HYPOTHESIS

H_0: $\overline{X}_1 = \overline{X}_2 = \overline{X}_3$
H_1: $\overline{X}_1 \neq \overline{X}_2 \neq \overline{X}_3$

4. SIGNIFICANCE LEVEL

.01

5. DECISION RULE

Reject null if F-ratio with 2, 18 df is equal to or greater than 6.01.

6. RESULT

The results are illustrated in Table 15.5. The observed F-ratio is 90.28. Means are 10 fps = 4.9, 20 fps = 8.8, 30 fps = 13.2.

7. CONCLUSION

Reject null; performance differs at different object speeds. It appears that error is greatest at higher speeds and least at the lower speeds. (This latter statement requires that a follow-up be used. These tests are presented in Chapter 19.)

**TABLE 15.5   Summary of Analysis of Variance for
Mean Distance Error Scores**

SOURCE OF VARIATION	SS	df	MS	F
Total	420.97	29	—	—
Between Subjects	41.64	9	—	—
Within Subjects	379.33	20	—	—
Treatments	344.87	2	172.44	90.28
Residual	34.46	18	1.91	

The calculation of the sum of squares between subjects, SS_{BS}, is shown in equation (15.2), where k = number of treatments, n = number of subjects, P = subject (row) sums:

$$SS_{BS} = \frac{\Sigma P^2}{k} - \frac{(\Sigma X)^2}{kn}$$

$$= \frac{(22)^2 + (26)^2 + \cdots + (22)^2}{3} - \frac{(269)^2}{30}$$

$$= \frac{7361}{3} - \frac{72,361}{30} \tag{15.2}$$

$$= 2453.67 - 2412.03$$

$$= 41.64$$

The calculation of the sum of squares within subjects, SS_{WS}, is shown in equation (15.3), where P = subject (row) sums, k = number of treatments:

$$SS_{WS} = \Sigma X^2 - \frac{\Sigma P^2}{k}$$

$$= 2833 - \frac{(22)^2 + (26)^2 + \cdots + (22)^2}{3}$$

$$= 2833 - \frac{7361}{3} \tag{15.3}$$

$$= 2833 - 2453.67$$

$$= 379.33$$

The SS_{WS} is further partitioned into the sum of squares for treatment, SS_{Tr}, and the sum of squares of the residual, SS_R, shown in equations (15.4) and (15.5), respectively, where T = treatment (column) sums, P = subject (row) sums, n = number of subjects, k = number of treatments:

$$SS_{Tr} = \frac{\Sigma\, T^2}{n} - \frac{(\Sigma\, X)^2}{kn}$$

$$= \frac{(49)^2 + (88)^2 + (132)^2}{10} - \frac{(269)^2}{30}$$

$$= \frac{27{,}569}{10} - \frac{72{,}361}{30} \qquad (15.4)$$

$$= 2756.9 - 2412.03$$

$$= 344.87$$

$$SS_R = \Sigma\, X^2 - \frac{\Sigma\, T^2}{n} - \frac{\Sigma\, P^2}{k} + \frac{(\Sigma\, X)^2}{kn}$$

$$= 2833 - \frac{(49)^2 + (88)^2 + (132)^2}{10}$$

$$- \frac{(22)^2 + (26)^2 + \cdots + (22)^2}{3} + \frac{(269)^2}{30} \qquad (15.5)$$

$$= 2833 - \frac{27{,}569}{10} - \frac{7361}{3} + \frac{72{,}361}{30}$$

$$= 2833 - 2756.9 - 2453.67 + 2412.03$$

$$= 34.46$$

EXERCISES

1. A researcher was interested in assessing the effect of the menstrual cycle on reaction time measured in milliseconds. Accordingly, ten females were tested on the first day, seventh day, ovulation day and last day of their cycle.

	FIRST DAY	SEVENTH DAY	OVULATION DAY	LAST DAY
S_1	20	18	21	20
S_2	22	20	20	22
S_3	21	20	18	20
S_4	18	19	21	20
S_5	17	17	19	16
S_6	24	23	22	20
S_7	16	16	15	17
S_8	28	30	31	29
S_9	27	28	30	28
S_{10}	25	24	26	24

2. A motor learning instructor used a card-sorting task to demonstrate the effect of number of choices on decision-making. The score for each of the 15 subjects for each task was the difference between a baseline task and the particular card-sort task.

	SORTS		
	COLOR	SUIT	PIC-NUM
S_1	10	20	11
S_2	12	19	13
S_3	15	25	15
S_4	11	18	13
S_5	18	31	16
S_6	20	30	19
S_7	15	25	12
S_8	14	20	15
S_9	12	17	15
S_{10}	10	17	15
S_{11}	13	18	12
S_{12}	15	22	17
S_{13}	10	19	10
S_{14}	9	20	8
S_{15}	11	25	12

CHAPTER SIXTEEN
ANALYZING
FACTORIAL
DESIGN

The one-way or simple analysis of variance considered in Chapter 14 and the total repeated-measures design presented in Chapter 15 are useful statistical tools. Unfortunately, as our knowledge about the factors that affect performance increases, these tools become as inappropriate to the questions we ask as the t-test was in a previous era. What we need is a statistical test or tests that can accommodate the complex designs dictated by the more sophisticated questions being asked by researchers. The extension of the concept of analysis of variance to factorial designs and to mixed designs requires a brief review in this chapter of underlying concepts. Then we will review procedures for analyzing and interpreting the results of factorial designs, and a model will be presented for extending the designs as needed for your research. Chapter 17 will review procedures for handling mixed designs and, again, a model for extending the basic design will be presented.

ANALYSIS OF VARIANCE:
CONCEPTS AND FOUNDATIONS

In an earlier chapter we characterized variance as a measure of the influences that produce differences in scores. We also presented the notion that research design should be viewed as focusing on maximizing treatment variance, controlling extraneous variance, and minimizing error variance. In our simple analysis-of-variance example we noted that the F-ratio, like the t-ratio, is based on a comparison of the treatment variance with the error variance. The extraneous variance is not represented because it is included either in the treatment variance, if we use the factors which produce the extraneous variance as variables, or in error variance, if we fail to control them by eliminating their effect. In the simple analysis of variance and the simple repeated measures we had no choice but to eliminate any extraneous variables, since the statistical test would not identify more than one source of treatment variance. The complex analyses possible with factorial analysis-of-variance tests enable researchers to observe and analyze multiple sources of variance. More important, perhaps, each source of treatment variance can be identified individually, as in its *main effect*, and jointly, as in its *interaction* with other factors.

Thus, analysis of variance provides a means for partitioning, or separating out, the differences in scores that are due to treatments, interactions of treatments, and error. Factorial analysis of variance enables us to accommodate multiple treatment factors, each having several levels. Analysis-of-variance techniques can be used to analyze between-subjects designs, within-subjects designs, or mixed designs. Some examples of these three types of designs are presented in Table 16.1. These factorial designs are labeled in a standard fashion. Each factor has a particular number of levels, depending upon the values it takes or is assigned. If one factor under study were subject gender, it would take two values: male or female. If the factor were cardiovascular respiratory fitness, it might have two levels (values): high and low, or three levels: high, medium, and low. These levels would have to be operationally defined by the researcher in terms of, for example, the score on a standardized test of CVR fitness. If we wanted to investigate the performance of males and females classified as high, medium, or low fit on a particular task, we would indicate that we employed a 2×3 factorial design in which the first factor was subject gender and the second factor was CVR fitness with three levels: high, medium, and low. Tables 16.1a and 16.1b are discussed in detail here. The remaining two parts, (c) and (d) are for contrast only and will be discussed in detail in Chapter 17.

In Table 16.1a we see a between-subjects design, a 3×2 factorial. We have labeled the age factor A and the teaching method factor B. Let us assume that there are 30 subjects in this study, 10 of each age. The students in each age group are randomly assigned to the task or the command teaching method. As a result there are 5 subjects in each age-teaching method combination. Each subject has only *one score*. That score, however, contains components due to age and due to teaching method in addition to components resulting from subject differences. In the analysis of variance we partition out the effects of age, teaching method, and age $\times$ teaching method by the way we use the subjects' scores. Recall that squaring the scores enabled us to estimate the variance due to individual differences. In this instance, too, we will square scores to estimate the variance due to the different variables. Notice, however, that in analysis of variance we do not get the variance directly. Rather, we calculate the sum of squares for each factor or combination and then use the *df* to estimate the mean square which is the equivalent of the variance. Thus, in the material which follows, the term "sum of squares" will be used to indicate the result of our calculations. Later, in the

TABLE 16.1   Model Factorial Designs

a. BETWEEN SUBJECTS

FACTOR	LEVELS	DESIGN
(A) Age	5, 10, 15 years of age	⎰
(B) Teaching method	Task, Command	⎱ 3 × 2 Factorial

DIAGRAM OF DESIGN

	TEACHING METHOD		
	TASK (B_1)	COMMAND (B_2)	
5 (A_1)	A_1B_1	A_1B_2	A_1
10 (A_2)	A_2B_1	A_2B_2	A_2
15 (A_3)	A_3B_1	A_3B_2	A_3
	B_1	B_2	

b. BETWEEN SUBJECTS

FACTOR	LEVELS	DESIGN
(A) Teaching method	Whole, Part	⎰
(B) Task type	Self-pace, Ext. pace	2 × 2 × 3 Factorial
(C) Imposed stress	High, Medium, Low	⎱

DIAGRAM OF DESIGN

		IMPOSED STRESS			
TEACHING METHOD	TASK TYPE	HIGH (C_1)	MEDIUM (C_2)	LOW (C_3)	
Whole (A_1) ⎰	Self-pace (B_1)	$A_1B_1C_1$	$A_1B_1C_2$	$A_1B_1C_3$	A_1B_1
⎱	Ext.-pace (B_2)	$A_1B_2C_1$	$A_1B_2C_2$	$A_1B_2C_3$	A_1B_2
Part (A_2) ⎰	Self-pace (B_1)	$A_2B_1C_1$	$A_2B_1C_2$	$A_2B_1C_3$	A_2B_1
⎱	Ext.-pace (B_2)	$A_2B_2C_1$	$A_2B_2C_2$	$A_2B_2C_3$	A_2B_2
		C_1	C_2	C_3	

c. WITHIN SUBJECTS

FACTOR	LEVELS	DESIGN
(A) Ball speed	10, 20, 30 fps	3 × 3 Factorial with
(B) Trial block	1, 2, 3	repeated measures on both

TABLE 16.1 **(Continued)**

DIAGRAM OF DESIGN

BALL SPEED (fps):	10(A_1)			20(A_2)			30(A_3)		
TRIAL BLOCK:	1	2	3	1	2	3	1	2	3
	B_1	B_2	B_3	B_1	B_2	B_3	B_1	B_2	B_3

SUBJECT:

S_1
S_2
S_3
$\vdots$
S_n

A_1B_1 A_1B_2 A_1B_3 A_2B_1 A_2B_2 A_2B_3 A_3B_1 A_3B_2 A_3B_3

d. MIXED DESIGN

FACTOR	LEVELS	DESIGN
(A) Age	5, 7, 9	$3 \times 3 \times 5$ Factorial
(B) Type of feedback	Spec., Dir., Mag.	with repeated mea-
(C) Practice block	1, 2, 3, 4, 5	sures on last factor

DIAGRAM OF DESIGN

		PRACTICE BLOCK				
		1 (C_1)	2 (C_2)	3 (C_3)	4 (C_4)	5 (C_5)
Age 5 (A_1)	Spec. FB (B_1)	$A_1B_1C_1$	$A_1B_1C_2$	$A_1B_1C_3$	$A_1B_1C_4$	$A_1B_1C_5$
	Dir. FB (B_2)	$A_1B_2C_1$	$A_1B_2C_2$	$A_1B_2C_3$	$A_1B_2C_4$	$A_1B_2C_5$
	Mag. FB (B_3)	$A_1B_3C_1$	$A_1B_3C_2$	$A_1B_3C_3$	$A_1B_3C_4$	$A_1B_3C_5$
Age 7 (A_2)	Spec. FB (B_1)	$A_2B_1C_1$	$A_2B_1C_2$	$A_2B_1C_3$	$A_2B_1C_4$	$A_2B_1C_5$
	Dir. FB (B_2)	$A_2B_2C_1$	$A_2B_2C_2$	$A_2B_2C_3$	$A_2B_2C_4$	$A_2B_2C_5$
	Mag. FB (B_3)	$A_2B_3C_1$	$A_2B_3C_2$	$A_2B_3C_3$	$A_2B_3C_4$	$A_2B_3C_5$
Age 9 (A_3)	Spec. FB (B_1)	$A_3B_1C_1$	$A_3B_1C_2$	$A_3B_1C_3$	$A_3B_1C_4$	$A_3B_1C_5$
	Dir. FB (B_2)	$A_3B_2C_1$	$A_3B_2C_2$	$A_3B_2C_3$	$A_3B_2C_4$	$A_3B_2C_5$
	Mag. FB (B_3)	$A_3B_3C_1$	$A_3B_3C_2$	$A_3B_3C_3$	$A_3B_3C_4$	$A_3B_3C_5$

presentation of the analysis-of-variance table, the mean square or estimated variance will be calculated.

To obtain the sum of squares due to age we square the numbers obtained at A_1, A_2, and A_3, divide by the number of scores in each A condition (10), and correct the estimate by subtracting an amount which represents the mean of the group. We are left with an estimate of the sum of squares due to age of subject.

In order to obtain the estimate of the sum of squares due to teaching method, B, we do the same thing but use the marginal values for B_1 and B_2. Similarly, we will subtract out an estimate of the mean of the group and be left with the sum of squares due to B. Achieving an estimate of AB is a bit more cumbersome but similar. In this instance, as you might guess, we need to use the AB values in the cells of the diagram. We similarly square each of the six values and divide by the number of scores (5) in each value. Then, since these scores contain estimates of A and estimates of B, we subtract the average of the squared values obtained for A and for B (before correction) from the average for AB. Now recall that when we wanted an estimate of A or B we had to subtract out a correction value which represented the mean of the group. Both the A and B amounts which we have just subtracted contain that same estimate. Thus, we have just subtracted this twice. Therefore, we must replace one, and so, instead of subtracting the correction factor as in A or B, we add it to AB.

Let us continue this line of reasoning for Table 16.1b. The estimates for A, B, and C and AB, AC, and BC are obtained as described for 16.1a. When we come to the three-way factor, ABC, represented by the nine values in the cells of the diagram of design, we must take out the estimates for AB, AC, and BC. However, if we reason as before that AB contains A and B, AC contains A and C, and BC contains B and C then we see that each of the factors A, B, and C has been taken twice, and so we add in the estimate of A, B, and C. Continuing the logic that each estimate contains a component representing the mean, we have subtracted that correction factor three times in AB, AC, and BC and added it three times in A, B, and C. Thus, the estimate of ABC still contains a component of the mean. Hence we subtract out the correction term.

After you have completed the estimates for all the factors and if you have calculated the total sum of squares as we did in the simple analysis of variance, then the sum of squares left when the values obtained for the factors are subtracted from the total is the error sum of squares. It is all the sums of squares that have not been accounted for by a treatment. The error sum of squares can also be obtained by calculating the sum of squares for each treatment group (AB or ABC) and adding the values to obtain the total. This is recommended as a check on your other calculations, since we know from previous information that the sum of squares for the individual components must sum to the total sum of squares. If the sum of the sums of squares for each component does not equal that for the total, there is an error in your calculations.

By following this logic you should have no difficulty generating statistical terms for factorial designs you have not yet seen. However, be forewarned. The more factors in a design, the more subjects are needed for each cell and the more difficult it will be to tease out the results if the factors interact significantly. Interaction will be discussed later in this chapter. For now let us consider an example. It is an extension of the stress example used in the simple analysis of variance.

A NUMERICAL EXAMPLE

While the simple analysis of variance represents a stride forward in our ability to find answers that will be meaningful, we must consider a more complex level of explanation. In the stress example that we used in a preceding chapter we noted that the ability to use three stress levels greatly increased our decision-making power. What if we could, in addition, vary another aspect of the situation—for example, the inherent anxiety or stress level of the subject? Would it not be relevant to ask, "Would different levels of stress result in different performance levels for individuals with different initial anxiety levels?" This is similar to asking, "Is it worthwhile to individualize our motivation techniques?" We know, for instance, that the coach should not use the same motivational procedures (pep talks are one) for all players at half-time. Some players may be too psyched and need to be calmed down before the second half. Some players are sufficiently "up" and need no extra motivation.

We can test this idea in a research study by employing a two-factor design. One factor is the stress level, which we have already used; the other is the player anxiety level. Thus, we have a two-factor design. Factor A is player anxiety and has two levels: high anxiety and low anxiety. Factor B is imposed stress and has three levels: high stress, moderate stress, and low stress. The design may be diagrammed as in Table 16.2.

As you can see from the table, we have a situation somewhat similar to what we had with the two-way chi-square. The difference, of course, is that we have scores of a number of individuals in each of the six resulting treatment combinations (or conditions). By using the two-factor design, we can obtain an estimate of the main effect of each of the variables (performer anxiety, imposed

TABLE 16.2   Diagram of Example

		IMPOSED STRESS (B)			
		B_1 (HIGH)	B_2 (MODERATE)	B_3 (LOW)	
Performer Anxiety (A)	A_1 (High)	A_1B_1	A_1B_2	A_1B_3	A_1
	A_2 (Low)	A_2B_1	A_2B_2	A_2B_3	A_2
		B_1	B_2	B_3	

stress) and the joint effect of the variables. In a two-factor design we ask three questions:

1. Does the main effect of A (in this case performer anxiety) make a difference?
2. Does the main effect of B (in this case imposed stress) make a difference?
3. Does the combination of A and B (into AB) make a difference? (Putting it another way, do A and B interact with each other to produce effects that we could not predict by knowing the effects of each?)

The calculations for a two-factor analysis of variance are designed to answer these questions. The difference between the one-way analysis of variance and the two-way is that in the two-way the treatment effect is partitioned further into the variance due to A, the variance due to B, and the variance due to AB. We obtain the error variance and the total variance in precisely the same way as before. The change is in the A, B, and AB partitioning of the treatment variance.

$$SS_A = \frac{(\Sigma\ A_1)^2 + (\Sigma\ A_2)^2}{bn} - \frac{(\Sigma\ X)^2}{abn} \tag{16.1}$$

(As before, the rule for unequal entries in calculating A applies.)

$$SS_B = \frac{(\Sigma\ B_1)^2 + (\Sigma\ B_2)^2 + (\Sigma\ B_3)^2}{an} - \frac{(\Sigma\ X)^2}{abn} \tag{16.2}$$

Equations (16.1) and (16.2) should be familiar to you, since they are the generalization of the technique used to get the main effect in the simple analysis. To obtain the interaction (AB) effect, use equation (16.3):

$$SS_{AB} = \frac{\begin{array}{c}(\Sigma\ A_1 B_2)^2 + (\Sigma\ A_1 B_2)^2 + (\Sigma\ A_1 B_3)^2 \\ + (\Sigma\ A_2 B_1)^2 + (\Sigma\ A_2 B_2)^2 + (\Sigma\ A_2 B_3)^2\end{array}}{n} - \frac{(\Sigma\ A_1)^2 + (\Sigma\ A_2)^2}{bn}$$
$$- \frac{(\Sigma\ B_1)^2 + (\Sigma\ B_2)^2 + (\Sigma\ B_3^2)}{an} + \frac{(\Sigma\ X)^2}{abn} \tag{16.3}$$

Several authors, to facilitate the calculation of the denominator value, assign lower-case letters to equal the number of levels of the factors. Thus, in equations (16.1), (16.2), and (16.3), the values given in (16.4) apply:

$a = 2$
$b = 3$
n = the number of subjects in each group when the groups are equal. Then the denominator is designated by the multi-plication of those levels not represented in the numerator. $\tag{16.4}$

In SS_A the denominator for the first term $= bn$ or $3 \times$ (number in each cell).
In SS_B the denominator for the first term $= an$ or $2 \times$ (number in each cell).
In SS_{AB} the denominator for the first term $= n$ or the number in each cell.
For the final term in each, the denominator $= abn$ or $2 \times 3 \times$ (number in each cell).

Let us work out the calculations for a simple example where there are only three subjects in each cell, as presented in Table 16.3. Note that the factors A, B are reversed from their order in Table 16.2.
To find the SS_{Total}, use equation (16.5):

$$SS_T = \Sigma \, X^2 - \frac{(\Sigma \, X)^2}{abn}$$

$$= 1198 - \frac{(126)^2}{18} \tag{16.5}$$

$$= 1198 - 882 = 316$$

To find the SS_A, use equation (16.6):

$$SS_A = \frac{(\Sigma \, A_1)^2 + (\Sigma \, A_2)^2}{bn} - \frac{(\Sigma \, X)^2}{abn}$$

$$= \frac{54^2 + 72^2}{9} - 882 \tag{16.6}$$

$$= 900 - 882 = 18$$

To find SS_B, use equation (16.7):

$$SS_B = \frac{(\Sigma \, B_1)^2 + (\Sigma \, B_2)^2 + (\Sigma \, B_3)^2}{an} - \frac{(\Sigma \, X)^2}{abn}$$

$$= \frac{(42)^2 + (30)^2 + (54)^2}{6} - 882 \tag{16.7}$$

$$= 930 - 882 = 48$$

TABLE 16.3   Data for Anxiety × Stress Study

IMPOSED STRESS	PERFORMER ANXIETY		TOTAL
	HIGH (A_1)	LOW (A_2)	
High Stress (B_1)	8, 4, 0	14, 10, 6	42
Moderate Stress (B_2)	10, 8, 6	4, 2, 0	30
Low Stress (B_3)	8, 6, 4	15, 12, 9	54
Total	54	72	126

TABLE 16.4   Decision-Making Steps for Factorial Analysis of Variance

1. THE PROBLEM

A teacher is interested in determining whether imposed stress and player anxiety, separately and in combination, affect performance on a motor task.

2. RESEARCH HYPOTHESIS

If different levels of stress are imposed, then performance of a motor task will differ.

If performers of differing anxiety levels are tested, then performance will differ.

If different levels of stress are imposed on performers of differing anxiety levels, then performance will differ.

3. STATISTICAL HYPOTHESES

    a. IMPOSED STRESS
    H_0: $\overline{X}_1 = \overline{X}_2 = \overline{X}_3$
    H_1: $\overline{X}_1 \neq \overline{X}_2 \neq \overline{X}_3$

    b. PLAYER ANXIETY

    H_0: $\overline{X}_1 = \overline{X}_2$
    H_1: $\overline{X}_1 \neq \overline{X}_2$

    c. IMPOSED STRESS × PLAYER ANXIETY

    H_0: $\overline{X}_1 = \overline{X}_2 = \overline{X}_3 = \overline{X}_4 = \overline{X}_5 = \overline{X}_6$
    H_1: $\overline{X}_1 \neq \overline{X}_2 \neq \overline{X}_3 \neq \overline{X}_4 \neq \overline{X}_5 \neq \overline{X}_6$

4. SIGNIFICANCE LEVEL

    .05

5. DECISION RULE

Anxiety: Reject null if F-ratio with 1 and 12 *df* equals or exceeds 4.75.

Stress: Reject null if F-ratio with 2 and 12 *df* equals or exceeds 3.89.

Anxiety × Stress: Reject null if F-ratio with 2 and 12 *df* equals or exceeds 3.89.

6. RESULTS

The results are presented in Table 16.5. Only the F-ratio for the interaction of anxiety and stress is significant. The means for the A × B interaction are presented in Table 16.6.

7. CONCLUSION

It appears that high-anxiety players performed better under moderate stress, while low-anxiety players performed better under low or high stress. (As with previous examples, follow-up tests should be used to confirm the observations. A follow-up test is likely to reveal that the means under imposed stress for the high-anxiety group do not differ.)

To find SS_{AB}, use equation (16.8):

$$SS_{AB} = \frac{\begin{aligned}(\Sigma\ A_1 B_1)^2 + (\Sigma\ A_1 B_2)^2 + (\Sigma\ A_1 B_3)^2 \\ + (\Sigma\ A_2 B_1)^2 + (\Sigma\ A_2 B_2)^2 + (\Sigma\ A_2 B_3)^2\end{aligned}}{n}$$

$$- \text{ first term } SS_A - \text{ first term } SS_B + \frac{(\Sigma\ X)^2}{abn} \qquad (16.8)$$

$$= \frac{(12)^2 + (24)^2 + (18)^2 + (30)^2 + (6)^2 + (36)^2}{3}$$

$$- 900 - 930 + 882$$

$$= 1092 - 900 - 930 + 882 = 144$$

To find SS_W (using the subtraction method, which you may verify by finding the sum of squares for each cell), use equation (16.9):

$$SS_W = SS_T - SS_A - SS_B - SS_{AB}$$

$$= 316 - 18 - 48 - 144 \qquad (16.9)$$

$$= 106$$

The decision steps for this problem are presented in Table 16.4 and the analysis of variance summary in Table 16.5.

In obtaining the required F-ratios from Table 6 in Appendix A we use the

TABLE 16.5   Analysis of Variance for Mean Performance Scores

SOURCE OF VARIATION	SS	df	MS	F
Total	316	17		
Performer anxiety (A)	18	1	18	2.04
Imposed stress (B)	48	2	24	2.72
AB	144	2*	72	8.15
Error	106	12†	8.83	

*To obtain the df for the interaction it is the same as for chi-square or (number of levels A − 1)(number of levels B − 1) = (2 − 1)(3 − 1) = (1)(2) = 2. Also (a − 1)(b − 1).
†To obtain the df for the error: each group loses one, and the total of the group df = the error df. That is, (3 − 1) + (3 − 1) + (3 − 1) + (3 − 1) + (3 − 1) + (3 − 1) = 12.

TABLE 16.6   Critical Values for Analysis of Variance

FACTOR	df	TABLED VALUE
A	1, 12	4.75
B	2, 12	3.89
AB	2, 12	3.89

TABLE 16.7   Mean Performance Scores

	STRESS			
	HIGH	MOD	LOW	OVERALL MEAN
High anxiety	4	8	6	6
Low anxiety	10	2	12	8
Overall mean	7	4	9	

same procedure as in the previous example. Thus, for each factor we have the tabled values shown in Table 16.6.

Therefore only the interaction, AB, is significant. If we look at the means presented in Table 16.7, we see that in players with high anxiety (A_j) moderate stress seemed to facilitate performance, while in players with low anxiety the moderate levels seemed to be associated with poorest performance, and they did best under high or low levels. The F-ratio tells you only what is significant; to determine what it means, you must look at the averages for the groups judged to be significant. Interpretation of interaction will be considered further in Chapter 17.

EXERCISES

1. A physical education teacher was interested in determining whether high-skilled and low-skilled performers' responses to task and command styles of teaching are different. *What would you conclude?*

	TASK METHOD	COMMAND METHOD
High Skilled	12	15
	14	10
	15	12
	17	14
	13	14
	15	10
Low Skilled	9	12
	8	14
	11	13
	9	10
	7	9
	8	11

2.   A researcher felt that individuals with different learning styles would benefit from different methods of skills presentation. Three learning-style groups of individuals were identified: a holistic group, a segmented group, and an average group. The groups were further divided into whole and part methods. *Did the groups respond differently?*

	PART	WHOLE
Holistic	4	9
	5	8
	6	10
	3	7
	7	6
Average	5	8
	6	7
	7	7
	4	6
	8	5
Segmented	10	4
	12	5
	10	6
	9	4
	13	7

CHAPTER SEVENTEEN
ANALYZING MIXED
MEASURES

In Chapter 16 we discussed analysis-of-variance procedures for designs with two or more factors having two or more levels. The major limitation of the purely between-subjects design presented there is that it does not enable the analysis of subject performance over time as in learning, or performance under several different, but compatible, conditions such as ball speed or object size or color. The limitation of the totally repeated-measures design, which would enable the comparisons mentioned, is that it cannot accommodate different types of subject, task, or environmental variables. Mixed designs enable the researcher to ask more complex questions and to obtain results which are likely to provide better answers to those questions.

The analysis of data for a mixed factorial design combines the statistical techniques reviewed in Chapter 16 and the techniques reviewed in Chapter 15. In Chapter 16 the analysis was focused on only treatment sums, A, B, C, AB, AC, BC, and ABC. In Chapter 15 there was emphasis on row or subject sums across treatments and column or treatment sums across subjects. A single score value must be conceived of as having many components—in fact one component for each factor in the study. This was illustrated in Table 16.1d, and since this design is one of those that will be used to present the statistical techniques for the mixed analysis of variance, it is repeated and extended in Table 17.1.

Each age × feedback between subjects treatment condition will have 4 subjects. The 12 subjects at each age level will be randomly assigned to the three feedback conditions. Each subject will be tested at all practice blocks, thus making this a within-subjects variable. The 5-year-olds have been shown with the subjects added to the table. The 7-, 9-, and 11-year-olds would be similarly

TABLE 17.1 Mixed Factorial Design

FACTOR	LEVELS	DESIGN
(A) Age	5, 7, 9, 11	$4 \times 3 \times 5$ Factorial
(B) Type of feedback	Spec., Dir., Mag.	with repeated measures
(C) Practice block	1, 2, 3, 4, 5	on last factor

DIAGRAM OF DESIGN
(AGE BY FEEDBACK BY PRACTICE BLOCK BY SUBJECTS)

PRACTICE BLOCK

		$1\ (C_1)$	$2\ (C_2)$	$3\ (C_3)$	$4\ (C_4)$	$5\ (C_5)$	ROW SUM (P)
	Spec. FB (B_1)	$A_1B_1C_1$	$A_1B_1C_2$	$A_1B_1C_3$	$A_1B_1C_4$	$A_1B_1C_5$	$A_1B_1S_1$
	S_1						$A_1B_1S_2$
	S_2						$A_1B_1S_3$
	S_3						$A_1B_1S_4$
	S_4						
	Dir. FB (B_2)	$A_1B_2C_1$	$A_1B_2C_2$	$A_1B_2C_3$	$A_1B_2C_4$	$A_1B_2C_5$	$A_1B_2S_1$
	S_1						$A_1B_2S_2$
	S_2						$A_1B_2S_3$
	S_3						$A_1B_2S_4$
Age 5	S_4						
(A_1)	Mag. FB (B_3)	$A_1B_3C_1$	$A_1B_3C_2$	$A_1B_3C_3$	$A_1B_3C_4$	$A_1B_3C_5$	$A_1B_3S_1$
	S_1						$A_1B_3S_2$
	S_2						$A_1B_3S_3$
	S_3						$A_1B_3S_4$
	S_4						
Age 7	Spec. FB (B_1)	$A_2B_1C_1$	$A_2B_1C_2$	$A_2B_1C_3$	$A_2B_1C_4$	$A_2B_1C_5$	
(A_2)	Dir. FB (B_2)	$A_2B_2C_1$	$A_2B_2C_2$	$A_2B_2C_3$	$A_2B_2C_4$	$A_2B_2C_5$	
	Mag. FB (B_3)	$A_2B_3C_1$	$A_2B_3C_2$	$A_2B_3C_3$	$A_2B_3C_4$	$A_2B_3C_5$	
Age 9	Spec. FB (B_1)	$A_3B_1C_1$	$A_3B_1C_2$	$A_3B_1C_3$	$A_3B_1C_4$	$A_3B_1C_5$	
(A_3)	Dir. B (B_2)	$A_3B_2C_1$	$A_3B_2C_2$	$A_3B_2C_3$	$A_3B_2C_4$	$A_3B_2C_5$	
	Mag. FB (B_2)	$A_3B_3C_1$	$A_3B_3C_2$	$A_3B_3C_3$	$A_3B_3C_4$	$A_3B_3C_5$	
Age 11	Spec. FB (B_1)	$A_4B_1C_1$	$A_4B_1C_2$	$A_4B_1C_3$	$A_4B_1C_4$	$A_4B_1C_5$	
(A_4)	Mag. FB (B_2)	$A_4B_2C_1$	$A_4B_2C_2$	$A_4B_2C_3$	$A_4B_2C_4$	$A_4B_2C_5$	
	Mag. FB (B_3)	$A_4B_3C_1$	$A_4B_3C_2$	$A_4B_3C_3$	$A_4B_3C_4$	$A_4B_3C_5$	

expanded. The table shown is a treatments-by-subjects table, since all the scores of each subject under their respective treatment conditions are shown. Note the last column of the table, which contains the ABS totals; these are the equivalent of the row sums (P) which we used in the repeated-measures analysis.

The calculation of the analysis of variance will be simplified by creation of a three-way table, the ABC table, which simply adds all the scores of all subjects in each ABC treatment condition together and creates a table like that in Table 16.1d. From this three-way table the three two-way tables, AB, AC, and BC, can be created. These tables will yield the main effects of A (A_1, A_2, A_3, A_4 and A_3), B (B_1, B_2, and B_3) and C (C_1, C_2, C_3, C_4, and C_5).

Let us consider a study in which the independent variables are those stated in Table 17.1 and the dependent variable is the number of correct responses on a particular task. Before proceeding to discuss the analysis in more detail, we present the $ABCS$ table as Table 17.2. Note that there is a P (row sum) column which contains the sum of the scores under the within-subjects independent variable for each subject individually

The ABC table is created from Table 17.2 by summing all subjects' scores in each ABC treatment condition. That is, the scores of the four subjects tested under condition $A_1 B_1 C_1$ (Age 5–Spec. FB–Practice Block 1) are summed ($9 + 5 + 2 + 0 = 16$) and entered in cell $A_1 B_1 C_1$ in the ABC table. The scores under treatment condition $A_4 B_3 C_5$ (Age 11–Mag. FB–Practice Block 5) are summed ($8 + 1 + 6 + 1 = 16$) and entered into the appropriate cell in the ABC table. When this is completed for all ABC treatment combinations, it yields the table presented as Table 17.3.

Table 17.3 is then used in similar fashion to generate the sums that make up the two-way tables. These are presented as Table 17.4 (Age × Feedback), Table 17.5 (Age × Practice Block), and Table 17.6 (Feedback × Practice Block). Taking Table 17.6 as an example, since it is perhaps a bit more difficult to conceptualize, let us see how this is done. For BC combination $B_1 C_1$ (Spec. FB × Practice Block 1), we would take all those ABC sums which have the factor value $B_1 C_1$. This necessitates ignoring the levels of A. We see that we obtain the values 16, 19, 50, and 63 in the column labeled Practice Block 1 that all are associated with the label "Spec." We sum these ($16 + 19 + 50 + 63 = 148$) and enter the total in the treatment condition $B_1 C_1$ in Table 17.6. In similar fashion, we generate the totals for all other conditions in that table. You should take the ABC table and generate the three two-way tables independently, then check your work against the tables presented here.

An important point is that all the scores in the cells of each of the tables represent different ways of summing *all* the scores in the ABC table. Thus, although the sums in the cells all differ, the marginal totals for the main effects— A, B, and C—should always be the same. You can check this by summing across the columns and the rows and verifying that all marginal totals for A_1–A_4 are the same: 146, 433, 739, and 680, respectively. In the same way you should verify the marginal totals for B and C. This is a good way of cross-checking your work in

TABLE 17.2   Age × Feedback × Practice Block × Subjects

			PRACTICE BLOCK					
			1	2	3	4	5	P (ROW SUM)
Age 5	Spec.	S_1	9	5	2	4	4	24
		S_2	5	3	5	9	7	29
		S_3	2	3	1	6	3	15
		S_4	0	0	1	1	0	2
	Dir.	S_1	3	0	2	3	1	9
		S_2	1	3	4	7	6	21
		S_3	4	0	1	0	0	5
		S_4	4	4	1	2	2	13
	Mag.	S_1	1	0	0	0	0	1
		S_2	2	1	1	1	0	5
		S_3	2	0	1	0	0	3
		S_4	0	0	0	7	12	19
Age 7	Spec.	S_1	8	11	18	23	20	80
		S_2	3	1	5	4	5	18
		S_3	5	9	10	20	18	62
		S_4	3	15	10	6	10	44
	Dir.	S_1	5	12	4	14	14	49
		S_2	8	8	10	13	12	51
		S_3	11	10	12	8	9	50
		S_4	4	4	3	5	11	27
	Mag.	S_1	3	1	0	0	2	6
		S_2	2	3	0	3	4	12
		S_3	0	0	1	0	0	1
		S_4	2	10	3	7	11	33
Age 9	Spec.	S_1	8	10	7	11	16	52
		S_2	10	12	9	7	11	49
		S_3	23	16	19	18	15	91
		S_4	9	10	20	24	20	83
	Dir.	S_1	11	7	14	15	14	61
		S_2	2	26	33	36	40	137
		S_3	13	18	16	11	17	75
		S_4	8	8	15	29	26	86
	Mag.	S_1	3	3	4	1	1	12
		S_2	0	5	2	12	14	33
		S_3	7	4	5	7	4	27
		S_4	9	8	6	10	0	33
Age 11	Spec.	S_1	14	24	19	22	22	101
		S_2	11	5	11	14	12	53
		S_3	24	19	25	25	26	119
		S_4	14	11	7	10	12	54
	Dir.	S_1	23	30	19	20	28	120
		S_2	15	9	11	21	11	67
		S_3	7	10	6	4	3	30
		S_4	1	2	2	14	14	33
	Mag.	S_1	3	12	17	9	8	49
		S_2	1	2	1	1	1	6
		S_3	11	3	7	7	6	34
		S_4	2	3	1	7	1	14

TABLE 17.3   Age × Feedback × Practice Block (*ABC*)

		PRACTICE BLOCK				
		1	2	3	4	5
Age 5	Spec.	16	11	9	20	14
	Dir.	12	7	8	12	9
	Mag.	5	1	2	8	12
Age 7	Spec.	19	36	43	53	53
	Dir.	28	34	29	40	46
	Mag.	7	14	4	10	17
Age 9	Spec.	50	48	55	60	62
	Dir.	34	59	78	91	97
	Mag.	19	20	17	30	19
Age 11	Spec.	63	59	62	71	72
	Dir.	46	51	38	59	56
	Mag.	17	20	26	24	16

TABLE 17.4   Age × Feedback (*AB*)

	SPEC.	DIR.	MAG.	
Age 5	70	48	28	146 (A_1)
Age 7	204	177	52	433 (A_2)
Age 9	275	359	105	739 (A_3)
Age 11	327	250	103	680 (A_4)
	876 (B_1)	834 (B_2)	288 (B_3)	

TABLE 17.5   Age × Practice Block

	PRACTICE BLOCK					
	1	2	3	4	5	
Age 5	33	19	19	40	35	146 (A_1)
Age 7	54	84	76	103	116	433 (A_2)
Age 9	103	127	150	181	178	739 (A_3)
Age 11	126	130	126	154	144	680 (A_4)
	316 (C_1)	360 (C_2)	371 (C_3)	478 (C_4)	473 (C_5)	

summing to obtain the cell totals. Finally, the sum of all the scores in the cells of each table you create should add to the grand total for the *ABCS* table. In this case it is 1998. This is another method of verifying that you have created the tables correctly. A last check involves summing the marginals for *A*, *B*, and *C* and verifying that these, too, add to 1998.

Conceptually, then, we take the raw *ABCS* scores of the study and, by summing them for various combinations of the independent variables of the

TABLE 17.6   Feedback × Practice Block

	PRACTICE BLOCK					
	1	2	3	4	5	
Spec. FB	148	154	169	204	201	876 (B_1)
Dir. FB	120	151	153	202	208	834 (B_2)
Mag. FB	48	55	49	72	64	288 (B_3)
	316 (C_1)	360 (C_2)	371 (C_3)	478 (C_4)	473 (C_5)	

study, we prepare to calculate the sums of squares due to each combination. When we are finished calculating, we will see that the sums of the squares for each of the combinations will add to the total sum of squares for the study which we obtain in the usual fashion.

Let us now consider the calculation of the values needed to obtain the sums of squares for each main effect and interaction and the total, between, within, and error sums of squares.

PRELIMINARY CALCULATIONS

In order to prepare the data for obtaining the various sums of squares needed to complete the analysis, we square and sum the scores in the cells of each of the tables we have created. We also square the sums for each of the levels of the main effects and for the row-sum (P) scores for each subject contained in Table 17.2, the $ABCS$ table. Since each of the interactions and the main effects represent sums of several scores, it is necessary to divide the sum of the squared values by the number of raw $(ABCS)$ scores that are contained in that value. We have previously used the small letters a, b, c, n to represent that and will continue to do so here.

First we sum the scores in the $ABCS$ table as in equation (17.1):

$$\Sigma\ X = (9 + 5 + 2 + 4 + \cdots + 3 + 1 + 7 + 1)$$

$$= 1998$$

(17.1)

We then square and sum the scores in the $ABCS$ table as shown in equation (17.2) (see Table 17.2 for scores):

$$\Sigma\ X^2 = (9^2 + 5^2 + 2^2 + 4^2 + \cdots + 3^2 + 1^2 + 7^2 + 1^2)$$

$$= (81 + 25 + 4 + 16 + \cdots + 9 + 1 + 49 + 1)$$

$$= 31,192$$

(17.2)

The next steps are similar in that we square and sum the totals for P, ABC, AB, AC, BC, A, B, and C. In these cases, however, we divide by the number which represents the number of score values included in each cell or total. These values are presented in equation (17.3):

$$a = 4, \qquad b = 3, \qquad c = 5, \qquad n = 4 \tag{17.3}$$

The calculations for P use Table 17.2 and are presented in equation (17.4). Each P value contains 5 scores which represent the levels c.

$$\frac{\Sigma\, P^2}{c} = \frac{P_1^2 + P_2^2 + P_3^2 + \cdots + P_{46}^2 + P_{47}^2 + P_{48}^2}{c}$$

$$= \frac{(24)^2 + (29)^2 + (15)^2 + \cdots + (6)^2 + (34)^2 + (14)^2}{5} \tag{17.4}$$

$$= \frac{138,354}{5}$$

$$= 27,670.8$$

The calculations for ABC are presented in equation (17.5) and use the cell sums from Table 17.3. The divisor is n, since there are 4 subjects in each cell sum in the ABC table.

$$\frac{\Sigma\,(ABC)^2}{n}$$

$$= \frac{(\Sigma\, A_1 B_1 C_1)^2 + (\Sigma\, A_1 B_1 C_2)^2 + \cdots + (\Sigma\, A_4 B_3 C_4)^2 + (\Sigma\, A_4 B_3 C_5)^2}{n}$$

$$= \frac{(16)^2 + (11)^2 + \cdots + (24)^2 + (16)^2}{4} \tag{17.5}$$

$$= \frac{256 + 121 + \cdots + 576 + 256}{4}$$

$$= \frac{100,534}{4}$$

$$= 25,133.5$$

The calculations for AB, AC, and BC are presented in equations (17.6),

(17.7), and (17.8), respectively. They use the values from the appropriate tables: AB (Table 17.4), AC (Table 17.5), and BC (Table 17.6).

$$\frac{\Sigma (AB)^2}{cn} = \frac{(\Sigma A_1 B_1)^2 + (\Sigma A_1 B_2)^2 + \cdots + (\Sigma A_4 B_2)^2 + (\Sigma A_4 B_3)^2}{cn}$$

$$= \frac{(70)^2 + (48)^2 + \cdots + (250)^2 + (103)^2}{20}$$

$$= \frac{4900 + 2304 + \cdots + 62{,}500 + 10{,}609}{20} \tag{17.6}$$

$$= \frac{479{,}206}{20}$$

$$= 23{,}960.3$$

$$\frac{\Sigma (AC)^2}{bn} = \frac{(\Sigma A_1 C_1)^2 + (\Sigma A_1 C_2)^2 + \cdots + (\Sigma A_4 C_4)^2 + (\Sigma A_4 C_5)^2}{bn}$$

$$= \frac{(33)^2 + (19)^2 + \cdots + (154)^2 + (144)^2}{12}$$

$$= \frac{1089 + 361 + \cdots + 23{,}716 + 20{,}736}{12} \tag{17.7}$$

$$= \frac{251{,}236}{12}$$

$$= 20{,}936.33$$

$$\frac{\Sigma (BC)^2}{an} = \frac{(\Sigma B_1 C_1)^2 + (\Sigma B_1 C_2)^2 + \cdots + (\Sigma B_3 C_4)^2 + (\Sigma B_3 C_5)^2}{an}$$

$$= \frac{(148)^2 + (154)^2 + \cdots + (72)^2 + (64)^2}{16}$$

$$= \frac{21{,}904 + 23{,}716 + \cdots + 5184 + 4096}{16} \tag{17.8}$$

$$= \frac{317{,}886}{16}$$

$$= 19{,}867.88$$

The calculations for A, B, and C are presented as equations (17.9)–(17.11) using the marginal totals from the appropriate tables.

$$\frac{\Sigma A^2}{bcn} = \frac{(\Sigma A_1)^2 + (\Sigma A_2)^2 + (\Sigma A_3)^2 + (\Sigma A_4)^2}{bcn}$$

$$= \frac{(146)^2 + (433)^2 + (739)^2 + (680)^2}{60}$$

$$= \frac{21{,}316 + 187{,}489 + 546{,}121 + 462{,}400}{60} \qquad (17.9)$$

$$= \frac{1{,}217{,}326}{60}$$

$$= 20{,}288.77$$

$$\frac{\Sigma B^2}{acn} = \frac{(\Sigma B_1)^2 + (\Sigma B_2)^2 + (\Sigma B_3)^2}{acn}$$

$$= \frac{(876)^2 + (834)^2 + (288)^2}{80}$$

$$= \frac{767{,}376 + 695{,}556 + 82{,}944}{80} \qquad (17.10)$$

$$= \frac{1{,}545{,}876}{80}$$

$$= 19{,}323.45$$

$$\frac{\Sigma C^2}{abn} = \frac{(\Sigma C_1)^2 + (\Sigma C_2)^2 + (\Sigma C_3)^2 + (\Sigma C_4)^2 + (\Sigma C_5)^2}{abn}$$

$$= \frac{(316)^2 + (360)^2 + (371)^2 + (478)^2 + (473)^2}{48}$$

$$= \frac{99{,}856 + 129{,}600 + 137{,}641 + 228{,}484 + 223{,}729}{48} \qquad (17.11)$$

$$= \frac{819{,}310}{48}$$

$$= 17{,}068.96$$

CALCULATING THE SUMS OF SQUARES

Using the values obtained in the preceding equations, we can proceed to calculate the sums of squares for each main effect and interaction as well as for the total, between, within, and error sums of squares. In general the procedure is the same as that presented in Chapter 16, in which we demonstrated that the sum of the squared scores due to main effects and appropriate interactions needed to be removed or added as appropriate and that the sum of squared scores representing the mean needed to be removed or added. These sums of squares are calculated in equations (17.12)–(17.23). The sum of squares for total is presented in equation (17.12):

$$SS_T = \Sigma\ X^2 - \frac{(\Sigma\ X)^2}{abcn}$$

$$= 31{,}192 - \frac{(1998)^2}{240}$$

$$= 31{,}192 - \frac{3{,}992{,}004}{240} \tag{17.12}$$

$$= 31{,}192 - 16{,}633.35$$

$$= 14{,}558.65$$

The sum of squares for between subjects is presented in equation (17.13):

$$SS_B = \frac{\Sigma\ P^2}{c} - \frac{(\Sigma\ X)^2}{abcn}$$

$$= 27{,}670.8 - 16{,}633.35 \tag{17.13}$$

$$= 11{,}037.45$$

The sum of squares within subjects is presented in equation (17.14):

$$SS_W = \Sigma\ X^2 - \frac{\Sigma\ P^2}{c}$$

$$= 31{,}192 - 27{,}670.8 \tag{17.14}$$

$$= 3521.2$$

In equations (17.15)–(17.18) we partition the between-subjects sum of squares further into the effects due to A, B, AB, and between-subjects error.

$$SS_A = \frac{\Sigma A^2}{bcn} - \frac{(\Sigma X)^2}{abcn}$$

$$= 20{,}288.77 - 16{,}633.35 \tag{17.15}$$

$$= 3{,}655.42$$

$$SS_B = \frac{\Sigma B^2}{acn} - \frac{(\Sigma X)^2}{abcn}$$

$$= 19{,}323.45 - 16{,}633.35 \tag{17.16}$$

$$= 2690.1$$

Recall that SS_{AB} requires correction by subtraction of the effects contained in AB which represent A and B. By doing this, we subtract out the effect due to the mean twice and therefore must add it back in as the fourth term in equation (17.17):

$$SS_{AB} = \frac{\Sigma AB^2}{cn} - \frac{\Sigma A^2}{bcn} - \frac{\Sigma B^2}{acn} + \frac{(\Sigma X)^2}{abcn}$$

$$= 23{,}960.3 - 20{,}288.77 - 19{,}323.45 + 16{,}633.35 \tag{17.17}$$

$$= 981.43$$

The SS for subjects within groups, also called error between, can then be obtained by subtraction of the sums of squares for each main effect and interaction from the sum of squares between subjects. This is shown in equation (17.18).

$$SS_{error\ between} = SS_B - SS_A - SS_B - SS_{AB}$$

$$= 11{,}037.45 - 3{,}655.42 - 2690.1 - 981.43 \tag{17.18}$$

$$= 3710.5$$

In equations (17.19)–(17.23) we partition the within-subjects sum of squares into the effects for C, since it is a within-subjects variable, and for C in combination with the other variables (AC, BC, ABC) and the error within.

$$SS_C = \frac{\Sigma \ C^2}{abn} - \frac{(\Sigma \ X)^2}{abcn}$$

$$= 17{,}068.96 - 16{,}633.35 \qquad\qquad (17.19)$$

$$= 435.61$$

$$SS_{AC} = \frac{(\Sigma \ AC)^2}{bn} - \frac{\Sigma \ A^2}{bcn} - \frac{\Sigma \ C^2}{abn} - \frac{(\Sigma \ X)^2}{abcn}$$

$$= 20{,}936.33 - 20{,}288.77 - 17{,}068.96 + 16{,}633.35 \qquad (17.20)$$

$$= 211.95$$

$$SS_{BC} = \frac{\Sigma \ (BC)^2}{an} - \frac{\Sigma \ B^2}{acn} - \frac{\Sigma \ C^2}{abn} + \frac{(\Sigma \ X)^2}{abcn}$$

$$= 19{,}867.88 - 19{,}323.45 - 17{,}068.96 + 16{,}633.35 \qquad (17.21)$$

$$= 108.82$$

$$SS_{ABC} = \frac{\Sigma \ (ABC)^2}{n} - \frac{\Sigma \ (AB)^2}{cn} - \frac{\Sigma \ (AC)^2}{bn} - \frac{\Sigma \ (BC)^2}{an}$$

$$+ \frac{\Sigma \ A^2}{bcn} + \frac{\Sigma \ B^2}{acn} + \frac{\Sigma \ C^2}{abn} - \frac{(\Sigma \ X)^2}{abcn} \qquad (17.22)$$

$$= 25{,}133.5 - 23{,}960.3 - 20.936.33 - 19.867.88$$
$$+ 20{,}288.77 + 19{,}323.45 + 17{,}068.96 - 16{,}633.35$$

$$= 416.82$$

$$SS_{\text{error within}} = SS_W - SS_C - SS_{AC} - SS_{BC} - SS_{ABC}$$

$$= 3521.20 - 435.61 - 211.95 - 108.82 - 416.82 \qquad (17.23)$$

$$= 2348$$

THE ANALYSIS-OF-VARIANCE TABLE

As in previous cases, we present the results of the analysis in table form. First, however, we should consider the determination of degrees of freedom. Using the a, b, c, n values presented in equation (17.3), we can calculate the df as in Table 17.7.

Now we can formulate the analysis-of-variance table and calculate the mean squares and the F-ratios. This is presented as Table 17.8.

The F-ratios in the table were calculated by dividing the MS for the effect of a particular variable by the MS for error between or within, depending upon whether the variable was a between-subjects variable (A, B, AB) or a within-subjects variable or interaction with a within-subjects variable (C, AC, BC, ABC). The critical values for the F-ratios are determined in exactly the same way

TABLE 17.7   Determining the Degrees of Freedom

SOURCE OF VARIATION	df (EQ.)	df (VALUE)	
Total	$abcn - 1$	$240 - 1$	$= 239$
Between subjects	$abn - 1$	$48 - 1$	$= 47$
Age	$a - 1$	$4 - 1$	$= 3$
Feedback	$b - 1$	$3 - 1$	$= 2$
Age × Feedback	$(a - 1)(b - 1)$	$(4 - 1)(3 - 1)$	$= 6$
Error between	$ab(n - 1)$	$(4)(3)(4 - 1)$	$= 36$
Within subjects	$abn(c - 1)$	$(4)(3)(4)(5 - 1)$	$= 192$
Practice blocks	$c - 1$	$5 - 1$	$= 4$
Age × Practice	$(a - 1)(c - 1)$	$(4 - 1)(5 - 1)$	$= 12$
Feedback × Practice	$(b - 1)(c - 1)$	$(3 - 1)(5 - 1)$	$= 8$
Age × Feedback × Practice	$(a - 1)(b - 1)(c - 1)$	$(4 - 1)(3 - 1)(5 - 1)$	$= 24$
Error within	$ab(c - 1)(n - 1)$	$(4)(3)(5 - 1)(4 - 1)$	$= 144$

TABLE 17.8   Analysis of Variance for Mean Correct Response Scores

SOURCE OF VARIATION	SS	df	MS	F
Total	14,558.65	239		
Between groups	11,037.45	47		
Age	3,655.42	3	1,215.14	11.79
Feedback	2,690.10	2	1,345.05	13.05
Age × Feedback	981.43	6	163.57	1.59
Error between	3,710.50	36	103.07	
Within groups	3,521.20	192		
Practice	435.61	4	108.90	6.68
Age × Practice	211.95	12	17.66	1.08
FB × Practice	108.82	8	13.60	1
Age × Feedback × Practice	416.82	24	17.37	1.06
Error within	2,348.00	144	16.31	

TABLE 17.9   Decision-Making Steps for Mixed Analysis of Variance

1. THE PROBLEM

If different age groups are provided different feedback over a series of practice trials, will
the number of correct responses vary? Accordingly, children of ages 5, 7, 9, and 11
were randomly assigned to one of three feedback conditions and then practiced a task
during five practice blocks. The number of correct responses in each practice block
was recorded.

2. RESEARCH HYPOTHESIS

If children of different ages are tested, then the number of correct responses will vary.
If different feedback is provided, then the number of correct responses will differ.
If practice is considered, then the number of correct responses will change.
(The interactions may be hypothesized as in Table 16.4.)

3. STATISTICAL HYPOTHESES

   a. AGE:
       H_0: $\bar{X}_1 = \bar{X}_2 = \bar{X}_3 = \bar{X}_4$
       H_1: $\bar{X}_1 \neq \bar{X}_2 \neq \bar{X}_3 \neq \bar{X}_4$

   b. FEEDBACK:

       H_0: $\bar{X}_1 = \bar{X}_2 = \bar{X}_3$
       H_1: $\bar{X}_1 \neq \bar{X}_2 \neq \bar{X}_3$

   c. PRACTICE:
       H_0: $\bar{X}_1 = \bar{X}_2 = \bar{X}_3 = \bar{X}_4 = \bar{X}_5$
       H_1: $\bar{X}_1 \neq \bar{X}_2 \neq \bar{X}_3 \neq \bar{X}_4 \neq \bar{X}_5$

(Statistical hypotheses for the interactions may be hypothesized as in Table 16.4.)

4. SIGNIFICANCE LEVEL

   .05

5. DECISION RULE

Age: Reject null if *F*-ratio with 3 and 36 *df* equals or exceeds 2.92.
Feedback: Reject null if *F*-ratio with 2 and 36 *df* equals or exceeds 3.32.
Practice: Reject null if *F*-ratio with 4 and 144 *df* equals or exceeds 2.45.
(Again, decision rules for the interactions should be provided in similar fashion.)

6. RESULTS

The results are presented in Table 17.8. Only main effects are significant, the interactions
are not. The mean correct responses for A_1 to A_4 are 2.4, 7.2, 12.3, and 11.33,
respectively. Follow-up tests as described in Chapter 18 should be done. The mean
correct responses for B_1 to B_3 are 10.95, 10.42, and 3.6, respectively. Follow-up tests
necessary. The mean correct responses over practice blocks are 6.6, 7.5, 7.7, 9.9, and
9.8 for C_1 to C_5, respectively. Again follow-up tests are necessary.

TABLE 17.9   (Continued)

7. CONCLUSIONS

On the basis of the analysis we conclude that age, feedback, and practice affect performance on the task. It appears that performance improves with age (except perhaps between 9 and 11). It appears that magnitudinal feedback is associated with poorer performance than either specific or directional feedback. Finally, performance appears to improve with practice—or at least from practice block 1 to practice blocks 4 and 5. These conclusions are tentative and would require follow-up tests such as those presented in Chapter 18.

as in the other analysis-of-variance examples we have considered. Thus, having completed the analysis and the table, we can review the decision-making steps for this problem. This is presented as Table 17.9.

EXTENSION OF THE EXAMPLE TO OTHER DESIGNS

The example we have presented can easily be extended to other mixed designs. Extension to a design in which there are more between-subject factors is the simplest and could be determined by adding terms, as we have already done, and following the conceptual model that was discussed in Chapter 16 and reviewed briefly here. Extension when there are other within-subjects variables is a bit more difficult because of the necessity to generate other row-sum values. If there were two within-subject variables, e.g., C and D, the analysis would require that the $ABCDS$ table be used to generate an overall row sum for each subject which would include C and D values *and* a row sum for each subject for each of the within variables, e.g., CP and DP. These values would then be used to calculate C and D sums of squares, while the overall value would be used to calculate the CD sum of squares. The interested reader is encouraged to consult Winer (1971) for a specific example of a design in which there are two within factors. It should be easy to follow, since the models used here draw on his methods of presentation.

INTERACTIONS

An interaction occurs when the joint effect of two or more factors is significant. That is, when the observed F-ratio for the combination AB, AC, or BC, or ABC is equal to or greater than the tabled value. In the numerical example used in the chapter there were no interactions, only main effects. That is, the main effects of Age (A), Feedback (B), and Practice (C) were significant, but joint effects were not. When interactions are not observed the interpretation of the observed results is straightforward. In this instance the mean correct responses for ages 5, 7, 9, and 11 are 2.4, 7.2, 12.3, and 11.33 respectively. Although follow-up tests are necessary to determine precise differences between and among age means, there is little difficulty of interpretation. The same is true for the effects of feedback and practice.

Such is not the case when interactions occur. An interaction occurs when the effect of one or more factors is not the same for all levels of another factor. Interactions between or among factors are independent of main effects. Interactions can occur whether or not main effects are significant. If interactions occur in the absence of main effects, there is little difficulty. If, however, main effects are also observed, they have little meaning since that effect appears to depend upon the particular level of another variable or variables. Thus, the presence of interactions precludes the interpretation of main effects. Additional information regarding interpretation of interaction is provided in Chapter 19 which considers the use of simple effects and individual comparisons as follow-up tests for significance.

Interactions are perhaps best described pictorially. Figure 17.1 provides several examples. Figure 17.1a, by way of contrast, illustrates a fictitious example in which the effect of age and of practice are significant but the interaction of the two, age × practice, is not. The five-year-olds make significantly more errors than the seven- or the nine-year-olds, and all improve with practice in an additive fashion. The lines representing the three age groups are parallel.

In Figure 17.1b we see a different picture. In this instance there is an interaction. The five-year-olds appear to make no improvement with practice, the nine-year-olds make some improvement, but the seven-year-olds show a marked improvement. There is clear deviation from parallel in the lines representing the three age groups. In this case there may be significant differences

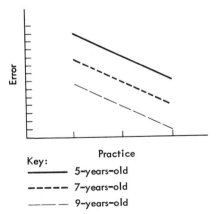

Key:
_____ 5-years-old
― ― ― ― 7-years-old
_ _ _ _ 9-years-old

FIGURE 17-1a   Significant Main Effects, No Interaction

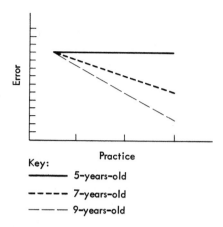

Key:

——————— 5-years-old

– – – – – 7-years-old

— — — 9-years-old

FIGURE 17-1b   Significant Main Effects, Interaction

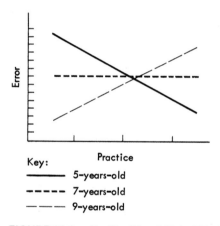

Key:

——————— 5-years-old

– – – – – 7-years-old

— — — 9-years-old

FIGURE 17-1c   No Significant Main Effects, Significant Interaction

among age groups and over practice. However, these significant differences are not interpretable. Taking practice effects as an example, the main effects may show that improvement occured over practice. This is certainly not true in the case of the five-year-olds, who make no discernable improvement at all. Thus, the main effect of practice is not legitimately interpretable since it has different effects for different age groups.

Figure 17.1c presents another example of interaction. In this case however, the main effects are not significant and the interaction is significant. The interaction occurs because the nine-year-olds do well in early practice and then poorly as practice continues, while the five-year-olds do poorly in early practice and improve as practice continues. Finally, the seven-year-olds do not improve at all. The averages for the main effects of age and of practice will be approximately equal.

EXERCISES

1. A researcher was interested in determining the effect of mental and physical practice, alone and in combination, on the learning and retention of an open and a closed skill.

		LEARNING	RETENTION
Open Skills			
	S_1	3	3
	S_2	10	13
Mental	S_3	7	9
	S_4	9	11
	S_5	7	6
	S_1	9	10
	S_2	9	11
Phys.	S_3	11	10
	S_4	8	8
	S_5	12	12
	S_1	15	15
	S_2	12	12
Ment.-	S_3	15	16
Phys.	S_4	13	12
	S_5	8	8
Closed Skills			
	S_1	10	8
	S_2	12	13
Mental	S_3	10	13
	S_4	13	16
	S_5	9	13
	S_1	15	17
	S_2	12	14
Phys.	S_3	16	16
	S_4	18	18
	S_5	11	10
	S_1	19	19
	S_2	15	14
Ment.-	S_3	19	19
Phys.	S_4	18	18
	S_5	13	16

2.   An instructor was interested in the effect of movement education, and length of time of instruction, on student performance and retention in basketball.

		PRETEST	POSTTEST	RETENTION
Traditional	S_1	3	4	5
Method	S_2	3	4	5
	S_3	4	6	5
	S_4	3	7	8
	S_5	3	5	6
4 weeks	S_6	6	7	8
	S_7	6	8	9
	S_8	4	8	8
	S_9	4	5	4
	S_{10}	3	4	5
	S_1	3	6	6
	S_2	3	5	4
	S_3	5	7	6
	S_4	3	5	4
8 weeks	S_5	6	9	9
	S_6	4	5	4
	S_7	6	9	8
	S_8	3	5	5
	S_9	5	8	9
	S_{10}	3	4	4
Movement	S_1	3	4	4
Education	S_2	4	6	7
	S_3	4	6	7
	S_4	4	5	5
4 weeks	S_5	3	5	7
	S_6	3	4	5
	S_7	5	8	8
	S_8	5	6	6
	S_9	5	8	9
	S_{10}	4	6	7
	S_1	3	6	6
	S_2	4	6	7
	S_3	7	9	7
	S_4	6	9	7
8 weeks	S_5	6	9	8
	S_6	4	7	7
	S_7	5	8	7
	S_8	3	5	5
	S_9	3	5	5
	S_{10}	4	7	6

REFERENCES

WINER, B. J. *Statistical principles in experimental design, 2nd ed.* New York: McGraw-Hill, 1971.

CHAPTER EIGHTEEN
ANALYZING
COVARIANCE
DESIGNS

An important consideration in experimental research is whether the treatment groups are equal at the outset. If, for some reason, they are not, the internal validity of the study has been compromised. We have seen, however, that the use of pretest, matching, and blocking procedures may compromise the external validity of the study.

Even if, in the early stages of investigation of an area, we are willing to risk compromise for the sake of internal validity, it is not always easy to establish equated groups. In addition, it is frequently necessary to study groups as they are—for example in recent studies involving the role of industrial fitness programs and employee productivity. The individuals in the experimental and control groups may vary widely in initial fitness levels. This variation will inflate the intersubject variability and will contribute to the error variance, perhaps masking treatment differences which might otherwise be statistically significant. Recall, if you will, that statistical significance is determined by the relationship:

$$\frac{\text{treatment variance}}{\text{error variance}}$$

Differences among subjects prior to treatment contribute to the error variance, unless they are accounted for in the group composition. Thus, some method of reducing variance among subjects would make possible greater sensitivity to between-group differences. Analysis of covariance is such a method.

Analysis of covariance tests the significance of adjusted mean differences between or among treatment groups. The adjusted mean differences are obtained by using the initial or pretest differences or the differences on some relevant variable to correct the final scores through use of correlational techniques. The score used in adjusting the final scores is called the *covariate*. The adjustment technique serves to remove from the final scores that portion which is due to the relation between the covariate and the final score, and, in doing so, adjusts for initial intersubject differences. The higher the correlation between the covariate and the final score, the more effective the analysis of covariance. Conversely, if the covariate and the final score yield a low or zero correlation, then use of analysis of covariance would be a waste of effort and time.

Analysis of covariance is generally employed (1) to increase precision in random-groups experiments, (2) to remove bias when subjects cannot be assigned at random to the treatment conditions, and (3) to remove variation due to unwanted factors. The use of analysis of covariance is a form of indirect (statistical) control of extraneous variability. By partitioning out the amount of variability in the final score accounted for by the covariate, we make the assessment of the effect of the independent variable(s) more precise. Thus, as indicated previously, the use of covariance analysis removes the effect of an extraneous source of variance that would otherwise inflate the experimental error.

Wildt and Ahtola (1978) have suggested that analysis of covariance is appropriate when the following conditions prevail:

1. There are one or more extraneous sources of variance believed to affect the dependent variable.
2. The extraneous source of variation can be measured on an interval or ratio scale.
3. The extraneous variable and the dependent variable are linearly correlated.
4. Direct control of extraneous sources of variation is not possible or not feasible.
5. It is possible to obtain a measure of extraneous variation that is free from treatment effects; that is, these measures are obtained prior to the imposition of the treatment (pretest), or observations on the covariate are obtained after treatment presentation but before the treatments have had a chance to affect it (early practice trials), or it can be assumed that the covariate is not affected by the treatment. (p. 15)

Further discussion of the covariate is in order, since textbooks rarely cover this topic adequately. The point has been made that the higher the correlation between the covariate and the dependent variable, the better the control. In fact, the adjusted mean scores obtained through analysis of covariance should be considered as residual scores, similar in nature to the residual variance obtained in the repeated-measures analysis of variance considered in Chapter 15. The adjusted mean scores represent the effect left after the portion of the score due to the covariate has been removed. The researcher using analysis of covariance wants to remove the effect of confounding or interfering variables without changing the nature of the dependent variable by removing portions of variability essential to its meaning. Thus, if the dependent variable was physical fitness and the measure included broad-jump performance, the researcher would not want to use broad-jump performance as a covariate, since it would remove a source of variance essential to the variation in the final scores. On the other hand, if a researcher were seeking to impose various training methods on subjects and compare their effect on broad-jump performance, the use of pretreatment broad-jump performance as a covariate might be a good way to eliminate initial subject differences. (It should be mentioned that the latter method is not a good procedure for dealing with pretreatment subject differences if other design-based methods can be found—for example, using pretreatment performance as an independent variable.)

As a further example of this last point: In the case where the covariate measures are obtained prior to treatment, a random-blocks design, a form of direct control of extraneous variance, would be preferable to the use of indirect control provided by analysis of covariance. A random-blocks design would be the only choice if the relationship beween the covariate and the dependent variable were nonlinear.

Another point that should be stressed is that the researcher should report the correlations between the covariate and the dependent variable for each group. In addition, the means and variances of the covariate for each group should not be significantly different, and this should be evaluated using a test of homogeneity. Finally, like the analysis of variance, the subjects should be randomly assigned to the treatment groups, or, at the very least, the assignment of treatments to groups should be random.

USING THE ANALYSIS-OF-COVARIANCE TECHNIQUE

Analysis of covariance is, as indicated previously, no substitute for a random-blocks design. In some cases, however, the use of a random-blocks design is not feasible. The most common example is when the researcher is constrained in forming the groups and must use existing groups.

In the example that follows, a researcher wishes to use existing classes to determine which of three training programs is most effective in producing changes in cardiovascular respiratory fitness and in promoting continued participation of students. Thus, the researcher uses four classes of students (one class serves as a control group). For ease of calculation, we assume small, equal classes of 8 students. The first program uses a bicycle ergometer; the second is basically a jogging program; and the third uses a variety of activities: swimming, jogging, racquetball. A fourth group serves as a control group. The

TABLE 18.1   Decision-making Steps for Analysis of Covariance

1. THE PROBLEM

A researcher wishes to determine which of three activity programs is more effective in developing initial levels of CVR fitness and in promoting continued participation. Is there a difference in the level of cardiovascular respiratory fitness achieved by participants in three different activity programs? Is there a difference in the level of continued participation of subjects in the three plans?

2. RESEARCH HYPOTHESIS

If groups participate in different types of activity programs, then they will differ in levels of CVR fitness and in continued participation.

3. STATISTICAL HYPOTHESES

H_0: $\overline{X}_1 = \overline{X}_2 = \overline{X}_3 = \overline{X}_4$

H_1: $\overline{X}_1 \neq \overline{X}_2 \neq \overline{X}_3 \neq \overline{X}_4$

4. LEVEL OF SIGNIFICANCE

.05

5. DECISION RULE

Reject null if F with 3 and 29 $df \geq 2.95$.

---

study is planned to evaluate two aspects of the programs: cardiovascular respiratory fitness after the first semester and at the end of one year; and continued participation in the semester following experimental treatment. For simplicity in illustrating the ANCOVA procedure the pretest and first-semester scores for CVR fitness will be used.

The decision-making procedure as applied to analysis of covariance is presented in Table 18.1. Consideration of the last two steps in the procedure—the value obtained, and the decision—will have to await the presentation of the calculation presented in Table 18.8.

ORGANIZING THE DATA

The data should be organized in column form as shown in Table 18.2. The information which needs to be culled from the raw data for X, Y, and XY and the method of obtaining it are presented in Table 18.3. Note that the procedures are exactly as presented for the analysis of variance in the previous chapter. The difference is that the solutions are obtained for X, Y, and XY. Thus, for each we obtain, under totals, values for the sum of the scores squared divided by the total number of observations—that is, $(\Sigma X)^2/N$; the sum of the

TABLE 18.2 Raw Scores (Minutes of Recovery) for Subjects

CYCLING GROUP 1		JOGGING GROUP 2		VARIETY GROUP 3		CONTROL GROUP 4	
X_1 PRE	Y_1 POST	X_2 PRE	Y_2 POST	X_3 PRE	Y_3 POST	X_4 PRE	Y_4 POST
8	6	9	6	8	4	8	7
6	4	6	4	6	3	6	7
10	7	8	7	7	4	5	5
13	10	11	6	8	5	9	10
7	6	9	4	9	4	4	5
5	3	10	7	13	10	11	9
6	4	7	5	6	2	7	6
14	9	12	9	10	8	12	11

TABLE 18.3 Preliminary Analysis-of-Covariance Calculations

(BY GROUP)

	X_1		Y_1	X_2		Y_2	X_3		Y_3	X_4		Y_4
$\Sigma(\ )$	69		49	72		48	67		40	62		60
$\Sigma(\ )^2$	675		343	676		308	599		250	536		486
ΣXY		479			449			376			506	
Err( )	79.9		42.9	28		20	37.9		50	55.5		36
ErrXY		56.4			17			41			41	

(TOTALS)

$(\Sigma X)^2/N$	$\dfrac{(69 + 72 + 67 + 62)^2}{32} = 2278.125$
ΣX^2	$675 + 676 + 599 + 536 = 2486$
$\Sigma(XG^2)$	$\dfrac{(69)^2 + (72)^2 + (67)^2 + (62)^2}{8} = 2284.75$
ErrorX	$79.9 + 28 + 37.9 + 55.5 = 201.3$
$(\Sigma Y)^2/N$	$\dfrac{(49 + 48 + 40 + 60)^2}{32} = 1212.7812$
ΣY^2	$343 + 308 + 250 + 486 = 1387$
$\Sigma(YG^2)$	$\dfrac{(49)^2 + (48)^2 + (40)^2 + (60)^2}{8} = 1238.125$
ErrorY	$42.9 + 20 + 50 + 36 = 148.9$
$(\Sigma X)(\Sigma Y)/N$	$\dfrac{(69 + 72 + 67 + 62)(49 + 48 + 40 + 60)}{32} = 1662.1875$
ΣXY	$479 + 449 + 376 + 506 = 1810$
$\Sigma(XYG)$	$\dfrac{(69)(49) + (72)(48) + (67)(40) + (62)(60)}{8} = 1654.625$
ErrorXY	$56.4 + 17 + 41 + 41 = 155.4$

squared scores, $\Sigma\ X^2$; the sum of each group total squared divided by the number in each group, $\Sigma\ (XG^2)/n$; and the error, ErrX, obtained by calculating the sum of squares for each group independently for each variable. These values will be used to calculate the analyses.

CALCULATING THE ANALYSIS

In order to calculate the analysis of covariance and the adjusted means, we first compute the analysis of variance for X and Y individually. To do this we proceed exactly as we did in the analysis of variance in the previous chapter. Calculate the total sum of squares as shown in equation (18.1), the between-groups sum of squares (18.2), and the within-groups sum of squares by subtraction (18.3).

For the variable X:

$$SS_T = \Sigma\ X^2 - \frac{(\Sigma\ X)^2}{N}$$

$$= 2486 - 2278.125 \tag{18.1}$$

$$= 207.875$$

$$SS_{BG} = \frac{\Sigma\ (G^2)}{n} - \frac{(\Sigma\ X)^2}{N}$$

$$= 2284.75 - 2278.125 \tag{18.2}$$

$$= 6.625$$

$$SS_{WG} = SS_T - SS_{BG}$$

$$= 207.875 - 6.625 \tag{18.3}$$

$$= 201.25$$

In similar fashion we can calculate the appropriate values for Y and XY. These are presented in Table 18.4. (Try calculating these from the data in Table 18.3.)

Using these values, we prepare an analysis-of-variance table for X and Y as shown in Table 18.5.

Using the values obtained for the XY and the X and Y, we calculate the values for the analysis-of-covariance table shown in Table 18.6. The total sum

TABLE 18.4   Sum of Squares for Y and XY

	VARIABLE Y	VARIABLE XY
SS_T	174.22	147.81
SS_{BG}	25.34	−7.56[a]
SS_{WG}	148.9	155.4

[a]In all other cases a negative sum of squares would indicate an error. In analysis of covariance a negative SS_{x-y} is possible.

TABLE 18.5   Analysis of Variance for X and Y

			X			Y	
SOURCE OF VARIATION	df	SS	MS	F	SS	MS	F
Total	31	207.9	—	—	174.2	—	—
Between groups	3	6.6	2.2	1	25.3	8.4	1.58
Within groups	28	201.2	7.2		148.9	5.3	

TABLE 18.6   Analysis of Covariance of Mean Recovery Scores

SOURCE OF VARIATION	df	SS	MS	F
Total	31	69.12	—	—
Between groups	3	40.22	13.40	13.01
Within groups	28	28.9	1.03	

of squares for Y as adjusted on the basis of the pretest scores is shown in equation (18.4):

$$SS_{T_{y \cdot x}} = SS_{TY} - \frac{(SS_{TXY})^2}{SS_{XT}}$$

$$= 174.22 - \frac{(147.81)^2}{207.88}$$

$$= 174.22 - 105.10$$

$$= 69.12$$

(18.4)

The within-groups sum of squares for Y as adjusted on the basis of the pretest scores is shown in equation (18.5):

$$SS_{WG_{y \cdot x}} = SS_{WY} - \frac{(SS_{WXY})^2}{SS_{XW}}$$

$$= 148.9 - \frac{(155.4)^2}{201.25} \tag{18.5}$$

$$= 148.9 - 119.996$$

$$= 28.9$$

The between-groups sum of squares is calculated by subtraction as in equation (18.6):

$$SS_{BG_{y \cdot x}} = SS_{T_{y \cdot x}} - SS_{WG_{y \cdot x}}$$

$$= 69.12 - 28.9 \tag{18.6}$$

$$= 40.22$$

An analysis-of-covariance table is formulated as shown in Table 18.6.

ADJUSTING THE TREATMENT MEANS

In order to determine the adjusted treatment means, we must calculate an unbiased estimate of the regression of X on Y. A within-group regression coefficient is the most nearly unbiased estimate. This is calculated as equation (18.7), where the within-groups sum of squares for XY is that calculated earlier for the variable XY:

$$b = \frac{SS_{XYWG}}{SS_{XWG}}$$

$$= \frac{155.4}{201.25} \tag{18.7}$$

$$= .77$$

The adjusted means are then calculated using equation (18.8):

$$M_{y \cdot x} = M_y - b_w (M_x - \text{Gen. } M_x) \tag{18.8}$$

TABLE 18.7 Adjusted Mean Recovery Time

GROUPS	n	M_x	M_y	$M_{y \cdot x}$
Cycling	8	8.6	6.1	5.98
Jogging	8	9	6	5.57
Variety	8	8.4	5	5.03
Control	8	7.8	7.5	7.99
Totals	32	8.44	6.16	6.14

As an example consider the mean for the cycling group shown in equation (18.9):

$$M_{y \cdot x} = 6.1 - .77 (8.6 - 8.44)$$

$$= 6.1 - .77 (.16)$$

$$= 6.1 - .12 \tag{18.9}$$

$$= 5.98$$

Thus, Table 18.7 is created.

COMPLETING THE ANALYSIS

Earlier in the chapter, in Table 18.1, we presented five of the seven decision-making steps for analysis of covariance; now we can complete the list. Starting from step 5, the decision rule, the final steps are shown in Table 18.8.

The results of the ANCOVA reveal that there is a difference among the

TABLE 18.8 Completion of Decision-Making Steps

5. DECISION RULE

Reject H_0 if $F_{(3, 29)} \geq 2.95$.

6. VALUE OBTAINED

$F = 13.01$.

7. CONCLUSION

Reject H_0; there are differences among the observed means, follow up tests necessary.

groups but they do not reveal the precise source of the significance. This is true in any instance in which there are more than two means. Recall that in the *t*-test, interpretation was simple; the difference was significant, there were two means, our interpretation was clear, one group was better than the other. In cases in which there are three or more means, statistical procedure dictates that a follow-up procedure for analyzing individual differences among means be employed. In this case the follow-up procedure would entail comparing the four group means to determine the source of the significant *F*-ratio. Since these procedures are general, they are considered in Chapter 19.

The purpose of considering analysis of covariance was to introduce you to the procedure and to help you understand the underlying concepts. The exercises at the end of the chapter will give you an opportunity to work through several examples and are intended to heighten your understanding of the procedure. In problems which involve larger groups, more than one variable, or repeated measures, manual computation is cumbersome and tedious—particularly since normal data are generally more complex than the simplistic data employed here for illustration. Thus, researchers will generally use standardized computer packages to analyze their data, as discussed in Chapter 20.

EXERCISES

1. The example given in the chapter considered two dependent variables: CVR fitness, and continued participation. The data given below are based on subject self-report. The pretest scores are based on information gathered on a questionnaire subjects filled out at the beginning of the semester; the posttest scores are based on information gathered at the time of the one-year testing. (The score is the hours per week the subject spends in vigorous physical activity.)

CYCLING GROUP 1		JOGGING GROUP 2		VARIETY GROUP 3		CONTROL GROUP 4	
X_1 PRE	Y_1 POST	X_2 PRE	Y_2 POST	X_3 PRE	Y_3 POST	X_4 PRE	Y_4 POST
4	7	4	8	3	6	3	4
2	5	5	9	2	9	4	4
4	6	5	7	2	7	6	5
2	4	4	8	3	8	3	3
3	5	3	7	4	8	5	6
2	4	1	5	4	7	2	3
5	7	2	6	2	6	5	3
6	8	5	8	6	9	4	5

2. The example given in the chapter further indicates that a follow-up test for CVR fitness will be given after one year. The results of this test are given below. (Note that the pretest score used for the covariate is the same one used in the initial end-of-semester analysis.)

CYCLING GROUP 1		JOGGING GROUP 2		VARIETY GROUP 3		CONTROL GROUP 4	
X_1 PRE	Y_1 POST	X_2 PRE	Y_2 POST	X_3 PRE	Y_3 POST	X_4 PRE	Y_4 POST
8	7	9	5	8	4	8	9
6	5	6	3	6	3	6	6
10	8	8	7	7	5	5	6
13	11	11	5	8	4	9	10
7	7	9	5	9	4	4	4
5	4	10	6	13	8	11	8
6	5	7	4	6	3	7	7
14	10	12	9	10	9	12	10

REFERENCES

WILDT, A. R. and AHTOLA, O. T. *Analysis of covariance.* Beverly Hills, Calif.: Sage, 1978.

CHAPTER NINETEEN CONSIDERING SIGNIFICANT FINDINGS: FOLLOW-UP TESTS

As noted previously, to compare two treatment means (as in the case of the t-test) we simply take the difference between them. The mean that is higher or lower, according to the particular measure employed, signifies the better treatment. Such is not the case when three or more means are involved. In this case, several standard statistical comparisons may be used. These tests, often called follow-up, post hoc, or a posteriori tests, are used to follow up significant differences in multigroup experiments for the purpose of ascertaining, more precisely, the source of the observed significance. We will consider five procedures: studentized range statistic; Tukey; Scheffe; Newman-Kuels; and Duncan multiple range. We will also consider additional procedures, simple effects, which must be employed prior to individual comparisons in multifactor experiments in which interactions are significant.

INDIVIDUAL COMPARISONS

You may ask, "Why do we need a follow-up test? Isn't it sufficient to report that the F-test was significant?" The F-test is an overall test. It merely indicates, in the case of a single variable with multiple levels, that the means do not fall on a straight line. Often this is not sufficient for interpretation or decision making. As an example, consider the results of the study reported in Chapter 17. Recall that the independent variable was type of activity program: cycling, jogging, variety, and nothing (control). The dependent variable used in the first analysis was CVR

TABLE 19.1   Analysis of Covariance for Mean Scores of Activity Groups

SOURCE OF VARIATION	df	SS	MS	F
Total	31	69.1148	—	—
Between groups	3	40.21	13.40	13.01
Within groups	28	28.9	1.03	—

ADJUSTED MEAN SCORES FOR ACTIVITY GROUPS

GROUP	n	$\overline{X}$
Cycling	8	5.98
Jogging	8	5.57
Variety	8	5.03
Control	8	7.99

fitness. The results of the analysis of covariance and the table of means are presented in Table 19.1.

Using only the reported means, the researcher might conclude that the experimental group involving a variety was better, in terms of CVR fitness, than the control group. Interpretations and discussions would be based on the largest differences observed. Without a follow-up procedure the researcher actually knows little more than that "there was a difference between the two most distant activity groups." To discuss further differences between the means for the particular activities is fallacious. Thus, the researcher employs an individual-comparisons procedure. Each test to be reviewed will be illustrated in terms of the data provided by this example.

Studentized Range Statistic

The hypothesis tested by the studentized range statistic is that $\overline{X}_1 = \overline{X}_2 = \overline{X}_3 = \overline{X}_4$. The test is defined by the formula (Winer, 1971) given in equation (19.1):

$$q = \frac{\overline{T}_{largest} - \overline{T}_{smallest}}{\sqrt{\dfrac{MS_{error}}{n}}} \tag{19.1}$$

where n is the number of observations in each treatment mean. This formula is read as: the difference between the largest and smallest treatment means (7.99 − 5.03) divided by the square root of the MS experimental error (1.03) over n (8). Thus, substituting as shown in equation (19.2):

$$q = \frac{7.99 - 5.03}{\sqrt{\dfrac{1.03}{8}}}$$

$$= \frac{2.96}{.36} \tag{19.2}$$

$$= 8.22$$

The critical value to which the observed value 8.22 is compared is found in Table 7, Appendix A, distribution of the studentized range statistic, with $df = 4, 28$, where 4 is the number of treatment means and 28 is the df associated with the MS_{error}. The tabled value, using the .05 level of significance, and the closest df without exceeding 28 is 3.90. Thus, since the obtained value (8.22) exceeds the tabled value, we conclude that there is a significant difference. Unfortunately, this procedure does not tell us any more than we already know as a function of our original F-test. What we really wish to do is to evaluate the statistical significance of all possible pairs of means. This procedure is called the Newman-Kuels test. It employs a version of the studentized range statistic.

Newman-Kuels

The major difference in this test is that it focuses on evaluating the set of ranked treatment means. The statistic is the same but the numerator changes as each new pair of means is compared. The ranked treatment means for our example are given in Table 19.2, where 1 is the smallest mean and 4 is the largest. The q statistic is calculated for each pairwise comparison. The T_4 mean is 4 steps (r) from T_1, 3 steps from T_2, and 2 steps from T_3. Similarly the T_3 mean is 3 steps from T_1 and 2 steps from T_2. Finally, the T_2 mean is 2 steps from the T_1 mean.

Perhaps the simplest way to proceed in preparing the data to perform the Newman-Kuels test is to create a table such as Table 19.3. The number in ( ) represents the number of steps (r) between the ordered pair. It is possible to use the formula presented earlier to calculate the q value for each pair of means, as shown in equation (19.3):

TABLE 19.2   Ordered Treatment Means

			ORDER	
	1	2	3	4
Means	5.03	5.57	5.98	7.99

TABLE 19.3   Differences Between Pairs of Ordered Means

ORDERED MEANS	3	2	1
	(STEPS)		
4	(2) 2.01	(3) 2.42	(4) 2.96
3	—	(2) .41	(3) .95
2	—	—	(2) .54

$$q = \frac{T_4 - T_1}{\sqrt{\dfrac{MS_{error}}{n}}} \qquad (19.3)$$

But it is far easier to transpose the formula as shown in equation (19.4):

$$T_4 - T_1 = q\sqrt{\frac{MS_{error}}{n}} \qquad (19.4)$$

Also the value will be the same for each pair of means that are the same distance apart. Thus, three equations will have to be calculated: for $r = 4$, $r = 3$, and $r = 2$. The MS_{error}/n will remain constant as calculated in equation (19.5):

$$\sqrt{\frac{MS_{error}}{n}} = \sqrt{\frac{1.03}{8}}$$

$$= \sqrt{.139} \qquad (19.5)$$

$$= .36$$

A table can be formed to ease your work using 9-values obtained from Table A7, as shown in Table 19.4. The values obtained are then compared to those in Table 19.3.

TABLE 19.4   Calculation of Comparison Values

r	q (FROM TABLE) (r, df_{error})	COMPARISON VALUE $(q\sqrt{MS_{error}/n})$
4	3.90	1.40
3	3.53	1.27
2	2.92	1.05

TABLE 19.5 Procedure For Evaluating Ordered Means

1. The first test is on the mean which represents the largest number of steps (4): that in the upper right-hand corner (2.96). The comparison value is 1.43; clearly the observed difference is significant. This is indicated by use of a single asterisk to designate significance at the .05 level. (If we were using the .01 level, we would designate this by a double asterisk.)

2. The next test is on all the mean differences which are 3 steps distant (2.42 and .95). In this instance the comparison value is 1.30. Thus the largest mean, for the control group, is significantly greater than that for the jogging group (5.57), but the mean for the cycling group (5.98) is not significantly different from that for the variety group. If there were additional differences of 3 steps, these could not be compared once a nonsignificant difference was encountered, for reasons explained above.

3. The next test is on all the mean differences which are separated by 2 steps. These are, in order to be compared: 2.01, .41, and .54. The value 2.01 clearly exceeds the required 1.08. Thus, a single asterisk is placed next to the difference. The value .41 does not exceed the critical value, so comparisons stop there.

In comparing the obtained values to those observed in Table 19.3 a prescribed sequence must be followed. This is important so that contradictions in decision-making do not occur. One example should suffice. In looking at the chart of comparison values it is clear that as the size of the step decreases, the value required for significance is smaller. Because of this it is possible that the difference between the largest and the smallest mean may not reach significance but the difference between the second largest and the smallest may reach significance. For example, the largest mean and the next largest mean might differ by only .02. Since the comparison value is likely to differ by .13, or even by as much as .22, as it did in Table 19.4, this would lead to a contradiction where the first comparison might not reach significance while the second, smaller actual difference might. This is not a valid inference. If the larger difference is not significant, then differences that follow, since by definition they are smaller, cannot be significant. The procedure is given in Table 19.5.

The revised table, including indicated levels of significance, is presented as Table 19.6.

The convention for presenting the differences schematically is to underline treatments that do not differ with a common line. Treatments not schematically

TABLE 19.6 Differences Between Pairs of Ordered Means

MEANS: 4—7.99   3—5.98   2—5.57   1—5.03

ORDERED MEANS	3	2	1
4	2.01*	2.42*	2.96*
3	—	.41	.95
2	—	—	.54

connected by a common line do differ from each other. Thus,

Variety	Jogging	Cycling	Control

would indicate that the three activity treatments do not differ from each other but that they all differ from the control group.

Tukey's Honestly Significant Difference (HSD)

In the test above, Newman-Keuls, the comparison value is computed separately for each stepwise comparison. That is, the comparison value decreases as the number of pairwise steps decrease. This increases the significance levels in effect as the number of steps increases. In order to account for this, Tukey suggests a more conservative procedure in which the comparison value is calculated once on the basis of the largest stepwise comparison. In the case of our example we would calculate it for the 4-step distance and use the comparison value obtained (1.40) to make all comparisons. This would make no difference at all in the conclusions, since all the pairwise differences that were significant in the previous method are significant for this more conservative method as well.

Duncan's Multiple-Range Test

The procedure for Duncan's Multiple-Range Test is exactly the same as that for the Newman-Kuels test. The difference is that the critical values, which are obtained from a table not included in the appendix, are less (except in the case of the 2-step values). The comparison values are obtained by equation (19.6):

$$\text{least significant range} = (\text{significant student range})(s_{\bar{X}}) \tag{19.6}$$

or

$$LSR = SSR(s_{\bar{X}})$$

Calculating, we obtain the results of equation (19.7):

$$(s_{\bar{X}}) = \sqrt{\frac{MS_{error}}{n}}$$

$$= \sqrt{\frac{1.03}{8}} \tag{19.7}$$

$$= \sqrt{.139}$$

$$= .36$$

TABLE 19.7   SSR's and Comparison Values

r	SSR	LSR
4	3.13	1.13
3	3.04	1.09
2	2.89	1.04

and

$$LSR = SSR(.36)$$

Using data from the appropriate table, we find the SSR's and comparison values for DMR in Table 19.7 (values obtained by r, df_{error}). These LSR values are then used in evaluating the observed pairwise differences. The table is the same as that for the Newman-Kuels test and the conclusions are the same for this example. Since there are differences in the comparison values for the larger step intervals, some difference in the results might be anticipated.

In the case of both the Newman-Kuels test and this test, the example has been for the instance in which the groups were equal. Often this is not the case. The necessary modification is accomplished in the denominator of the fraction, as shown by the transition from equation (19.8) to (19.9):

$$\sqrt{\frac{MS_{error}}{n}} \qquad (19.8)$$

$$\sqrt{\frac{MS_{error}}{.5(n_a + n_b)}} \qquad (19.9)$$

where n_a and n_b are the numbers in each of two unequal groups. This multiplier must be calculated individually for each pair of unequal groups. As an illustration, consider the fictitious example of Table 19.8.

Scheffe's Test

The final test of individual comparisons to be considered is the Scheffe test. It is similar to the Tukey test in that a single critical value is used for comparison. The major difference between this test and the others which have been considered is that it uses the readily available F table rather than a specialized table as in the case of the other tests. The comparison difference (CD) to be used is calculated as in equation (19.10):

$$CD = \sqrt{(a - 1)F} \sqrt{\frac{2(MS_{error})}{n}} \qquad (19.10)$$

where a = the number of experimental groups

TABLE 19.8   Example of Calculations With Unequal _n_

$$MS_{error} = 2.00$$

GROUP	_n_	MEAN
1	5	10
2	10	15
3	7	18
4	9	12

Thus, for each pair:

GROUPS	$\sqrt{\dfrac{MS_{error}}{.5(n_a + n_b)}}$
1 and 2	$\sqrt{\dfrac{2.00}{.5(5 + 10)}} = \sqrt{\dfrac{2.00}{7.5}} = .52$
1 and 3	$\sqrt{\dfrac{2.00}{.5(5 + 7)}} = \sqrt{\dfrac{2.00}{6}} = .58$
1 and 4	$\sqrt{\dfrac{2.00}{.5(5 + 9)}} = \sqrt{\dfrac{2.00}{7}} = .53$
2 and 3	$\sqrt{\dfrac{2.00}{.5(10 + 7)}} = \sqrt{\dfrac{2.00}{8.5}} = .48$
2 and 4	$\sqrt{\dfrac{2.00}{.5(10 + 9)}} = \sqrt{\dfrac{2.00}{9.5}} = .46$
3 and 4	$\sqrt{\dfrac{2.00}{.5(7 + 9)}} = \sqrt{\dfrac{2.00}{8}} = .50$

Then, individually for each comparison:

GROUPS	MULTIPLIER	STEPS	TAB. VAL.	REQ. DIFF.	OBS. DIFF.	_s/ns_
1 and 2	.52	2	2.89	1.50	5	s
1 and 3	.58	3	3.04	1.76	8	s
1 and 4	.53	4	3.13	1.66	2	s
2 and 3	.48	2	2.89	1.39	3	s
2 and 4	.46	3	3.04	1.40	3	s
3 and 4	.50	2	2.89	1.44	6	s

Thus, all observed differences are significant.

TABLE 19.9   Mean Scores For Fitness

GROUP	_n_	$\overline{X}$
Cycling	8	5.98
Jogging	8	5.57
Variety	8	5.03
Control	8	7.99

F = the tabled value for df_b, df_w

n = the number of subjects in each group (if unequal, use procedure presented previously or harmonic mean)

Using the earlier example (in which $MS_{error} = 1.03$), we have the data in Table 19.9, and we calculate the CD as shown in equation (19.11).

$$CD = \sqrt{3(2.95)} \; \sqrt{\frac{2(1.03)}{8}} \tag{19.11}$$

$$= \sqrt{8.85} \; \sqrt{\frac{2.06}{8}}$$

$$= 2.97\sqrt{.26}$$

$$= 2.97(.51)$$

$$= 1.51$$

The actual pairwise differences would be compared to this value. It is clear that the obtained value is larger than the values obtained by any of the previous procedures. Hence, this is the most stringent test of any, and significance is more difficult to obtain.

SIMPLE EFFECTS

In the previous section we considered tests which are used to ascertain the source of significant differences in a multigroup experiment. Typically, we are referring to a one-way analysis-of-variance design. Frequently, however, researchers need to use follow-up procedures (post hoc tests) to tease out the source or sources of significance in a multifactor experiment. An example which will provide a good basis for discussion is a 2×3 factorial design. In this case both factors are between-group factors. Using our standard decision-making and statistical procedures, we obtain Table 19.10.

The overall analysis, using a two-way analysis of variance, has indicated that personality does not seem to affect performance. However, motivation condition, and the interaction of the subject's personality and the motivation condition, seem to have a strong effect on performance. You will recall that in the t-test the results of a significant t-ratio were immediately interpretable by comparing the two mean scores and simply indicating that the group with the higher or lower mean score, depending on the dependent measure, was better. When comparisons involve three or more means, as do all ANOVAs, it is necessary to use additional statistical tests to tease out where the significance lies. Earlier in

TABLE 19.10   Decision-Making Steps With Simple Effects

1. THE PROBLEM

A researcher wished to determine whether motivational techniques matched to the personality of the subject would have a positive effect on performance.

Is there a difference in the level of performance of subject as a result of application of different motivational techniques?

It there a difference in the performance of subjects of different personality type?

Does the combination of motivational technique and personality make a difference?

2. RESEARCH HYPOTHESES

Groups will differ in performance as a result of motivational technique.

Groups will differ in performance as a result of personality.

Groups will differ in performance as a result of the interaction of motivational technique and personality.

3. STATISTICAL HYPOTHESES

Motivation:

$$H_0: \quad \overline{M}_1 = \overline{M}_2 = \overline{M}_3, \qquad H_1: \quad \overline{M}_1 \neq \overline{M}_2 \neq \overline{M}_3$$

Personality:

$$H_0: \quad \overline{P}_1 = \overline{P}_2, \qquad H_1: \overline{P}_1 \neq \overline{P}_2$$

Motivation $\times$ Personality:

$$H_0: \quad \overline{M}_1\overline{P}_1 = \overline{M}_1\overline{P}_2 = \overline{M}_2\overline{P}_1 = \overline{M}_2\overline{P}_2 = \overline{M}_3\overline{P}_1 = \overline{M}_3\overline{P}_2$$

$$H_1: \quad \overline{M}_1\overline{P}_1 \neq \overline{M}_1\overline{P}_2 \neq \overline{M}_2\overline{P}_1 \neq \overline{M}_2\overline{P}_2 \neq \overline{M}_3\overline{P}_1 \neq \overline{M}_3\overline{P}_2$$

4. LEVEL OF SIGNIFICANCE

.01

5. DECISION RULE

Reject H_0 if $F(1, 54) \geq 7.31$

Reject H_0 if $F(2, 54) \geq 5.18$

6. RESULTS

The values obtained are presented in Tables 19.11 and 19.12.

7. CONCLUSION

The main effect of personality does not make a difference in performance.

The main effect of motivation does make a difference in performance, with the *S/C* and *T/C* groups apparently better than the *none* group.

The interaction of personality and motivational technique is significant; ind. perform better with *S/C* motivation and *dep.* perform better with *T/C* motivation.

TABLE 19.11   Analysis-of-Variance Table for Mean Scores

SOURCE OF VARIATION	df	MS	F
Total	59		
Personality (A)	1	1.07	1.07
Motivation (B)	2	33.95	33.95
Pers. × Moti. (AB)	2	20.02	20.02
Error	54	1.00	

TABLE 19.12   Table of Mean Scores for Personality/Motivation

		MOTIVATION CONDITION			
		STUDENT-CENTERED	TEACHER-CENTERED	NONE	
Personality	Ind.	5.3	3.5	2.1	3.63
	Dep.	3.0	5.2	1.9	3.37
		4.15	4.35	2.0	

TABLE 19.13   Mean Difference Among Groups

$TC - SC = 4.35 - 4.15 = .20$ ns
$TC - No = 4.35 - 2.00 = 2.35$ sig
$SC - No = 4.15 - 2.00 = 2.15$ sig

this chapter we explored individual comparisons as a technique to be used when comparing means of several levels of a single experimental variable. In the case of the significant difference in groups using different motivational conditions, individual comparisons would be the appropriate technique to employ. Using the Scheffe test, we obtain the results of equation (19.12) and Table 19.13.

$$CD = \sqrt{2(5.18)} \; \sqrt{\frac{2(1.00)}{10}}$$

$$= \sqrt{10.36} \; \sqrt{\frac{2.00}{10}}$$

$$= \sqrt{10.36} \; \sqrt{.2}$$

$$= 3.22(.45)$$

$$= 1.45$$

(19.12)

Thus, we note that the no-motivation group evidenced significantly lower performance scores than either the teacher-centered motivation group or the student-centered motivation group.

TABLE 19.14   Comparisons to be Made

1. Levels of personality at SC motivation
2. Levels of personality at TC motivation
3. Levels of personality at No motivation
4. Levels of motivation at Ind. personality
5. Levels of motivation at Dep. personality

The significant interaction between motivation condition and personality is a different matter, and it requires different statistical treatment. The appropriate follow-up technique for significant interactions is *simple effects*. This technique involves comparing the means for each of the levels of the experimental variables across the levels of the other variable or variables. In this experiment there are five comparisons to be made as indicated in Table 19.14. Each of the comparisons involves calculating the total sum of squares for each comparison, using the equation (19.13):

$$SS \text{ for } P \text{ at } M_1 = \frac{P_1^2 + P_2^2}{n} - \frac{(P_1 + P_2)^2}{N} \qquad (19.13)$$

where n = number of subjects in each group
        N = total subjects in this comparison

For each of the comparisons we find the results in equations (19.14)–(19.18).

1. Levels of P at SC:

$$SS = \frac{(53)^2 + (30)^2}{10} - \frac{(53 + 30)^2}{20} \qquad (19.14)$$

$$= 370.9 - 344.45 = 26.45$$

2. Levels of P at TC:

$$SS = \frac{(35)^2 + (52)^2}{10} - \frac{(35 + 52)^2}{20} \qquad (19.15)$$

$$= 392.9 - 378.45 = 14.45$$

3. Levels of P at No:

$$SS = \frac{(21)^2 + (19)^2}{10} - \frac{(21 + 19)^2}{20} \qquad (19.16)$$

$$= 80.2 - 80 = 0.2$$

4.   Levels of M at Ind.:

$$SS = \frac{(53)^2 + (35)^2 + (21)^2}{10} - \frac{(53 + 35 + 21)^2}{30} \tag{19.17}$$

$$= 447.5 - 396.03 = 51.47$$

5.   Levels of M at Dep.:

$$SS = \frac{(30)^2 + (52)^2 + (19)^2}{10} - \frac{(30 + 52 + 19)^2}{30} \tag{19.18}$$

$$= 396.5 - 340.03 = 56.47$$

A summary table, Table 19.15, is then completed for the simple effects of Motivation $\times$ Personality. The mean square for error is the same as that for the original ANOVA, since only between-factor comparisons are made. (If the ANOVA employed within-subjects comparisons as well, the error term appropriate to the comparison would be used.) In each of the P comparisons which were significant, having exceeded the required value $(F_{1,54})\,p < .01 = 7.31$, there are only two means. Therefore, we can interpret the findings by simply inspecting the means. For the M comparisons at Ind. and Dep., three means are involved; thus, individual comparisons are required before interpretations can be made. Using the Scheffe test, we obtain the results of equation (19.19) and Table 19.16. For both M at Ind. and M at Dep. the CD will be the same:

$$CD = \sqrt{(a-1)F}\ \sqrt{\frac{2(MS_{\text{error}})}{n}}$$

$$= \sqrt{(3-1)5.18}\ \sqrt{\frac{2(1.00)}{10}}$$

$$= \sqrt{10.36}\ \sqrt{.2} \tag{19.19}$$

$$= 3.22(.45)$$

$$= 1.45$$

(This value is the same as used previously for individual comparisons of the main effect of motivation.)

The observed differences between the means are presented in Table 19.16. The interpretation of these findings would be that in the case of the Ind. personality, teacher-centered motivation is not significantly better than nothing; for the Dep. personality, student-centered motivation is not significantly better than nothing. In addition, and more simply, the most effective motivation for the Ind.

TABLE 19.15 Simple Effects for Mean Performance Scores for Personality × Motivation Interaction

COMPARISON	df	MS	F	
P at SC	1	26.45	26.45	sig
P at TC	1	14.45	14.45	sig
P at No	1	.20	.20	ns
M at Ind.	2	25.74	25.74	sig
M at Dep.	2	28.24	28.24	sig
Error	54	1.00		

TABLE 19.16 Significance of Mean Differences

COMPARISON	M AT IND.		M AT DEP.	
SC − TC	5.3 − 3.5 = 1.8	sig	3.0 − 5.2 = −2.2	sig
SC − No	5.3 − 2.1 = 2.2	sig	3.0 − 1.9 = 1.1	ns
TC − No	3.5 − 2.1 = 1.4	ns	5.2 − 1.9 = 3.3	sig

group seems to be student-centered, while the most effective technique for the Dep. group appears to be teacher-centered motivation. Although this is similar to what was concluded by simple inspection of the means, statistical support is required.

EXERCISES

For each of the exercises on one-way analysis of variance in Chapter 14, calculate individual comparisons using:

a Tukey's test.
b Scheffe's test.
c Newman-Kuels test.
d Duncan multiple-range test.

Compare the results obtained using each of these tests.

CHAPTER TWENTY
META-ANALYSIS:
USING RESEARCH TO
INFLUENCE PRACTICE

The purpose of this chapter is not to discuss *whether* research and theory should or should not be used to influence practice or even whether it is possible to do so; those aspects have been argued time and again since 1967 by others (Broderick, 1971; Fraleigh, 1979; Hoffman, 1977; Kneer, 1981; Ley, 1977; Locke, 1967, 1969a, 1969b, 1970, 1979; Miller, 1969; Rothstein, 1973, 1977, 1980; Seidentop, 1977; Sloan, 1977; Stadulis, 1973; Zeigler, 1979). Rather the chapter will focus on *how* research and theory *can be* translated (or transduced) and applied to practice. It is clear, therefore, that I have resolved the argument of whether it is possible to use research and theory to influence practice. I believe that the proper question is; *How can research be used to influence practice?*

It would be foolish to deny that the problems associated with application sometimes appear insurmountable. However, I adamantly refuse to simply throw up my hands and retreat without trying to ameliorate the problems and proceed with the task of application. The problems have been well documented: lack of a systematic procedure for carrying out research, development, dissemination, demonstration, implementation, and evaluation; failure to identify critical field-based problems as foci for application; failure to understand what research can and cannot do; the knowledge explosion and proliferation of journals and publications; development of subdisciplines within physical education and concomitant lack of integration of areas; lack of systematic procedures for synthesizing the results of research; limited, strained, or nonexistent communication between researchers and practitioners; failure to prepare individuals to act as synthesizers; failure to incorporate synthesis and application activities within the existing academic reward system; and failure to market the potential benefits of research and theory in a meaningful way to practitioners. It would be impossible and inappropriate to consider all these problems in a textbook that focuses on research design and statistics. Thus, this chapter is organized around the central theme of using research and statistics creatively in influencing practice in physical eduction. The intent is to utilize examples in which research provides immediately useful information that "can be used to select from alternative courses of action those procedures offering a high probability of producing a desired effect" (Locke, 1969, p. 3).

RESEARCH: APPLICATION TO PRACTICE

Many activities within sport situations, specifically designed to influence practice, may be called research. Shot charts in basketball, analysis of game films, analysis of player errors, surveys of coaching practices, surveys of training methods are all forms of research (data gathering) which can be used to improve practice. These activities produce results which are clear and are directly applicable to sport situations. At the opposite end of the research spectrum are studies conducted in the laboratory, under highly controlled conditions, on a limited aspect of behavior or performance. Analysis of muscle firing patterns in a simple movement, effect of environmental conditions on performance of a dart throw, and cardiac function during maximal exercise are examples of research studies in which the results are not directly applicable to practice.

The differences in applicability are directly related to the necessity for control, as discussed earlier in this text. The directly applicable studies are designed to produce answers for immediate use in the situation or with the individuals with whom the research was done. Studies in the second group seek to gather information that is generalizable to a variety of individuals in a variety of situations. It is clear that one study cannot provide a universal answer; it is also clear that groups of studies may differ on critical aspects which preclude direct synthesis. Meta-analysis, the technique to be discussed at length in this chapter, is a method by which differences between and among studies can be subsumed in arriving at general conclusions which are applicable to practice.

META-ANALYSIS

Use of a method of combining, synthesizing, and applying research findings is critical, since the research literature in and relevant to physical education has been increasing geometrically. Although this is positive, in that more and more complete information is available, it is also negative, because the research represents "unorganized and unrelated bits of information or highly abstract theory far removed from real life experiences." (Fraleigh, 1979, p. 20). Ley (1977) also indicated that "New knowledge in the form of ideas and concepts has developed much faster than we can devise ways to apply it . . ." (p. 69). Further, a survey of the research on some topics in sport psychology, exercise physiology, motor learning, biomechanics, motor development, and curriculum and teaching often yields contradictory findings.

In recent years researchers in the subdisciplines have generated more and more data on more and more topics. This information often goes unused for the lack of someone or some way to interrelate, reanalyze, and interpret it in a way that would bring order out of chaos. In some areas of research in physical education, the findings are unstable due to variations in the task, the subjects, the environment, the research design, and countless other factors. Where ten studies might suffice to resolve a matter in some areas in which events and such can be precisely controlled, the results in sport psychology, for example, may be disparate enough to make extrapolation impossible. In some areas in which there are hundreds of studies, simple summary is impossible. Some technique for organizing, depicting, and interrelating the studies must be found.

The purpose of this section is to introduce you to a way of thinking about research synthesis which utilizes the statistical techniques you have already learned; you will use these techniques to draw conclusions about a topic in research in the same way that you have used them to draw conclusions about the results of a single study. I specifically chose to use the phrase "a way of thinking" because that is the key element in *meta-analysis*. The central idea in meta-analysis is that the unit of analysis (the score) is derived from a study rather than a subject. In the same way that you previously derived a score by, for example, calculating the mean for 10 trials, you derive a score through calculation. In the same way that you classified a particular subject for a chi-square analysis, you classify a particular study and then calculate statistical values.

The remainder of the section answers four questions: (1) What is meta-analysis? (2) How is it done? (3) How has it been used and what did we find out? (4) Does it have a role in our field? For those of you who are interested in more information than can be provided here an extensive bibliography of studies, books, and commentaries on meta-analysis techniques is provided at the end of this chapter.

What Is Meta-Analysis

In defining the term *meta-analysis*, consider what the parts mean. *Analysis* refers to the act of breaking up the whole into its constituent parts in order to determine its nature. We do this in a statistical analysis, in which the data are separated into various components to reveal the factors underlying the observations. *Meta* can be used in the sense of higher or beyond or in the sense of changed or transformed. For the purpose of research synthesis we are hoping to do both—first, to go beyond the breaking up of the original wholes into parts by using the wholes as the parts in a higher-order analysis; second, to change or transform the original analyses so that formerly incompatible findings can be brought into closer agreement and ultimately combined to reveal information that may not have been forthcoming, had the results been left in the original form. In actual practice the first task is to transform the information from each original study and then combine that transformed information into a new whole. It is instructive to consider the description of meta-analysis provided by Glass (1977):

> The approach to research integration referred to as "meta-analysis" is nothing more than an attitude of data analysis applied to quantitative summaries of individual experiments. By recording the properties of studies and their findings in quantitative terms, the meta-analysis of research invites one who would integrate numerous and diverse findings to apply the full power of statistical techniques to the task. [Meta-analysis] . . . is a perspective that uses many techniques of measurement and statistical analysis. (p. 354)

It is tempting for some to dismiss meta-analysis as the same old literature review given a new, pretentious name (Eysenck, 1978; Gallo, 1978; Gallo and Lynn, 1981; Mansfield and Bussey, 1977; Paul and Licht, 1978). However, meta-analysis is something more. It is characterized by system, sophistication, and statistics. It is quantitative; it does not prejudge in terms of research quality (though quality can be a factor in the analysis); and it seeks general conclusions (Glass, McGaw, and Smith, 1981). It can assist us in raising the cumulative impact of the evidence available from previous research in a way that traditional forms of review cannot. The operating principle of meta-analysis is that by combining the results from many studies, the "noise"—i.e., unsystematic bias—is canceled out. It is as different from a literature review as we know it as descriptive analytic research on teaching (DART) is from casual observation. This analogy is deliberate, since both meta-analysis and DART incorporate structured observation and recording according to a coding scheme developed prior to observation. The system may be as simple or as complex as desired or necessary. In my opinion, the coding system should be designed as exhaustively as possible, so you won't have to return to the same set of studies later when you find that you require additional information. (This is especially true when the analysis requires that you receive copies of completed theses and dissertations on interlibrary loan.)

Rothstein has suggested (1980) that successful application of research demands that the level of sophistication of the techniques used to integrate findings match the level of sophistication of the studies we integrate. Three methods, which vary in sophistication but which utilize the power of statistical analysis, are the critical-factors approach (Rothstein and Arnold,

1976); the combining-results approach (Gage, 1978; Glass, 1981; Rosenthal, 1978); and the Bayesian approach (Drayton, 1978). Although these methods have different names, they all are variations on the same theme: meta-analysis.

Critical-factors approach.   The critical-factors approach involves the use of the chi-square statistic and is the most simplified approach to meta-analysis to be considered. First, a coding scheme is developed. The study on videotape replay (Rothstein and Arnold, 1976) used a very simple scheme: study identification, sex, age, task, skill level, treatment condition, length of study (or number of trials), evaluation method (test), and result. A portion of the data table is presented as Table 20.1. In order to answer the central question: "Which factors were related to effective use of videotape replay?" the individual studies were sorted according to significance (significant versus nonsignificant). Then two-way chi-square tables were formed using the variable significant/nonsignificant in combination with the other variables. The chi-square statistic was then incorporated to determine which factors statistically differentiated the studies.

One of the comparisons for which the chi-square value was significant was treatment condition. This is presented in Table 20.2. In this comparison VTR + cues was more effective in producing performance differences than VTR alone. In other comparisons the length of the study and the skill level of the subjects were found to be significantly related to performance improvement. Other comparisons did not yield significance.

It is also possible to calculate chi-square values for combinations of variables. For example, Table 20.2 could be structured for beginners and intermediates separately to see if the cueing factor was similar in both cases. When this is done, it appears that cueing is more critical for beginners.

Combining-results approach.   Rosenthal (1978) has provided a comprehensive summary of methods of combining the results of independent studies. His two tables, reproduced as Tables 20.3 and 20.4, provide a good illustration of nine methods: adding logs, adding probabilities, adding ts, adding Zs, adding weighted Zs, testing the mean p, testing the mean Z, counting, and blocking; and they provide criteria for selection: advantages, limitations, and applicability. Interested readers should consult his article for further information.

Since the method to be reviewed in detail here is based on *effect sizes* (Glass, 1976, 1977; Glass and McGaw, 1980; Glass, McGaw, and Smith, 1981), it is reasoned that extensive consideration of these other methods would needlessly lengthen this section. It should also be noted that Gage (1978) has suggested a method which converts the exact probability value of each single study into a chi-square statistic. These values are then summed across studies to estimate the statistical significance of a group of individual studies. Again, those who are interested should consult this reference.

The method suggested by Glass and co-workers (1976, 1977, 1980, 1981) has been employed in over 100 studies since 1976. (Some of these studies are included in the bibliography.) The statistic which he uses, *effect size,* is in fact a z-score calculated as follows:

$$ES = \frac{\overline{X}_{treat} - \overline{X}_{con}}{s_{con}}$$

These effect sizes are then averaged to determine the standard deviation units which separate the treatment group and the control group. In an illustration of the effect-size procedure using 13 studies dealing with the use of psychotherapy in asthma (Glass et al., 1981, pp. 26–31), the average effect was $.86s_{\overline{X}}$. Therefore, the average subject receiving psychotherapy evidenced fewer symptoms than 80% of the control group subjects. A specific and detailed illustration of the use and computation of effect sizes in carrying out a meta-analysis will be presented after we briefly consider the Bayesian approach (Drayton, 1978) to meta-analysis.

Bayesian Approach.   In her introduction to the use of the Bayesian model to accomplish meta-analysis in education, Drayton (1978) discusses the notion that replication, through its repeated testing of a common cause-effect relationship, is the preferred method of achieving consensus in research. Since the preplanning and coordination needed to achieve this necessary replication are not likely to occur, she suggests a combining procedure which simulates replication using data from individual studies. In her estimation the Bayesian model, which is additive, allows for mathematical transformations, and for differential weightings of the data it appears to be a good choice. She outlines the three steps of a Bayesian analysis (pp. 7–9):

a)   As a first step in a Bayesian analysis, the researcher states a prior belief as to what the truth is and translates this into three statistical qualifiers: expected mean, expected variance, and strength of belief in the prior opinion . . . . The three statistical qualifiers can be based either on previous experience, prior research, or a combination of both . . . . There is nothing to prevent the use of previous research as a prior if it can be expressed in terms of the mean, the standard deviation, and a hypothetical sample size.

b)   The second step . . . is collecting the results of experimentation or observation . . . . In meta-analysis, this step can be acquiring the summary statistics of a subsequent experimental research study similar to the one designated as the "prior." This second collection of data is called the "likelihood" or the "sample."

c)   Step three is the act of combining the prior and the likelihood to yield a "posterior." That obtained posterior can become a new and more informed prior, with an additional research study becoming a new likelihood.

It is clear that the procedure is iterative. New studies which have the

TABLE 20.1 Videotape Replay (Significance)

AUTHOR (YEAR)	SEX	AGE	TASK	SKILL LEVEL	TREATMENT CONDITIONS	TIME	TEST	RESULT
Armstrong, W. (1971)	F	Col.	Tennis	Beginner	Lec-Demo Lec-Demo VTR ea. class Lec-Demo VTR 1/wk.	2×/wk. 10 wk.	Broer Miller	Rate of improvement sig. diff.
Beverly, L. (1973)	?	?	Archery	Beginner	Lec/Demo rat VTR + corr. ea. pd. VTR + corr. e/o pd.[a]	Term	Accur. Form	VTR ea. pd. not sig. on acc. e/o pd. VTR ea. pd. sig. on form from lec/demo and e/o pd. VTR ea. pd. sig. from lec/demo ALL groups imp. sig.
Caine, J. E. (1966)	M&F	Col.	Bowl.	Beginner	Verbal Demo VTR VTR + analysis	?	Score	Sig. imp. in VTR groups not in conventional groups
Carr, N.J. (1971)	W	Col.	Badm.	Beginner	Control TV obj. TV subj.	?	Written & Short serve	Sig. gains in TV groups Cognitive ability affected by subjective TV
Cooper, W.E. (1969)	M	7 Gr.	BB	Blocked	Auditory Aud + VTR VTR No FB Control	8×	Johnson BB	Dribble—VTR, Comb, No FB sig. better Lay-up—no sig. Pass-catch-combo sig. Push—same as dribble

Author (Year)	Sex	Level	Skill	Subjects	Treatment	Duration	Measure	Results
Del Rey, P. (1970)	W	Col.	Fencing Lunge O/C	Beginner	Open skill (O) Video as KP / No VTR / Closed skill (C) Video as KP / No VTR	3 da.	Accur. Form Time	Form and latency, O/C sig. / Testing pd. sig. / Accuracy O/C sig.
Green, W. (1970)	?	?	Swim.	Beg. + Ad. beg.	Traditional / VTR	16 wk. 3 da.	Form ARC	VTR better than trad. / Ad. beg. more gain than beg. / VTR depend upon tchr. + ability group
Hegman, E. II (1973)	?	Col.	Tennis stroke & serve	Beginner	VTR training VS. no / Inst. FB during VTR vs. no	?	Form	Sig. diff. favor of trained for stroking not serve / No effect for inst. FB
Jackson, C.H. (1973)	M	Col.	Novel skill	Beginner	VTR / Audio-VTR / Control	6 wk.	Vary	VTR sig. effects acquisition of wall volley / VTR sig. effects retention of tennis ball toss
Lewis, G. Jr. (1970)	?	?	Ski.	Inter.	Traditional / VTR	6 wk. 2/wk.	Form	Sig. for instr. treat., raters interaction
McLaren, J.D. (1971)	M	7 Gr.	High jump	Beginner	Control / Practice only / Traditional Tching. / VTR	?	Height	Gain in TV and trad. sig. / 10 bet. control and 3 others
Morgan, N.A. (1970)	W	Col.	Swim. but'fly	Beginner	VTR / Movement cue / VTR & movement cue / Control	3 pds.	Speed Power	Both groups with VTR improved sig. / Sig. diff. bet. control and VTR + MC in power

TABLE 20.1 (Continued)

AUTHOR (YEAR)	SEX	AGE	TASK	SKILL LEVEL	TREATMENT CONDITIONS	TIME	TEST	RESULT
Paulat, J.G. (1969)	M&F	Col.	Tennis FH dr.	Beginner	Sex Male Female Loop film VTR	2×/wk.[a]	Object. skill & judges	No sig. diff. M/F, loop film Sig. VTR for objective test & judging
Plese, E.R. (1968)	M	JHS	Gymnas.	Beginners	Traditional Trad. + VTR	7 wk.	Compl. of routine	VTR group sig. better
Pohl, P. (1971)	M	9 Gr.	High jump	Beginners	Initial instruct. (11) 11 + verbal 11 + VTR + coach 11 + VTR	?	Height	No sig. imp. for 11 Sig. imp. for other 3 VTR + coach most favorable
Stephens, M. (1972)	W	Col.	Badm.	Beg. + Ad. Beg.	Traditional VTR	12 wk.	Long S. Clear	VTR more beneficial in serve VTR best in Ad. Beg.
Taylor, W. (1971)	M	Col.	Swim. whip K.	See Treat.	Skill level Adv. Inter. Beg. Treatment VTR VTR + verbal Verbal Control	Term	?	High skill all equally effective Low skill: VTR + verbal superior to verbal alone or none

[a]Every other pd.

Excerpted from A.L. Rothstein and R.K. Arnold, Bridging the gap: Application of research on videotape replay and bowling. *Motor Skills: Theory into Practice,* 1976, **1**, 35–62.

TABLE 20.2   Videotape Replay and Treatment Condition

	SIGNIFICANCE	
TREATMENT	SIGNIFICANT	NONSIGNIFICANT
VTR alone	12	28
VTR + cues	8	5

appropriate characteristics and data can be added as they are found. As Drayton (1978) indicates, "Sampling could continue until the whole population is exhausted, or could be stopped whenever the last adversary had been convinced" (p. 11). The procedure is flexible in the use of differential weightings and transformations, and Bayesian theory is sensitive to the size of the n. It is a procedure that deserves further consideration.

HOW TO DO A META-ANALYSIS

The procedures used in preparing for and doing a meta-analysis are (Rothstein, 1981):

a Choose an area in which the results are equivocal and/or confusing;
b Select several good review articles for the purpose of identifying major variables and factors;
c Consult several authorities (via books, letters or interview) to evaluate selection of major variables and factors;
d Delimit area of interest by specifying what will be included in the meta-analysis;
e Design a preliminary coding scheme containing a number of items in each of the following categories:
  1. study identification
  2. subject identification
  3. instrumentation
  4. design specifications
  5. treatment information
  6. major variables
  7. major outcome variables
  8. statistical outcomes
  9. effect sizes
f Formulate specific questions within the area of consideration;
g Prepare a working bibliography (use computer search procedures with one or more data bases)
h Select 10 or so representative studies to test the coding scheme;
i Revise the coding scheme as necessary and develop coding conventions;
j Code all relevant studies;
k Use the data in conjunction with various statistical procedures to interpret the findings.

TABLE 20.3 Advantages and Limitations of Nine Methods of Combining Probabilities

METHOD	ADVANTAGES	LIMITATIONS	APPLICABLE WHEN
Adding logs	Well established	Cumulates poorly; can support opposite conclusions	N of studies is small (≤ 5)
Adding ps	Good power	Inapplicable when N of studies (or ps) is large, unless complex corrections are introduced	N of studies is small ($\Sigma\,p \leq 1.0$)
Adding ts	Unaffected by N of studies, given minimum df per study	Inapplicable when ts are based on very few df	Studies are not based on too few df
Adding Zs	Routinely applicable, simple	Assumes unit variance when under some conditions Type I or Type II errors may be increased	Anytime
Adding weighted Zs	Routinely applicable, permits weighting	Assumes unit variance when under some conditions Type I or Type II errors may be increased	Whenever weighting is desired
Testing mean p	Simple	N of studies should not be less than four	N of studies ≥ 4
Testing mean Z	No assumption of unit variance	Low power when N of studies is small	N of studies ≥ 5
Counting	Simple and robust	Large N of studies is needed; may be low in power	N of studies is large
Blocking	Displays all means for inspection, thus facilitating search for moderator variables	Laborious when N is large; insufficient data may be available	N of studies is not too large

Reprinted from R. Rosenthal, Combining the results of independent studies. Psychological Bulletin, 1978, **86**, 185-193. Copyright 1978 by the American Psychological Association. Reprinted by permission of the author.

TABLE 20.4   Conversion to Chi-Square

STATISTIC	$\chi^2 = -2 \log_e p$ EXACT p	$-2 \log_e p$
$t = 2.00$	.0254	7.35
$F_{1,348} = .65$	.3103	3.12
$\chi^2 = 7.11$	.0077	9.73

$\chi^2_{(df=2N)} = -2 \log_e p_i$ (N = number of studies)

$\chi^2_6 = 20.20, p\ .0001$

Two aspects of this outline deserve further consideration: selecting the variables and factors and preparing a working bibliography. The question most frequently asked in regard to the former is, "How are the factors and variables to be coded identified?" This is the point of reading the several review articles. What are the factors most frequently mentioned? What are all the factors mentioned? What factors are thought to make a difference in outcomes? What factors are identified as confounding interpretation? Most of the factors and variables identified will fit into the categories mentioned under item(e) above. There is no substitute for expertise with an area of study. Do not hesitate to consult individuals who are knowledgeable about an area.

The second aspect, preparing a working bibliography, is likely to be the most difficult and uncertain. Information on using computerized literature retrieval systems is given in Chapter 21. Since meta-analysis is akin to survey research, where the unit is the study rather than the subject, the methods by which studies are located and the delineation of those methods is critical. Glass and others (1981) have stated that

> Documenting the methods used in finding research literature takes more space than custom traditionally allocates to describing one's search. How one searches determines what one finds; and what one finds is the basis of the conclusions of one's integration of studies. Searches should be more carefully done and documented than is customary. (p. 61)

The majority of criticisms of meta-analysis center around the problem of the studies used. One major criticism relates to the assumption that there would be major differences between the results of studies which were published and those which were unpublished. While there is some difference, these differences are not always in the same direction. Overall, however, the effect size appears to be larger for published studies than for theses or unpublished studies. This criticism has also been addressed by Rosenthal (1979), who showed mathematically that as the average effect size increases and as the number of studies used in a meta-analysis increases, the number of studies averaging null results ($\bar{z} = .00$) which would be required before it could be concluded that the overall results were the result of sampling bias would increase almost geometrically. In a meta-analysis of studies on experimenter bias ($N = 311$) Rosenthal (1976) noted a mean z of 1.18. He concluded that nearly 50,000 studies averaging a null result would be necessary to reasonably ascribe the results to sampling error.

Another criticism related to the studies centers around the potential biasing effect of design flaws. This can be dealt with by incorporating a description of design and analysis features in the coding system and including this factor in an analysis. Glass (1977) has suggested that because of randomization of design flaws and problems across a set of studies, it is possible that "many weak studies can add up to a strong conclusion.... Respect for parsimony and good sense demands an acceptance of the notion that imperfect studies can converge on a true conclusion." (p. 356).

Calculating Effect Sizes

As indicated previously, when you calculate the effect size (*ES*), you are calculating a z-score using the mean of the control group as a z-score of 0 and their standard deviation as the estimate of the population standard deviation. Although McGaw and Glass (1980) provide techniques for calculating the effect sizes for various statistics, it is preferable to use means and standard deviations when they are given, since, even in cases where more than one experimental group is present, each can be compared to the control group. It is also possible to calculate effect sizes from test statistics as shown in Table 20-5.

TABLE 20.5   Computation of Effect Sizes

If two means (control and treatment) are given and standard deviation is available:

$$ES = \frac{\bar{Y}_T - \bar{Y}_C}{s_C}$$

If *t*-test statistic is given:

$$ES = t \sqrt{\frac{1}{n_T} + \frac{1}{n_C}}$$

If *F*-test statistic is given:

$$ES = 2 \sqrt{\frac{F}{n_T + n_C}}$$

If proportion achieving some criterion is given:

$$ES = Z_C - Z_T$$

For correlated *t*-test:

$$ES = t_G \sqrt{2(1 - r_{XY}) \frac{1}{n_T} + \frac{1}{n_C}}$$

TABLE 20.6   Example of Effect-Size Calculation Using Means and Standard Deviations

| | TREATMENT GROUP | | | | |
| | EXPERIMENTAL | | CONTROL | | |
STUDY	MEAN	SD	MEAN	SD	ES
A	65.75	19.92	62.00	19.75	.19
B	89.71	8.58	85.71	8.56	.47
C	41.15	10.79	41.01	10.01	.01
D	39.42	12.89	41.41	12.52	−.16
E	50.58	14.33	35.88	12.70	1.16
F	39.13	7.11	38.59	7.42	.07
G	38.40	14.06	31.69	7.64	.88
				Sum:	2.62
				Avg.:	.37

In order to provide an example, data from Drayton (1978) has been used. The independent variable under consideration was individualized versus traditional instruction in math. The dependent variable was achievement, and the score was obtained through a standardized achievement test. The data are presented in Table 20.6.

Recall that *ES* is calculated from the means and standard deviation using the following formula:

$$ES = \frac{(\overline{X}_T - \overline{X}_C)}{s_C}$$

Using the notion of superimposed normal curves representing the control and treatment groups, we would conclude that the average member of the experimental group would do better than 64% of the control group. (The proportion from the mean to z under the normal curve at $z=.37$ is about 14%. The average control-group member is at 50%, thus the figure 64%.)

When the procedures are used in this straightforward way, it is not readily apparent that the influence of various factors and variables can be teased out. It is possible to code a study on a number of different factors, as in the feedback example where the factors were age, sex, skill level, treatment condition, length of study, etc., and then use a more sophisticated statistical analysis with *ES* as the dependent variable to evaluate the effect of different factors on the outcome. As is the case with more complex statistical analysis, as the number of factors increases, the number of subjects (or in this case studies) must increase concomitantly.

Two complex examples

Feltz and Landers (1983) completed a meta-analysis which focused on mental practice. They used a total of 60 different studies; of these, 26 were published and yielded 146 effect sizes; the others were unpublished master's or doctoral theses. In addition, 39 studies on mental practice were not used because they did not meet the criteria for inclusion. The coding sheets Feltz and Landers used, along with the effect sizes, are presented in Table 20.7. Using the *ES*s, the studies were compared on nine different characteristics. These comparisons are presented in Table 20.8. Using the following formula, it is possible to calculate *t* for the various factors and ascertain whether significant differences in effect sizes are present:

$$t = \frac{\overline{ES}_1 - \overline{ES}_2}{s_{\bar{x}_1 - \bar{x}_2}}$$

where

$$s_{\bar{x}_1 - \bar{x}_2} = SEM_1^2 + SEM_2^2$$

The *t*-ratios presented in the last column of Table 20.8 indicate that the following comparisons are significant:

> *Motor vs. cognitive vs. strength.* The effect size was significantly greater for cognitive tasks in comparison to either motor or strength tasks and significantly greater for the motor tasks when compared to the strength tasks.
> *Theses vs. publications.* The effect size was significantly greater for the published studies than for the theses.

Feltz and Landers (1983) also conducted polynomial regression analyses to assess the influence of number of practice sessions, length of practice sessions, and number of practice trials per session on effect sizes. There was no relationship between effect size and number of practice sessions. A significant relationship was noted for length of practice session, in which practice sessions under 1 minute or between 15 and 25 minutes produced the largest mental practice effects. In the case of trials per session a significant relationship was also noted; studies which employed less than 6 or between 36 and 46 trials per practice session were associated with larger effect sizes. They also noted an interaction between type of task and practice session trials; cognitive tasks required fewer trials, motor or strength tasks required many more trials.

Another recent meta-analysis of interest to physical educators was conducted by Kavale and Mattson (1983) to assess the efficacy of perceptual-motor training. They synthesized the results of 180 individual studies which yielded 637 individual effect sizes. Of the 180 studies, 110 came from journals, 39 were dissertations or theses, and 31 were from other sources, e.g., *ERIC*. The studies were then coded according to a number of treatment, subject, test, and outcome variables, which are evident in Tables 20.9 through 20.12.

The average effect size for the 637 individual values obtained was .082. This means that if the control group is assumed to be at the 50% of the normal curve, the control group would be at the 53%. Although specific guidelines for interpreting the average effect size are not available, common sense would suggest that a 3% difference is hardly adequate to suggest real differences between control and treated groups. In fact, the authors report, 48% of the effect sizes were negative (indicating that the treated group did worse than the control group), suggesting that the likelihood of perceptual-motor training programs having a positive effect is only slightly better than chance. Table 20.9 presents data for perceptual-motor outcome classes and categories. In each case the number of effect sizes obtained, the average effect size, the standard deviation, and the percentile equivalent are given. For the perceptual-motor classes, for example, the percentile equivalents are: perceptual-motor (56%), academic (50%), congnitive (51%), and adaptive (61%). These percentile equivalents indicate that, in the case of perceptual-motor outcomes, for example, an average subject in the treated group scores 6 percentiles higher than an average subject in the control or untreated group. Another way of saying the same thing is that for each 100 students in the treated group, 6 would do better than expected (based on the figures for the control group) as a result of having been treated. Is this outcome sufficient for the time and effort expended? The average effect sizes and percentile equivalents for other comparisons are not much better, as seen in Table 20-10, specific perceptual-motor outcome categories; Table 20-11, individual outcome measures; and Table 20-12, specific perceptual-motor training programs.

The authors conclude that, on the basis of their analyses, perceptual-motor training programs are not effective and that children exposed to such programs are likely to gain little compared to children receiving no intervention. Although the data appear strong as presented, the authors do not seem to go far enough in analyzing the data. It would seem that some cross-tabulating of the effect sizes obtained might yield some combinations which would lead to different interpretations and recommendations. What about studies in which treatments were geared toward a particular outcome? Might not analysis of type of treatment by type of outcome yield some interesting results? What types of programs work best for children who are trainable? Are the effect sizes larger for some subject-treatment combinations than for others? Since one of the most consistent comments regarding perceptual-motor training studies is that the length of the study is too short, what about the interaction between length of study and outcomes? If length of study were analyzed individually, would longer studies be associated with larger effect sizes? Perhaps a synthesis aimed at identifying the critical factors that make programs work or the conditions under which programs work best would have been more helpful. As the report is presented, however, it clearly suggests caution in expending scarce resources on perceptual-motor programs.

Before we review additional meta-analyses pertinent to physical education and sport, a cautionary note is in order. In a series of articles, Hedges (1981, 1982a, 1982b, 1982c, 1982d, 1983a, 1983b), Hedges and Olkin (1983), and Hedges and Stock (1983) have commented on meta-analysis techniques with

TABLE 20.7 Summary of Characteristics and Effect Sizes for Mental Practice Studies

STUDY	TASK AND TASK TYPE	n	SEX†	AGE GROUP†	EXPERIENCED OR NOVICE	PRACTICE SESSIONS	LENGTH OF PRACTICE	CONTROL	IMMEDIATE POSTTEST	EFFECT SIZE
Arnold (1965)	Dart throwing Motor/self-paced	18	F	Coll	Novice	9	50 trials	Pre/post	No	.330
Bagg (1966)	Baseball Motor/reactive	10	M	Coll	Experienced	9	9 trials	Simple	No	.258
Beckow (1967)	Badminton short serve Motor/self-paced	15	M	Coll	Novice	6	6 min	Motivation	No	.553
	Badminton long serve Motor/self-paced	15	M	Coll	Novice	6	6 min	Motivation	No	.341
Bissonette (1965)	Speed skating Motor/neither	10	M	Elem	Experienced	10	10 min	Pre/post	No	1.780
Browning (1972)	Tap dance skill Motor/self-paced	12	F	Coll	Novice	6	15 min	Motivation	No	.079
Burns (1962)	Dart throw Motor/self-paced	62	F	High school	Novice	14	30 trails	Simple	No	.521
Clark (1960)*	Foul shooting Motor/self-paced	72	M	High school	Novice	14	30 trials	Pre/post	No	.908
Corbin (1967a)*	Wand juggling Motor/reactive	10	M	High school	Novice / Intermediate / Experienced	21	10 min and 30 trials	Simple	No	-.032 / .133 / .132
Corbin (1967b)*	Wand juggling Motor/reactive	10	M	Coll	Novice	13	30 trials	Pre/post	No	1.711
Cronk (1967)	Cable tensiometer Strength	6	F	Coll	Novice	24	10 trials	Simple	No	-.547
Egstrom (1964)*	Novel ball-striking task Motor/reactive	20	M	Coll	Novice / Experienced	5	5 min	Simple	Yes	.068 / .882
Eideness (1965)	Basketball free throw Motor/self-paced	11	M	Coll	Novice	16	25 trials	Pre/post	No	1.595

Study	Task / Type	N	Sex	Level	Experience	No.	Time	Condition	Motivation	Value
Epstein (1980)*	Dart throw Motor/self-paced	12 15 18 14	F M	Coll	Novice	1	3 min	Motivation	Yes	−.796 −.384 −.135 −.306
Gondola (1966)	Base test of dynamic balance Motor/reactive	35	F	Coll	Novice	5	5 min	Simple	No	.419
Hall (in press)	Basketball free throw Motor/reactive	4	F	Coll	Experienced	5	20 min	Pre/post	No	2.565
Hammerslough (1971)	Softball pitch Motor/self-paced	33	M F	Coll	Novice	10	5 min	Pre/post	No	.726 .487
	Golf chip shot Motor/self-paced	33	M F	Coll	Novice	10	5 min	Pre/post	No	.645 .459
	Soccer dribble Motor/self-paced	33	M F	Coll	Novice	10	5 min	Pre/post	No	.619 .742
Harby (1952)*	Underhand free throw Motor/self-paced	15	M	Coll	Novice	7 14 20	Not given	Simple	No	−.364 .380 −.178
Howe (1967)	Ball juggling Motor/reactive	24	M&F	Coll	Novice	6	10 min	Pre/post	No Yes	.425 .359 .180 .345
Johnson (1967)	One-wall handball serve Motor/self-paced	133	M&F	Elem	Novice	5	5 min	Simple	No	.185
Kelly (1965)	Overhand volleyball serve	26	F	High school	Novice	10	7-9 min and 20 trials	Motivation	No	.365
Kelsey (1961)*	Sit-ups Strength	12	M	Coll	Novice	20	5 min	Simple	No	.205 .582
Kohl & Roenker (1980)	Pursuit rotor Motor/neither	21	M	Coll	Novice	1	30 sec and 25 trials 30 sec and 18 trials	Motivation	Yes	1.751 .795
Kovar (1969)	Underhand free throw Motor/self-paced	16	F	Coll	Novice	6	5 min	Simple	No	.387

TABLE 20.7 (Continued)

STUDY	TASK AND TASK TYPE	n	SEX	AGE GROUP	EXPERIENCED OR NOVICE	PRACTICE SESSIONS	LENGTH OF PRACTICE	CONTROL	IMMEDIATE POSTTEST	EFFECT SIZE
Kuhn (1971)	Soccer dribble Motor/reactive	18	M	Coll	Novice	10	10 trials	Motivation	Yes	-.567
LaLance (1974)	Power handball serve Motor/self-paced	15	M	Coll	Experienced	8	Not given	Simple	No	.399
										-.066
	Lob handball Motor/self-paced									1.048
Levy (1969)	Center football snap Motor/self-paced	20	M	Coll	Novice	18	6 trials	Motivation	No	-.462
Maxwell (1968)	Volleyball serve Motor/self-paced	16	F	Coll	Novice	8	10 trials	Pre/post	No	.738
Mendoza & Wichman (1978)*	Dart throw Motor/self-paced	7	M&F	Coll	Experienced	12	15 min	Simple	No	2.222
Moritani (1975)	Jump board Motor/self-paced	16	F	Coll	Novice	10	6 min	Pre/post	No	.235
Morrisett (1956)	Finger dexterity Motor/self-paced	24	M&F	Coll	Novice	1	7 min	Motivation	Yes	.258
	Dial-a-maze Cognitive	24	M&F	Coll	Novice	4	7 min	Motivation	Yes	.273
	Dart throw Motor/self-paced	10	M	Coll	Novice	3	21 min	Motivation	Yes	.390
	Card sorting Low cognitive High cognitive	8	M	Coll	Novice	1	5 min	Motivation	Yes	.265 1.215
Murphy (1977)	Jumpshot Motor/self-paced	9	M	High school	Experienced	12	Not given	Motivation	No	.781
Perry (1939)*	Three-hole tapping Motor/neither	16	M	Elem	Novice	5	30 sec	Motivation	No	.527
	Card-sorting Cognitive	16	M	Elem	Novice	5	60 sec	Motivation	No	1.347

Study	Task	Age	Sex	Level	Experience	N	Duration	Design		Effect size
	Peg-board test Cognitive	12	M	Elem	Novice	5	60 sec	Motivation	No	2.327
	Symbol digit test Cognitive	15	M	Elem	Novice	5	60 sec	Motivation	No	2.008
	Mirror tracing Motor/neither	14	M	Elem	Novice	5	60 sec	Motivation	No	.858
Phipps & Morehouse (1969)*	Hockey swing Motor/self-paced	36	M	Coll	Novice	5	10 trials	Motivation	Yes	.511
	Jumpfoot Motor/self-paced	36	M	Coll	Novice	5	10 trials	Motivation	Yes	.571
	Soccer hitch kick Motor/self-paced	36	M	Coll	Novice	5	10 trials	Motivation	Yes	.025
Rawlings & Rawlings (1974)*	Rotary pursuit Motor/neither	17	F	Coll	Novice	1	3 min	Motivation	Yes	1.051
Razor (1966)	Hand-grip Dominant hand Nondominant hand Strength	17	M	Coll	Novice	18	10 sec and 10 trials	Pre/post	No	.090 .197
Rodriguez (1967)	Sit-ups Strength	14	F	Coll	Novice	17	5 min	Simple	No	.063
Ryan & Simons (1981)*	Dial-a-maze Cognitive	13	M	Coll	Novice	1	30 sec and 9 trials	Motivation	Yes	1.478
	Stabilometer Motor/reactive	13	M	Coll	Novice	1	30 sec and 9 trials	Motivation	Yes	.690
Sackett (1934)*	Maze learning Cognitive	20	M	Coll	Novice	7	5 trials	Simple	No	2.455
Sackett (1935)*	Finger maze Cognitive	25	F	Coll	Novice	7 21 35	1 trial 3 trials 5 trials	Simple	No	1.880 1.057 3.310
Seaborne (1981)	Karate competition Motor/reactive	8	M	Coll	Novice	35	10 min	Motivation	Yes	.438
	Karate skills Motor/self-paced	8	M	Coll	Novice	35	10 min	Motivation	Yes	−.143
Shappell (1977)	Maze tracing Cognitive	15	M	Coll	Novice	20	34 sec	Simple	Yes	1.110

TABLE 20.7 (Continued)

STUDY	TASK AND TASK TYPE	n	SEX	AGE GROUP	EXPERIENCED OR NOVICE	PRACTICE SESSIONS	LENGTH OF PRACTICE	CONTROL	IMMEDIATE POSTTEST	EFFECT SIZE
Sheldon (1963)	Breaststroke Motor/neither	14	F	Coll	Experienced	9	5 trials	Pre/post	No	.984
	Breaststroke kick Motor/neither	14	F	Coll	Experienced	9	5 trials	Pre/post	No	1.120
Sheldon & Mahoney (1978)*	Basketball free throw Motor/self-paced	15	F	Coll	Experienced	15	3 min	Pre/post	Yes	-.260
Schick (1970)*	Wall volley Motor/reactive	5	F	Coll	Experienced	10	3 min	Simple	No	.083
	Volleyball serve Motor/self-paced	5	F	Coll	Experienced	10	3 min	Simple	No	-.068
Smith & Harrison (1962)*	Accuracy/speed task Motor/reactive	10	M	Coll	Novice	6	10 sec	Motivation	Yes	1.531
										.487
Smyth (1975)*	Mirror drawing Motor/neither	10	M&F	Coll	Novice	1	5 trials 5 min	Simple	Yes	.420
										.293
	Pursuit rotor Motor/neither	10	M&F	Coll	Novice	1	4 min	Simple	Yes	.373
Spears (1966)	High jump Motor/self-paced	15	F	Coll	Novice	10	20 min	Simple	No	.187
Standridge (1971)	Swimming whipkick Motor/self-paced	10	F	Coll	Novice	8	30 min	Pre/post	Yes	.316
Start (1962)*	Underarm basketball throw Motor/self-paced	38	M	High school	Novice	9	5 min	Simple	No	1.356
Stebbins (1968)*	Target throw Motor/self-paced	21	M	Coll	Experienced	18	25 trials	Simple	No	.020
Stephens (1966)	Accuracy throw Motor/self-paced	8	F	Coll	Novice	1	9 trials	Motivation	Yes	.052
						2				.244
						3				.204
						4				.684
						5				.440
						6				.307

Study	Task	Type	N	Sex	Level	Experience	No.	Time	Motivation		Correlations
Surburg (1968)*	Forehand tennis	Motor/self-paced	25	M	Coll	Novice	24	Not given	Motivation	No	.480 / 1.214 / .531 / .900 / 1.367 / .582 / .027
Tufts (1963)	Bowling	Motor/self-paced	12	F	Coll	Experienced	9	15 min	Pre/post	No	1.097
Twining (1949)	Target throw	Motor/self-paced	12	M	Coll	Novice	20	15 min	Not given	No	.502
Whitehill (1964)	Handball serve	Motor/self-paced	19	M	Elem	Novice	8	7 min	Simple	No	-.053
Whitehill (1965)	Handball toss	Motor/self-paced	36 / 27	M&F	Elem	Novice	5	5 min	Simple	No	-.203 / -.047
	Ball throw	Motor/self-paced	36 / 27	M&F	Elem	Novice	5	5 min	Simple	No	-.322 / -.293 / -.047
	Paddleboard serve	Motor/self-paced	36 / 27	M&F	Elem	Novice	5	5 min	Simple	No	-.148 / .016 / .274
Wills (1966)	Hand grip	Strength	10	M	Coll / High school / Elem	Novice	6	Not given	Simple	Yes	.103 / -.322
				F	Coll / High school / Elem						.092 / .598 / .559
	Standing long jump	Strength	10	M	Coll / High school / Elem	Novice	6	Not given	Simple	Yes	-.224 / .377 / -.073
				F	Coll / High school / Elem						.784 / .643 / -.580 / .381

TABLE 20.7 (Continued)

STUDY	TASK AND TASK TYPE	n	SEX	AGE GROUP	EXPERIENCED OR NOVICE	PRACTICE SESSIONS	LENGTH OF PRACTICE	CONTROL	IMMEDIATE POSTTEST	EFFECT SIZE
Wills (1966)	Hand grip Strength	6	M	Coll	Novice	8	Not given	Simple	No	-.382
				High school						-.156
			F	Elem						-.390
				Coll						.495
				High school						-.154
	Standing long jump Strength	6	M	Coll	Novice	8	Not given	Simple	No	1.056
				High school						.758
				Elem						-.793
			F	Coll						-.408
				High school						.805
				Elem						.914
Wills (1965)	Football pass Motor/self-paced	20	M	Elem	Novice	15	30 trials	Motivation	No	.291
										.802
Wilson (1960)	Tennis forehand and backhand Motor/self-paced	14	F	Coll	Experienced	6	28 trials	Simple	No	-.073
		15			Novice					.293
Wrisberg & Ragsdale (1979)	Block test Cognitive	20	F	Coll	Novice	1	3 min	Motivation	Yes	.364
	Stabilometer Motor/reactive	20	F	Coll	Novice	1	3 min	Motivation	Yes	.204

Reprinted with permission from D. Feltz and D. Landers, The effects of mental practice on motor skills learning and performance. *Journal of Sport Psychology*, 1983, **5**, 25-57. Copyright 1983 by Human Kinetics Publishers, Inc.
*Published.

†M = male; F = female; Coll = college; Elem = elementary.

TABLE 20.8   Comparisons of Effect Sizes Among Various Coding Characteristics

CODING CHARACTERISTIC	n	MEAN EFFECT SIZE	MEAN SD	F	t'	p
Subject characteristics						
Male	70	.50	.68		.08	
Female	52	.49	.70			
Elementary	26	.45	.74	1.01		
High School	17	.29	.54			
College	103	.52	.68			
Experienced	18	.77	.88		1.54	.18
Novice	128	.44	.63			
Type of task						
Motor	104	.43	.57	40.12*	3.64*	.008
Cognitive	13	1.44	.98			
Strength	29	.20	.49		4.33*	.001
Self-paced	79	.39	.58		1.21	
Reactive	16	.25	.38			
Design characteristics						
Motivational control	49	.46	.63	1.37		.25
Simple control	70	.42	.72			
Pre/post design	27	.67	.62			
Immediate	55	.32	.48		2.45	.02
Later	91	.57	.76			
Unpublished	91	.32	.46		3.31*	.01
Published	55	.74	.87			

*$p \leq .01$

Reprinted with permission from D. Feltz and D. Landers. The effects of mental practice on motor skills learning and performance. *Journal of Sport Psychology*, 1983, **5**, 25-57. Copyright 1983 by Human Kinetics Publishers, Inc.

reference to statistical analysis and interpretation of effect sizes. In general they caution that some statistical methods used to ascertain relationships and effects through analysis of effect sizes may be suboptimal and may lead to erroneous conclusions. Hedges indicates that several factors may contribute to the problem. Published studies often fail to provide adequate information to complete a meta-analysis using optimal methods; thus the researcher can either discard the unit or use suboptimal methods for estimating effect sizes. Studies often have unequal subjects. A series of studies may share common design flaws. Statistical techniques may be inappropriate. This distribution of effect sizes may not be homogeneous. In addition to his criticism of current techniques he offers alternative methods for analyzing categorical data (1982c) and continuous data (1982d). Individuals either planning to use the results of meta-analyses completed by others or preparing to conduct their own studies should become familiar with his critical analysis of research, and of research and statistical methods.

TABLE 20.9   Average Effect Sizes for Perceptual-Motor Outcomes: (a) Classes, (b) Categories

a. AVERAGE EFFECT SIZES FOR PERCEPTUAL-MOTOR OUTCOME CLASSES

OUTCOME CLASS	NUMBER OF EFFECT SIZES	MEAN	STANDARD ERROR	PERCENTILE EQUIVALENT
Perceptual/sensory motor	233	.166	.017	56
Academic achievement	283	.013	.018	50
Cognitive/aptitude	95	.028	.023	51
Adaptive behavior	26	.267	.072	61

b. AVERAGE EFFECT SIZES FOR PERCEPTUAL-MOTOR GENERAL OUTCOME CATEGORIES

GENERAL OUTCOME CATEGORIES	NUMBER OF EFFECT SIZES	MEAN	STANDARD ERROR	PERCENTILE EQUIVALENT
Perceptual/sensory motor				
Gross motor	44	.214	.046	58
Fine motor	28	.178	.039	57
Visual perception	145	.149	.022	56
Auditory perception	16	.122	.062	55
Academic achievement				
Readiness	69	.076	.024	53
Reading	142	−.039	.022	48
Arithmetic	26	.095	.076	54
Language	18	.031	.057	51
Spelling	16	.021	.055	51
Handwriting	12	.053	.052	52
Cognitive/aptitude				
Verbal IQ	53	−.007	.031	50
Performance IQ	34	.068	.040	53

Reprinted by special permission of The Professional Press, Inc. from K. Kavale and D. Mattson, One jumped off the balance beam: Meta-analysis of perceptual-motor training. *Journal of Learning Disabilities*, 1983, **16,** 165-173. Copyright 1983 by The Professional Press, Inc.

USES AND FINDINGS OF META-ANALYSIS TO DATE

There are, at this time, to the best of my knowledge, only three completed meta-analyses specific to questions in physical education and sport. Besides the two mentioned previously, Feltz and Landers (1983) and Rothstein and Arnold (1976), Sparling (1980) published a meta-analysis of studies comparing maximal oxygen uptake in men and women. He suggested that a meta-analysis on this topic was needed because samples used in various published studies differed on critical factors, such as age and level of conditioning, thus confounding conclusions concerning the magnitude of the sex differences on this variable. In selecting studies for analysis he used the following criteria (p. 544):

TABLE 20.10   Average Effect Sizes for Perceptual-Motor Specific Outcome Categories

SPECIAL OUTCOME CATEGORIES	NUMBER OF EFFECT SIZES	MEAN	STANDARD ERROR	PERCENTILE EQUIVALENT
Gross motor skills				
Body awareness/image	22	.256	.070	60
Balance/posture	14	.263	.096	60
Locomotor skills	8	−.017	.122	49
Visual perceptual skills				
Visual discrimination	31	.146	.068	56
Figure-ground discrimination	28	.173	.047	57
Visual-motor ability	26	.222	.051	59
Visual integration	17	.086	.097	54
Visual spatial perception	16	.144	.079	56
Visual memory	15	.062	.098	53
Reading achievement				
Word recognition	36	−.016	.049	49
Comprehension	33	−.055	.059	48
Oral reading	17	−.037	.103	48
Vocabulary	25	−.012	.035	50
Speed/rate	8	−.038	.172	48

Reprinted by special permission of The Professional Press, Inc. from K. Kavale and D. Mattson. One jumped off the balance beam: Meta-analysis of perceptual-motor training. *Journal of Learning Disabilities,* 1983, **16,** 165-173. Copyright 1983 by the Professional Press, Inc.

a.   Study included both males and females.
b.   Subjects were late adolescent or older.
c.   Measures of body composition were obtained.
d.   Measures of V_{O_2} max were given.

Studies which met these guidelines were evaluated relative to the following:

a.   Habitual level of physical activity/conditioning of subjects.
b.   Physical and physiological description of subjects.
c.   Statistical analysis and interpretation.

These studies are shown in Tables 20.13 and 20.14.

The *ES* for each study was obtained by using a formula (Glass and Stanley, 1970) for converting the *t* value to a point-biserial correlation. He located 13 studies which met the criteria stipulated above. He concluded that the average effect size for V_{O_2} max expressed in liters/minute was .81. When this measure is expressed relative to body weight, the effect size was reduced to .70. The *ES* was further reduced to .59 when expressed relative to fat-free weight. When studies which tested only trained subjects were used for comparison, the *ES* was reported as smaller (the actual figure is not given).

The one drawback in the procedures used in the study involves the elimination of *ES*s for studies in which the comparisons were not significant. This

TABLE 20.11 Average Effect Sizes for Individual Outcome Measures

MEASURE	NUMBER OF EFFECT SIZES	MEAN	STANDARD ERROR	PERCENTILE EQUIVALENT
Perceptual/sensory motor				
PPMS	19	.212	.085	58
FDTVP-PQ	23	.163	.051	56
EM	18	.243	.068	59
FG	18	.182	.055	57
FC	16	.077	.050	56
PS	16	.077	.050	53
SR	14	.134	.088	55
Academic achievement				
MRT	26	.084	.024	53
MAT	27	.058	.039	52
SAT	21	−.074	.047	47
WRAT	23	−.065	.040	47
SRT	17	−.022	.057	49
GMRT	16	−.205	.057	42
Cognitive/aptitude				
WISC-T	9	.017	.092	51
V	21	−.021	.067	49
P	16	.059	.049	52
PPVT	15	−.023	.065	49
ITPA	10	.124	.102	55

```
PPMS  = Purdue Perceptual Motor Survey
FDTVP = Frostig Developmental Test of Visual Perception
  PQ  = Perceptual Quotient
  EM  = Eye-Motor Coordination
  FG  = Figure-Ground Discrimination
  FC  = Form Consistency
  PS  = Position in Space
  SR  = Spatial Relationships
 MRT  = Metropolitan Readiness Test
 MAT  = Metropolitan Achievement Test
 SAT  = Stanford Achievement Test
WRAT  = Wide Range Achievement Test
 SRT  = Stanford Reading Test
GMRT  = Gates-MacGinitie Reading Test
WISC  = Wechsler Intelligence Scale for Children
   T  = Total IQ
   V  = Verbal IQ
   P  = Performance IQ
PPVT  = Peabody Picture Vocabulary Test
ITPA  = Illinois Test of Psycholinguistic Abilities
```

TABLE 20.12   Average Effect Sizes for Perceptual-Motor Training Programs

TRAINING PROGRAM	NUMBER OF EFFECT SIZES	MEAN	STANDARD ERROR	PERCENTILE EQUIVALENT
Barsch	18	.157	.053	56
Cratty	27	.113	.041	54
Delacato	79	.161	.025	56
Frostig	173	.096	.015	54
Getman	48	.124	.029	55
Kephart	132	.064	.016	52
Combination	78	.057	.037	52
Other	82	−.021	.014	49

Reprinted by special permission of the Professional Press, Inc. from K. Kavale and D. Mattson. One jumped off the balance beam: Meta-analysis of perceptual-motor training. *Journal of Learning Disabilities,* 1983, **16**, 165-173. Copyright 1983 by the Professional Press, Inc.

defeats the purpose of the meta-analysis. In some of the instances where differences were not significant small sample size was cited as a possible reason. In order to minimize the effect of this, a weighting procedure might be used in which less weight would be given to studies which reported smaller *n*s, this regardless of significance. In addition, the *ES* statistic employed is not as easily interpreted as that based on the *z* statistic. Finally, the small number of studies and the lack of specific information in some of the reports made the task of interpretation extremely difficult and limited the types of comparisons that might be made. In his conclusion Sparling (1980) makes a plea similar to that made by Rosenthal (1978) that researchers publish their work with its potential use in a meta-analysis in mind and include sufficient descriptive and statistical data to enable calculation of effect sizes and coding of critical factors. Certainly the recent trend toward sparse reporting of data is a drawback to the synthesis of research. I would make an additional plea that minimal, but useful, statistical information be included in *Dissertation Abstracts* and *Completed Research in HPERD.*

Although studies which consider specific questions in physical education are few, a number of meta-analyses consider areas of research which are of interest in physical education and sport. Rosenthal and Rubin (1978), for example, published a completed meta-analysis of 345 studies on interpersonal expectancy effects. This is commonly known as self-fulfilling prophecy and concerns the notion that experimenters (or teachers, employers, coaches) influence the behavior (performance) of subjects (or pupils, employees, athletes) through communication of expectancies. Their purpose for undertaking this analysis was to statistically "encompass the results of all the existing studies that have investigated the effects of the interpersonal self-fulfilling prophecy" (p. 377). The studies that are potentially most interesting for physical educators are those which deal with learning and ability. There have been 34 studies (9 before 1969 and 25 since 1969). Of these, approximately 10 studies reached $p \leq .05$. For these studies the mean *ES* is reported as .54. Using a normal distribution table,

TABLE 20.13 Summary of Maximal Oxygen Uptake Expressions for Males and Females and the Magnitude of the Sex Difference from Selected Studies[a]

STUDY	TEST	UNITS	MAXIMAL OXYGEN UPTAKE MALE	MAXIMAL OXYGEN UPTAKE FEMALE	% DIFFERENCE $\frac{M-F}{F} \times 100$	t	p	r	r²
von Dobeln, 1956	Bicycle ergometer[b]	l/min	3.90 ± .56	3.04 ± .54	28	6.5	.001	.62	.39
		ml/min·kg BW	56.5 ± 6.9	48.7 ± 8.8	16	4.1	.001	.45	.20
		ml/min·kg FFW	63.3 ± 6.6	60.6 ± 10.2	4	1.3	n.s.	—	—
Hermansen & Anderson, 1965	Bicycle ergometer	l/min	4.80 ± .53	3.30 ± .43	45	5.2[d]	.001	.78	.61
		ml/min·kg BW	71.0 ± 6.8	55.0 ± 3.1	29	4.8[d]	.001	.76	.58
		ml/min·kg FFW	80.7 ± 7.5[c]	67.8 ± 3.4[c]	18	3.3[d]	.01	.63	.39
Cotes et al., 1969	Bicycle ergometer	l/min	3.43 ± .53[c]	2.14 ± .38[c]	60	8.9[d]	.001	.81	.66
		ml/min·kg BW	48.5 ± 7.9[c]	39.2 ± 6.5[c]	24	4.1[d]	.001	.54	.29
		ml/min·kg FFW	55.8 ± 8.7[c]	53.5 ± 7.4[c]	4	<1.0[d]	n.s.	—	—
McNab et al., 1969	Treadmill	l/min	3.92 ± .58	2.32 ± .41	69	11.0	.001	.85	.73
		ml/min·kg BW	51.7 ± 5.1	39.1 ± 5.1	32	8.6	.001	.78	.62
		ml/min·kg FFW	59.4 ± 5.9	50.4 ± 6.0	18	7.1	.001	.72	.52
	Bicycle ergometer	l/min	3.52 ± .61	2.12 ± .41	66	9.3	.001	.81	.66
		ml/min·kg BW	46.5 ± 6.3	35.7 ± 5.6	30	6.3	.001	.68	.46
		ml/min·kg FFW	53.3 ± 6.6	46.9 ± 7.2	14	5.1	.001	.60	.36
Dill et al., 1972	Bicycle ergometer	l/min	3.21 ± .49	1.92 ± .27	67	7.4	.001	.86	.74
		ml/min·kg BW	45.2 ± 6.4	35.9 ± 3.3	26	4.1	.001	.81	.65
		ml/min·kg FFW	52.9 ± 5.0	46.0 ± 4.7	15	3.3	.01	.60	.36
Davies et al., 1973	Bicycle ergometer	l/min	2.76 ± .39	2.00 ± 2.4	38	10.0[d]	.001	.72	.52
		ml/min·kg BW	47.0 ± 5.2	40.2 ± 4.8	17	6.1[d]	.001	.54	.29
		ml/min·kg FFW	53.4 ± 5.6	52.8 ± 6.0	1	<1.0[d]	n.s.	—	—

Study	Device	Unit							
Mayhew, 1976	Treadmill	l/min	3.89 ± .45	2.70 ± .34	44	9.9	.001	.83	.69
		ml/min·kg BW	63.8 ± 5.7	47.5 ± 4.1	34	10.8	.001	.85	.73
		ml/min·kg FFW	69.8 ± 6.1	59.1 ± 7.4	18	5.4	.001	.63	.40
Dill et al., 1977	Treadmill	l/min	3.63 ± .60[c]	2.13 ± .50[c]	70	6.6[d]	.001	.80	.64
		ml/min·kg BW	54.0 ± 8.7	36.9 ± 4.1	46	6.0[d]	.001	.77	.60
		ml/min·kg FFW	61.0 ± 8.3	51.1 ± 6.9	19	3.1[d]	.001	.53	.29
Kitagawa et al., 1977	Treadmill	l/min	3.22 ± .56	2.08 ± .21	55	10.9[d]	.001	.79	.63
		ml/min·kg BW	51.8 ± 6.6	39.2 ± 3.0	32	10.0[d]	.001	.77	.59
		ml/min·kg FFW	59.7 ± 6.9	50.0 ± 3.9	19	7.1[d]	.001	.65	.42
Diaz et al., 1978	Treadmill	l/min	3.78 ± .37	2.41 ± 4.7	57	5.2[d]	.001	.85	.73
		ml/min·kg BW	50.7 ± 4.2	40.5 ± 8.7	25	2.5[d]	.05	.62	.38
		ml/min·kg FFW	57.5 ± 4.2	52.3 ± 10.8	10	1.1[d]	n.s.	—	—
	Bicycle ergometer	l/min	3.68 ± .42	2.21 ± .38	67	5.7[d]	.001	.87	.76
		ml/min·kg BW	49.8 ± 4.8	37.7 ± 7.8	32	3.0[d]	.05	.69	.47
		ml/min·kg FFW	56.4 ± 4.8	48.6 ± 9.2	16	1.7[d]	n.s.	—	—
Daniels et al., 1978	Treadmill	l/min	4.19 ± .54	2.64 ± .31	58	13.4[d]	.001	.87	.75
		ml/min·kg BW	59.4 ± 5.9	46.0 ± 5.1	29	9.2[d]	.001	.77	.59
		ml/min·kg FFW	68.3 ± 5.7[c]	60.0 ± 5.2[c]	14	5.7[d]	.001	.60	.36
Vogel and Patton, 1978	Treadmill	l/min	3.36 ± .48[c]	2.25 ± .32[c]	63	20.1[d]	.001	.83	.69
		ml/min·kg BW	50.8 ± 3.5	38.1 ± 3.5	33	20.1[d]	.001	.83	.69
		ml/min·kg FFW	60.4 ± 3.7[c]	52.9 ± 3.5[c]	14	11.5[d]	.001	.65	.42
Sparling, 1979	Treadmill	l/min	4.29 ± .47	2.75 ± .40	56	14.6	.001	.87	.76
		ml/min·kg BW	61.0 ± 4.9	51.9 ± 5.1	18	7.5	.001	.68	.46
		ml/min·kg FFW	68.6 ± 5.5	65.1 ± 5.6	5	2.6	.05	.31	.09

Reprinted with permission from P. B. Sparling. A meta-analysis of studies comparing maximal oxygen uptake in men and women. *Research Quarterly for Exercise and Sport*, 1980, **51**, 542-552.

[a] Maximal oxygen uptake values are means ± standard deviations.
[b] Maximal oxygen uptake estimated from submaximal heart rates.
[c] Standard deviations estimated from the range as suggested by Baumgartner and Jackson (1975, p. 38)
[d] Values estimated from means and standard deviations according to Blommers and Lindquist (1960, p. 348).

TABLE 20.14 Summary of Physical Characteristics for Male and Female Subjects in Studies Selected for Meta-Analysis[a]

STUDY	SEX	n	ACTIVITY STATUS	AGE, YEARS	HEIGHT, cm	WEIGHT, kg	FAT, %
von Dobeln, 1956	M	35	Physical education, students and teachers, Swedish	26.1 ± 4.7	177.9 ± 6.9	69.4 ± 8.2	10.6[b]
	F	34		22.6 ± 3.3	169.6 ± 3.8	62.8 ± 6.5	20.3[b]
Hermansen & Anderson, 1965	M	14	National-level cross-country skiers, Norwegian	27.7 ± 3.1	174.8 ± 6.3	66.7 ± 5.0	10.0[c,d]
	F	5		25.1 ± 5.9	169.0 ± 5.7	61.6 ± 6.2	20.9[c,d]
Cotes et al., 1969	M	23	Factory workers: M—fairly heavy work, F—fairly light work, British	25.0	176.0	71.4	13.9[c,d]
	F	20		23.7	162.0	55.0	27.2[c,d]
MacNab et al., 1969	M	24	Physical education/recreation students, Canadian	20.0 ± 1.2	179.3 ± 6.1	76.1 ± 8.8	12.7[b]
	F	24		18.7 ± 0.6	165.8 ± 5.3	59.2 ± 5.9	23.4[b]
Dill et al., 1972	M	11	High school students, American	17.9 ± 1.5	181.3 ± 7.6	73.1 ± 16.4	14.5[b]
	F	10		16.7 ± 1.1	166.5 ± 6.3	53.8 ± 8.2	21.7[b]
Davies et al., 1973	M	62	Activity level not stated, African	22.7 ± 2.7	165.9 ± 6.7	58.0 ± 5.7	11.6[c,d]
	F	32		27.0 ± 9.5	153.5 ± 5.7	50.1 ± 7.3	26.1[c,d]
Mayhew, 1976	M	24	High school track athletes, American	16.7 ± 0.9	176.0 ± 4.9	61.2 ± 7.6	8.2[b]
	F	21		16.5 ± 0.8	168.9 ± 5.9	56.4 ± 5.7	17.2[b]
Dill et al., 1977	M	14	High school athletes, American		178.0 ± 5.4	67.3 ± 9.4	11.8[b]
	F	12			166.0 ± 7.8	57.7 ± 6.7	27.4[b]
Kitagawa et al., 1977	M	39	University students, Japanese	19.3 ± 0.8	172.1 ± 5.0	62.0 ± 6.7	13.1[b]
	F	33		18.7 ± 0.3	157.0 ± 4.5	53.2 ± 5.1	21.6[b]
Diaz et al., 1978	M	7	Activity level not stated, American	28.6	177.0	74.4	12.0[b]
	F	5		29.0	163.0	59.2	22.6[b]
Daniels et al., 1978	M	30	First-year West Point cadets, American			70.6 ± 7.6	13.1[c]
	F	30				57.7 ± 6.0	23.8[c]
Vogel & Patton, 1978	M	92	Untrained Army recruits, American	21.0 ± 4.0		7.20 ± 11.0	15.8[c]
	F	92		20.0 ± 2.0		59.0 ± 7.0	27.9[c]
Sparling, 1979	M	34	Trained runners, American	26.6 ± 4.0	180.5 ± 6.8	70.3 ± 6.8	10.8[b]
	F	34		25.0 ± 4.6	162.5 ± 6.9	52.9 ± 6.8	19.8[b]

From Sparling (1980, p. 545).

[a]Values are means ± standard deviations.
[b]Values estimated from body density as measured by hydrostatic weighing.
[c]Values estimated from multiple skinfold measurements.
[d]Values computed from average fat-free weight values.

Reprinted with permission from P. B. Sparling. A meta-analysis of studies comparing maximal oxygen uptake in men and women. *Research Quarterly for Exercise and Sport* 1980, 51, 542-552.

this indicates that the average individual in the treated group was better than 71% of the nontreated group. They also provided the statistics for dissertations and nondissertations. For the former the *ES* was .11, lowering the percentage to 54%; for the nondissertation group the *ES* was .76, raising the percentage to 78%. On the basis of these findings and those in eight other areas of research—reaction time; inkblot tests; animal learning; laboratory interviews; psychophysical judgments; person perception; and everyday situations—the authors conclude that the expectancy effect is alive and operating.

I recommend this article highly because of the explanations provided and also because the journal in which it appears, *The Behavioral and Brain Sciences*, is special in that each article is accompanied by peer commentary. In this instance there are 29 commentaries which focus on substantive issues, rival hypotheses, general methodological issues, and specific methodological issues. The specific methodological issues are of special interest since they concern the technique of meta-analysis: mixing apples and oranges; exclusion of poorly done studies; issues related to pooling studies; computation of *ES*; and inconsistency of direction of effects. The commentary by Glass (pp. 394–395) is particularly interesting and informative on the subject of meta-analysis.

Another study (Hall, 1978) summarized the results of 75 studies relative to gender effects in decoding nonverbal cues. She coded the following attributes of the studies:

a. Year.
b. Sample size.
c. Age of judges.
d. Sex of stimulus person(s).
e. Age of stimulus person(s).
f. Medium and channel of communication.
g. Sex of subject(s).

She examined the attributes using three outcome indices:

a. Direction of effect.
b. Effect size (in SD units).
c. Significance level.

Hall's purpose for conducting a meta-analysis in this area was that "Despite the intuitive and theoretical importance of learning about differences between the sexes in ability to judge nonverbal communication, there exists considerable uncertainty over the facts" (p. 845). Her sample consists of studies published or known to be submitted for publication. She carefully delineates those types of studies that were excluded (pp. 846–847). In addition, she describes the stimuli used in the studies and then proceeds to provide a complete listing of all the studies and their coded attributes (pp. 848–850). In the discussion Hall concludes that "The present review clarifies a previously confused issue and establishes that on a variety of conceptually similar tasks of decoding nonverbal cues females are reliably more accurate than males. The mean difference of .40 SD is not, however, a large difference. An average effect of this size means that the upper 50% of the female distribution exceeds about 65% of the male distribution . . ." (p. 854). In her tables, however, she does indicate that for visual cues only the mean ES is .32, for auditory cues it is .18, but for visual plus auditory cues the mean is 1.02. All of these favor females. The last indicates that the upper 50% of the female distribution exceeds about 85% of the male distribution. In regard to this she suggests that the "visual plus auditory stimuli probably (have) more ecological validity than visual or auditory stimuli alone" (p. 852).

The effects of cooperation, competition, and individual goal setting on achievement were studied by Johnson, Maruyama, Johnson, Nelson, and Skon (1981). This analysis is of value because of the interest in these treatments within physical education and sport. The authors' purpose in completing the meta-analysis was to allow for "more precise and confident statements about the relative effects of cooperative, competitive, and individualistic efforts on achievement and productivity" (p. 49). Their study is worth reading because of the findings and because of the types of analyses they did on the data. In addition, they contrasted three types of methods: the voting method, the ES, and the z-score method. Generally, the results favored cooperation against treatments which included competition, whether those treatments were individual competition or cooperation with intergroup competition. In a series of ANOVAs used to determine the role of group and individual characteristics it was noted that: age was a significant factor, with results stronger for precollege students; the smaller the groups within the cooperative condition, the greater the superiority of cooperation; and tasks which demand decision making, cognitive rehearsal, and encouragement (i.e., group cooperation) favor cooperation over tasks which tend to be rote.

The interested reader should review the list of studies in the bibliography at the end of this chapter and should consult those which appear interesting in order to gain perspective on how the technique is done and how the results are reported. You will find studies on computer-assisted instruction (Hartley, 1977); individual instruction (Kulik, Kulik, and Cohen, 1979); psychotherapy (Smith, Glass, and Miller, 1980); special education (Carlberg, 1979, Kavale and Glass, 1982); student ratings of instruction and student achievement (Cohen, 1980); computer-based teaching (Kulik, Kulik, and Cohen, 1980, Kulik, Kulik and Cohen, 1983); and visual-based teaching (Cohen, Ebeling, and Kulik, 1981). A search of back issues of the *American Educational Research Journal* and the *Review of Educational Research* will yield an average of one meta-analysis per issue on various topics.

As mentioned previously, I know of only three meta-analyses specific to physical education. There is a clear need for more on such topics as whole versus part learning, schema theory, feedback, coincidence-anticipation, attribution, psychological sex-role, achievement motivation, audience effect, and transfer of training, among others. Why is this avenue not being pursued? One problem, I am certain, involves the lack of respect accorded synthesis in comparison to "original research." In fact, much "original" research is misnamed and merely adds to the already fragmented nature of research results. A well-planned, sophisticated, extensive meta-analysis can provide much more in the way of originality and creativity and can make a lasting contribution to the field by providing research problems related to the testing of the conclusions drawn. It has been suggested (Arnold, 1981) that "meta-analysis, followed by a series of systematic studies to test the effect of the variables identified would seem to provide an ideal context, for example, for graduate students to conduct meaningful, structured research within an ongoing series of investigations."

ROLE OF META-ANALYSIS IN PHYSICAL EDUCATION

Apprehending the meaning of the collected research in an area of study has become a technical problem. The findings of a collection of studies have become too varied and numerous to be grasped readily, as for example one might readily understand a theory by reading it. The confusion that arises from irregularity and sheer numbers can be tamed by coding, ordering, and arranging instances in search of patterns and gross features (Glass, 1978). Meta-analysis does this by applying to a collection of studies the same rigorous, objective, replicable methods that researchers use in analyzing the results of the individual studies. Thus, the conclusions of the meta-analyst are likely to be reproducible, reliable, and general. Paraphrasing Cooper and Rosenthal (1980), some of the confusion and confounding we often convey regarding research in motor learning, sport psychology, motor development, biomechanics, exercise physiology, curriculum and teaching may not be a function of the studies we have done but rather of the way we have chosen to synthesize them.

The majority of research in physical education is conducted on human subjects. It should not therefore be surprising that the research literature breeds confusion. The lack of agreement may be due to differences in characteristics of the sample groups, to the context of the research, or to the specific procedures used. A meta-analysis approach to combining data enables the identification of underlying factors which may have influenced the results and precipitated the confusion.

The statistical techniques used in meta-analysis are not highly sophisticated; rather it is the total procedure of coding, selecting, calculating, and combining data that yields the sophistication. As we have noted above, the statistics are not any more complex than the z-score statistic you previously learned and used.

The findings of the meta-analysis have potential for both the researcher and the practitioner. For the researcher, the identification of the critical set of variables, independent or interactive, can suggest a research design that is most likely to produce a definitive or clarifying result in the future. For the practitioner meta-analysis of research can "a) bring order and harmony to what appears to be a mass of conflicting results, b) indicate under what set of conditions certain training and learning effects can be expected, and c) foster an attitude of analytical observation of the effects of critical variables in the gymnasium or on the athletic field" (Arnold, 1981).

Not only does meta-analysis have a role in physical education, the times demand it. We need to use the research we have; we need to shorten the lag time from research to practice; individual studies are not generalizable to physical education and sport but conclusions based on statistical synthesis of groups of studies are. The answer to the initial question posed in this chapter, *How can research be used to influence practice?*, is simply *By doing it*. At this time meta-analysis in some form is clearly the best way of doing it.

STATISTICAL ANALYSIS OF GAME STATISTICS

This technique has something in common with both DART and meta-analysis. In truth, it is a form of meta-analysis which uses the game as the unit of analysis and employs a coding scheme to identify variables of interest associated with game outcome (win or lose). It is also a form of descriptive analytic research in that it describes what is, rather than attempting to impose conditions and then measure their effect. The statistical analysis of game statistics has been pursued by Arnold and her colleagues and students in the analysis of wrestling (Kushner, 1978; Cervino, 1979; Gallione, 1980); tennis (Capobianco, 1978; Mizerik, 1980); soccer (Lash, 1980); and field hockey (Chrobock, 1980) as cited in Arnold (1982).

The technique, as proposed by Arnold (1982), involves the following:

a. Clearly define the question(s) to be investigated.
b. Identify specific players or teams to be observed.
c. Establish categories which are jointly exhaustive and mutually exclusive.
d. Develop a coding form.
e. Pilot the form (includes developing coding conventions).
f. Identify source of observed data (scorebooks, game films, direct observation).
g. Train recorders (or practice recording).
h. Evaluate the reliability of the form and the recorder(s).
i. Collect the data.
j. Evaluate the data statistically, using chi-square techniques.
k. Draw conclusions about the relationship between the factors identified and game outcome.

An Illustration

The following illustration is from Arnold (1982) who used the data of Capobianco (1978) to demonstrate the technique of game stat analysis. The intent of the study was to investigate three aspects of tennis play:

a. The relationship between winning the fifth point in a game tied at 30–30 and winning the game.
b. The relationship between winning the seventh game in a set tied at 3–3 and subsequently winning the set.
c. The relationship between winning the second set, creating a 1–1 tie, and winning the match.

The hypothesis was that these situations were pivotal and that the winner in each case would go on to win the game, set, or match, respectively. The data were obtained from scorecards of singles matches in the 1977 U.S. Open tennis tournament. The cards used indicate the sequence in which points were won by the players. The matrices used in tallying the data are illustrated below (the sample given is for men's data):

WINNING THE FIFTH POINT OF GAME

OUTCOME OF GAME	ABSOLUTE FREQUENCY	RELATIVE FREQUENCY
Win	626**	75.2%
Lose	206	24.8%
Total	832	100.0%

The table illustrates that 75.2% of the time the individual who won the fifth point of a 30–30 game went on to win the game. (The expected percent, you will remember from the chapter on chi-square, is 50%.) Thus, the chi-square value is significant at the .01 level, as indicated by the double asterisk. The same procedure would be followed in the case of each of the hypotheses. For each tie situation, 30–30 game, 3–3 set, 1–1 match, Capobianco ascertained who won the point, game, and set (to create the 1–1 tie) and then noted whether that person went on to win the game, set, or match, respectively. These relationships were appropriately cross-tabulated, and chi-square statistics were calculated.

It is clear that the analysis of game statistics has much in common with meta-analysis and in fact could be called meta-analysis of game statistics. In a sense it serves some of the same purposes. It synthesizes the data about selected variables (events) across a wide variety of game situations for a single sport in an attempt to extract the commonality from the "noise" of the inconsistencies within, between, and among games. I recommend the Arnold article highly and encourage the use of this procedure in connection with game statistics.

In her article Arnold also provides suggestions for additional, more sophisticated uses of the meta-analysis of game statistics. She suggests that this method may be used to determine: (a) the best method of breaking ties in soccer; (b) the relationship between time of offensive possession and winning in football, lacrosse, field hockey; (c) the extent to which season success in a sport is related to number of contests per week, game conditions, and environmental factors; (d) the relationship between violations in basketball and winning at various levels of play; or (e) the relationship between the winning of a close game and the winning of the next game. The potential questions are endless; you are limited only by your imagination and the availability of or possibility of recording appropriate game statistics.

SUMMARY

This chapter has illustrated the various ways in which research and research techniques could be used to influence practice. The three aspects considered were: descriptive analytic research on teaching; meta-analysis of research data; and statistical analysis (meta-analysis) of game statistics. Emphasis was on how research and research techniques could be used rather than on whether they could be used, since I am firmly convinced, and feel that I have amply demonstrated, that research can and should be used to influence practice. I would qualify my presentation only by stipulating that the appropriate individual to prepare the application by using the sequential processes of development, dissemination, demonstration, implementation, and evaluation does not now exist, and a mechanism or curriculum will have to be created to prepare such persons.

REFERENCES AND BIBLIOGRAPHY

ANDERSON, W.G.   Teacher behavior in physical education classes. Part I. Development of a descriptive system. Unpublished paper, Teachers College, Columbia University, 1974.
————.   Introduction. In W.G. Anderson and G. T. Barrette (eds.), *What's going on in gym*. Newtown, CT: Motor Skills: Theory into Practice, 1978, 1–10.
ARKIN, R., COOPER, H., and KOLDITZ, T.   A statistical review of the literature concerning the self-serving bias attribution in interpersonal situations. *Journal of Personality*, **48** (1980), 435–448.
ARNOLD, R.K.   Game stats analysis. Paper presented at the American Alliance for Health, Physical Education, Recreation and Dance Conference, 1981.
————.   Game stats analysis I and II. *Journal of Physical Education, Recreation and Dance*, 1983, **54**:5, 18-20. 62; **54**:9, 47-50
BRODERICK, R.   Bridging the gap: The teacher's view. Paper presented at the AAHPER National Conference, Detroit, MI, 1971.
CHEFFERS, J.T.F.   The validation of an instrument designed to expand the Flanders system of interaction analysis to describe non-verbal interaction, different varieties

of teacher behavior, and pupil responses. Unpublished doctoral dissertation, Temple University, 1972.

COHEN, P.A., KULIK, J.A., and KULIK, C.C. Educational outcomes of tutoring. *American Educational Research Journal*, **19** (1982), 237–248.

COOK, T.D., and LEVITON, L.C. Reviewing the literature: A comparison of traditional methods with meta-analysis. *Journal of Personality*, **48** (1980), 449–472.

COOPER, H.M. Statistically combining independent studies: A meta-analysis of sex differences in conformity research. *Journal of Personality and Social Psychology*, **37** (1979), 131–146.

————. Scientific guidelines for conducting integrative research reviews. *Review of Educational Research*, **52** (1982), 291–302.

COOPER, H.M., and ARKIN, R.M. On quantitative reviewing. *Journal of Personality* **49** (1981), 225–230.

COOPER, H.M., and ROSENTHAL, R. Statistical versus traditional procedures for summarizing research findings. *Psychological Bulletin*, **87** (1980), 442–449.

DRAYTON, M.A. A Bayesian meta-analytic demonstration: Mathematics achievement in seventh and eighth grade. Unpublished doctoral dissertation, Northern Illinois University, 1978.

EDDINGTON, E.S. An additive method for combining probability values from independent experiments. *Journal of Psychology*, **80** (1972), 351–363.

————. A normal curve method for combining probability values from independent experiments. *Journal of Psychology*, **82** (1972), 85–89.

EYSENCK, H.J. An exercise in mega-silliness. *American Psychologist*, **33** (1978), 517.

FELTZ, D., and LANDERS, D. The effects of mental practice on motor skill learning and performance: A meta-analysis. *Journal of Sport Psychology*, **5** (1983), 25–57.

FISHMAN, S. A procedure for recording augmented feedback in physical education classes. Unpublished doctoral dissertation, Teachers College, Columbia University, 1974.

FRALEIGH, W.P. A philosophic basis for curriculum content in physical education in the 1980s. In M. Gladys Scott (ed.), *Issues and challenges: A kaleidoscope of change*. Washington, D.C.: American Academy of Physical Education, 1979, 20–26.

GAGE, N.L. The yield of research on teaching. *Phi Delta Kappan*, **60** (1978), 229–235.

————. *The scientific basis of the art of teaching*. New York: Teachers College Press, 1978.

GALLO, P.S. Meta-analysis—A mixed meta-phor? *American Psychologist*, **33** (1978), 515–517.

GALLO, P.S., and LYNN, E. The variance accounted for in meta-analysis of psychotherapy outcomes—A reply to Wilson. *American Psychologist*, **36** (1981), 1196–1198.

GLASS, G.V. Primary, secondary, and meta-analysis of research. *Educational Reseacher*, **5** (1976), 3–8.

————. Integrating findings: Meta-analysis of research. *Review of Research in Education*, **5** (1977), 351–379.

GLASS, G.V., McGAW, B., and SMITH, M.L. *Meta-analysis in social research*. Beverly Hills, CA: Sage, 1981.

HALL, J.A. Gender effects in decoding nonverbal cues. *Psychological Bulletin*, **85** (1978), 845–857.

HALL, J.L., and BROWN, M.J. *Online Bibliographic Databases: An International Directory*. London: Aslib, 1981.

HEDGES, L.V. Distribution theory for Glass's estimator of effect size and related estimators. *Journal of Educational Statistics*, **6** (1981), 107–128.

————. Estimation of effect size from a series of independent experiments. *Psychological Bulletin*, **92** (1982a), 490–499.

————. Estimation and testing for differences in effect size: A comment on Hsu. *Psychological Bulletin*, **91** (1982b), 691–693.

————. A random effects model for effect sizes. *Psychological Bulletin*, **93** (1983a), 388–395.

————. Combining independent estimators in research synthesis. *British Journal of Mathematical and Statistical Psychology*, **36** (1983b), 123–131.

————. Fitting categorical models to effect sizes from a series of experiments. *Journal of Educational Statistics*, **7** (1983c), 119–137.

————. Fitting continuous models to effect size data. *Journal of Educational Statistics*, **7** (1982d), 245–270.

HEDGES, L.V., and OLKIN, I. Clustering estimates of effect magnitude from independent studies. *Psychological Bulletin*, **93** (1983), 563–573.

HEDGES, L.V., and STOCK, W. The effects of class size: An examination of rival hypotheses. *American Educational Research Journal*, **20** (1983), 63–85.

HOFFMAN, S.J. Observing and reporting on learner responses: The teacher as a reliable feedback agent. In L.I. Gedvilas and M.E. Kneer (eds.), *Proceedings of the NAPECW/NCPEAM national conference*. Chicago: University of Illinois at Chicago Publications, 1977, 153–159.

HUNTER, J.E., SCHMIDT, F.L., and JACKSON, G.B. *Meta-analysis: Cumulating research findings across studies*. Beverly Hills, CA: Sage, 1982.

JACKSON, G.B. Methods for integrative reviews. *Review of Educational Research*, **50** (1980), 438–460.

JOHNSON, D.W., MARUYAMA, G., JOHNSON, R., NELSON, D., and SKON, L. The effects of cooperative, competitive, and individualistic goal structures on achievement: A meta-analysis. *Psychological Bulletin*, **89** (1981), 47–62.

JONES, L.V., and FISKE, D.W. Models for testing the significance of combined results. *Psychological Bulletin*, **50** (1953), 375–381.

KAVALE, K.A. and GLASS, G.V. The efficacy of special education interventions and practices: A compendium of meta-analysis findings. *Focus on Exceptional Children*, **15** (1982), 1–14.

KAVALE, K.A., and MATTSON, D. "One jumped off the balance beam": Meta-analysis of perceptual-motor training. *Journal of Learning Disabilities*, **16** (1983), 165–173.

KULIK, J.A., BANGERT, R.L. and WILLIAMS, G. Effects of computer-based teaching on secondary school students. *Journal of Educational Psychology*, **75** (1983), 19–26.

KULIK, J.A., KULIK, C.C., and COHEN, P.A. Effectiveness of computer-based college teaching: A meta-analysis of findings. *Review of Educational Research*, **50** (1980), 525–544.

————. A meta-analysis of outcome studies of Keller's personalized system of instruction. *American Psychologist*, **34** (1979), 307–318.

LADAS, H. Summarizing research: A case study. *Review of Educational Research*, **50** (1980), 597–624.

LAUBACH, S.A. The development of a system for coding student behavior in physical education classes. Unpublished doctoral dissertation, Teachers College, Columbia University, 1975.

LEVISON, M.E. A descriptive system to investigate teacher references to the task environment during the facilitation of perceptual-motor skills. Unpublished doctoral dissertation, Teachers College, Columbia University, 1978.

LEVITON, L.C., and COOK, T.D. What differentiates meta-analysis from other forms of review? *Journal of Personality*, **49** (1981), 231–236.

LEY, K.L. Reaction of a teacher-coach to Johnson's "A viewpoint from exercise physiology." In M. Gladys Scott (ed.), *Relationships in physical education.* Washington, D.C.: American Academy of Physical Education, 1977, 69–73.

LIGHT, R.J., and SMITH, P.V. Accumulating evidence: Procedures for resolving contradictions among different research studies. *Harvard Educational Review,* **41** (1971), 429–471.

LOCKE, L.F. Research quarterly: Caveat emptor. *New York State Journal of Health, Physical Education and Recreation,* 1967, Fall, 30–36.

————. Researchers and teachers at the OK corral. In NCPEAM, *Proceedings of the 72nd annual meeting.* Washington, D.C.: NCPEAM, 1969a, 160–168.

————. *Research in physical education.* New York: Teachers College Press, 1969b.

————. From research and the disciplines to practice and the professions: One more time. In L.I. Gedvilas and M.E. Kneer (eds.), *Proceedings of the NAPECW/ NCPEAM National Conference.* Chicago: University of Illinois at Chicago Publications, 1977, 34–44.

————. Learning from teaching. In J.J. Jackson (ed.), *Theory into practice.* Victoria, BC: University of Victoria, 1979, 133–152.

MANSFIELD, R.S., and BUSSE, T.V. Meta-analysis of research: A rejoinder to Glass. *Educational Researcher,* **6** (1977), 3.

McGAW, B., and GLASS, G.V. Choice of the metric for effect size in meta-analysis. *American Educational Research Journal,* **17** (1980), 325–337.

MILLER, R.I. Some aspects of research and practice. In NCPEAM, *Proceedings of the 72nd annual meeting.* Washington, D.C.: NCPEAM, 1969, 172–177.

MORGENEGG, B.L. The pedagogical functions of physical education teachers. Unpublished doctoral dissertation, Teachers College, Columbia University, 1978.

PAUL, G.L., and LICHT, M.H. Resurrection of uniformity assumption myths and the fallacy of statistical absolutes in psychotherapy research. *Journal of Consulting and Clinical Psychology,* **46** (1978), 1531–1534.

PILLEMAR, D.B., and LIGHT, R.J. Synthesizing outcomes: How to use research evidence from many studies. *Harvard Educational Review,* **50** (1980), 176–195.

ROSENTHAL, R. *Experimenter effects in behavioral research.* New York: Irvington Press, 1976.

————. Combining results of independent studies. *Psychological Bulletin,* **86** (1978), 185–193.

————. The "File Drawer Problem" and tolerance for null results. *Psychological Bulletin,* **86** (1979), 638–641.

————. On telling tales when combining results of independent studies. *Psychological Bulletin,* **88** (1980), 496–497.

ROSENTHAL, R., and RUBIN, D.B. Interpersonal expectancy effects: The first 345 studies. *Behavioral and Brain Sciences,* **3** (1978), 377–415.

ROSENTHAL, R., and RUBIN, D.B. A simple, general purpose display of magnitude of experimental effect. *Journal of Educational Psychology,* **74** (1982), 166–169.

————. Comparing effect sizes of independent studies. *Psychological Bulletin,* **92** (1982), 500–504.

ROTHSTEIN, A.L. Practitioners and the scholarly enterprise. *Quest,* **20** (1973), 56–59.

————. Instructional design in open skills. In L.I. Gedvilas and M.E. Kneer (eds.), *Proceedings of the NAPECW/NCPEAM National Conference.* Chicago: University of Illinois at Chicago Publications, 1977, 160–166.

———— (ed.) The role of research in practice. *Journal of Physical Education and Recreation,* **51** (1980), 39–64.

ROTHSTEIN, A.L., and ARNOLD, R.K. Bridging the gap: Application of research on videotape feedback and bowling. *Motor Skills: Theory into Practice,* 1 (1976), 35–62.

SEIDENTOP, D.   Motor learning and instructional design: Why the shotgun wedding? In L.I. Gedvilas and M.E. Kneer (eds.), *Proceedings of the NAPECW/NCPEAM National Conference.* Chicago: University of Illinois at Chicago Publications, 1977, 145–152.

SEIDENTOP, D., and RUSHALL, B.   *The development and control of behavior in physical education and sport.* Philadelphia: Lea & Febiger, 1972.

SLOAN, M.R.   Relationships in physical education: A viewpoint from motor learning-skill acquisition. In M. Gladys Scott (ed.), *Relationships in physical education.* Washington, D.C.: American Academy of Physical Education, 1977, 29–39.

SMITH, M.L., and GLASS, G.V.   Meta-analysis of psychotherapy outcome studies. *American Psychologist,* 32 (1977), 752–760.

————.   Meta-analysis of research on class size and its relationship to attitudes and instruction. *American Educational Research Journal,* 17 (1980), 419–433.

SOHN, D.   Critique of Cooper's meta-analytic assessment of the findings on sex differences in conformity behavior. *Journal of Personality and Social Psychology,* 39 (1980), 1215–1221.

SPARLING, P.B.   A meta-analysis of studies comparing maximal oxygen uptake in men and women. *Research Quarterly for Exercise and Sport,* 51 (1980), 542–552.

STADULIS, R.E.   Bridging the gap: A lifetime of waiting and doing. *Quest,* 20 (1973), 47–55.

STOCK, W.A., OKUN, M.A., HARING, M.J., MILLER, W., KINNEY, C., and CEURVORST, R.W.   Rigor in data-synthesis: A case study of reliability in meta-analysis. *Educational Researcher,* 11 (1982), 10–14, 20.

STRUBE, M.J.   The application of meta-analysis to cross-cultural comparisons: Sex differences in child competitiveness. *Journal of Cross Cultural Psychology,* 12 (1981), 3–20.

VATZA, E.J., BYATT, S.E., KAY, E.J., KERCHNER, M., RICHTER, M.L., and SEAY, M.B.   Comment on "Combining results of independent studies." *Psychological Bulletin,* 88 (1980), 494–495.

WALBERG, H.J., and HAERTEL, E.H. (eds.)   Research integration: The state of the art. *Evaluation in Education,* 4 (1980), 1–142.

WILLIAMS, P.A., HAERTEL, E.H., HAERTEL, G.D., and WALBERG, H.J.   The impact of leisure-time television on school learning: A research synthesis. *American Educational Research Journal,* 19 (1982), 19–50.

WILSON, V.L.   The variance accounted for in meta-analysis of psychotherapy outcomes. *American Psychologist,* 35 (1980), 467.

WILSON, V.L., and PUTNAM, R.R.   A meta-analysis of pretest sensitization effects in experimental design. *American Educational Research Journal,* 19 (1982), 249–258.

ZEIGLER, E.F.   Past, present and future development of physical education and sport. In M. Gladys Scott (ed.), *Issues and challenges: A kaleidoscope of change.* Washington, D.C.: American Academy of Physical Education, 1979, 9–19.

CHAPTER TWENTY-ONE
USING COMPUTERS IN RESEARCH IN PHYSICAL EDUCATION

The age of computers is upon us. Children in elementary schools are becoming computer literate. In some schools, such as Carnegie-Mellon Institute, computers are a necessary tool for coursework. And computer prices have been dropping dramatically: a stripped-down microcomputer can be had for what a sophisticated calculator cost a few years ago—$100 or less.

Unfortunately, manufacturers' claims to the contrary, the average person cannot take a computer home, plug it in, and be up and running within the hour. Learning to use a computer takes time. It is not the purpose of this chapter to teach you how to use a computer; rather the intent is to show you what computers can do, using some programs as illustration, and to explore the potential for computing in research in physical education. This includes action research (the daily data collection and summarization that is part of every teacher's job) as well as experimental research, literature search, data analysis, report writing, and interfacing with a mainframe computer in order to use more powerful statistical packages like SPSS, BMDP, and SAS. In addition, some terminology will be introduced to ease your transition into the computer age.

COMPUTER LITERACY

Computer literacy entails some fundamental understanding of what computers do and how they do it. It is not merely feeling comfortable in using computers. In truth we all use computers every day—in appliances, cars, toys, video games, phones, radios, TVs, and such. Microchips in such devices enable them to do seemingly intelligent things, such as redial busy numbers, forward calls, change channels at a specified time, and speak. These uses do not make us computer literate, because the microchips and special circuitry are "transparent to the user"—we use them but don't know they are there. Some observers argue that specific instruction in computing is unnecessary, because soon home computers will be programmed, as some dedicated devices already are, so that people will use them as tools much in the way that they use their automobiles. Apple Computer, for example, has designed its Macintosh to be significantly more "user friendly" than any other computer currently on the market.

Suhor (1983) uses the example of the automobile to warn educators against embracing the computer as the central focus of educational curricula. A brief section from his article will make the point:

> The implications of the automobile for education are mindboggling. And yet it is clear that our schools are not preparing students for the world in which they will live. This is especially ironic, because young people seem to have a natural affinity toward cars, far outstripping their parents in openmindedness and eagerness to learn. The curriculum must be drastically overhauled to serve the new car-rich environment.
>
> Here are some moves that must be implemented immediately: mandatory courses in car maintenance and repair, . . . in reading programs emphasis on rapid decoding of street signs, traffic markers, . . . in mathematics, emphasis on auto economics—calculation of miles between communities, miles per gallon, . . . in the sciences, on the complex principles of physics and chemistry involved in the workings of the automobile. (pp. 30–31)

What is probable is that, as they do with the automobile, people will interact with computers at different levels. Some will be *aware* of computers and will be able to differentiate computer hardware and software, use both, and understand the implications of computer technology. Others will have an *applications* knowledge of computers; they will be able to evaluate hardware and software for use in particular situations, understand what computers can and cannot do, assist students in using computers, integrate computers into instruction, locate sources of information on computer hardware and software, and counsel students regarding career opportunities in computing. Finally, fewer individuals will have a *programming* knowledge of computers. They will have all the competencies mentioned and in addition be able to write applications programs for use in computer-assisted learning and computer-managed learning, assist students in writing and debugging programs, teach courses on programming, and utilize peripheral devices.

It has been suggested that a computer literacy course for teachers include the following units: computer operations; computer literacy strands (history, concepts, process, applications); incorporation of the computer into the curriculum; educational applications of the computer; computer programs; and development of problem solving/logical thinking skills (Dearborn, 1983).

Computers have the potential to influence positively what we do in physical education and sport (and already are exerting this influence, as we shall see later in the chapter). It is important, however, that we control the uses of the computer in education rather than the reverse. In order to control we must understand. We must be able to make reasonable decisions based on information. That is part of what this chapter is about.

SOME USEFUL TERMINOLOGY

BASIC An abbreviation for Beginners' All-purpose Symbolic Instruction Code. A high-level user-oriented language.

Binary The number system with a base of two. This system uses only the digits 0 or 1. It is used to code (represent) letters, numbers, in the computer, using positive or negative electrical charges. (See *Byte*)

Bit A binary digit. A single character in a binary number.

Byte A contiguous set of bits acted on as a unit—that is, an 8-bit or 6-bit byte. Each position represents a power of 2. Numbers can be represented as indicated in the 4-bit chart below (1 = on; 0 = off). The decimal number 1 is represented by the binary number 0001—zero 8's plus zero 4's plus zero 2's plus one 1. The decimal number 15 is represented by the binary number 1111—one 8 plus one 4 plus one 2 plus one 1.

DECIMAL NUMBER	(8) 2^3	(4) 2^2	(2) 2^1	(1) 2^0
1	0	0	0	1
2	0	0	1	0
3	0	0	1	1
4	0	1	0	0
5	0	1	0	1
6	0	1	1	0
7	0	1	1	1
8	1	0	0	0
9	1	0	0	1
10	1	0	1	0
11	1	0	1	1
12	1	1	0	0
13	1	1	0	1
14	1	1	1	0
15	1	1	1	1

Card reader An input device that enables information to be transmitted to the computer via punched cards.

Central processing unit Sometimes abbreviated CPU, this is the working unit of the computer. It follows the instructions provided by a program and executes them as interpreted.

Command mode   This mode allows the user to instruct the computer to carry out various operations.

Compiler   A computer program which translates the program you write, using a high-level language like FORTRAN, COBOL, PL-1, BASIC, into a machine-language program.

Computer   A device capable of accepting information, processing it, and supplying the results. Usually consists of input device, central processor, output device, and storage unit.

Computer-assisted instruction   Interaction of the student with the computer according to a preprogrammed plan.

Data   The information which the computer works on; input.

Debugging   The process of detecting, locating, and removing errors from a computer program.

Disk   A magnetic storage unit which can store programs and data for future use.

Error messages   Messages generated by the system with regard to programming errors made by the operator.

Flowchart   A formal representation of the sequence and logic of operations you wish the program to perform. Used as a preliminary step in structuring the program.

FORTRAN   A programming language originally conceived for use in science and mathematical operations. Acronym for Formula Translation.

Hard copy   A printed copy of computer output.

Hardware   The electronic, electric, and mechanical equipment used to process data.

Input   Information to be transferred into the computer via an input device such as a card reader, terminal with keyboard, disk reader.

Input routine   That portion of the program which contains instructions on reading or inputting data.

Instruction   A statement, usually in a program, which calls for a specific computer operation.

Iterate   To repeat the same series of steps until a predetermined point is reached; to loop.

Output   The final results provided by the computer after processing. The device used to present the final results to the user.

Printer   An output device which prints results on paper (hard copy). Letter-quality printers may be desired for word-processing functions.

Program   The plan and instructions used to produce the desired results. Usually consists of an input routine, a processing routine, and an output routine.

RAM (Random-Access Memory)   A storage area that contains instructions for the particular task to be performed. These are entered from the keyboard or a disk and are lost when the power is turned off. To save your programs they must be permanently stored on a disk.

ROM (Read-Only Memory)   A storage area that contains the instructions for starting up the computer. This is a permanent memory; its contents are not erased when the power is turned off. The number of "built-in" functions a machine has affects the size of ROM needed. A machine advertised as having 48K memory may use as much as 10K or more of that for ROM, leaving a usable memory (RAM) of only 38K.

Routine   A sequence of machine instructions which carry out a specific processing function. May also be a program routine.

Software   The collection of programs and specific instructions used to solve problems with a computer.

Subroutine   A routine that is used repeatedly throughout a program and thus is accessed from different sections of the program as necessary. For example, a study involving timing of responses might use a subroutine to read a clock at various times in the program execution. Thus, rather than repeating the set of instructions each time, a subroutine is accessed.

Terminal   A device, connected to a computer, which may be used to send/ receive input and output from a remote or adjacent location. Typically phone lines are used to transmit data from one location to another.

Word processing   The use of computers, or specialized equipment, to input, process, and output text materials. The key element in word processing with computers is software. (See the discussion in the chapter for further information.)

A LITTLE BACKGROUND

Since many persons are unfamiliar with computers and how they work, a short introduction is in order. Most of the background will relate to microcomputers, since they are similar to larger systems but are easier to explain. The simplest computer system consists of an input device (keyboard), a processing device (central processing unit), and an output device (monitor). The central processing unit consists of both ROM (read-only memory) and RAM (random-access memory). The ROM contains permanently stored information for starting up the computer. The RAM is cleared each time the machine is turned off, and we must reset it each time the machine is activated by loading a program. The program has the effect of setting the RAM to do what you want it to do. If you were to write a program to calculate the average of a set of scores and type the program into the computer, it would reside in RAM. If you used the program to calculate the averages for a class and then shut the machine off, the program you wrote would be erased from RAM, so next time you wished to use that program you would have to type it in again after you activated the computer. To avoid having to do this, it is useful to have a means for saving programs which you wish to use again and again. There are two ways to do this: on floppy dish or on magnetic tape. Disk systems are much faster, more reliable, and easier to use.

A disk system uses a control card and one or more disk drives, devices which "read" the magnetic signals on the disk and transfer the information to the RAM. This system enables you to store programs which you write or purchase for repeated use. It also enables the storage of data for later analysis.

Another added device is a printer. This enables you to obtain hard copy of your programs, data, program output, texts, and reports. The printer also requires a control card to provide an interface between the computer and the external device. Some machines require that you install additional "interface cards," and some machines have the control devices included. (Microcomputers which come with many of the interface capabilities "wired in" will have less RAM because these functions are in ROM. Thus, a computer which begins with 64K memory and has the interface capability for printers, modems, and other peripheral devices will have less useable memory, RAM, for you to access than one in which you must add the interface cards.)

Another added device is a modem or coupler. This enables you to use your computer as a terminal to communicate with other computers or with data services such as The Source or Dialog. In many cases the same interface card (a serial interface) which the printer uses will also be sufficient for the coupler.

Other devices include game paddles, a joystick, a light pen, a mouse, a graphics tablet, a clock, a digitizer, an analog-to-digital converter, and an 80-column card. A cursory glance at the ads in any popular computer magazine (such as *Byte, Creative Computing,* or *Personal Computing*) will reveal many other possible additions.

How It Works

The heart of any computer is the central processing system (CPU). This is the system which controls all operations. The computer logic is based on Boolean logic. This system uses three logical operators: AND, OR, and NOT.

> AND: X AND Y is TRUE if both X and Y are TRUE; otherwise it is FALSE.
> OR: X OR Y is TRUE if X is TRUE or if Y is TRUE or if both are TRUE; otherwise it is FALSE.
> NOT: Not X is TRUE if X is FALSE; otherwise it is FALSE.

This logic system can be simulated using a binary code—a code based on sequences of 0's and 1's, which the computer represents as sequences of switches that are off or on; thus, the computer can use this system to perform logical operations.

The computer is made up of bits, on-off switches, which are organized into bytes. Each byte may be made up of 8 or 16 bits, giving rise to the label of 8-bit machine or 16-bit machine. The Apple II Plus, for example is an 8-bit machine, while the IBM PC is a 16-bit machine. This means that the IBM PC is about twice as fast as the Apple II Plus.

Hardware vs. Software

It is useful to think about the computer system as being made up of hardware and software. The hardware is the physical machine and the peripheral devices connected to it. The software is the programs, the instructions that control the machine and make it do your bidding. The human body might be used as an analogy: Your bones, muscles, tendons, and joints might be thought of as your hardware, and the commands your brain issues to control the action of these components the software. To carry the analogy further, at times you may issue commands (software) to your muscles, tendons, and joints (hardware) to perform a particular action, but what comes out is not quite what you intended. The probability is that your program was incorrect in some way. Thus, your body did what it was told, rather than what you intended. So too with the computer. In an issue of *Science 82* the following complaint was quoted:

> I really hate this damn machine
> I wish that they would sell it
> It never does quite what I want
> But only what I tell it.

What Is a Program?

In order to get the computer to do useful things, you must use a program—one that you write or one that has been written by someone else. A program is a set of logical instructions which contains a section for getting input into the computer, a section which tells the computer what to do with the input, and a section for indicating what to do with the output. A simple program is illustrated below:

```
10 Input "What is your grade for exam 1? "; E1
20 Input "What is your grade for exam 2? "; E2
30 Input "What is your grade for exam 3? "; E3
40 TTL=E1 + E2 + E3
50 Print "The total of your grades is: "; TTL
60 AVG=TTL/3
70 Print "The average of your grades is: "; AVG
80 End
```

Instructions 10, 20, and 30 request that the student enter the grade received on each of three examinations. Instruction 40 causes the computer to add the numbers in variables E1, E2, and E3 and put them into a variable TTL. Instruction 50 prints the statement in quotes and then prints whatever is in TTL. Instruction 60 divides the number in TTL by 3 and then puts that into a variable AVG. Finally, instruction 70 prints the statement in quotes and then prints whatever is in AVG. Instruction 80 tells the computer that the main part of the program is ended. (This is useful when there are subroutines—repetitive sets of instructions—which are accessed by the main program.

Programs are written in different languages, each having its own syntax and grammar. Each machine, such as the Apple II Plus or the IBM PC or the Commodore 64 or the TRS-80, has its own machine language, the binary

TABLE 21.1:   Overview of Programming Languages

LANGUAGE	EASE OF PROGRAM CREATION AND EDITING	EXECUTION SPEED	APPLICATIONS AND FEATURES
BASIC	Excellent	Slow	General
Compiled BASIC	Excellent	Fast	General
Pascal	Good	Fast	General and excellent graphics
FORTRAN	Good	Fast	General and number crunching
Forth	Average	Very fast	High-speed tasks
Assembler or machine	Poor	Fastest	High-speed tasks

Reprinted with permission from Richards and Engelhorn, 1983, p. 19.

electrical code of 0's and 1's used to represent elementary computer operations. In order to communicate with the computer, you must communicate with a compiler, which translates your instructions into machine language. In the early days of computing, programmers used what are referred to as *low-level languages,* instructions which are translated directly into machine language. Currently available languages, such as BASIC, COBOL, and FORTRAN, are called *high-level languages;* they are easier for humans to use but harder for the computer to translate, via compiler, into machine-language code. It also takes longer for high-level instructions to be translated. Thus, where speed is required, programmers will sometimes program in *assembler.* For reaction-time programs, for example, assembler might be a more effective language to use. An overview of programming languages (Richards and Engelhorn, 1983) is presented as Table 21.1.

Summary

This section has presented a brief overview of the computer system and an introduction to how the computer works. Since most of you probably will be using the computer as a tool and will be more concerned about communicating your needs to specialists who can assist you, the remainder of this chapter takes an applied approach to computing by introducing you to what computers can do and how they can be used to maximize your own research efforts.

USING COMPUTERS IN LITERATURE SEARCH

Research in physical education and sport is proliferating at an astounding pace. Simply considering the number of scientific journals boggles the mind:

. . . the number of scientific journals has increased from 1 in 1665 to over 100,000 today. The number of scientific papers published annually has doubled every 12–15 years for the past 250 years. If science continues to grow at this current rate, 1 million scientific journals will be available by the end of the century. (Kulik, Kulik and Cohen, 1979, p. 307)

These remarks refer to published papers. What about theses, dissertations, papers presented at conferences, monographs, books, ERIC, and so on? It seems clear that a thorough literature review will *require* that the reviewer employ computerized search procedures. The need for access to literature is being treated through a number of sources: ISI (Institute for Scientific Information), which publishes *Current Contents* and *Science Citation Index,* in addition to *ASCATOPICS,* specific summaries on areas of interest in research; SRI (Sport and Recreation Index); PE/SI (Physical Education/Sports Index); PF/SM (Physical Fitness/Sports Medicine); Dissertation Abstracts International (DATRIX); and SIRLS (System of Information Retrieval for Leisure and Sport). While these sources are created with the assistance of available computerized retrieval systems, you can mount an individualized computer search on your own through access to *Lockheed Dialog* and *Medlars.* These systems provide access to over 100 databases and can, in a relatively short period, provide information about journal articles, books, conference papers, dissertations, and research abstracts.

While use of computer data bases for information retrieval is appealing, effective and efficient use does involve learning. As the system user you must supply certain information to delimit or specify the search. You might wish to access information from books, periodicals, reports, dissertations, conference proceedings, newspaper articles, or other sources. You can select on the basis of subject, author, keywords, combinations of keywords, specific data base, specialities, specific phrases or terms, or other items.

Hall and Brown (1981) have suggested that bibliographic data bases provide an on-line knowledge pool. On-line retrieval has the potential to become a powerful tool when used appropriately and to full advantage. These authors state:

Increasingly, the data base and on-line industries are becoming more ready and technically able to respond to the needs of everyday users. The individual technologies will improve, and in the future will no doubt offer further enhancements: storage in even more compact devices; full-text data bases, more reliable telecommunications, improved and more standardized access protocols, better access terminals, routine retrieval via domestic television receivers, and so on. For the present, however, it can truly be said that information retrieval from on-line data bases is now so powerful it can be considered a mature tool of the information age.

On-line retrieval can closely approach the desirable ideal of putting the inquirer instantly in touch with a substantial part of mankind's collective memory.

Stoan (1982) also believes that all researchers should become familiar with online searching and its potential for their teaching and for their research. He provides a good summary of the procedures for conducting a literature search. Briefly:

1. To use an online service
   a) user must subscribe to a communications service which inter-faces between the user and the database (e.g. Tymshare, Telenet).
   b) user must have a terminal with an acoustic coupler.
   c) user must be trained in appropriate language.
   d) user must have telephone number.
   e) user must have a password.
2. Once online
   a) user selects file to be used.
   b) user conducts search by using any or a combination of the following:
      1. author
      2. title words
      3. journal name
      4. year of publication
      5. descriptors (keywords)
      6. words in the text of abstract
      7. language
      8. document type (e.g. book, article, government publication)
      9. others, which vary

The plus in the computer search is that the user can employ combinations of factors in "and," "or," and "not" relationships. Suppose, for example, that you are interested in articles on reaction time but only those which used children as subjects. You could search for all articles in which reaction time *and* children were descriptors. You might employ "or" in a search to access articles that deal with coincidence-anticipation, knowing that many different labels are used to describe this behavior. You would therefore ask for articles with descriptors of coincident timing, or coincidence-anticipation, or coincidence anticipation, or timing, or transit reaction, or perceptual anticipation.

Often authors choose their own descriptors, and some may lack descriptiveness. We can broaden the search by looking for words in the abstract or title. Stoan refers to this as a dirty search and indicates that it usually gives about a 60% relevance rate in contrast to a clean search, with an average relevance rate of 88%. In the latter search, however, the researcher may lose potentially useful citations.

Different searchers and searches may yield different results because of (1) use of a clean, dirty, or combination search; (2) choice of data-base file; (3) strategy used by the searcher: "The computer yields only what the online searcher has been skillful enough to draw out with the available search keys."

Stoan provides a concise analysis of the positive and negative aspects of online searches:

> Computer searching, then, though it can be of supplemental value to research in any discipline, assumes an approach to research based solely on the "rational." In it, scholars and students find little or no room for browsing and serendipitous discovery that exists with print indexes, imperfect as they are. It does not provide the broad education in the discipline that print indexes do. It assumes a precision in definition and an accuracy in assigning descriptors that often do not exist. It can be useful in tracking down citations of value, but it is only one more technique to be added to the broad array of approaches used by the research scholar. Improperly used, it could pose real dangers to the world of scholarship and teaching. (p. 15)

USING COMPUTERS TO DO RESEARCH

A key concept in experimental design is control. One aspect of control is that achieved during the experiment itself. The procedures used for each subject should be as nearly identical as possible, differing only in regard to the specific treatment(s). Another aspect relates to measurement of the dependent variable. Measurements should differ in response to the treatment variable only; random variation or error in measurement due to errors in observation or recording should be avoided. Computers can be used to control the experimental situation, and, because these devices are specialized for carrying out repetitive operations without error (if programmed properly and tested adequately), high levels of experimental control can be readily achieved. Some ways in which computers have been and could be used in research are:

> To vary the warning interval and record reaction time to combinations of visual and auditory signals.
>
> To produce simulated motion and measure coincidence-anticipation performance.
>
> To determine psychophysical thresholds.
>
> To measure movement time for total movements or segments of movements.
>
> To vary aspects of a movement, such as angle of release of an object, and determine the effect that such variation will have on the outcome.
>
> To monitor and control environmental conditions relative to temperature, humidity, and altitude in physiological studies.
>
> To identify the common elements in a variety of successful performances by high-level athletes.
>
> To totally control onset and offset of experimental procedures, even in the

absence of the researcher, as in a study where initiation of successive exercise bouts is determined by the pulse rate of the subject.

To measure movement extents, locations, and durations in two- and three-dimensional space using digitizers, electrogoniometers, motion analyzers.

To simulate limb motion through stimulation of motor neurons via external or implanted electrodes (Wright State University work with quadriplegics).

To monitor subject performance of single motor unit firing and to administer visual and auditory feedback re: performance.

To administer feedback in connection with biofeedback studies.

To record performance and provide feedback based on that performance based on parameters such as specificity of feedback, sensory channel (visual, auditory, tactile), number of trials summarized, and so on.

To monitor and control workload according to physiological measures of exercise intensity.

To administer feedback to high-level athletes relative to the kinematics of their movements, including information about speed, direction, acceleration, deceleration, accuracy, consistency over trials.

To record kinematics of movement for the same subject under varying external conditions and as learning proceeds.

To analyze the kinematics associated with high-level performance.

To administer, record, score, and store psychological test data.

To design curricula or courses.

To administer, record, score, and store psychomotor performance data.

To conduct social psychology studies involving games stressing co-acting, interacting, and parallel acting.

To study the effects of cooperation and competition alone and in groups on performance.

The studies that can be conducted totally by the computer or with the assistance of the computer are limited only by the imagination of the researcher, the capability of the programmer, and the availability of funds. (Additional uses are presented in a special feature in the *Journal of Physical Education, Recreation, and Dance,* November–December 1983.) We have noted that the degree to which the results of research can be generalized to other populations, other settings, and other tasks is of considerable interest in determining the external validity of the study. As yet, few studies have been conducted to determine whether the results of studies conducted with the aid of computers are correlated with the results of similar studies conducted using traditional methods. An interesting set of studies could involve using a computer-controlled coincidence-anticipation task, a Bassin Timer (Lafayette Instruments), a batting task, and batting averages to measure coincidence-anticipation performance under various conditions and then determining whether the results of the various tasks were correlated. (One of the demonstration programs included in this chapter tests coincidence-anticipation performance.)

Although psychological research involving testing using various scales seems natural for computerization, there is a potential problem involving copyright. Someone who uses psychological tests such as Catell's 16 Personality Factor, Bem's Sex Role Inventory (BSRI), Spence and Helmrich's PAQ, or Rotter's I-E scale generally obtains a copy or copies of the scale from the author of the scale or from the company which publishes the test. It would seem then that anyone wishing to use a computerized version of the test would have to obtain permission. Another problem concerns the format of the test. Most psychological tests are scored with the notion that the subject reads each question once and answers it. In reality, written tests give the subject the opportunity (unless like the SAT test, they are structured otherwise) to go back to previous items later in the test. Computerized versions of the test do not permit this behavior and so may be more like what the test designer originally intended. As in the case of the coincidence-anticipation studies, research which correlates the paper-and-pencil version of the psychological scale with the coputerized version must be completed to see whether the results are comparable. (A computerized version of the BSRI is included here.)

Computers
in Biomechanics Research

A recent article (Stewart, 1982), "Coached by computer," describes the techniques which Gideon Ariel (Computerized Biomechanical Analysis, Inc.) uses in biomechanics research and application. "He uses cameras, digitizers, magnetic pens and computer graphics to . . . record and quantify dynamic factors affecting athletic performance." (p. 34) In brief his use of the computer in analysis of the biomechanics of movement involves:

1. Filming the athlete with high-speed cameras from two or more angles;
2. Projecting films on a digitizing screen and tracing the limbs frame by frame with a magnetic pen;
3. Using a computer to process the information;
4. Producing a simulated three-dimensional stick figure on a graphics terminal; and
5. Quantifying forces, angles, velocities, and distances.

The computer can turn and rotate the image, simulating viewing from any vantage point. In addition, the computer can simulate changes in the athletes technique and evaluate the effect of the change on the force, angle velocity, and distance.

The article describes a biophysics program which Ariel uses to scientifically recruit top athletes by analyzing an individual's reaction to certain conditions. It also points out that he has amassed floppy-disk "recordings" of Jack Nicklaus, Jimmy Connors, Bill Rodgers, and Muhammed Ali. He has developed a computerized technique called "formation analysis" which has potential application to team sports. In the world of biomechanical application of computer technology Gideon Ariel is a forerunner.

Miller (1975) considers the topic of computer simulation. She indicates that computers may be used in statistical fashion with actual data to provide evidence on questions such as: "Do left-handed batters have a greater probability of obtaining a hit off right-handed pitchers than do right-handed batters?" "What is the relationship between the score in a particular inning and winning the game?" These types of questions were considered in Chapter 20, so we will not consider them further here.

Another type of simulation treats the athlete as a linked system and considers either external forces as they act on the system, or internal forces, or a combination of both. Miller (1971) used computer simulation to develop a mathematical model that defined the "position and orientation of the body during the flight portion of a dive." She was able to use the model to investigate how the total performance of the dive would be affected by altering body proportions, initial conditions, and limb movements. The computer output involved numerical values as well as three-dimensional graphic display of the diver.

Similar simulations have been used to investigate: the golf swing (Cochran and Stobbs, 1968; Jorgensen, 1970; Williams, 1967), swimming (Gallenstein and Huston, 1973; Seireg and Baz, 1971), long jump (Ramey, 1973; 1972), sprinting (Dillman, 1971), weight lifting (Chaffin, 1969), downhill skiing (Quigley and Chaffin, 1971), and locomotion. The application of the considerable work on locomotion was demonstrated on the TV show, "60 Minutes," when a quadriplegic, Nan Davis, walked with the aid of braces, a harness, and a computer program which created the appropriate sequence of electrical impulses to simulate walking behavior. These impulses were transmitted through surface electrodes to the muscles of the leg. Researchers have investigated the possibility of teaching movement through activation of muscles, but this research is still embryonic.

Initially, this simulation required more memory than is currently available in personal computers. However, an article in *Science82* (Menosky, 1982) reports on efforts to enable dancers to (1) notate, using labonotation, a dance as fast as they can type it into a computer; (2) print a copy of the score to study; (3) reproduce copies as needed; and (4) transform the score into a graphic display of movement using a silhouette figure; a stick figure; a bubble man or woman, a figure of overlapping spheres; or a sausage woman, a figure of overlapping ellipsoids. There are difficulties with regard to the look of the movements, but these may be resolved, since the technology is currently in use in animation and the interest in extending the technology to dance is high.

A special feature on computers and dance edited by Gray (1983) reviews applications in recording and analyzing dance-teacher behaviors (Gray, 1983); notating dance (Sealy, 1983); animating dance, as in the computer animation of a character in Twyla Tharp's "The Catherine Wheel" (Allen, 1983);

simulating dance composition and choreography (Boettcher, 1983); and quantifying dance criticism (Alter, 1983).

Computers in Exercise Physiology Research

Computers are ideally suited for research in exercise physiology. They can be used to precisely control experimental conditions, to simultaneously record multiple measures from subjects, to simulate change in physiological parameters or work output under various conditions, to vary workload in accordance with a subject's response, and to reduce various data to composite scores. Most of the interesting uses in exercise physiology, however, demand the capability to interface peripheral equipment. This means that the external signal, such as blood pressure, must be transformed so that the computer can understand it, and that the transformed signal be transmitted to the computer for processing. The type of interface unit commonly used to do this is an analog-to-digital converter (ADC).

An ADC is an input device that supplies instantaneous digital readings from some continuous variable. As an example, consider the galvanic skin response (GSR), which produces a continuous voltage. The ADC can take 60,000 readings per second, which are conveyed as binary numbers to the central processing unit. The values conveyed to the computer are proportional to the voltage. Respiration rate and pulse rate may be transformed into electrical signals by mechanical means, since they are already digital signals, and the computer can merely count the number of signals per unit time. The majority of researchers know what they need to do for their research design and would like to make maximal use of computers, but they need the services of a good technician to solve the problem of getting the signal into the computer.

Another problem the researcher faces relates to the priority of the measures. In a study in which a subject's heart rate is the signal to change the workload (reduce workload if above a certain level, raise workload if below a certain level), heart rate would have the first priority for monitoring so that changes in it have a maximal chance of detection. Other measures (blood pressure, respiration rate, EKG) would be given a lower priority.

In a simpler example, the computer can be used to calculate a subject's body fat percentage based on skinfold or circumference measures. A program might prompt the subject or researcher by asking for the measurements at the required sites and the sex of the subject, calculate the percentage of body fat by using the appropriate formula, and then print out the percentage of body fat with some appropriate comment. Or a computer might tell a student the percentile rank for particular performance items on a physical fitness test and prescribe an exercise regimen based on the subject's composite index (see Donnelly, 1983).

A computer, with appropriate peripheral devices and interfaces, might even be used to monitor minute-to-minute changes in lactic acid levels in muscle tissue or carbon monoxide levels in exhaled air. It is even reasonable to imagine that a cross-country runner might wear a microprocessor in a pack during a long-distance run or marathon and that this microprocessor would record various physiological parameters during the course of the race. At the end of the race the pack could be turned in and the data read directly into a microcomputer, which would process the data minute by minute.

Computers in Motor Learning Research

The availability of programs for use in motor learning research is much greater than for some other areas. Programs have been developed, for example, to measure memory, perception, reaction time, choice reaction time serial learning, coincidence-anticipation, psychometrics, feedback, and error analysis. In addition, with the exception of serial learning, most of the areas can be studied without the use of peripheral equipment, thus simplifying the task of programming.

A feature in the *Journal of Physical Education and Recreation* provides specific examples of the use of the computer in motor learning research (Engelhorn, 1983). The beauty of using the computer is that the experimental conditions are exactly the same for each subject, since the computer controls the conditions, which are written into the program, and the computer records the data. Thus, the possibility of error is much less than if the experimenter or research assistant controls the conditions and reads and records the data.

Lest all seem too simple, I must report an unfortunate incident which has made me more careful and will reinforce some recommendations I have to make. The particular coincidence-anticipation program which was in use does not provide feedback to the subject or to the researcher during the experiment. The student researcher, having had a particularly good day in getting subjects, was able to test the last five or six needed to complete the study. After all had been tested, the student dutifully submitted the disk to me so that I could return a printed copy of the names of the subjects with the stimulus speeds and error scores for each trial. In printing out the data I noticed that there were only two values of scores, 0 or −.066. This is highly improbable, and I wondered what could have gone wrong. It became clear to me that the clock had not been running and that, because the student had neglected to run a simple test before initiating the experiment, the whole session had been wasted and another five or six subjects had to be located.

If you look at the program which controls this experiment presented in Appendix B1, you will see that the instruction in line 370 indicates that if a variable called FLAG = 0 and the value of a particular location which indicates whether a key has been pressed (PEEK −16384) is more than 127, then the program control passes to instruction 570, the subject's response, which reads the clock. When the control returns, the variable FLAG is set to 1. In statement 400 we see that if the variable FLAG is equal to 1, the subject's response time (T3IME) is reduced by .066. This is because it takes that long for the program to cycle from control of the line to reading the clock and back again, causing the total travel time (T2IME) to be .066 too long. If the subject's response occurs after the line has passed the barrier (see 410), the clock time has already been read for the T2IME, statement 390, and the score will be 0 if the clock is not running. Thus, scores of 0 and −.066 indicate only that a subject was early, or late or on time. It would have been possible to use a nonparametric test to analyze these data (for example, a two-way chi-square test for speed by early/late response).

Since this unfortunate occurrence, the experimenter is instructed to ascertain whether the clock is running before testing subjects for the day by typing the instruction "IN#4." This instructs the computer to input the information from the device in slot #4 to the screen. The information includes the month, date, hour, minutes, and seconds. If the seconds do not change row by row, then the clock is not working, and a special program can be run to correct that situation. In addition, it is possible to have a separate source of power to the clock so that it runs continuously, even when the computer is off. This reduces the possibility that the same problem will recur.

Clearly the best strategy for any research effort is to have a mini-program that can be run prior to the day's testing to see whether the system is operating properly. Much frustration, time, and effort will be saved.

Use of Computers
in Sport Psychology

A use of computers in sport psychology mentioned earlier, which is illustrated by the program for the administration of the Bem Sex Role Inventory, is that of psychological testing. Several articles (Johnson, 1981; Katz and Dalby, 1981a, 1981b; Marshall-Goodell and others, 1981) indicate that the correlation between paper-and-pencil administrations and computerized administrations of a number of psychological tests is high.

In addition, the computer can provide for multiple time-keyed recording of data during an experiment. That is, the particular conditions created (such as levels of stress) and measurements obtained (such as GSR, performance scores) can be keyed to a time scale. It is also possible to create programs in which two or more individuals or groups interact or coact in competitive or cooperative fashion. The success or failure of individuals could be manipulated.

The recording of data in field-based studies would be simpler if the computer were used as a recording device in a manner similar to that described for recording dance. Interactions between team members, between coaches and players, between coaches, between coaches and referees, between referees and players, as well as audience behaviors and player performance could be coded using various observation instruments keyed to computerized recording. Some suggestions are given in the next section.

Descriptive Analytic Research on Teaching

The purpose of descriptive analytic research on teaching is to describe teacher behavior under classroom/gymnasium conditions. One of the first scales to be used was the Flander's Interaction Analysis System. This instrument codes 10 categories of verbal behavior. It could easily be adapted to a computerized recording scheme, and, if timed entries were desired, the computer could signal the recorder through an audio signal to enter the next behavior. If, as with some systems, entries are necessary at each behavior change and/or every five seconds, the computer could time the entries as desired. Many of the instruments developed and used at Columbia University Teachers College (Anderson and Barrette, 1978) could be computerized for use in the classroom or with videotape recordings from the data bank. A system developed at Arizona State University uses a computerized system to record coaches' behavior and is very successful.

It would be possible, of course, to code more than one dimension at a time. It might also be possible to use the computer to track student or teacher movement in the gymnasium and to use a timing signal to match the various aspects, teacher/student movement, teacher/student behavior for analysis.

USING THE COMPUTER IN ANALYZING THE RESULTS OF RESEARCH

The very first use of computerlike devices was in 1801 to direct looms for weaving of cloth. The earliest use for analysis and compilation of data was in the 1890 census. This involved the use of key punch machines, card sorters, tabulating machines, and other equipment. Early machines were massive and extremely slow, since they worked with the aid of vacuum tubes. Not until the recent development of electronic chips with large-scale integrated circuits did home microcomputers became feasible. (Memory size in computers is generally measured in bytes. Thus a computer might be said to have 48K memory; this is 48,000 bytes. Chips are currently available which can store 64K.) Most electronic games are run by a single chip that controls the game, aided by additional chips which may control the graphics and the audio.

The primary use for computers is in number crunching. They quickly, accurately, and effectively reduce masses of data to manageable size (see also Mayhew and Rankin, 1983). The availability of computers for data analysis has both positive and negative aspects. The positive aspect relates to the ability of researchers to design more complex and realistic experiments in which more dependent measures are taken. The negative aspect is that when research designs become overly complex, explanation may become virtually impossible. This is particularly true when a complex design yields high-level interactions. The Williams (1968) example cited in our discussion of research design illustrates the difficulties encountered when many of the experimental variables interact.

Computer capability enables researchers and students to concentrate on understanding what the statistical results mean and on the interpretation and application of results. It is important to be aware, however, particularly in cases where the computer administers the experiment, records the data, and then analyzes the results, that the computer does not think or act on its own. It only does what you tell it. It does not pause to evaluate whether a particular value is reasonable (unless you tell it to do so); it merely processes whatever it receives. Researchers are encouraged to plot the individual scores to determine whether there are any outliers—scores which are lower or higher than would reasonably be expected or which are widely disparate in relation to other scores. These scores may be the result of some misunderstanding by the subject, or some lapse in attention, or possibly some malfunction in the computer or the program. The outliers obtained in studies which are fully computerized are likely to be real values (that is, the error was not in the measuring or recording of the data or in the administration of the treatment but the result of the subject's behavior—provided, of course, that the program has been fully pilot tested and debugged prior to the experiment. The researcher must decide whether these scores will be kept or discarded and must have a good reason for the decision.

Examples of programs to analyze data are provided in the appendix to this chapter. One difficulty in using a microcomputer in data analysis is that with large data sets you will quickly get an out-of-memory error. Thus, programmers need to be especially alert to the designing of programs which can take the data from disks and manipulate it as it is read. This can be particularly difficult in instances in which data must be sorted or ranked, since sort programs typically require large amounts of memory. A problem I ran into with the PAQ Analyzer program was the need to keep tabs on the scale scores (for six different scales) for each subject in the study. Also, the program was set up so that the experimenter would not have to enter the scale to which each item belonged. Thus, it was necessary to code the 40 questions for each of the subjects to be summarized. A version of the program shown in the appendix, which also had DIM statements for the scales, gave an out-of-memory error when 100 subjects were run. However, it could be used to run smaller numbers. If there were many subjects, they could be run in small sets. It is also possible to revise the program to eliminate this problem.

The development of statistical packages (generic programs which can conduct a specific statistical test on your data after you set the parameters such as the number of factors, the number of levels of each factor, the number of subjects in each treatment) for use on computers enabled researchers to quickly analyze the results of highly complex studies. These packages also became more and more sophisticated. Early analysis-of-variance programs, for example, would analyze data only in studies where the number in each group was equal. Current programs can handle unequal groups. The advent of statistical packages has also enabled highly sophisticated analyses of very complex designs (multiple correlation, multivariate analysis of variance, path analysis, factor analysis, discriminant analysis). Unfortunately, the computer does only what you instruct it to do, and so it cannot evaluate the appropriateness of the statistical test you are using or the accuracy of the data. Much hard experience lies behind the outcry: *To err is human; but to really foul things up you need a computer.*

You can conduct statistical analyses on micro- or mini-computers by using programs which are self-written or purchased, or you can access a mainframe computer, through an on-line terminal or card reader and use statistical packages such as Statistical Package for Social Science (SPSS), Biomedical Computer Programs (BMDP), Statistical Analysis System (SAS), and Multivariance. This chapter will not attempt to teach you how to run computer packages, but a brief introduction here may help you feel more comfortable in communicating with others in getting assistance. Every statistical package has an associated User Manual which describes the types of programs the package contains. After you determine the statistical program you wish to use, you instruct the computer (job control cards) that you wish to run a program and tell it what statistical package you are using and the particular program in that package you want. The job control cards will vary according to the computer system you are using.

The next portion of the program sets the parameters—that is, number of factors, levels of each, names of factors, form of the data, number of subjects in each group, research design, type of analysis, title of study, and so on.

The third portion of the program generally is the data (unless the program has been instructed to obtain the data from an existing computer file). This data must be in the same form as was indicated in the program. The computer will read only what you tell it to. The same data can read very differently when different format statements are given. A format statement for decimal numbers may read (in FORTRAN) F4.2. This indicates that the number is a floating-point number, that four spaces are taken by the number, including the decimal, and that there are two places after the decimal. The format statement 3F3.1 indicates that there are three numbers, each taking three spaces, including the decimal, with one place following the decimal. (The data need not include the decimal; the illustration below does not.) Most packages will report an error if there are fewer data than the instructions indicate but not if there are more. Thus, it is a good idea to have the program print out the data and to inspect the data to see if they are what you intended.

Data: 1234567891011121314151617181920

Format	What is read
F5.3	12.34
4F3.2	.12, .34, .56, .78
3F4.1, 2F2.0, F6.2	12.3, 45.6, 78.9, 10, 11, 12, 131.41

Can you think of one or more format statements that will cause the computer to read all the data?

Finally, all programs have job control cards that should be included at the conclusion of the data to indicate that the input is completed. (In the case of SPSS programs it is usual to place additional requests for data analysis after the actual data which are part of the program.) In order to give you an idea of the format of the actual programs and to illustrate the output which the programs provide, examples from the BMDP, SAS, and SPSS packages is included in the appendix. The actual computer output has been annotated to aid your understanding.

It was mentioned that micro- and mini-computers can also be used to analyze research data. Several programs written for the Apple II Plus computer are presented in an appendix by way of illustration. The complete program is included together with an example of the output. These programs are less flexible than the commercial statistical packages, but generally micro- and mini-computers have the advantage of quick turn-around. That is, your results are immediately available; your job is not placed in a queue for analysis and then for printing; execution and printing are immediate. A software package for micro-computers has just became available. The publisher (Wadsworth) claims that the package does all that SPSS does but on an Apple or IBM-PC. The cost is about $2000.00.

USING THE COMPUTER
FOR WORD PROCESSING

The last use to be considered here is that of word processing. The computer can be used to compose, store, edit, revise, and print various reports and papers that result from research. This book was, in fact, composed on an Apple II Plus Computer using EasyWriter Professional (a text-editing package) and a

Diablo Printer (Xerox). Word processing on a computer is not very different from typing, since the computer keyboard is the same as that of the typewriter. Most people who are introduced to the word-processing function of the computer are very quickly hooked. For one thing, errors are very easy to correct. Once an error is corrected, the mistake will not appear in the next printed draft.

Word processing calls for two important items: a text-editing package and a printer. The package is the software and the printer is an additional piece of hardware. The editing package and printer you choose depends on what you plan to do. If you merely want to produce draft copy or even to produce research papers for submission to journals, a dot-matrix printer is the least costly way to go. The dot-matrix printer produces letters by moving a boxlike component containing blunt needles in front of the ribbon, shooting out only those needles that are needed to make the desired letter or character. Early printers had rather poor-quality output but were generally less expensive and faster than letter-quality printers. Letter-quality printers use either a daisy wheel or a thimble element and produce letters much in the same way your typewriter does. In the case of a daisy wheel, for example, the wheel is rotated until the proper letter is in position; then a hammer strikes the spoke, forcing it against the ribbon and leaving an impression on the page. Letter-quality printers are more expensive and much slower than dot-matrix printers. The quality of the dot-matrix printer image has been markedly improved, and for some models only an expert could tell the difference. Another benefit of the dot-matrix printer is that the user can program it to obtain different types and sizes of printing (within limits, of course). In addition, some dot matrix printers have graphics capabilities. Thus, with appropriate software and interfaces charts, pictures, and graphs can be produced in addition to text. Whatever you decide to do, be sure to actually try the printer you intend to purchase with your computer.

Many software packages are available; a 1980 book which evaluates word-processing packages for the Apple II lists nine, and I am aware of at least six others. In choosing a software package, you need to evaluate how well it fits your application; how you move from one section of the manuscript to another in terms of speed and ease; how easy it is to insert and delete text; how easy it is to move blocks of text; whether you can search and replace text; how the text looks on the screen (do you see what will print out, or do the words wrap around?); ease of saving and revising files; ease of formatting the output; overall friendliness of the package; documentation, including the manual and the on-screen assistance; and special features such as spelling checker, mailing capability. You also need to find out whether you will require additional hardware to run a particular software program or to interface your computer with a particular printer. With a software package, as with a printer, you should try before you buy.

USING THE COMPUTER
TO ENHANCE INSTRUCTION

In addition to applications in research, the computer can be used to enhance instruction. Computer-managed learning can free the teacher to spend more time with individual students by facilitating instructional management (testing, record keeping, grading, data analysis, report writing) and can help the teacher to individualize instruction by directing student learning through instructional games, simulations, drill-and-practice, testing, and remediation. Although many packaged programs can be adapted for use in instructional management, many are difficult to use, since the user must tailor them, and the manual often is poorly written. Colleagues may have written their own programs that they are willing to share. Students may be willing to write programs for specific purposes such as analyzing bowling averages, calculating class averages on fitness tests, computing intramural standing. In addition, course-authoring languages are available which enable teachers to design computer-managed instruction.

A good overview of computer application in assisting student learning is provided by Barlow and Baylis (1983). They describe programs developed at the University of Delaware for instruction in health and nutrition, lifetime sports, anatomy and physiology, and sport science. Programs simulate muscle contraction, provide instruction in sport strategy, teach biomechanical analysis, fitness concepts, and muscle identification, and teach basic mathematics. Programs which can be used with high school students, perhaps in connection with concepts introduced in the Basic Stuff Series (National Association for Sport and Physical Education, 1981), should be developed. Physical participation in sport for learning and for the development of fitness are critical, but cognitive learning and understanding are an integral part of physical education. The use of computer-managed learning can free the teacher to provide information and feedback on a more individualized basis, while the computer individualizes instruction and feedback in areas in which it can be most effective.

A PERSONAL NOTE

Computers are not for everyone. Contrary to the current hype, there will be people who function quite well without them. Everyone is affected by computers in some way, however, and so should have an *awareness* of them. Computers have certainly made my life easier, more fun, and more challenging. They have helped me in writing this book, chapters, and articles, creating data bases, doing research, analyzing results, teaching my classes, writing reports, keeping track of students, editing and reviewing articles for journals, and creating tests. They have allowed me to play computer games (that I wouldn't play in public), made my work time more productive, put me in contact with people I might not otherwise have met, opened new areas of inquiry for me, and made my work time more interesting. The computer has also challenged and in some respects frustrated me. I want to be able to use it in more and better ways, to design new applications, to try different software packages, to be able to answer questions asked of me, to produce simulations for research that are more like reality, to control the simulations to answer more complex questions, to write programs that do what I want, to have more time to spend, to try many different computers and to be able to use them in ways I have only dreamed about.

I learned about computers from friends and colleagues and by making mistakes and having the computer correct me. Perhaps the most significant contribution of the personal computer is its provision of instant feedback. If you wonder whether a particular command will work, you try it out and know instantly whether it does or not. You can write a program and monitor its operation to determine whether it works as you intended. Commercial software is often written to provide feedback when you make an error. There is excellent software that provides computerized instruction on how to use and program personal computers. The most rapidly growing area of publishing is books on personal computers. Many journals and magazines contain program listings that you can enter and use. Most work. Some don't—and that can be frustrating. If you still fear that computing is not for you because you won't be able to learn, don't despair—computers of the future will be designed to make using them as easy as turning them on. (Perhaps you won't even have to do that much, since they can be programmed to recognize you approach, your touch, or your voice and to turn themselves on as you come near.)

Hopefully this chapter has made you more knowledgeable about computers and what they can do. The programs and the information about statistical packages are included in the appendices in order to give you someplace to start, if you want to. Computing will continue to be an important aspect of research and statistics in physical education and sport—in some areas, a critical aspect. If you don't want to get involved in computing, at least you can be a more knowledgeable user of computer services.

BIBLIOGRAPHY

ALLEN, J. F. Quantified analysis. *Journal of Physical Education, Recreation, and Dance,* **54** (1983), 38–39.

ALTER, J. F. Quantified analysis. *Journal of Physical Education, Recreation, and Dance,* **54** (1983), 41–42.

ANDERSON, W. G., and BARRETTE, G. (eds.). *What's Going on in Gym.* Newton, CT: Motor Skills: Theory into Practice, 1978.

APTER, M. J., and WESTBY, G. *The Computer in Psychology.* New York: Wiley, 1973.

BASIC STUFF SERIES. National Association for Sport and Physical Education, American Alliance for Health, Physical Education, Recreation and Dance. 1981.

BARLOW, D. A. and BAYLISS, P. A. Computer facilitated learning. *Journal of Physical Education, Recreation, and Dance* **54** (1983), 27–29.

BENEDICT, J. O., and BUTTS, B. O. Computer simulation or real experimentation: Is one better for teaching experimental design? *Teaching of Psychology,* **8** (1981), 35–37.

BOETTCHER, J. W. Dance education. *Journal of Physical Education, Recreation, and Dance,* 1983, **54,** 40.

BUSINESS WEEK. Information Processing: The coming shakeout in personal computers. November 22, 1982, 72–85.

CASTELLAN, N. J. Computers in psychology: A survey of instructional applications. *Behavior Research Methods & Instrumentation,* in press.

CHAFFIN, D. B. A computerized biomechanical model—Development of and use in studying gross body actions. *Journal of Biomechanics,* **2** (1969), 429–441.

CICCIARELLA, C. F. Enter—The microcomputer. *Journal of Physical Education, Recreation and Dance,* **52:** 6 (1981), 60–61.

COCHRAN, A., and STOBBS, J. *The Search for the Perfect Swing.* New York: Lippincott, 1968.

DEARBORN, D. E. Computer literacy. *Educational Leadership,* **41** (1983), 32–34.

DILLMAN, C. J. A kinetic analysis of the recovery leg during sprint running. In J. M. Cooper (ed.), *Selected Topics on Biomechanics.* Chicago: The Athletic Institute, 1971.

DONNELLY, J. E. Physiology and fitness testing. *Journal of Physical Education, Recreation, and Dance,* **54** (1983), 24–26.

ENGELHORN, R. Motor learning and control. *Journal of Physical Education, Recreation, and Dance,* **54** (1983), 30–32.

FRIEDMAN, P. *Computer Programs in BASIC.* Englewood Cliffs, NJ: Prentice-Hall, Inc., 1981.

GALLENSTEIN, J., and HUSTON, R. L. Analysis of swimming motions. *Human Factors,* **15** (1973), 91–98.

GRAY, J. A. Introduction. *Journal of Physical Education, Recreation, and Dance,* **54** (1983), 33.

―――― The dance teacher. *Journal of Physical Education, Recreation, and Dance,* **54** (1983), 34–35.

HALL, J. L., and BROWN, M. J. *Online Bibliographic Databases: An International Directory.* London: Aslib, 1981.

HUTTON, S. S., and HUTTON, S. R. Microcomputer data base management of bibliographic information. *Sociological Methods & Research,* **9** (1981), 461–472.

JOHNSON, M. A. The analysis of multiphasic signals with the Apple II/FIRST microprocessor system. *Behavior Research Methods & Instrumentation,* **13** (1981), 276–280.

JORGENSEN, L. On the dynamics of the swing of a golf club. *American Journal of Physics,* **38** (1970), 644–651.

KATZ, L., and DALBY, J. T. Computer and manual administration of the Eysenck Personality Inventory. *Journal of Clinical Psychology,* **37** (1981a), 586–588.

―――― Computer-assisted and traditional psychological testing of elementary-school-aged children. *Contemporary Education Psychology,* **6** (1981b), 314–322.

KULIK, J. A., KULIK, C. C., and COHEN, P. A. A meta-analysis of outcome studies of Keller's personalized system of instruction. *American Psychologist,* **34** (1979), 307–318.

LANGA, F. S. Be your own programmer. *New Shelter,* 3:7 (1982), 37–40.

LEHMAN, R. S. What simulation can do to the statistics and design course. *Behavior Research Methods and Instrumentation,* **12** (1980), 157–159.

MARSHALL-GOODELL, B.; GORMEZANO, I.; SCANDRETT, J.; and CACI-OPPO, J. T. The microcomputer in social-psychological research. *Sociological Methods & Research,* **9** (1981), 502–512.

MATSUDA, M., and MATSUDA, F. Computer application to error factor analysis in learning. *Psychologia,* **15** (1972) 167–174.

MAYHEW, J. L. and RANKIN, B. A. Date management. *Journal of Physical Education, Recreation, and Dance,* **54** (1983), 22–23.

MENOSKY, J. Video graphics and Grand Jetes. *Science82,* **3**:4 (1982), 24–33.

MILLER, D. I. Computer simulation of human motion. In D. W. Grieve, et al., *Techniques for the analysis of human movement.* Princeton, NJ: Princeton Book Company, 1975, 69–108.

—— A computer simulation model of the airbourne phase of diving. In J. M. Cooper (ed.), *Selected topics on Biomechanics.* Chicago: The Athletic Institute, 1971.

MONEY. Choosing the best computer for you. November 1982, 68–117.

QUIGLEY, B. M., and CHAFFIN, D. B. A computerized biomechanical model applied to the analysis of skiing. *Medicine and Science in Sports,* **3** (1971), 89–96.

RAMEY, M. R. The significance of angular momentum in long jumping. *Research Quarterly,* **44** (1973), 35–42.

—— Effective use of force plates for long jump studies. *Research Quarterly,* **43** (1972), 247–252.

RAWLINGS, R. The ultimate tool: But for what? *New Shelter,* **3**:7 (1982), 26–31.

RICHARDS, J. G., and ENGELHORN, R. Selecting a microcomputer. *Journal of Physical Education, Recreation, and Dance,* **54** (1983), 19–21.

SEALY, D. Computer programs for dance notation. *Journal of Physical Education, Recreation, and Dance,* **54** (1983), 36–37.

SEIREG, A., and BAZ, A. A mathematical model for swimming mechanics. In L. Lewillie and J. P. Clarys (eds.), *Proceedings of the First International Symposium on Biomechanics in Swimming.* Brussels: Université Libre de Bruxelles, 1971.

STEWART, D. M. Coached by computer. *American Way,* November 1982, 34–38.

STOAN, S. K. Computer searching: A primer for the uninformed scholar. *Academe,* **68**:6 (1982), 10–15.

SUHOR, C. Cards, Computers, and curriculum. *Educational Leadership,* **41** (1983), 30–32.

THORNE, M. P. The specification and design of educational microcomputer systems. *British Journal of Educational Technology,* **11** (1981), 178–184.

TIME. The computer moves in. **121** (1983), 12–39.

WILLIAMS, D. The dynamics of the golf swing. *Quarterly Journal of Mechanics and Applied Mathematics,* **20** (1967), 247–264.

Appendix A

TABLE A1: AREAS UNDER THE NORMAL CURVE

z	mean to z area	larger area	smaller area	z	mean to z area	larger area	smaller area
0.00	.0000	.5000	.5000	0.40	.1554	.6554	.3446
0.01	.0040	.5040	.4960	0.41	.1591	.6591	.3409
0.02	.0080	.5080	.4920	0.42	.1628	.6628	.3372
0.03	.0120	.5120	.4880	0.43	.1664	.6664	.3336
0.04	.0160	.5160	.4840	0.44	.1700	.6700	.3300
0.05	.0199	.5199	.4801	0.45	.1736	.6736	.3264
0.06	.0239	.5239	.4761	0.46	.1772	.6772	.3228
0.07	.0279	.5279	.4721	0.47	.1808	.6808	.3192
0.08	.0319	.5319	.4681	0.48	.1844	.6844	.3156
0.09	.0359	.5359	.4641	0.49	.1879	.6879	.3121
0.10	.0398	.5398	.4602	0.50	.1915	.6915	.3085
0.11	.0438	.5438	.4562	0.51	.1950	.6950	.3050
0.12	.0478	.5478	.4522	0.52	.1985	.6985	.3015
0.13	.0517	.5517	.4483	0.53	.2019	.7019	.2981
0.14	.0557	.5557	.4443	0.54	.2054	.7054	.2946
0.15	.0596	.5596	.4404	0.55	.2088	.7088	.2912
0.16	.0636	.5636	.4364	0.56	.2123	.7123	.2877
0.17	.0675	.5675	.4325	0.57	.2157	.7157	.2843
0.18	.0714	.5714	.4286	0.58	.2190	.7190	.2810
0.19	.0753	.5753	.4247	0.59	.2224	.7224	.2776
0.20	.0793	.5793	.4207	0.60	.2257	.7257	.2743
0.21	.0832	.5832	.4168	0.61	.2291	.7291	.2709
0.22	.0871	.5871	.4129	0.62	.2324	.7324	.2676
0.23	.0910	.5910	.4090	0.63	.2357	.7357	.2643
0.24	.0948	.5948	.4052	0.64	.2389	.7389	.2611
0.25	.0987	.5987	.4013	0.65	.2422	.7422	.2578
0.26	.1026	.6026	.3974	0.66	.2454	.7454	.2546
0.27	.1064	.6064	.3936	0.67	.2486	.7486	.2514
0.28	.1103	.6103	.3897	0.68	.2517	.7517	.2483
0.29	.1141	.6141	.3859	0.69	.2549	.7549	.2451
0.30	.1179	.6179	.3821	0.70	.2580	.7580	.2420
0.31	.1217	.6217	.3783	0.71	.2611	.7611	.2389
0.32	.1255	.6255	.3745	0.72	.2642	.7642	.2358
0.33	.1293	.6293	.3707	0.73	.2673	.7673	.2327
0.34	.1331	.6331	.3669	0.74	.2704	.7704	.2296
0.35	.1368	.6368	.3632	0.75	.2734	.7734	.2266
0.36	.1406	.6406	.3594	0.76	.2764	.7764	.2236
0.37	.1443	.6443	.3557	0.77	.2794	.7794	.2206
0.38	.1480	.6480	.3520	0.78	.2823	.7823	.2177
0.39	.1517	.6517	.3483	0.79	.2852	.7852	.2148

TABLE A1: AREAS UNDER THE NORMAL CURVE (continued)

z	mean to z area	larger area	smaller area	z	mean to z area	larger area	smaller area
0.80	.2881	.7881	.2119	1.30	.4032	.9032	.0968
0.81	.2910	.7910	.2090	1.31	.4049	.9049	.0951
0.82	.2939	.7939	.2061	1.32	.4066	.9066	.0934
0.83	.2967	.7967	.2033	1.33	.4082	.9082	.0918
0.84	.2995	.7995	.2005	1.34	.4099	.9099	.0901
0.85	.3023	.8023	.1977	1.35	.4115	.9115	.0885
0.86	.3051	.8051	.1949	1.36	.4131	.9131	.0869
0.87	.3078	.8078	.1922	1.37	.4147	.9147	.0853
0.88	.3106	.8106	.1894	1.38	.4162	.9162	.0838
0.89	.3133	.8133	.1867	1.39	.4177	.9177	.0823
0.90	.3159	.8159	.1841	1.40	.4192	.9192	.0808
0.91	.3186	.8186	.1814	1.41	.4207	.9207	.0793
0.92	.3212	.8212	.1788	1.42	.4222	.9222	.0778
0.93	.3238	.8238	.1762	1.43	.4236	.9236	.0764
0.94	.3264	.8264	.1736	1.44	.4251	.9251	.0749
0.95	.3289	.8289	.1711	1.45	.4265	.9265	.0735
0.96	.3315	.8315	.1685	1.46	.4279	.9279	.0721
0.97	.3340	.8340	.1660	1.47	.4292	.9292	.0708
0.98	.3365	.8365	.1635	1.48	.4306	.9306	.0694
0.99	.3389	.8389	.1611	1.49	.4319	.9319	.0681
1.00	.3413	.8413	.1587	1.50	.4332	.9332	.0668
1.01	.3438	.8438	.1562	1.51	.4345	.9345	.0655
1.02	.3461	.8461	.1539	1.52	.4357	.9357	.0643
1.03	.3485	.8485	.1515	1.53	.4370	.9370	.0630
1.04	.3508	.8508	.1492	1.54	.4382	.9382	.0618
1.05	.3531	.8531	.1469	1.55	.4394	.9394	.0606
1.06	.3554	.8554	.1446	1.56	.4406	.9406	.0594
1.07	.3577	.8577	.1423	1.57	.4418	.9418	.0582
1.08	.3599	.8599	.1401	1.58	.4429	.9429	.0571
1.09	.3621	.8621	.1379	1.59	.4441	.9441	.0559
1.10	.3643	.8643	.1357	1.60	.4452	.9452	.0548
1.11	.3665	.8665	.1335	1.61	.4463	.9463	.0537
1.12	.3686	.8686	.1314	1.62	.4474	.9474	.0526
1.13	.3708	.8708	.1292	1.63	.4484	.9484	.0516
1.14	.3729	.8729	.1271	1.64	.4495	.9495	.0505
1.15	.3749	.8749	.1251	1.65	.4505	.9505	.0495
1.16	.3770	.8770	.1230	1.66	.4515	.9515	.0485
1.17	.3790	.8790	.1210	1.67	.4525	.9525	.0475
1.18	.3810	.8810	.1190	1.68	.4535	.9535	.0465
1.19	.3830	.8830	.1170	1.69	.4545	.9545	.0455
1.20	.3849	.8849	.1151	1.70	.4554	.9554	.0446
1.21	.3869	.8869	.1131	1.71	.4564	.9564	.0436
1.22	.3888	.8888	.1112	1.72	.4573	.9573	.0427
1.23	.3907	.8907	.1093	1.73	.4582	.9582	.0418
1.24	.3925	.8925	.1075	1.74	.4591	.9591	.0409
1.25	.3944	.8944	.1056	1.75	.4599	.9599	.0401
1.26	.3962	.8962	.1038	1.76	.4608	.9608	.0392
1.27	.3980	.8980	.1020	1.77	.4616	.9616	.0384
1.28	.3997	.8997	.1003	1.78	.4625	.9625	.0375
1.29	.4015	.9015	.0985	1.79	.4633	.9633	.0367

TABLE A1: AREAS UNDER THE NORMAL CURVE (continued)

z	mean to z area	larger area	smaller area	z	mean to z area	larger area	smaller area
1.80	.4641	.9641	.0359	2.30	.4893	.9893	.0107
1.81	.4649	.9649	.0351	2.31	.4896	.9896	.0104
1.82	.4656	.9656	.0344	2.32	.4898	.9898	.0102
1.83	.4664	.9664	.0336	2.33	.4901	.9901	.0099
1.84	.4671	.9671	.0329	2.34	.4904	.9904	.0096
1.85	.4678	.9678	.0322	2.35	.4906	.9906	.0094
1.86	.4686	.9686	.0314	2.36	.4909	.9909	.0091
1.87	.4693	.9693	.0307	2.37	.4911	.9911	.0089
1.88	.4699	.9699	.0301	2.38	.4913	.9913	.0087
1.89	.4706	.9706	.0294	2.39	.4916	.9916	.0084
1.90	.4713	.9713	.0287	2.40	.4918	.9918	.0082
1.91	.4719	.9719	.0281	2.41	.4920	.9920	.0080
1.92	.4726	.9726	.0274	2.42	.4922	.9922	.0078
1.93	.4732	.9732	.0268	2.43	.4925	.9925	.0075
1.94	.4738	.9738	.0262	2.44	.4927	.9927	.0073
1.95	.4744	.9744	.0256	2.45	.4929	.9929	.0071
1.96	.4750	.9750	.0250	2.46	.4931	.9931	.0069
1.97	.4756	.9756	.0244	2.47	.4932	.9932	.0068
1.98	.4761	.9761	.0239	2.48	.4934	.9934	.0066
1.99	.4767	.9767	.0233	2.49	.4936	.9936	.0064
2.00	.4772	.9772	.0228	2.50	.4938	.9938	.0062
2.01	.4778	.9778	.0222	2.51	.4940	.9940	.0060
2.02	.4783	.9783	.0217	2.52	.4941	.9941	.0059
2.03	.4788	.9788	.0212	2.53	.4943	.9943	.0057
2.04	.4793	.9793	.0207	2.54	.4945	.9945	.0055
2.05	.4798	.9798	.0202	2.55	.4946	.9946	.0054
2.06	.4803	.9803	.0197	2.56	.4948	.9948	.0052
2.07	.4808	.9808	.0192	2.57	.4949	.9949	.0051
2.08	.4812	.9812	.0188	2.58	.4951	.9951	.0049
2.09	.4817	.9817	.0183	2.59	.4952	.9952	.0048
2.10	.4821	.9821	.0179	2.60	.4953	.9953	.0047
2.11	.4826	.9826	.0174	2.61	.4955	.9955	.0045
2.12	.4830	.9830	.0170	2.62	.4956	.9956	.0044
2.13	.4834	.9834	.0166	2.63	.4957	.9957	.0043
2.14	.4838	.9838	.0162	2.64	.4959	.9959	.0041
2.15	.4842	.9842	.0158	2.65	.4960	.9960	.0040
2.16	.4846	.9846	.0154	2.66	.4961	.9961	.0039
2.17	.4850	.9850	.0150	2.67	.4962	.9962	.0038
2.18	.4854	.9854	.0146	2.68	.4963	.9963	.0037
2.19	.4857	.9857	.0143	2.69	.4964	.9964	.0036
2.20	.4861	.9861	.0139	2.70	.4965	.9965	.0035
2.21	.4864	.9864	.0136	2.71	.4966	.9966	.0034
2.22	.4868	.9868	.0132	2.72	.4967	.9967	.0033
2.23	.4871	.9871	.0129	2.73	.4968	.9968	.0032
2.24	.4875	.9875	.0125	2.74	.4969	.9969	.0031
2.25	.4878	.9878	.0122	2.75	.4970	.9970	.0030
2.26	.4881	.9881	.0119	2.76	.4971	.9971	.0029
2.27	.4884	.9884	.0116	2.77	.4972	.9972	.0028
2.28	.4887	.9887	.0113	2.78	.4973	.9973	.0027
2.29	.4890	.9890	.0110	2.79	.4974	.9974	.0026

TABLE A1: AREAS UNDER THE NORMAL CURVE (continued)

z	mean to z area	larger area	smaller area	z	mean to z area	larger area	smaller area
2.80	.4974	.9974	.0026	3.05	.4989	.9989	.0011
2.81	.4975	.9975	.0025	3.06	.4989	.9989	.0011
2.82	.4976	.9976	.0024	3.07	.4989	.9989	.0011
2.83	.4977	.9977	.0023	3.08	.4990	.9990	.0010
2.84	.4977	.9977	.0023	3.09	.4990	.9990	.0010
2.85	.4978	.9978	.0022	3.10	.4990	.9990	.0010
2.86	.4979	.9979	.0021	3.11	.4991	.9991	.0009
2.87	.4979	.9979	.0021	3.12	.4991	.9991	.0009
2.88	.4980	.9980	.0020	3.13	.4991	.9991	.0009
2.89	.4981	.9981	.0019	3.14	.4992	.9992	.0008
2.90	.4981	.9981	.0019	3.15	.4992	.9992	.0008
2.91	.4982	.9982	.0018	3.16	.4992	.9992	.0008
2.92	.4982	.9982	.0018	3.17	.4992	.9992	.0008
2.93	.4983	.9883	.0017	3.18	.4993	.9993	.0007
2.94	.4984	.9984	.0016	3.19	.4993	.9993	.0007
2.95	.4984	.9984	.0016	3.20	.4993	.9993	.0007
2.96	.4985	.9985	.0015	3.21	.4993	.9993	.0007
2.97	.4985	.9985	.0015	3.22	.4994	.9994	.0006
2.98	.4986	.9986	.0014	3.23	.4994	.9994	.0006
2.99	.4986	.9986	.0014	3.24	.4994	.9994	.0006
3.00	.4987	.9987	.0013	3.30	.4995	.9995	.0005
3.01	.4987	.9987	.0013	3.40	.4997	.9997	.0003
3.02	.4987	.9987	.0013	3.50	.4998	.9998	.0002
3.03	.4988	.9988	.0012	3.60	.4998	.9998	.0002
3.04	.4988	.9988	.0012	3.70	.4999	.9999	.0001

TABLE A2: TABLE OF VALUES FOR t-TEST OF SIGNIFICANCE

df	5%	1%	df	5%	1%
1	12.706	63.657	21	2.080	2.831
2	4.303	9.925	22	2.074	2.819
3	3.182	5.841	23	2.069	2.807
4	2.776	4.604	24	2.064	2.797
5	2.571	4.032	25	2.060	2.787
6	2.447	3.707	26	2.056	2.779
7	2.365	3.499	27	2.052	2.771
8	2.306	3.355	28	2.048	2.763
9	2.262	3.250	29	2.045	2.756
10	2.228	3.169	30	2.042	2.750
11	2.201	3.106	35	2.030	2.724
12	2.179	3.055	40	2.021	2.704
13	2.160	3.012	45	2.014	2.690
14	2.145	2.977	50	2.008	2.678
15	2.131	2.947	60	2.000	2.660
16	2.120	2.921	70	1.994	2.648
17	2.110	2.898	80	1.990	2.638
18	2.101	2.878	90	1.987	2.632
19	2.093	2.861	100	1.984	2.626
20	2.086	2.845		1.960	2.576

TABLE A3: PEARSON PRODUCT MOMENT CORRELATION

df	5%	1%	df	5%	1%
1	.997	1.000	24	.388	.496
2	.950	.990	25	.381	.487
3	.878	.959	26	.374	.478
4	.811	.917	27	.367	.470
5	.754	.874	28	.361	.463
6	.707	.834	29	.355	.456
7	.666	.798	30	.349	.449
8	.632	.765	35	.325	.418
9	.602	.735	40	.304	.393
10	.576	.708	45	.288	.372
11	.553	.684	50	.273	.354
12	.532	.661	60	.250	.325
13	.514	.641	70	.232	.302
14	.497	.623	80	.217	.283
15	.482	.606	90	.205	.267
16	.468	.590	100	.195	.254
17	.456	.575	125	.174	.228
18	.444	.561	150	.159	.208
19	.433	.549	200	.138	.181
20	.423	.537	300	.113	.148
21	.413	.526	400	.098	.128
22	.404	.515	500	.088	.115
23	.396	.505	1000	.062	.081

TABLE A4: SPEARMAN RANK ORDER CORRELATION

N	5%	1%
5	1.000	-----
6	.886	1.000
7	.786	.929
8	.738	.881
9	.683	.833
10	.648	.794
12	.591	.777
14	.544	.714
16	.506	.665
18	.475	.625
20	.450	.591
22	.428	.562
24	.409	.537
26	.392	.515
28	.377	.496
30	.364	.478

TABLE A5: CHI-SQUARE VALUES FOR SIGNIFICANCE

df	5%	1%	df	5%	1%
1	3.84	6.64	16	26.30	32.00
2	5.99	9.21	17	27.59	33.41
3	7.82	11.34	18	28.87	34.80
4	9.49	13.28	19	30.14	36.19
5	11.07	15.09	20	31.41	37.57
6	12.59	16.81	21	32.67	38.93
7	14.07	18.48	22	33.92	40.29
8	15.51	20.09	23	35.17	41.64
9	16.92	21.67	24	36.42	42.98
10	18.31	23.21	25	37.65	44.31
11	19.68	24.72	26	38.88	45.64
12	21.03	26.22	27	40.11	46.96
13	22.36	27.69	28	41.34	48.28
14	23.68	29.14	29	42.56	49.59
15	25.00	30.58	30	43.77	50.89

TABLE A6: F DISTRIBUTION

df for numerator

df for denom.		1	2	3	4	5	6	7	8	9	10	11	12	15	20	24	30	40	50	60
1	.95	161	200	216	225	230	234	237	239	241	242	243	244	246	248	249	250	251	252	252
2	.95	18.5	19.0	19.2	19.2	19.3	19.3	19.4	19.4	19.4	19.4	19.4	19.4	19.4	19.4	19.5	19.5	19.5	19.5	19.5
	.99	98.5	99.0	99.2	99.2	99.3	99.3	99.4	99.4	99.4	99.4	99.4	99.4	99.4	99.4	99.5	99.5	99.5	99.5	99.5
3	.95	10.1	9.55	9.28	9.12	9.10	8.94	8.89	8.85	8.81	8.79	8.76	8.74	8.70	8.66	8.64	8.62	8.59	8.58	8.57
	.99	34.1	30.8	29.5	28.7	28.2	27.9	27.7	27.5	27.3	27.2	27.1	27.1	26.9	26.7	26.6	26.5	26.4	26.4	26.3
4	.95	7.71	6.94	6.59	6.39	6.26	6.16	6.09	6.04	6.00	5.96	5.94	5.91	5.86	5.80	5.77	5.75	5.72	5.70	5.69
	.99	21.2	18.0	16.7	16.0	15.5	15.2	15.0	14.8	14.7	14.5	14.4	14.4	14.2	14.0	13.9	13.8	13.7	13.7	13.7
5	.95	6.61	5.79	5.41	5.19	5.05	4.95	4.88	4.82	4.77	4.74	4.71	4.68	4.62	4.56	4.53	4.50	4.46	4.44	4.43
	.99	16.3	13.3	12.1	11.4	11.0	10.7	10.5	10.3	10.2	10.1	9.96	9.89	9.72	9.55	9.47	9.38	9.29	9.24	9.20
6	.95	5.99	5.14	4.76	4.53	4.39	4.28	4.21	4.15	4.10	4.06	4.03	4.00	3.94	3.87	3.84	3.81	3.77	3.75	3.74
	.99	13.7	10.9	9.78	9.15	8.75	8.47	8.26	8.10	7.98	7.87	7.79	7.72	7.56	7.40	7.31	7.23	7.14	7.09	7.06
7	.95	5.59	4.74	4.35	4.12	3.97	3.87	3.79	3.73	3.68	3.64	3.60	3.57	3.51	3.44	3.41	3.38	3.34	3.32	3.30
	.99	12.2	9.55	8.45	7.85	7.46	7.19	6.99	6.84	6.72	6.62	6.54	6.47	6.31	6.16	6.07	5.99	5.91	5.86	5.82
8	.95	5.32	4.46	4.07	3.84	3.69	3.58	3.50	3.44	3.39	3.35	3.31	3.28	3.22	3.15	3.12	3.08	3.04	3.02	3.01
	.99	11.3	8.65	7.59	7.01	6.63	6.37	6.18	6.03	5.91	5.81	5.73	5.67	5.52	5.36	5.28	5.20	5.12	5.07	5.03
9	.95	5.12	4.26	3.86	3.63	3.48	3.37	3.29	3.23	3.18	3.14	3.10	3.07	3.01	2.94	2.90	2.86	2.83	2.80	2.79
	.99	10.6	8.02	6.99	6.42	6.06	5.80	5.61	5.47	5.35	5.26	5.18	5.11	4.96	4.81	4.73	4.65	4.57	4.52	4.48
10	.95	4.96	4.10	3.71	3.48	3.33	3.22	3.14	3.07	3.02	2.98	2.94	2.91	2.85	2.77	2.74	2.70	2.66	2.64	2.62
	.99	10.0	7.56	6.55	5.99	5.64	5.39	5.20	5.06	4.94	4.85	4.77	4.71	4.56	4.41	4.33	4.25	4.17	4.12	4.08
11	.95	4.84	3.98	3.59	3.36	3.20	3.09	3.01	2.95	2.90	2.85	2.82	2.79	2.72	2.65	2.61	2.57	2.53	2.51	2.49
	.99	9.65	7.21	6.22	5.67	5.32	5.07	4.89	4.74	4.63	4.54	4.46	4.40	4.25	4.10	4.02	3.94	3.86	3.81	3.78

TABLE A6: F DISTRIBUTION (continued)

df for numerator

df for denom.		1	2	3	4	5	6	7	8	9	10	11	12	15	20	24	30	40	50	60
12	.95	4.75	3.89	3.49	3.26	3.11	3.00	2.91	2.85	2.80	2.75	2.72	2.69	2.62	2.54	2.51	2.47	2.43	2.40	2.38
	.99	9.33	6.93	5.95	5.41	5.06	4.82	4.64	4.50	4.39	4.30	4.22	4.16	4.01	3.86	3.78	3.70	3.62	3.57	3.54
13	.95	4.67	3.81	3.41	3.18	3.03	2.92	2.83	2.77	2.71	2.67	2.63	2.60	2.53	2.46	2.42	2.38	2.34	2.31	2.30
	.99	9.07	6.70	5.74	5.21	4.86	4.62	4.44	4.30	4.19	4.10	4.02	3.96	3.82	3.66	3.59	3.51	3.43	3.38	3.34
14	.95	4.60	3.74	3.34	3.11	2.96	2.85	2.76	2.70	2.65	2.60	2.57	2.53	2.46	2.39	2.35	2.31	2.27	2.24	2.22
	.99	8.86	6.51	5.56	5.04	4.69	4.46	4.28	4.14	4.03	3.94	3.86	3.80	3.66	3.51	3.43	3.35	3.27	3.22	3.18
15	.95	4.54	3.68	3.29	3.06	2.90	2.79	2.71	2.64	2.59	2.54	2.51	2.48	2.40	2.33	2.29	2.25	2.20	2.18	2.16
	.99	8.68	6.36	5.42	4.89	4.56	4.32	4.14	4.00	3.89	3.80	3.73	3.67	3.52	3.37	3.29	3.21	3.13	3.08	3.05
16	.95	4.49	3.63	3.24	3.01	2.85	2.74	2.66	2.59	2.54	2.49	2.46	2.42	2.35	2.28	2.24	2.19	2.15	2.12	2.11
	.99	8.53	6.23	5.29	4.77	4.44	4.20	4.03	3.89	3.78	3.69	3.62	3.55	3.41	3.26	3.18	3.10	3.02	2.97	2.93
17	.95	4.45	3.59	3.20	2.96	2.81	2.70	2.61	2.55	2.49	2.45	2.41	2.38	2.31	2.23	2.19	2.15	2.10	2.08	2.06
	.99	8.40	6.11	5.18	4.67	4.34	4.10	3.93	3.79	3.68	3.59	3.52	3.46	3.31	3.16	3.08	3.00	2.92	2.87	2.83
18	.95	4.41	3.55	3.16	2.93	2.77	2.66	2.58	2.51	2.46	2.41	2.37	2.34	2.27	2.19	2.15	2.11	2.06	2.04	2.02
	.99	8.29	6.01	5.09	4.58	4.25	4.01	3.84	3.71	3.60	3.51	3.43	3.37	3.23	3.08	3.00	2.92	2.84	2.78	2.75
19	.95	4.38	3.52	3.13	2.90	2.74	2.63	2.54	2.48	2.42	2.38	2.34	2.31	2.23	2.16	2.11	2.07	2.03	2.00	1.98
	.99	8.18	5.93	5.01	4.50	4.17	3.94	3.77	3.63	3.52	3.43	3.36	3.30	3.15	3.00	2.92	2.84	2.76	2.71	2.67
20	.95	4.35	3.49	3.10	2.87	2.71	2.60	2.51	2.45	2.39	2.35	2.31	2.28	2.20	2.12	2.08	2.04	1.99	1.97	1.95
	.99	8.10	5.85	4.94	4.43	4.10	3.87	3.70	3.56	3.46	3.37	3.29	3.23	3.09	2.94	2.86	2.78	2.69	2.64	2.61
22	.95	4.30	3.44	3.05	2.82	2.66	2.55	2.46	2.40	2.34	2.30	2.26	2.23	2.15	2.07	2.03	1.98	1.94	1.91	1.89
	.99	7.95	5.72	4.82	4.31	3.99	3.76	3.59	3.45	3.35	3.26	3.18	3.12	2.98	2.83	2.75	2.67	2.58	2.53	2.50
24	.95	4.26	3.40	3.01	2.78	2.62	2.51	2.42	2.36	2.30	2.25	2.21	2.18	2.11	2.03	1.98	1.94	1.89	1.86	1.84
	.99	7.82	5.61	4.72	4.22	3.90	3.67	3.50	3.36	3.26	3.17	3.09	3.03	2.89	2.74	2.66	2.58	2.49	2.44	2.40

df for numerator

df for denom.		1	2	3	4	5	6	7	8	9	10	11	12	15	20	24	30	40	50	60
26	.95	4.23	3.37	2.98	2.74	2.59	2.47	2.39	2.32	2.27	2.22	2.18	2.15	2.07	1.99	1.95	1.90	1.85	1.82	1.80
	.99	7.72	5.53	4.64	4.14	3.82	3.59	3.42	3.29	3.18	3.09	3.02	2.96	2.81	2.66	2.58	2.50	2.42	2.36	2.33
28	.95	4.20	3.34	2.95	2.71	2.56	2.45	2.36	2.29	2.24	2.19	2.15	2.12	2.04	1.96	1.91	1.87	1.82	1.79	1.77
	.99	7.64	5.45	4.57	4.07	3.75	3.53	3.36	3.23	3.12	3.03	2.96	2.90	2.75	2.60	2.52	2.44	2.35	2.30	2.26
30	.95	4.17	3.32	2.92	2.69	2.53	2.42	2.33	2.27	2.21	2.16	2.13	2.09	2.01	1.93	1.89	1.84	1.79	1.76	1.74
	.99	7.56	5.39	4.51	4.02	3.70	3.47	3.30	3.17	3.07	2.98	2.91	2.84	2.70	2.55	2.47	2.39	2.30	2.25	2.21
40	.95	4.08	3.23	2.84	2.61	2.45	2.34	2.25	2.18	2.12	2.08	2.04	2.00	1.92	1.84	1.79	1.74	1.69	1.66	1.64
	.99	7.31	5.18	4.31	3.83	3.51	3.29	3.12	2.99	2.89	2.80	2.73	2.66	2.52	2.37	2.29	2.20	2.11	2.06	2.02
60	.95	4.00	3.15	2.76	2.53	2.37	2.25	2.17	2.10	2.04	1.99	1.95	1.92	1.84	1.75	1.70	1.65	1.59	1.56	1.53
	.99	7.08	4.98	4.13	3.65	3.34	3.12	2.95	2.82	2.72	2.63	2.56	2.50	2.35	2.20	2.12	2.03	1.94	1.88	1.84
120	.95	3.92	3.07	2.68	2.45	2.29	2.17	2.09	2.02	1.96	1.91	1.87	1.83	1.75	1.66	1.61	1.55	1.50	1.46	1.43
	.99	6.85	4.79	3.95	3.48	3.17	2.96	2.79	2.66	2.56	2.47	2.40	2.34	2.19	2.03	1.95	1.86	1.76	1.70	1.66
200	.95	3.89	3.04	2.65	2.42	2.26	2.14	2.06	1.98	1.93	1.88	1.84	1.80	1.72	1.62	1.57	1.52	1.46	1.41	1.39
	.99	6.76	4.71	3.88	3.41	3.11	2.89	2.73	2.60	2.50	2.41	2.34	2.27	2.13	1.97	1.89	1.79	1.69	1.63	1.58
∞	.95	3.84	3.00	2.60	2.37	2.21	2.10	2.01	1.94	1.88	1.83	1.79	1.75	1.67	1.57	1.52	1.46	1.39	1.35	1.32
	.99	6.63	4.61	3.78	3.32	3.02	2.80	2.64	2.51	2.41	2.32	2.25	2.18	2.04	1.88	1.79	1.70	1.59	1.52	1.47

TABLE A7: STUDENTIZED RANGE STATISTIC

r=number of steps between ordered means

df for error		2	3	4	5	6	7	8	9	10	11	12	13	14	15
1	.95	18.0	27.0	32.8	37.1	40.4	43.1	45.4	47.4	49.1	50.6	52.0	53.2	54.3	55.4
	.99	90.0	135	164	186	202	216	227	237	246	253	260	266	272	277
2	.95	6.09	8.3	9.8	10.9	11.7	12.4	13.0	13.5	14.0	14.4	14.7	15.1	15.4	15.7
	.99	14.0	19.0	22.3	24.7	26.6	28.2	29.5	30.7	31.7	32.6	33.4	34.1	34.8	35.4
3	.95	4.50	5.91	6.82	7.50	8.04	8.48	8.85	9.18	9.46	9.72	9.95	10.2	10.4	10.5
	.99	8.26	10.6	12.2	13.3	14.2	15.0	15.6	16.2	16.7	17.1	17.5	17.9	18.2	18.5
4	.95	3.93	5.04	5.76	6.29	6.71	7.05	7.35	7.60	7.83	8.03	8.21	8.37	8.52	8.66
	.99	6.51	8.12	9.17	9.96	10.6	11.1	11.5	11.9	12.3	12.6	12.8	13.1	13.3	13.5
5	.95	3.64	4.60	5.22	5.67	6.03	6.33	6.58	6.80	6.99	7.17	7.32	7.47	7.60	7.72
	.99	5.70	6.97	7.80	8.42	8.91	9.32	9.67	9.97	10.2	10.5	10.7	10.9	11.1	11.2
6	.95	3.46	4.34	4.90	5.31	5.63	5.89	6.12	6.32	6.49	6.65	6.79	6.92	7.03	7.14
	.99	5.24	6.33	7.03	7.56	7.97	8.32	8.61	8.87	9.10	9.30	9.49	9.65	9.81	9.95
7	.95	3.34	4.16	4.69	5.06	5.36	5.61	5.82	6.00	6.16	6.30	6.43	6.55	6.66	6.76
	.99	4.95	5.92	6.54	7.01	7.37	7.68	7.94	8.17	8.37	8.55	8.71	8.86	9.00	9.12
8	.95	3.26	4.04	4.53	4.89	5.17	5.40	5.60	5.77	5.92	6.05	6.18	6.29	6.39	6.48
	.99	4.74	5.63	6.20	6.63	6.96	7.24	7.47	7.68	7.87	8.03	8.18	8.31	8.44	8.55
9	.95	3.20	3.95	4.42	4.76	5.02	5.24	5.43	5.60	5.74	5.87	5.98	6.09	6.19	6.28
	.99	4.60	5.43	5.96	6.35	6.66	6.91	7.13	7.32	7.49	7.65	7.78	7.91	8.03	8.13
10	.95	3.15	3.88	4.33	4.65	4.91	5.12	5.30	5.46	5.60	5.72	5.83	5.93	6.03	6.11
	.99	4.48	5.27	5.77	6.14	6.43	6.67	6.87	7.05	7.21	7.36	7.48	7.60	7.71	7.81
11	.95	3.11	3.82	4.26	4.57	4.82	5.03	5.20	5.35	5.49	5.61	5.71	5.81	5.90	5.99
	.99	4.39	5.14	5.62	5.97	6.25	6.48	6.67	6.84	6.99	7.13	7.26	7.36	7.46	7.56
12	.95	3.08	3.77	4.20	4.51	4.75	4.95	5.12	5.27	5.40	5.51	5.62	5.71	5.80	5.88
	.99	4.32	5.04	5.50	5.84	6.10	6.32	6.51	6.67	6.81	6.94	7.06	7.17	7.26	7.36

TABLE A7: STUDENTIZED RANGE STATISTIC (continued)

r=number of steps between ordered means

df for error		2	3	4	5	6	7	8	9	10	11	12	13	14	15
13	.95	3.06	3.73	4.15	4.45	4.69	4.88	5.05	5.19	5.32	5.43	5.53	5.63	5.71	5.79
	.99	4.26	4.96	5.40	5.73	5.98	6.19	6.37	6.53	6.67	6.79	6.90	7.01	7.10	7.19
14	.95	3.03	3.70	4.11	4.41	4.64	4.83	4.99	5.13	5.25	5.36	5.46	5.55	5.64	5.72
	.99	4.21	4.89	5.32	5.63	5.88	6.08	6.26	6.41	6.54	6.66	6.77	6.87	6.96	7.05
16	.95	3.00	3.65	4.05	4.33	4.56	4.74	4.90	5.03	5.15	5.26	5.35	5.44	5.52	5.59
	.99	4.13	4.78	5.19	5.49	5.72	5.92	6.08	6.22	6.35	6.46	6.56	6.66	6.74	6.82
18	.95	2.97	3.61	4.00	4.28	4.49	4.67	4.82	4.96	5.07	5.17	5.27	5.35	5.43	5.50
	.99	4.07	4.70	5.09	5.38	5.60	5.79	5.94	6.08	6.20	6.31	6.41	6.50	6.58	6.65
20	.95	2.95	3.58	3.96	4.23	4.45	4.62	4.77	4.90	5.01	5.11	5.20	5.28	5.36	5.43
	.99	4.02	4.64	5.02	5.29	5.51	5.69	5.84	5.97	6.09	6.19	6.29	6.37	6.45	6.52
24	.95	2.92	3.53	3.90	4.17	4.37	4.54	4.68	4.81	4.92	5.01	5.10	5.18	5.25	5.32
	.99	3.96	4.54	4.91	5.17	5.37	5.54	5.69	5.81	5.92	6.02	6.11	6.19	6.26	6.33
30	.95	2.89	3.49	3.84	4.10	4.30	4.46	4.60	4.72	4.83	4.92	5.00	5.08	5.15	5.21
	.99	3.89	4.45	4.80	5.05	5.24	5.40	5.54	5.56	5.76	5.85	5.93	6.01	6.08	6.14
40	.95	2.86	3.44	3.79	4.04	4.23	4.39	4.52	4.63	4.74	4.82	4.91	4.98	5.05	5.11
	.99	3.82	4.37	4.70	4.93	5.11	5.27	5.39	5.50	5.60	5.69	5.77	5.84	5.90	5.96
60	.95	2.83	3.40	3.74	3.98	4.16	4.31	4.44	4.55	4.65	4.73	4.81	4.88	4.94	5.00
	.99	3.76	4.28	4.60	4.82	4.99	5.13	5.25	5.36	5.45	5.53	5.60	5.67	5.73	5.79
120	.95	2.80	3.36	3.69	3.92	4.10	4.24	4.36	4.48	4.56	4.64	4.72	4.78	4.84	4.90
	.99	3.70	4.20	4.50	4.71	4.87	5.01	5.12	5.21	5.30	5.38	5.44	5.51	5.56	5.61
	.95	2.77	3.31	3.63	3.86	4.03	4.17	4.29	4.39	4.47	4.55	4.62	4.68	4.74	4.80
	.99	3.64	4.12	4.40	4.60	4.76	4.88	4.99	5.08	5.16	5.23	5.29	5.35	5.40	5.45

Appendix B

ANNOTATED COMPUTER PROGRAMS AND OUTPUT

This section contains annotated computer programs and sample output for use
on Apple Microcomputers and for use at computer installations that support
one or more of BMDP, SAS, SPSS. These stand for <u>Biomedical Programs,</u>
<u>Statistical Analysis System,</u> and <u>Statistical Package for the Social</u>
<u>Sciences,</u> respectively. The types of programs are listed below. Due to
limited space only a sampling of Applesoft programs have been included.
Others are available on disk or in printed form from the author.

APPLESOFT PROGRAMS

Dice throw statistics..296
Independent groups t-test.......................................297
Pearson Product Moment correlation..............................299
One-way Analysis of Variance....................................301
Two factor between subjects Analysis of Variance................304
Two factor-one repeated measure Analysis of Variance............307
Program for coincidence anticipation study......................311
Scoring the Personal Attributes Questionnaire...................313
Administering and scoring the BSRI..............................315

STATISTICAL SOFTWARE PACKAGE PROGRAMS

Space does not permit inclusion of output for all of the sample programs. Only one sample output is given for each package. In general
the output is easily understood and well-marked. Some of the statistical
tests are shown with more than one package since installations may not
have all packages. The programs presented are basic programs for conducting the tests. In general the BMDP, SAS, and SPSS systems are
capable of very elaborate data handling and transformations. These jobs
are intended to introduce you to how to run the statistical tests covered
in this book. It is highly recommended that you purchase the manual for
the system(s) used at your installation. The job control language,
usually in the first 3 or 4 and the last two lines of the input, is
unique to every installation. Therefore, you should check at your
computer center before you run these jobs. Finally, annotations are
included only if they further clarify. In general, however, the input
is explained. (Please note that the SPSS-X jobs shown here will only
run at an installation which has installed SPSS-X. It will not run on
SPSS since there have been significant changes.

BMDP ANALYSES

One factor Analysis of Variance.....................................
Two- factor between Analysis of Variance............................
Two factor-one repeated measure Analysis of Variance................

294

SAS ANALYSES

Descriptive statistics...
Pearson Correlation..
One factor Analysis of Variance..................................
Two factor between Analysis of Variance..........................

SPSS-X ANALYSES

Descriptive statistics with Histogram............................
Independent groups t-test..
Pearson correlation with Scattergram.............................
Two factor chi-square..
One factor Analysis of Variance..................................
Two factor between Analysis of Variance..........................

APPLESOFT BASIC PROGRAM FOR CALCULATING DICE THROW STATISTICS

This program was used to generate the tables in the chapter on
statistical inference. It provides the average, standard deviation, and standard error of the mean for a given number of
dice throws.

```
10  INPUT "WHAT IS THE TOTAL NUMB
ER OF THROWS OF THE DICE YOU
   WISH TO RECORD? ";N
20  FOR I = 1 TO N
30  X =  RND (6) * 10
40  X =  INT (X)
50  IF X > 6 OR X < 1 GOTO 30
60  Y =  RND (6) * 10
70  Y =  INT (Y)
80  IF Y > 6 OR Y < 1 GOTO 60
90  ROLL = X + Y
100  SUM = SUM + ROLL
110  RT = RT + (ROLL * ROLL)
120  NEXT I
130  STD =  SQR ((RT - ((SUM * SUM
) / N)) / N)
140  AVG = SUM / N
150  SEM = STD /  SQR (N)
160  PRINT "THE AVERAGE IS: ";AVG

170  PRINT "THE STANDARD DEVIATIO
N IS: ";STD
180  PRINT "THE STD ERROR OF THE
MEAN IS: ";SEM
190  END
```

Statement 10 sets N to the number
of throws you wish to produce.

Statements 20–120 cause random
numbers to be generated, rejects
them if they are under 1 or over 6
and then adds them to obtain one
roll. In addition the sum of the
rolls and the sum of the squared
rolls are calculated.

Statements 130–180 calculate
descriptive statistics for the set
of throws generated.

PROGRAM OUTPUT

```
WHAT IS THE TOTAL NUMBER OF THROWS OF THE DICE YOU WISH TO RECORD?   36
THE AVERAGE IS: 6.27777778
THE STANDARD DEVIATION IS: 2.65215961
THE STD ERROR OF THE MEAN IS: .442026602


WHAT IS THE TOTAL NUMBER OF THROWS OF THE DICE YOU WISH TO RECORD? 360
THE AVERAGE IS: 6.9
THE STANDARD DEVIATION IS: 2.25363903
THE STD ERROR OF THE MEAN IS: .118777206


WHAT IS THE TOTAL NUMBER OF THROWS OF THE DICE YOU WISH TO RECORD? 3600
THE AVERAGE IS: 6.88944445
THE STANDARD DEVIATION IS: 2.41545941
THE STD ERROR OF THE MEAN IS: .0402576568
```

APPLESOFT BASIC PROGRAM TO CALCULATE AN INDEPENDENT
GROUPS t-TEST

This program completes an independent groups t-test.   It handles
unequal groups.   The data used to illustrate this program were:
Group A: 2,4,5,3,6,5,7,8,5,6
Group B: 3,7,8,9,8,10,12,7,9,8,11,9

```
10   INPUT "HOW MANY SUBJECTS IN G
ROUP A? ";NA
20   INPUT "HOW MANY SUBJECTS IN G
ROUP B? ";NB
30   DIM A(NA),B(NB)
40   FOR I = 1 TO NA
50   INPUT "ENTER A SCORE FOR GROU
P A. ";A(I)
60   NEXT I
65   GOSUB 380
70   FOR I = 1 TO NB
80   INPUT "ENTER A SCORE FOR GROU
P B. ";B(I)
90   NEXT I
100  GOSUB 650
110  FOR I = 1 TO NA
120  AALL = AALL + A(I)
130  AROOT = AROOT + A(I) * A(I)
140  NEXT I
150  FOR J = 1 TO NB
160  BALL = BALL + B(J)
170  BROOT = BROOT + B(J) * B(J)
180  NEXT J
190  AMEAN = AALL / NA
200  BMEAN = BALL / NB
210  ASD =  SQR ((AROOT / NA) - AM
EAN ^ 2)
220  BSD =  SQR ((BROOT / NB) - BM
EAN ^ 2)
230  AERM = ASD /  SQR (NA)
240  BERM = BSD /  SQR (NB)
250  T = (AMEAN - BMEAN) /  SQR (A
ERM ^ 2 + BERM ^ 2)
260  PRINT "ASUM=",AALL
270  PRINT "BSUM=",BALL
280  PRINT "ASUM OF SQUARES=",ARO
OT
290  PRINT "BSUM OF SQUARES=",BRO
OT
300  PRINT "AMEAN=",AMEAN
310  PRINT "BMEAN=",BMEAN
320  PRINT "'A' STANDARD DEVIATIO
N=",ASD
330  PRINT "'B' STANDARD DEVIATIO
N=",BSD
340  PRINT "ASEM=",AERM
350  PRINT "BSEM=",BERM
360  PRINT "T RATIO=",T
370  END
```

Statements 10-100 set RAM for the
size of the groups, enables the
user to enter scores, and allows
checking and correction of errors
through GOSUB 380 or 650.

Statements 110-180 calculate the
sum of scores and the sum of the
squared scores for groups A and B.

Statements 190-250 calculate
necessary statistics and the
t-ratio.

Statements 260-360 cause the values
for the t-test to be printed.

Statements 380-900 enable the
correction of data which has been
improperly entered.

```
380  REM  START DISPLAYING VALUES
     FOR CORRECTIONS IN GROUP A
390  KK = 1
400  TEXT : HOME
410  FOR I = KK TO NA
420  PQ = PQ + 1
430  PRINT I;"  ";
440  PRINT "A= ";
450  PRINT A(I)
460  IF PQ = 14 OR (I = NA) THEN
     GOSUB 490:PQ = 0: HOME : REM
     MAKE CORRECTIONS
470  NEXT I
480  RETURN
490  REM  SUB CORRECTIONS
500  PRINT "CHANGES IN THIS GROUP
     ? "
510  INPUT "Y OR N ";TT$: IF TT$ <
     > "Y" AND TT$ <  > "N" THEN
     510
520  IF TT$ = "N" THEN  RETURN
530  PRINT "WHICH I ";
540  PRINT "DO YOU WISH";
550  INPUT " TO CHANGE ";IC
560  PRINT "OLD VALUE= ";
570  PRINT A(IC)
580  INPUT "NEW VALUE= ";A(IC)
590  PRINT "ANY MORE CHANGES";
600  PRINT " IN THIS LOT"
605  PRINT I
610  INPUT "Y OR N ";TT$
620  IF TT$ = "Y" THEN  GOTO 530
630  IF TT$ = "N" THEN  RETURN
640  GOTO 610: REM  BAD RESPONSE
650  REM  START DISPLAYING VALUES
     FOR CORRECTIONS IN GROUP B
660  KK = 1
670  TEXT : HOME
680  FOR I = KK TO NB
685  PQ = PQ + 1
690  PRINT I;"  ";
700  PRINT "B= ";
710  PRINT B(I)
720  IF PQ = 14 OR (I = NB) THEN
     GOSUB 750:PQ = 0: HOME : REM
     MAKE CORRECTIONS
730  NEXT I
740  RETURN
750  REM  SUB CORRECTIONS GROUP B
760  PRINT "CHANGES IN THIS GROUP
     ? "
770  INPUT "Y OR N ";TT$: IF TT$ <
     > "Y" AND TT$ <  > "N" THEN
     770
780  IF TT$ = "N" THEN  RETURN
790  PRINT "WHICH I ";
800  PRINT "DO YOU WISH ";
810  INPUT "TO CHANGE? ";IC
820  PRINT "OLD VALUE= ";
830  PRINT B(IC)
840  INPUT "NEW VALUE= ";B(IC)
850  PRINT "ANY MORE CHANGES";
860  PRINT " IN THIS LOT "
870  INPUT "Y OR N ";TT$
880  IF TT$ = "Y" THEN  GOTO 790
890  IF TT$ = "N" THEN  RETURN
900  GOTO 870: REM  BAD RESPONSE
```

PROGRAM OUTPUT

```
HOW MANY SUBJECTS IN GROUP A? 10
HOW MANY SUBJECTS IN GROUP B? 12
ENTER A SCORE FOR GROUP A. 2
ENTER A SCORE FOR GROUP A. 4
 9  A= 5
10  A= 6
CHANGES IN THIS GROUP?
Y OR N N

ENTER A SCORE FOR GROUP B. 3
ENTER A SCORE FOR GROUP B. 7
ENTER A SCORE FOR GROUP B. 8
11  B= 11
12  B= 9
CHANGES IN THIS GROUP?
Y OR N N
ASUM=51
BSUM=101
ASUM OF SQUARES=289
BSUM OF SQUARES=907
AMEAN=5.1
BMEAN=8.41666667
'A' STANDARD DEVIATION=1.69999999
'B' STANDARD DEVIATION=2.17785571
ASEM=.5375872
BSEM=.628692789
T RATIO=-4.00952529
```

APPLESOFT BASIC PROGRAM TO CALCULATE A PEARSON PRODUCT MOMENT
CORRELATION

This program calculates a correlation coefficient using the
pearson product moment test. The data used to illustrate the
program were:

Variable X	2	3	3	7	6	5	6	7	3	5
Variable Y	6	5	2	9	8	4	9	8	6	7

```
10 XM = YM = XS = YS = R = Ø
20  INPUT "HOW MANY PAIRS OF SCOR
ES DO YOU WISH TO ENTER? ";N

25  DIM X(N),Y(N)
30  FOR I = 1 TO N
40  INPUT "ENTER EACH PAIR OF SCO
RES, X,Y: ";X(I),Y(I)
44  NEXT I
45  GOSUB 1070
46  FOR I = 1 TO N
50  XM = XM + X(I)
60  YM = YM + Y(I)
70  XS = XS + X(I) ^ 2
80  YS = YS + Y(I) ^ 2
90  R = R + X(I) * Y(I)
100   NEXT I
110  XAVG = XM / N
120  YAVG = YM / N
130  XERR = XS / N - XAVG ^ 2
140  YERR = YS / N - YAVG ^ 2

150  COEFR = (R / N - XAVG * YAVG)
/ ( SQR (XERR * YERR))
160   PRINT "THE SUM OF SCORES FOR
X IS: ";XM
170   PRINT "THE SUM OF SCORES FOR
Y IS: ";YM
175   PRINT "THE SUM OF SCORES FOR
XY IS: ";R
180   PRINT "THE SUM OF SQUARED SC
ORES FOR X IS: ";XS
190   PRINT "THE SUM OF SQUARED SC
ORES FOR Y IS: ";YS
200   PRINT "THE MEAN FOR X IS: ";
XAVG
210   PRINT "THE MEAN FOR Y IS: ";
YAVG
220   PRINT "THE VARIANCE FOR X IS
: ";XERR
230   PRINT "THE VARIANCE FOR Y IS
: ";YERR
240   PRINT "THE CORRELATION BETWE
EN X,Y IS:";COEFR
250  END
```

Statements 10-25 set initial values
to zero, indicate the number of
pairs of scores to be entered and
reserve RAM for the scores.

Statements 30-45 enable the user to
enter scores and then allow for
checking the pairs for accuracy
through a correction subroutine.

Statements 46-150 calculate the
necessary values for computing the
correlation and computes the
coefficient.

Statements 160-240 print the values
used for calculating the
correlation.

Statements 1070-1340 constitute the correction subroutines.

```
1070  REM  START DISPLAYING VALUE
S              FOR CORREC
TIONS
1080  KK = 1
1085  TEXT : HOME
1090  FOR I = KK TO N
1095  PQ = PQ + 1
1097  PRINT I;"  ";
1100  PRINT "X= ";
1110  PRINT X(I);
1120  PRINT "   Y= ";
1130  PRINT Y(I)
1140  IF PQ = 14 OR I = N THEN
GOSUB
1200:PQ = 0: HOME : REM  MAK
E CORRECTIONS
1150  NEXT I
1160  RETURN
1200  REM  SUB CORRECTIONS
1205  PRINT "CHANGES IN THIS GROU
P?"
1206  INPUT "Y OR N ";TT$: IF TT$
< > "Y" AND TT$ < > "N" THEN
1206
1207  IF TT$ = "N" THEN  RETURN
1210  PRINT "WHICH I ";
1220  PRINT "DO YOU WISH";
1240  INPUT " TO CHANGE ";IC
1250  PRINT "OLD VALUES= ";
1260  PRINT X(IC);",";
1270  PRINT Y(IC)
1280  INPUT "X,Y ";X(IC),Y(IC)
1290  PRINT "ANY MORE CHANGES";
1300  PRINT " IN THIS LOT"
1310  INPUT "Y OR N ";TT$
1320  IF TT$ = "Y" THEN I = I - P
Q: RETURN
1330  IF TT$ = "N" THEN  RETURN
1340  GOTO 1310: REM  BAD RESPONS
E
```

PROGRAM OUTPUT

HOW MANY PAIRS OF SCORES DO YOU WISH
TO ENTER?
ENTER EACH PAIR OF SCORES, X,Y: 2,6
ENTER EACH PAIR OF SCORES, X,Y: 4,5
 9 X= 3   Y= 6
10 X= 5   Y= 7
CHANGES IN THIS GROUP?
Y OR N Y
WHICH I DO YOU WISH TO CHANGE 2
OLD VALUES= 4,5
X,Y 3,5
ANY MORE CHANGES IN THIS LOT
Y OR N N

THE SUM OF SCORES FOR X IS: 47
THE SUM OF SCORES FOR Y IS: 64
THE SUM OF SCORES FOR XY IS: 327
THE SUM OF SQUARED SCORES FOR X IS: 251
THE SUM OF SQUARED SCORES FOR Y IS: 456
THE MEAN FOR X IS: 4.7
THE MEAN FOR Y IS: 6.4
THE VARIANCE FOR X IS: 3.01000001
THE VARIANCE FOR Y IS: 4.63999996
THE CORRELATION BETWEEN X,Y IS:.7010662

APPLESOFT BASIC PROGRAM TO CALCULATE A ONE-WAY ANALYSIS OF
VARIANCE

This program conducts an analysis of variance for a three
group design. The program may be expanded to handle more
groups and may also be modified to print the final analysis
of variance tables. The data used to illustrate this program
were:

Group A:	12,13,14,12,15
Group B:	13,15,16,15,16
Group C:	15,16,17,16,17

```
10  INPUT "HOW MANY SUBJECTS IN G
ROUP A? ";NA
20  INPUT "HOW MANY SUBJECTS IN G
ROUP B? ";NB
25  INPUT "HOW MANY SUBJECTS IN G
ROUP C? ";NC
30  DIM A(NA),B(NB),C(NC)
40  FOR I = 1 TO NA
50  INPUT "ENTER A SCORE FOR GROU
P A. ";A(I)
60  NEXT I
70  GOSUB 490
80  FOR I = 1 TO NB
90  INPUT "ENTER A SCORE FOR GROU
P B. ";B(I)
100  NEXT I
110  GOSUB 770
120  FOR I = 1 TO NC
130  INPUT "ENTER A SCORE FOR GRO
UP C. ";C(I)
140  NEXT I
150  GOSUB 1040
160  FOR I = 1 TO NA
170  AALL = AALL + A(I)
180  AROOT = AROOT + A(I) * A(I)
190  NEXT I
200  FOR J = 1 TO NB
210  BALL = BALL + B(J)
220  BROOT = BROOT + B(J) * B(J)
230  NEXT J
240  FOR K = 1 TO NC
250  CLL = CLL + C(K)
260  CROOT = CROOT + C(K) * C(K)
270  NEXT K
```

Statements 10-30 set the size for
the three groups and save RAM for
the scores.

Statements 40-270 enable the user
to enter the scores for each group,
make corrections as necessary, and
then calculate the sum of scores
and the sum of squared scores for
each group.

```
280  AMEAN = AALL / NA
290  BMEAN = BALL / NB
300  CMEAN = CLL / NC
310  ASD =  SQR ((AROOT / NA) - AM
EAN ^ 2)
320  BSD =  SQR ((BROOT / NB) - BM
EAN ^ 2)
330  CSD =  SQR ((CROOT / NC) - CM
EAN ^ 2)
340  STTL = (AROOT + BROOT + CROOT
) - ((AALL + BALL + CLL) ^ 2
) / (NA + NB + NC)
350  SBTN = (((AALL ^ 2) / NA) + (
(BALL ^ 2) / NB) + ((CLL ^ 2
) / NC)) - ((AALL + BALL + C
LL) ^ 2) / (NA + NB + NC)
360  SWS = STTL - SBTN
370  PRINT "ASUM=",AALL
380  PRINT "BSUM=",BALL
385  PRINT "CSUM = ",CLL
390  PRINT "ASUM OF SQUARES=",ARO
OT
400  PRINT "BSUM OF SQUARES=",BRO
OT
405  PRINT "CSUM OF SQUARES=",CRO
OT
410  PRINT "AMEAN=",AMEAN
420  PRINT "BMEAN=",BMEAN
425  PRINT "CMEAN=",CMEAN
430  PRINT "'A' STANDARD DEVIATIO
N=",ASD
440  PRINT "'B' STANDARD DEVIATIO
N=",BSD
445  PRINT "'C' STANDARD DEVIATIO
N=",CSD
450  PRINT "TOTAL SUM OF SQ=",STT
L
460  PRINT "BETWEEN SUM OF SQUARE
S=",SBTN
470  PRINT "WITHIN SUBJECTS SUM O
F SQ=",SWS
480  END
490  REM  START DISPLAYING VALUES
 FOR CORRECTIONS IN GROUP A
500  KK = 1
510  TEXT : HOME
520  FOR I = KK TO NA
530  PQ = PQ + 1
540  PRINT I;"   ";
550  PRINT "A= ";
560  PRINT A(I)
570  IF PQ = 14 OR (I = NA) THEN
 GOSUB 600:PQ = 0: HOME : REM
 MAKE CORRECTIONS
580  NEXT I
590  RETURN
```

Statements 280–470 calculate the values needed for each group and then the values needed for the analysis of variance. The sum of squares within subjects (statement 360) is calculated by subtraction but could be calculated by obtaining the sum of squares for each group and adding them.

Statements 490–1300 constitute the correction subroutines for each of the three groups.

```
600   REM  SUB CORRECTIONS
610   PRINT "CHANGES IN THIS GROUP
?  "
620   INPUT "Y OR N ";TT$: IF TT$ <
> "Y" AND TT$ < > "N" THEN
620
630   IF TT$ = "N" THEN  RETURN
640   PRINT "WHICH I ";
650   PRINT "DO YOU WISH";
660   INPUT " TO CHANGE ";IC
670   PRINT "OLD VALUE= ";
680   PRINT A(IC)
690   INPUT "NEW VALUE= ";A(IC)
700   PRINT "ANY MORE CHANGES";
710   PRINT " IN THIS LOT"
730   INPUT "Y OR N ";TT$
740   IF TT$ = "Y" THEN  GOTO 640
750   IF TT$ = "N" THEN  RETURN
760   GOTO 730: REM  BAD RESPONSE
770   REM     START DISPLAYING VALU
ES FOR CORRECTIONS IN GROUP
B
780   KK = 1
790   TEXT : HOME
800   FOR I = KK TO NB
810   PQ = PQ + 1
820   PRINT I;"   ";
830   PRINT "B= ";
840   PRINT B(I)
850   IF PQ = 14 OR (I = NB) THEN
GOSUB 880:PQ = Ø: HOME : REM
MAKE CORRECTIONS
860   NEXT I
870   RETURN
880   REM  SUB CORRECTIONS GROUP B

890   PRINT "CHANGES IN THIS GROUP
?  "
900   INPUT "Y OR N ";TT$: IF TT$ <
> "Y" AND TT$ < > "N" THEN
900
910   IF TT$ = "N" THEN  RETURN
920   PRINT "WHICH I ";
930   PRINT "DO YOU WISH ";
940   INPUT "TO CHANGE? ";IC
950   PRINT "OLD VALUE= ";
960   PRINT B(IC)
970   INPUT "NEW VALUE= ";B(IC)
980   PRINT "ANY MORE CHANGES";
990   PRINT " IN THIS LOT "
1000  INPUT "Y OR N ";TT$
1010  IF TT$ = "Y" THEN  GOTO 920

1020  IF TT$ = "N" THEN  RETURN
1030  GOTO 1000: REM  BAD RESPONS
E
```

```
1040  REM  START DISPLAYING VALUE
S FOR CORRECTIONS IN GROUP C

1050  KK = 1
1060  TEXT : HOME
1070  FOR I = KK TO NC
1080  PQ = PQ + 1
1090  PRINT I;"   ";
1100  PRINT "C= ";
1110  PRINT C(I)
1120  IF PQ = 14 OR (I = NC) THEN
GOSUB 1150:PQ = Ø: HOME : REM
MAKE CORRECTIONS
1130  NEXT I
1140  RETURN
1150  REM  SUB CORRECTIONS GROUP
C
1160  PRINT "CHANGES IN THIS GROU
P?  "
1170  INPUT "Y OR N ";TT$: IF TT$
< > "Y" AND TT$ < > "N" THEN
900
1180  IF TT$ = "N" THEN  RETURN
1190  PRINT "WHICH I ";
1200  PRINT "DO YOU WISH ";
1210  INPUT "TO CHANGE? ";IC
1220  PRINT "OLD VALUE= ";
1230  PRINT C(IC)
1240  INPUT "NEW VALUE= ";C(IC)
1250  PRINT "ANY MORE CHANGES";
1260  PRINT " IN THIS LOT "
1270  INPUT "Y OR N ";TT$
1280  IF TT$ = "Y" THEN  GOTO 119
Ø
1290  IF TT$ = "N" THEN  RETURN
1300  GOTO 1270: REM  BAD RESPON
SE
```

PROGRAM OUTPUT

```
]ASUM=66
BSUM=75
CSUM = 81
ASUM OF SQUARES=878
BSUM OF SQUARES=1131
CSUM OF SQUARES=1315
AMEAN=13.2
BMEAN=15
CMEAN=16.2
'A' STANDARD DEVIATION=1.1661903
'B' STANDARD DEVIATION=1.09544511
'C' STANDARD DEVIATION=.748331361
TOTAL SUM OF SQ=38.3999982
BETWEEN SUM OF SQUARES=22.7999997
WITHIN SUBJECTS SUM OF SQ=
15.5999985
```

APPLESOFT BASIC PROGRAM FOR A TWO-FACTOR ANALYSIS OF VARIANCE

The program illustrated here performs a two-factor anova for between subjects factors. Each factor can have several levels which the user specifies. The example is taken from Hopkins and Glass, 1978 page 377.

	B_1	B_2
A_1	4,5,6,8,10,3,5,6,8,7	5,5,7,8,9,4,5,6,7,8
A_2	7,5,7,8,9,3,4,8,6,9	4,5,3,4,9,3,5,6,8,7

```
1  PRINT "THIS PROGRAM DOES AN AN
OVA FOR A"
2  PRINT "TWO FACTOR DESIGN."
3  PRINT "A=THE LEVELS OF THE FIR
ST BETWEEN S FACTOR"
4  PRINT "B=THE LEVELS OF THE SEC
OND BETWEEN S FACTOR"
5  PRINT "C=THE NUMBER OF SUBJECT
S IN EACH AB TREATMENT."
6  INPUT "HOW MANY LEVELS OF THE
BETWEEN FACTOR A? ";A
7  INPUT "HOW MANY LEVELS OF THE
BETWEEN FACTOR B? ";B
8  INPUT "HOW MANY SUBJECTS IN EA
CH AB TREATMENT COMBINATION?
 ";C
```

Statements 1-8 request input from the user specifying the design values.

```
10  DIM X(A,B,C),A(A),B(B),COL(A,
B),RSSQ(A,B)
```

Statement 10 dimensions the variables.

```
20   FOR I = 1 TO A
30   FOR K = 1 TO B
35   FOR J = 1 TO C
40   PRINT "ENTER A SCORE FOR "
41   PRINT "A";I;"B";K;"C";J;
42   INPUT X(I,K,J)
45   NEXT J
50   NEXT K
60   NEXT I
```

Statements 20-60 enable the user to enter score values for each subject in each treatment combination.

```
70   FOR I = 1 TO A
80   FOR K = 1 TO B
85   FOR J = 1 TO C
90  COL(I,K) = COL(I,K) + X(I,K,J)
100 RSSQ(I,K) = RSSQ(I,K) + (X(I,
K,J) * X(I,K,J))
105   NEXT J
110   NEXT K
120   NEXT I
125   FOR I = 1 TO A
130   FOR K = 1 TO B
135 TTL = TTL + COL(I,K)
140   NEXT K: NEXT I
145   FOR I = 1 TO A
150   FOR K = 1 TO B
155 A(I) = A(I) + COL(I,K)
160   NEXT K: NEXT I
```

Statements 70-120, 125-140, 145-160, and 175-190 constitute individual loops which calculate the values for the main factors.

```
170   FOR I = 1 TO A
175   FOR K = 1 TO B
180   B(K) = B(K) + COL(I,K)
190   NEXT K: NEXT I
200   FOR I = 1 TO A: PRINT A(I): NEXT
I
210   FOR K = 1 TO B: PRINT B(K): NEXT
K
270   GOSUB 500
450   END
500   REM   THIS DOES THE ACTUAL AN
OVA
520   T1 = (TTL * TTL) / (A * B * C
)
530   FOR I = 1 TO A: FOR K = 1 TO
B
532   T2 = T2 + RSSQ(I,K)
534   NEXT K: NEXT I
538   FOR I = 1 TO A
540   T3 = T3 + (A(I) * A(I))
542   NEXT I
545   T3 = T3 / (B * C)
550   FOR K = 1 TO B:T4 = T4 + (B(
K) * B(K)): NEXT K
555   T4 = T4 / (A * C)
560   FOR I = 1 TO A
570   FOR K = 1 TO B
580   T5 = T5 + (COL(I,K) * COL(I,K
))
590   NEXT K: NEXT I
600   T5 = T5 / C
630   PRINT T1
640   PRINT T2
650   PRINT T3
660   PRINT T4
670   PRINT T5
700   PRINT "TOTAL SUM OF SQUARES=
";T2 - T1
710   PRINT "SUM OF SQUARES BETWEE
N SUBJECTS= ";T5 - T1
720   PRINT "SUM OF SQUARES FOR A=
";T3 - T1
730   PRINT "SUM OF SQUARES FOR B=
";T4 - T1
740   PRINT "SUM OF SQUARES FOR AB
= ";T5 - T3 - T4 + T1
750   PRINT "SUM OF SQUARES FOR ER
ROR= ";T2 - T5
```

Statements 200 and 210 print the values for the main factors.

Statements 500–600 calculate the values for each term needed to compute the variance for the ANOVA. The terms are from Winer (1972).

Statements 630–670 print the values of the terms.

Statements 700–750 print the source of variation and the sum of squares for each of the terms needed in the ANOVA table. The user must calculate the df, MS, and F-ratio. The program could be modified to do this and to print the actual table.

```
THIS PROGRAM DOES AN ANOVA FOR A
TWO FACTOR DESIGN.
A=THE LEVELS OF THE FIRST BETWEEN S FACTOR
B=THE LEVELS OF THE SECOND BETWEEN S FACTOR
C=THE NUMBER OF SUBJECTS IN EACH AB TREATMENT.
HOW MANY LEVELS OF THE BETWEEN FACTOR A? 2
HOW MANY LEVELS OF THE BETWEEN FACTOR B? 2
HOW MANY SUBJECTS IN EACH AB TREATMENT COMBINATION? 10
ENTER A SCORE FOR                    A2B1C1?7
A1B1C1?4                             ENTER A SCORE FOR
ENTER A SCORE FOR                    A2B1C2?5
A1B1C2?5                             ENTER A SCORE FOR
ENTER A SCORE FOR                    A2B1C3?7
A1B1C3?6                             ENTER A SCORE FOR
ENTER A SCORE FOR                    A2B1C4?8
A1B1C4?8                             ENTER A SCORE FOR
ENTER A SCORE FOR                    A2B1C5?9
A1B1C5?10                            ENTER A SCORE FOR
ENTER A SCORE FOR                    A2B1C6?3
A1B1C6?3                             ENTER A SCORE FOR
ENTER A SCORE FOR                    A2B1C7?4
A1B1C7?5                             ENTER A SCORE FOR
ENTER A SCORE FOR                    A2B1C8?8
A1B1C8?6                             ENTER A SCORE FOR
ENTER A SCORE FOR                    A2B1C9?6
A1B1C9?8                             ENTER A SCORE FOR
ENTER A SCORE FOR                    A2B1C10?9
A1B1C10?7                            ENTER A SCORE FOR
ENTER A SCORE FOR                    A2B2C1?4
A1B2C1?5                             ENTER A SCORE FOR
ENTER A SCORE FOR                    A2B2C2?5
A1B2C2?5                             ENTER A SCORE FOR
ENTER A SCORE FOR                    A2B2C3?3
A1B2C3?7                             ENTER A SCORE FOR
ENTER A SCORE FOR                    A2B2C4?4
A1B2C4?8                             ENTER A SCORE FOR
ENTER A SCORE FOR                    A2B2C5?9
A1B2C5?9                             ENTER A SCORE FOR
ENTER A SCORE FOR                    A2B2C6?3
A1B2C6?4                             ENTER A SCORE FOR
ENTER A SCORE FOR                    A2B2C7?5
A1B2C7?5                             ENTER A SCORE FOR
ENTER A SCORE FOR                    A2B2C8?6
A1B2C8?6                             ENTER A SCORE FOR
ENTER A SCORE FOR                    A2B2C9?7
A1B2C9?7                             ENTER A SCORE FOR
ENTER A SCORE FOR                    A2B2C10?8
A1B2C10?8                            1512.9
ENTER A SCORE FOR                    1662
                                     1513.8
                                     1515.4
TOTAL SUM OF SQUARES= 149.1          1521.2
SUM OF SQUARES BETWEEN SUBJECTS= 8.29999972
SUM OF SQUARES FOR A= .900000095
SUM OF SQUARES FOR B= 2.5
SUM OF SQUARES FOR AB= 4.89999962
SUM OF SQUARES FOR ERROR= 140.8
```

APPLESOFT BASIC PROGRAM FOR A TWO-FACTOR ANOVA WITH REPEATED
MEASURES ON THE SECOND FACTOR

This program is to be used in conjunction with the material
presented in Chapter 17 and may be used to check your work of
the examples in that chapter. As explained in the annotation
it can be used with data that is included in DATA statements
in the program or can be used with direct entry of data.

```
1   PRINT "THIS PROGRAM DOES AN AN
OVA FOR A TWO FACTOR"
2   PRINT "DESIGN WITH REPEATED ME
ASURES ON THE SECOND"
3   PRINT "FACTOR. A=THE LEVELS OF
  THE BETWEEN S FACTOR"
4   PRINT "B=THE LEVELS OF THE REP
EATED FACTOR"
5   PRINT "C=THE NUMBER OF SUBJECT
S IN EACH A LEVEL."
6   INPUT "HOW MANY LEVELS OF THE
BETWEEN FACTOR? ";A
7   INPUT "HOW MANY LEVELS OF THE
REPEATED MEASURE? ";B
8   INPUT "HOW MANY SUBJECTS IN EA
CH GROUP? ";C
10  DIM A(A,B,C)
20  FOR I = 1 TO A
30  FOR K = 1 TO B
35  FOR J = 1 TO C
40  PRINT "ENTER A SCORE FOR "
41  PRINT "A";I;"B";K;"C";J;
42  INPUT A(I,K,J)
45  NEXT J
50  NEXT K
60  NEXT I
70  FOR I = 1 TO A
80  FOR K = 1 TO B
85  FOR J = 1 TO C
90  COL(I,K) = COL(I,K) + A(I,K,J)

100  RSSQ(I,K) = RSSQ(I,K) + (A(I,
K,J) * A(I,K,J))
105  NEXT J
110  NEXT K
120  NEXT I
140  FOR I = 1 TO A
145  FOR J = 1 TO C
147  FOR K = 1 TO B
150  ROW(I,J) = ROW(I,J) + A(I,K,J
)
170  NEXT K
175  NEXT J
180  NEXT I
```

Statements 1-8 provide informa-
to the program user about the
coding. They also obtain the
information about the levels
of A,B and C needed for the
program.

Statement 10 dimensions an array
for the scores according to the
input of the user.

Statements 20-60 enable the user
to input scores going across the
rows. By changing statement 42
to READ A(I,K,J) the program
will read data from the DATA
statements in the program.

Statements 70-120 serve to sum
and square and sum the scores.

Statements 140-170 sums the
rows to obtain totals for
each subject.

(continued)

TWO FACTOR RM ANOVA (continued)

```
220   FOR KK = 1 TO A
225   FOR LL = 1 TO B
236   SMALL = SMALL + COL(KK,LL)
237   SQSM = SQSM + RSSQ(KK,LL)
238   SCLM = SCLM + (COL(KK,LL) * C
OL(KK,LL))
240   NEXT LL: NEXT KK
247   GOSUB 500
248   END
250   DATA  21,16,9,4,2,5,1,0,0,7,
17,19,18,19,5,5,2,1,20,18,33
,18,18,5,11,0,15,7,28,11
260   DATA  8,7,0,12,7,7,26,11,13,
9,2,11,0,9,13,8,4,10,20,14,9
,22,8,0,7,2,9,20,23,20
270   DATA  0,3,5,19,11,5,4,5,2,4,
0,21,3,10,10,9,12,7,5,14,1,1
9,0,5,4,10,8,35,6,15
500   REM  THIS DOES THE ACTUAL AN
OVA
520   T1 = (SMALL * SMALL) / (A * B
 * C)
530   FOR I = 1 TO A: FOR K = 1 TO
B
532   T2 = T2 + RSSQ(I,K)
534   NEXT K: NEXT I
540   FOR J = 1 TO A
550   FOR K = 1 TO B
560   PART(J) = PART(J) + COL(J,K)
561   IF K = 1 THEN P(1) = P(1) +
COL(J,K)
562   IF K = 2 THEN P(2) = P(2) +
COL(J,K)
563   IF K = 3 THEN P(3) = P(3) +
COL(J,K)
564   IF K = 4 THEN P(4) = P(4) +
COL(J,K)
565   IF K = 5 THEN P(5) = P(5) +
COL(J,K)
566   IF K = 6 THEN P(6) = P(6) +
COL(J,K)
567   IF K = 7 THEN P(7) = P(7) +
COL(J,K)
568   IF K = 8 THEN P(8) = P(8) +
COL(J,K)
569   IF K = 9 THEN P(9) = P(9) +
COL(J,K)
570   T5 = T5 + (COL(J,K) * COL(J,K
))
571   NEXT K: NEXT J
```

Statements 220-240 sum and square and sum the column totals.

250-270 contains the raw data used by the program if READ statement is used in 42. If the data is included in the program then it can be checked for correctness before running. It should be entered in the same way as the example.

Statements 500-571 perform the computations necessary to obtain values for the ANOVA

(continued)

TWO FACTOR RM ANOVA (continued)

```
572 T5 = T5 / C
580  FOR L = 1 TO A:T3 = T3 + (PA
RT(L) * PART(L)): NEXT L
585 T3 = T3 / (B * C)

587 T4 = T4 + (P(K) * P(K))
588  NEXT K
595 T4 = T4 / (A * C)
600  FOR I = 1 TO A
610  FOR J = 1 TO C
620 T6 = T6 + (ROW(I,J) * ROW(I,J
))
621  NEXT J: NEXT I
625 T6 = T6 / B
630  PRINT T1
640  PRINT T2
650  PRINT T3
660  PRINT T4
670  PRINT T5
680  PRINT T6
690  PRINT "BETWEEN SUBJECTS SS=
";(T6 - T1)
700  PRINT "PRACTICE SS= ";(T3 -
T1)
710  PRINT "BETWEEN S ERROR= ";(T
6 - T3)
720  PRINT "WITHIN S SS= ";(T2 -
T6)
730  PRINT "TRIALS SS= ";(T4 - T1
)
740  PRINT "PRACTICE X TRIALS SS=
";(T5 - T3 - T4 + T1)
750  PRINT "WITHIN GROUPS ERROR=
";(T2 - T5 - T6 + T3)
760  RETURN
```

Statements 572-565 compute the values needed to obtain the sums of squares for the sources of variance.

Statements 630-680 cause the values obtained above to be printed out.

Statements 690-760 compute and print the sums of squares for the ANOVA.

SAMPLE OUTPUT FOR THIS PROGRAM IS PROVIDED ON NEXT PAGE

TWO FACTOR REPEATED MEASURES ANOVA - PROGRAM OUTPUT
]RUN
THIS PROGRAM DOES AN ANOVA FOR A TWO FACTOR
DESIGN WITH REPEATED MEASURES ON THE SECOND
FACTOR. A=THE LEVELS OF THE BETWEEN S FACTOR
B=THE LEVELS OF THE REPEATED FACTOR
C=THE NUMBER OF SUBJECTS IN EACH A LEVEL.
HOW MANY LEVELS OF THE BETWEEN FACTOR? 2
HOW MANY LEVELS OF THE REPEATED MEASURE? 4
HOW MANY SUBJECTS IN EACH GROUP? 3
ENTER A SCORE FOR
A1B1C1?0
ENTER A SCORE FOR
A1B1C2?3
ENTER A SCORE FOR   Example from Winer (1971:525)
A1B1C3?4
ENTER A SCORE FOR   B1   B2   B3   B4
A1B2C1?0   S1   0   0   5   3
ENTER A SCORE FOR   A1   S2   3   1   5   4
A1B2C2?1   S3   4   3   6   2
ENTER A SCORE FOR
A1B2C3?3   S1   4   2   7   8
ENTER A SCORE FOR   A2   S2   5   4   6   6
A1B3C1?5   S3   7   5   8   9
ENTER A SCORE FOR
A1B3C2?5
ENTER A SCORE FOR
A1B3C3?6
ENTER A SCORE FOR
A1B4C1?3
ENTER A SCORE FOR
A1B4C2?4
ENTER A SCORE FOR
A1B4C3?2
ENTER A SCORE FOR
A2B1C1?4
ENTER A SCORE FOR
A2B1C2?5
ENTER A SCORE FOR
A2B1C3?7
ENTER A SCORE FOR
A2B2C1?2
ENTER A SCORE FOR   477.041667
A2B2C2?4   615
ENTER A SCORE FOR   528.083333
A2B2C3?5   524.5
ENTER A SCORE FOR   583
A2B3C1?7   545.25
ENTER A SCORE FOR   BETWEEN SUBJECTS SS= 68.2083334
A2B3C2?6   PRACTICE SS= 51.0416666
ENTER A SCORE FOR   BETWEEN S ERROR= 17.1666668
A2B3C3?8   WITHIN S SS= 69.75
ENTER A SCORE FOR   TRIALS SS= 47.4583334
A2B4C1?8   PRACTICE X TRIALS SS= 7.45833338
ENTER A SCORE FOR   WITHIN GROUPS ERROR= 14.8333333
A2B4C2?6
ENTER A SCORE FOR
A2B4C3?9

APPLESOFT BASIC PROGRAM FOR COINCIDENCE-ANTICIPATION RESEARCH

This program is used with an internal clock (in slot #4) to test coincidence-anticipation performance. The line moves at different speeds. The program administers 90 trials and then writes the results to a file. There is a high-resolution graphics version available also.

Statements 10-105 serve to instruct the subject in the testing procedures. GET T$ causes the program to pause while the subject reads the instructions. The operation resumes when the subject presses any key.

```
5   D$ = CHR$ (4)
10  HOME
11  VTAB 3
20  PRINT "THIS PROGRAM TESTS YOUR ABILITY TO "
30  PRINT "PREDICT THE ARRIVAL OF A MOVING LINE "
40  PRINT "AT AN INTERCEPT POINT INDICATED BY "
50  PRINT "A LINE TO THE RIGHT OF THE SCREEN. "
51  PRINT
52  PRINT "YOU SHOULD PRESS ANY KEY SO THAT IT "
53  PRINT "REACHES THE DEPRESSED POSITION AT THE "
54  PRINT "SAME TIME THE LINE CONTACTS THE BAR. "
55  PRINT
56  PRINT "FOR FURTHER INSTRUCTION PRESS ANY LETTER. "
57  GET T$
90  PRINT "YOU MAY PRESS ANY KEY BUT WE SUGGEST
91  PRINT "THAT YOU ALWAYS USE THE SAME KEY FOR "
92  PRINT "CONSISTENCY.
93  PRINT
94  PRINT "A BLINKING SQUARE ON THE SCREEN MEANS "
95  PRINT "THAT YOU MUST PRESS THE LETTER KEY TO "
96  PRINT "CONTINUE. "
97  GET T$
98  HOME : VTAB 3
99  PRINT "BEFORE EACH TRIAL THE NUMBER OF THE "
100 PRINT "TRIAL WILL APPEAR AT THE BOTTOM OF "
101 PRINT "SCREEN AND A BLINKING SQUARE AT THE "
```

Statements 200-210 obtain the subjects name and reserve space in RAM for the 90 scores and speed codes.

```
102 PRINT "LOWER LEFT.
103 PRINT
104 PRINT "WHEN YOU PRESS THE KEY THE FIRST TRIAL "
105 PRINT "WILL BEGIN. "
110 GET T$
181 PRINT
190 HOME
195 VTAB 3
200 INPUT "PLEASE WRITE YOUR FULL NAME. ";SNAME$
210 DIM SCRE(90),SPD(90)
220 FOR EE = 1 TO 90
230 VTAB 20
240 HTAB 20
250 PRINT EE
260 GET T$
261 PRINT
270 GR : COLOR= 3
280 READ X
290 SPD(EE) = X
300 PLOT 37,20: PLOT 37,21: PLOT 37,19
310 GOSUB 510: REM  READCLOCK
320 T1IME = S2EC
330 FLAG = 0: POKE ( - 16368),0
340 FOR I = 3 TO 37
350 FOR KK = 1 TO 1 * X: NEXT KK
360 PLOT I,20
370 IF FLAG = 0 AND  PEEK ( - 16384) > 127 THEN  GOSUB 570:FLAG = 1
380 NEXT I
390 GOSUB 510
400 T3IME = S2EC: IF FLAG = 1 THEN T3IME = T3IME - .066
410 IF FLAG = 0 THEN  GET T$: GOSUB 570
420 TEXT
430 HOME
440 POKE ( - 16368),0
450 SCRE(EE) = T2IME - T3IME
460 NEXT EE
470 GOTO 590
```

Statements 220-460 control the actual task which operates in low resolution graphics. The GOSUB 510 occurs just prior to the line beginning and just after the line is completed. The subject's response may occur early, in which case statement 370 causes the clock to be read. If the subject's response occurs late the program reads the clock first, 400 and then waits for the subject to press a key before the clock is read for the subject's response. Finally, statement 450 calculates the subjects score by determining when the subject responded in relation to when the line reached the intercept point.

Statement 470 causes the speed code and the scores to be written to a data file which can be recalled later for analysis.

Statements 480-495 provide the speed codes used in 290 to control the line.

```
480  DATA  1,13,29,13,1,29,1,13,2
9,13,1,13,29,13,1,29,1,29,13
,1,29,13,29,1,29,13,1
485  DATA  29,13,1,13,29,1,13,29,
1,29,13,29,1,29,1,29,13,1,13,1,13
,1,29,1,29,13,29,13,1
490  DATA  13,29,1,13,1,13,29,1,2
9,1,13,1,29,13,29,13,1,29,13
,1,29,13,29,1,13,29,1
495  DATA  13,29,1,13,1,29,1,13,2
9
500  END
```

Statements 510-560 cause the clock to be read.

Statements 570-580 cause the clock to be read but it is the subject's response.

```
510  REM  READCLOCK
520  PR# 4: IN# 4
530  INPUT " ";T1$
540  S2EC = 60 *  VAL ( MID$ (T1$,
10,2)) +  VAL ( MID$ (T1$,13
,6))
550  PR# 0: IN# 0
560  RETURN
570  REM  SUBJECTS RESPONSE
580  GOSUB 510:T2IME = S2EC: RETURN

590  CALL 1002
600  N$ = "ASCRES"
610  D$ =  CHR$ (4)
620  PRINT D$;"APPEND ";N$
630  PRINT D$;"WRITE ";N$
640  PRINT SNAME$
650  FOR I = 1 TO 90
660  PRINT SPD(I)
665  PRINT SCRE(I)
670  NEXT I
680  PRINT D$"CLOSE ";N$
```

Statements 590-680 cause the data and speed codes to be written to a data file. The first time the program operates 620 should indicate "OPEN", afterwards the proper instruction is "APPEND" as written.

This program enables you to read the data files created as part of this program and as part of the BSRI program presented previously.

```
1  I = 90
5  DIM SPD(I),SCRE(I)
10  D$ =  CHR$ (4): REM  CTRL D
12  PRINT "THIS PROGRAM RETRIEVES
 TEXT FILES"
14  PRINT "CREATED BY THE 'CREATE
 TEXT' PROGRAM."
16  PRINT "MON C,I,O IS IN EFFECT
."
18  PRINT
20  INPUT "NAME OF TEXT FILE? ";Z
$
22  PRINT D$;"MON C,I,O"
24  PRINT
30  PRINT D$;"OPEN ";Z$
40  PRINT D$;"READ ";Z$
45  INPUT SNAME$
46  FOR J = 1 TO 90
52  INPUT SPD(J)
53  INPUT SCRE(J)
54  NEXT J
90  PRINT D$;"CLOSE ";Z$
100  PRINT D$;"NOMON C,I,O"
```

APPLESOFT BASIC PROGRAM FOR SCORING THE PERSONAL ATTRIBUTES
QUESTIONNAIRE (PAQ)

This program accepts answers from the paper and pencil version
of the PAQ and returns a total score for each of 6 scales.

Statements 10-30 provide the
option of the user having
instruction in how to use the
program.

Statements 35-40 set the number of
subjects and reserve an area of the
correct size in RAM for the values
to be entered.

Statements 50-56 cause the
program to read the scale for the
PAQ contained in the DATA statement
400.

Statements 210-260 print out the
scores by subject by each scale.
Statements 399-502 contain test data
as indicated.

```
10   PRINT "DO YOU WISH INSTRUCTIO
NS?"
20   INPUT "TYPE YES OR NO AFTER ?
 ";RES$
30   IF RES$ = "YES" THEN  GOSUB 1
000
35   INPUT "HOW MANY SUBJECTS? ";N

40   DIM SCLE(40),ANS$(N,40),ANS(N
,40)
50   FOR J = 1 TO 40
55   READ SCLE(J)
56   NEXT J
60   FOR I = 1 TO N
70   FOR J = 1 TO 40
80   READ ANS$(I,J)
85   REM  NUMBERS 1-6 EQUAL M+ F+
M-F+ M- FVA- AND FC- RESPECT
IVELY
90   IF SCLE(J) = 1 THEN  GOSUB 20
00
100  IF SCLE(J) = 2 THEN  GOSUB 2
100
110  IF SCLE(J) = 3 THEN  GOSUB 2
200
120  IF SCLE(J) = 4 THEN  GOSUB 2
300
130  IF SCLE(J) = 5 THEN  GOSUB 2
400
140  IF SCLE(J) = 6 THEN  GOSUB 2
500
150  NEXT J
160  NEXT I
170  I = 1
```

Statements 60-160 read the
subject's answers (A-F) and cause
the value to be added to the
appropriate scale.

```
210  PRINT "SUBJECT ";I;" MASC PO
S= ";MPSRE(I)
220  PRINT "SUBJECT ";I;" FEM POS
= ";FPSRE(I)
230  PRINT "SUBJECT ";I;" MAS-FEM
 POS= "MFPSRE(I)
240  PRINT "SUBJECT ";I;" MAS NEG
= ";MNSRE(I)
250  PRINT "SUBJECT ";I;" FVA NEG
= ";FVANSRE(I)
260  PRINT "SUBJECT ";I;" FC NEG=
 ";FCNSRE(I)
270  END
399  REM  SCALE ITEM IDENTIFICATI
ON
400  DATA  3,5,1,4,2,3,4,3,1,4,2,
6,2,5,2,1,6,3,4,2,3,4,3,5,2,
1,5,1,4,3,1,4,1,4,2,2,6,3,6,
1
501  REM  TEST DATA
502  DATA  E,A,E,E,E,A,A,E,E,E,
E,E,E,E,E,A,E,A,E,A,A,A,E,E,
A,A,E,A,A,E,E,E,E,E,A,A,E,
E
1000 PRINT "THIS PROGRAM ANALYZE
S THE RESULTS OF THE 40-ITEM
 EXTENDED PAQ"
1010 PRINT "IT DOES THIS BY USIN
G TWO VARIABLES"
1020 PRINT "ONE VARIABLE INDICAT
ES THE SCALE TO WHICH THE IT
EM BELONGS"
1030 PRINT "THE SECOND VARIABLE
INDICATES THE SUBJECTS ANSWE
R ON THAT ITEM"
1040 PRINT
1050 PRINT "(TO CONTINUE INTRODU
CTION HIT ANY KEY)": GET T$
1060 PRINT
1070 PRINT "THE DATA ARE ENTERED
 AT THE END OF THE PROGRAM A
ND ARE PART OF IT"
1080 PRINT "ENTER DATA BY TYPING
 A NUMBER IN THE 6000 RANGE"
```

Statements 1000-1170 contain the
instructions which are accessed
from the main program.

1090 PRINT "THEN TYPE THE WORD
DATA' FOLLOWED BY THE SUBJEC
TS ENTRY FOR EACH ITEM"
1100 PRINT "DO THIS FOR ALL SUBJ
ECTS, ENTERING ALL ANSWERS F
OR EACH SUBJECT ON A SINGLE
LINE"
1170 RETURN

Statements 2000–2550 constitute
the part of the program that sums
the scale values for each subject.
Within each scale the values are
sometimes reversed, the subroutines 3000
and 4000, which are called from the
program, serve to assign the appropriate
values as necessary.

2000 REM M+ SCALE
2010 GOSUB 4000
2020 IF J = 26 THEN GOSUB 3000
2030 MPSRE(I) = MPSRE(I) + ANS(I,
J)
2050 RETURN
2100 REM F+ SCALE
2110 GOSUB 4000
2120 FPSRE(I) = FPSRE(I) + ANS(I,
J)
2160 RETURN
2200 REM M-F+ SCALE
2210 GOSUB 3000
2255 IF J = 1 THEN   GOSUB 4000
2256 IF J = 18 THEN GOSUB 4000
2257 IF J = 6 THEN   GOSUB 4000
2260 MFPSRE(I) = MFPSRE(I) + ANS(
I,J)
2270 RETURN
2300 REM M- SCALE
2310 IF J = 4 THEN   GOSUB 4000
2315 IF J = 7 THEN   GOSUB 3000
2320 IF J = 10 THEN GOSUB 4000
2330 IF J = 19 THEN GOSUB 3000
2340 IF J = 22 THEN GOSUB 3000
2350 IF J = 29 THEN GOSUB 3000
2360 IF J = 32 THEN GOSUB 4000
2370 IF J = 34 THEN GOSUB 4000
2375 MNSRE(I) = MNSRE(I) + ANS(I,
J)
2380 RETURN
2400 REM FVA- SCALE
2410 IF J = 2 THEN   GOSUB 3000
2420 IF J = 14 THEN GOSUB 4000
2430 IF J = 24 THEN GOSUB 4000
2440 IF J = 27 THEN GOSUB 3000
2445 FVANSRE(I) = FVANSRE(I) + AN
S(I,J)
2450 RETURN

2500 REM FC- SCALE
2510 IF J = 12 THEN GOSUB 4000
2520 IF J = 17 THEN GOSUB 3000
2530 IF J = 37 THEN GOSUB 3000
2540 IF J = 39 THEN GOSUB 4000
2545 FCNSRE(I) = FCNSRE(I) + ANS(
I,J)
2550 RETURN

Statements 3000–4060 serve to
assign the appropriate values to the
alphabetic answers as dictated by
the scale.

3000 REM A-E/4-0
3010 IF ANS$(I,J) = "A" THEN ANS
(I,J) = 4
3020 IF ANS$(I,J) = "B" THEN ANS
(I,J) = 3
3030 IF ANS$(I,J) = "C" THEN ANS
(I,J) = 2
3040 IF ANS$(I,J) = "D" THEN ANS
(I,J) = 1
3050 IF ANS$(I,J) = "E" THEN ANS
(I,J) = 0
3060 RETURN
4000 REM A-E/0-4
4010 IF ANS$(I,J) = "A" THEN ANS
(I,J) = 0
4020 IF ANS$(I,J) = "B" THEN ANS
(I,J) = 1
4030 IF ANS$(I,J) = "C" THEN ANS
(I,J) = 2
4040 IF ANS$(I,J) = "D" THEN ANS
(I,J) = 3
4050 IF ANS$(I,J) = "E" THEN ANS
(I,J) = 4
4060 RETURN

APPLESOFT BASIC PROGRAM FOR ADMINISTERING, SCORING, AND SAVING
    SUBJECT DATA FOR THE BEM SEX ROLE INVENTORY   (BSRI)

This program was designed to administer, score and record the
results of the Bem Sex Role Inventory. It does not interpret
these results but communicates these results to the researcher.
Although the researcher must RUN the program the HELLO program
on the particular disk could be modified to automatically run
the program when the disk is booted. If the inventory was
administered as a paper and pencil test the program could be
modified to score the test.

```
10   INPUT "WRITE YOUR FULL NAME "
;NAME$
20   DIM X(20,3),N(20,3),A$(20,3)
30   FOR I = 1 TO 20
40   FOR J = 1 TO 3
50   READ N(I,J),A$(I,J)
60   HOME
70   PRINT "RATE YOURSELF ON A SCA
LE OF 1 TO 7 FOR EACH ADJECT
IVE"
80   PRINT "1 = NEVER OR ALMOST NE
VER TRUE "
90   PRINT "2 = USUALLY NOT TRUE "

100  PRINT "3 = SOMETIMES BUT INF
REQUENTLY TRUE "
110  PRINT "4 = OCCASSIONALLY TRU
E "
120  PRINT "5 = OFTEN TRUE "
130  PRINT "6 = USUALLY TRUE "
140  PRINT "7 = ALWAYS OR ALMOST
ALWAYS TRUE "
150  PRINT "            ";A$(I,J)
160  INPUT "WHAT WOULD YOU RATE Y
OURSELF? ";X(I,J)
170  IF J = 1 THEN   GOSUB 410
180  IF J = 2 THEN   GOSUB 450
190  IF J = 3 THEN   GOSUB 490
200  NEXT J
210  NEXT I
220  FOR KK = 1 TO 20
230  FOR JJ = 1 TO 3
240  PRINT A$(KK,JJ),X(KK,JJ)
250  IF KK = 5 AND JJ = 3 OR KK =
10 AND JJ = 3 OR KK = 15 AND
JJ = 3 THEN   GET T$
260  NEXT JJ
270  NEXT KK
280  PRINT COUNTER,C2OUNTER,C3OUN
TER
290  PRINT A1SUM,B1SUM,C1SUM,AQ,B
Q,CQ
```

Statements 10-20 serve to enter
the subject's name and to save RAM
for data to be entered.

Statements 30-210 constitute a loop
which prints the response scale,
the stimulus word, and requests a
response. Then the control is
sent to the appropriate subroutine
(410, 450 or 490) for scoring.

Statements 220-270 print the
answers given by the subject.

Statements 280-290 print various
values generated by the program.

```
300  GOSUB 530
310  PRINT TTEST
320  PRINT "MEAN FOR MASCULINE IT
EMS= ";AMEAN
330  PRINT "MEAN FOR FEMININE ITE
MS= ";BMEAN
331  GOSUB 8000
340  END
350  DATA  1, SELF RELIANT,2, YIE
LDING, 3,HELPFUL,4,DEFENDS O
WN BELIEFS,5,CHEERFUL,6,MOOD
Y,7,INDEPENDENT,8,SHY,9,CONS
CIENTIOUS,10, ATHLETIC
360  DATA  11,AFFECTIONATE,12,THE
ATRICAL,13,ASSERTIVE,14,FLAT
TERABLE,15,HAPPY,16,STRONG P
ERSONALITY,17,LOYAL,18,UNPRE
DICTABLE,19,FORCEFUL,20,FEMI
NINE
370  DATA  21,RELIABLE,22,ANALYTI
CAL,23,SYMPATHETIC,24,JEALOU
S,25,HAS LEADERSHIP ABILITIE
S,26,SENSITIVE TO THE NEEDS
OF OTHERS,27,TRUTHFUL,28,WIL
LING TO TAKE RISKS,29,UNDERS
TANDING,30,SECRETIVE
380  DATA  31,MAKES DECISIONS EAS
ILY,32,COMPASSIONATE,33,SINC
ERE,34,SELF SUFFICIENT,35,EA
GER TO SOOTHE HURT FEELINGS,
36,CONCEITED,37,DOMINANT,38,
SOFT SPOKEN,39,LIKABLE,40,MA
SCULINE
```

Statement 300 sends program to a subroutine.
Statements 310-330 cause the results of the ttest performed in response to 300 to be printed with means.
Statement 331 causes the results to be printed to a data file.
Statements 350-400 contain the stimulus words for the scale.

```
390   DATA  41,WARM,42,SOLEMN,43,W
ILLING TO TAKE A STAND,44,TE
NDER,45,FRIENDLY,46,AGGRESSI
VE, 47,GULLIBLE, 48,INEFFICI
ENT,49,ACTS AS A LEADER,50,C
HILDLIKE
400   DATA  51,ADAPTABLE,52,INDIVI
DUALISTIC,53,DOES NOT USE HA
RSH LANGUAGE,54,UNSYSTEMATIC
,55,COMPETITIVE,56,LOVES CHI
LDREN,57,TACTFUL,58,AMBITIOU
S,59,GENTLE,60,CONVENTIONAL
410   COUNTER = COUNTER + 1
420   A1SUM = A1SUM + X(I,J)
430   AQ = AQ + X(I,J) * X(I,J)
440   RETURN
450   C2OUNTER = C2OUNTER + 1
460   B1SUM = B1SUM + X(I,J)
470   BQ = BQ + X(I,J) * X(I,J)
480   RETURN
490   C3OUNTER = C3OUNTER + 1
500   C1SUM = C1SUM + X(I,J)
510   CQ = CQ + X(I,J) * X(I,J)
520   RETURN
```

Statements 410-520 sum the scores for the three scales of the BSRI.

Statements 530-610 perform the ttest on the data.

Statements 8000-8050 cause the data to be written to a file. This data can then be retrieved using another program illustrated in a subsequent program.

```
530   REM   TTEST
540   AMEAN = A1SUM / COUNTER
550   BMEAN = B1SUM / C2OUNTER
560   ASD =  SQR ((AQ / COUNTER) -
(AMEAN ^ 2))
570   BSD =  SQR ((BQ / C2OUNTER) -
(BMEAN ^ 2))
580   AEM = ASD / ( SQR (COUNTER))
590   BEM = BSD / ( SQR (C2OUNTER))

600   TTEST = (AMEAN - BMEAN) / ( SQR
(AEM ^ 2 + BEM ^ 2))
610   RETURN
8000  D$ =  CHR$ (4)
8010   PRINT D$;"APPEND BEM DATA"
8020   PRINT D$;"WRITE BEM DATA"
8030   PRINT NAME$
8031   PRINT AMEAN
8032   PRINT BMEAN
8033   PRINT TTEST
8040   PRINT D$;"CLOSE BEM DATA"
8050   RETURN
```

One factor ANOVA BMDP
INPUT

```
 1.    // JOB
 3.    // EXEC BMDP,PROG=1V,REGION=350K
 4.    //SYSIN DD *
 5.    /PROBLEM     TITLE IS 'ONE-WAY ANOVA BMDP1V EXAMPLE'.
 6.    /INPUT       VARIABLES ARE 2.
 7.                 FORMAT IS '(F1.0,F2.0)'.
 9.    /VARIABLE    NAMES ARE GROUP,SCORE.
14.                 GROUPING IS GROUP.
15.    /GROUP       CODES (1) ARE      1,    2,    3,    4.
16.                 NAMES (1) ARE     A1,   A2,   A3,   A4.
17.    /DESIGN      DEPENDENT IS SCORE.
18.    /END
20.    109
21.    110
22.    112
23.    114
24.    115
25.    108
26.    107
27.    115
28.    112
29.    113
30.    114
31.    113
32.    115
33.    216
34.    215
35.    214
36.    217
37.    214
38.    212
39.    209
40.    215
41.    214
42.    216
43.    214
44.    215
45.    210
46.    217
47.    316
48.    317
49.    318
50.    319
51.    313
52.    314
53.    317
54.    315
55.    314
56.    317
57.    318
58.    409
59.    408
60.    410
61.    407
62.    406
63.    409
64.    405
65.    409
66.    411
67.    410
68.    412
69.    408
70.    407
100.   //
101.   /*
```

Statements 1,3 and 4 are job control language (JCL) and are unique to the particular system on which this job is being run. This is true for all of the programs which follow. In some cases there are more than three lines of JCL.

All BMPD programs are divided into paragraphs which are defined by the slash (/) which begins each new section. Each so-called sentence in the paragraph ends with a period (.) as shown.

The problem paragraph is on line 5. It contains the title which is used on each page of the output.

The input paragraph, statements 6 and 7, indicates how many variables are included in the data. In 6 two variables are indicated. In 7 the program information provides a guide to how to read the data. In this case there are two fields, one a one number field and the other a two number field (F1.0 and F2.0 respectively).

The variable paragraph, statements 9 and 14 name the variables in the order indicated in the input paragraph. That is, the first variable is the group code and is the F1.0 field, the second is the score and is the F2.0 field.

The group paragraph, 15 and 16 indicate the codes for the groups and the group names.

Statement 17 comprises the design paragraph. For a one-way ANOVA it is sufficient to indicate the name of the dependent variable. This is because the BMDP,PROG=1V statement in line 3 calls the ANOVA program specialized for this design.

Statement 18 tells the system that this is the end of the program and that the data is coming.

Lines 20-70 are the data.

Lines 100-101 contain system JCL.

```
 1.     // JOB
 3.     // EXEC BMDP,PROG=2V,REGION=500K
 4.     //SYSIN DD *
 5.     /PROBLEM      TITLE IS 'TWO-WAY ANOVA BETWEEN SUBJECTS'.
 6.     /INPUT        VARIABLES ARE 3.
 7.                   FORMAT IS '(3F1.0)'.
 8.     /VARIABLE     NAMES ARE FACTORA, FACTORB, SCORE.
 9.     /DESIGN       DEPENDENT IS SCORE.
10.                   GROUPING ARE FACTORA, FACTORB.
11.     /GROUP        CODES (1) ARE      1,        2,        3.
12.                   NAMES (1) ARE      A1,       A2,       A3.
13.                   CODES (2) ARE   1,     2,     3,     4,     5
14.                   NAMES (2) ARE   B1,    B2,    B3,    B4,    B5
15.     /END
17.     113
18.     112
19.     114
20.     112
21.     124
22.     124
23.     124
24.     123
25.     133
26.     135
27.     135
28.     133
29.     144
30.     145
31.     144
32.     142
33.     155
34.     155
35.     155
36.     153
37.     213
38.     212
39.     213
40.     214
41.     224
42.     223
43.     224
44.     225
45.     234
46.     233
47.     234
48.     236
49.     245
50.     243
51.     246
52.     246
53.     256
54.     254
55.     256
56.     257
57.     314
58.     313
59.     313
60.     314
61.     325
62.     325
63.     324
64.     325
65.     337
66.     336
67.     334
68.     336
69.     348
70.     348
71.     345
72.     347
73.     359
74.     357
75.     356
76.     357
77.     //
78.     /*
```

Two factor between ANOVA BMDP
INPUT

As before 1,3 and 4 are JCL.

The BMDP program is 2V, which handles the multifactor ANOVAS.

The problem, input and variable paragraphs as similar to those in the previous BMDP job.

Lines 9–10 constitute the design paragraph which indicates both the dependent variable and the grouping factor.

Lines 11–14 indicate the values and names that each of the two grouping factors, factora and factorb can take. (It would have been better to use afactor and bfactor as indicated by the assignment made by the program.)

Line 15 again signals the end of the program and the beginning of the data.

17–76 contain the data, 77–78 JCL.

Two factor-one repeated
measure ANOVA   BMDP   INPUT

```
1.     // JOB  BMDP,PROG=2V,REGION=500K
3.     // EXEC BMDP,PROG=2V,REGION=500K
4.     //SYSIN DD *
5.     /PROBLEM   TITLE IS 'TWO-WAY ANOVA REPEATED MEASURES BMDP EXAMPLE'.
6.     /INPUT     VARIABLES ARE 6.
7.                FORMAT IS '(6F1.0)'.
8.     /VARIABLE  NAMES ARE FACTORA,T1,T2,T3,T4,T5.
9.     /DESIGN    DEPENDENT ARE 2 TO 6.
10.               LEVEL IS 5.
11.               GROUPING IS FACTORA.
12.               NAME IS TRIALS.
15.    /END
17.    1343 45
18.    1245 55
19.    1445 45
20.    1233 23
21.    2344 56
22.    2233 34
23.    2344 66
24.    2456 67
25.    3457 89
26.    3356 87
27.    3344 56
28.    3456 77
29.    /*
30.
```

This input is similar to the
two previous ones. The program
is again the BMDP 2V. The
major difference in is the
design paragraph. It indicates
that this is a repeated
measures design because it
indicates that dependent are 2
to 6 and the level is 5.
Statement 12 indicates that the
name of the repeated measures
variable is trials.

Two factor-one repeated
measure ANOVA   BMDP

OUTPUT

PROGRAM CONTROL INFORMATION

```
94.    /PROBLEM   TITLE IS 'TWO-WAY ANOVA REPEATED MEASURES BMDP EXAMPLE'.
95.    /INPUT     VARIABLES ARE 6.
96.               FORMAT IS '(6F1.0)'.
97.    /VARIABLE  NAMES ARE FACTORA,T1,T2,T3,T4,T5.
98.    /DESIGN    DEPENDENT ARE 2 TO 6.
99.               LEVEL IS 5.
100.               GROUPING IS FACTORA.
102.               NAME IS TRIALS.
103.
104.    /END
```

319

PROBLEM TITLE IS
TWO-WAY ANOVA REPEATED MEASURES BMDP EXAMPLE

NUMBER OF VARIABLES TO READ IN. 6
NUMBER OF VARIABLES ADDED BY TRANSFORMATIONS. . . . 0
TOTAL NUMBER OF VARIABLES. 6
NUMBER OF CASES TO READ IN. . . . . TO END
CASE LABELING VARIABLES. . . . . NEITHER
MISSING VALUES CHECKED BEFORE OR AFTER TRANS. . . . MISSING
BLANKS ARE. MISSING
INPUT UNIT NUMBER. 5
REWIND INPUT UNIT PRIOR TO READING. . DATA. . . . NO
NUMBER OF WORDS OF DYNAMIC STORAGE. 27546
NUMBER OF CASES DESCRIBED BY INPUT FORMAT. 1

VARIABLES TO BE USED
 1 FACTORA   2 T1   3 T2   4 T3   5 T4
 6 T5

INPUT FORMAT IS
(6F1.0)
MAXIMUM LENGTH DATA RECORD IS   6 CHARACTERS.
INPUT VARIABLES

VARIABLE INDEX	NAME	RECORD NO.	COLUMNS BEGIN	END	FIELD WIDTH	TYPE
1	FACTORA	1	1	1	1	F
2	T1	1	2	2	1	F
3	T2	1	3	3	1	F
4	T3	1	4	4	1	F
5	T4	1	5	5	1	F
6	T5	1	6	6	1	F

DESIGN SPECIFICATIONS

       GROUP = 1
       DEPEND = 2   3   4   5   6
       LEVEL = 5
BASED ON INPUT FORMAT SUPPLIED   1 RECORDS READ PER CASE.

VARIABLE NO. NAME	MINIMUM LIMIT	MAXIMUM LIMIT	MISSING CODE	CATEGORY CODE	CATEGORY NAME	INTERVAL RANGE GREATER THAN	LESS THAN OR = TO
1 FACTORA							
				1.00000	*1.00000		
				2.00000	*2.00000		
				3.00000	*3.00000		

NOTE--CATEGORY NAMES BEGINNING WITH * WERE GENERATED BY THE PROGRAM.

NUMBER OF CASES READ-- 12
PAGE 2 BMDP2V TWO-WAY ANOVA REPEATED MEASURES BMDP EXAMPLE

GROUP STRUCTURE

FACTORA	COUNT
*1.00000	4.
*2.00000	4.
*3.00000	4.

SUMS OF SQUARES AND CORRELATION MATRIX OF THE ORTHOGONAL COMPONENTS POOLED FOR ERROR

2 IN ANOVA TABLE BELOW

5.27500	1.000			
3.33929	-0.458	1.000		
1.22500	-0.659	-0.491	-1.000	
2.66071	0.159	-0.078	-0.215	1.000

SPHERICITY TEST APPLIED TO ORTHOGONAL COMPONENTS - TAIL PROBABILITY   0.2808

CELL MEANS FOR 1-ST DEPENDENT VARIABLE

FACTORA = TRIALS	*1.00000	*2.00000	*3.00000	MARGINAL
T1 1	2.75000	3.00000	3.50000	3.08333
T2 2	3.75000	4.25000	4.75000	4.16667
T3 3	4.00000	4.25000	5.75000	4.66667
T4 4	3.75000	5.00000	7.00000	5.25000
T5 5	4.50000	5.75000	7.25000	5.83333
MARGINAL	3.75000	4.40000	5.65000	4.60000
COUNT	4	4	4	12

STANDARD DEVIATIONS FOR   1-ST DEPENDENT VARIABLE

FACTORA =   *1.00000   *2.00000   *3.00000

TRIALS
T1   1   0.95743   0.81650   0.57735
T2   2   0.50000   0.81650   0.50000
T3   3   1.15470   1.25831   1.25831
T4   4   1.25831   1.41421   1.41421
T5   5   1.00000   1.25831   1.25831

PAGE   3   BMDP2V TWO-WAY ANOVA REPEATED MEASURES BMDP EXAMPLE

ANALYSIS OF VARIANCE FOR   1-ST
DEPENDENT VARIABLE -   T1   T2   T3   T4   T5

SOURCE	SUM OF SQUARES	DEGREES OF FREEDOM	MEAN SQUARE	F	TAIL PROB.
MEAN	1269.60000	1	1269.60000	289.28	0.0000
FACTORA	37.30000	2	18.65000	4.25	0.0502
1 ERROR	39.50000	9	4.38889		
TRIALS	53.23333	4	13.30833	38.33	0.0000
TF	9.86667	8	1.23333	3.55	0.0040
2 ERROR	12.50000	36	0.34722		

ERROR   EPSILON FACTORS FOR DEGREES OF FREEDOM ADJUSTMENT
TERM   GREENHOUSE-GEISSER   HUYNH-FELDT
2   0.6137   1.0000

NUMBER OF INTEGER WORDS OF STORAGE USED IN PRECEDING   PROBLEM   1209
CPU TIME USED   0.220 SECONDS

PAGE   4

BMDP2V - ANALYSIS OF VARIANCE AND COVARIANCE WITH REPEATED MEASURES.

JULY 3, 1984 AT 10:49:59

NO MORE CONTROL LANGUAGE.

PROGRAM TERMINATED

Descriptive Statistics   SAS
INPUT

```
  1.      // JOB
  3.      // EXEC SAS,REGION=512K
  4.      //SYSIN DD *
  5.      DATA;
  6.         INPUT   GROUP 1 SCORE 2-3;
 19.         CARDS;
 20.      109
 21.      110
 22.      112
 23.      114
 24.      115
 25.      108
 26.      107
 27.      115
 28.      112
 29.      113
 30.      114
 31.      113
 32.      115
 33.      216
 34.      215
 35.      214
 36.      217
 37.      214
 38.      212
 39.      209
 40.      215
 41.      214
 42.      216
 43.      214
 44.      215
 45.      210
 46.      217
 47.      316
 48.      317
 49.      318
 50.      319
 51.      313
 52.      314
 53.      317
 54.      315
 55.      314
 56.      317
 57.      318
 58.      409
 59.      408
 60.      410
 61.      407
 62.      406
 63.      409
 64.      405
 65.      409
 66.      411
 67.      410
 68.      412
 69.      408
 70.      407
 71.      PROC PRINT;
 72.         TITLE DESCRIPTIVE PROCEDURES SAS EXAMPLE;
 73.      PROC MEANS;
 73.5        BY GROUP;
 74.         TITLE OUTPUT FROM MEANS PROCEDURE;
100.      //
101.      /*
```

The SAS package is, in certain respects easier to use than SPSS-X or BMDP. It is organized more logically in that the data are presented first and then the procedures to be done, called PROC, are indicated. In general, like the other packages most of the statements are repetitive.

Lines 1,3 and 4 and 100 and 101 are system JCL cards and are unique to the system used to run these jobs.

Statements 5,6 and 19 are the same in all the SAS programs illustrated. In addition, like BMDP, the statements are organized by main and sub-statements. Each statement ends with a semi-colon (;). Line 5, DATA; alerts the computer that the data is coming, the INPUT statement tells the computer how to read the data on the cards or how the data is displayed. It does so by indicating in which columns particular data appears. The CARDS; statement indicates that the data is coming.

Lines 20-70 contain the data.

Line 71 indicates that the PROC (procedure) to be carried out is the PRINT operation. This is a command which cases the data to be listed. Line 72 has the title to be used in the listing.

Lines 73 indicates that PROC MEANS; is to be carried out. This tells the program to calculate descriptive statistics. The BY GROUP; sub-command indicates to print them by groups as determined from the data input statement (line 6). Line 74 indicates the title to be used on the output.

It should be noted that the numbers on the lines have little meaning except as a way of identifying the particular statement and its relative order. Numbers are sometimes missing because in adapting the data for one package or another there are more or less statements.

Pearson correlation   SAS

INPUT

```
//  JOB
//  EXEC SAS,REGION=512K
//SYSIN DD *
DATA;
INPUT VARA 1-2 VARB 3-4;
CARDS;
2 6
3 2
7 9
6 8
5 4
6 9
7 8
3 6
5 7
PROC CORR;
VAR VARA VARB;
//
/*
```

Lines 29.5 and 30 indicate that the procedure to be run is correlation and that the variables to be used, which have been identified in the input paragraph, are vara and varb.

Pearson correlation   SAS

OUTPUT

```
1       DATA;
2         INPUT VARA 1-2 VARB 3-4;
3         CARDS;
NOTE: DATA SET WORK.DATA1 HAS 10 OBSERVATIONS AND 2 VARIABLES. 953 OBS/TRK.
NOTE: THE DATA STATEMENT USED 0.07 SECONDS AND 208K.
14      PROC CORR;
15        VAR VARA VARB;
NOTE: THE PROCEDURE CORR USED 0.16 SECONDS AND 208K AND PRINTED PAGE 1.
NOTE: SAS USED 208K MEMORY.
```

VARIABLE	N	MEAN	STD DEV	SUM	MINI/
VARA	10	4.70000000	1.82878223	47.00000000	2.00000
VARB	10	6.40000000	2.27058485	64.00000000	2.00000

CORRELATION COEFFICIENTS / PROB > |R| UNDER H0:ρHD=0 / N = 10

	VARA	VARB
VARA	1.00000	0.70107
	0.0000	0.0239
VARB	0.70107	1.00000
	0.0239	0.0000

One factor ANOVA   SAS
INPUT

```
  1.      //  JOB
  3.      //  EXEC  SAS,REGION=512K
  4.      //SYSIN  DD  *
  5.      DATA;
  6.        INPUT    GROUP  1  SCORE  2-3;
 19.        CARDS;
 20.      109
 21.      110
 22.      112
 23.      114
 24.      115
 25.      108
 26.      107
 27.      115
 28.      112
 29.      113
 30.      114
 31.      113
 32.      115
 33.      216
 34.      215
 35.      214
 36.      217
 37.      214
 38.      212
 39.      209
 40.      215
 41.      214
 42.      216
 43.      214
 44.      215
 45.      210
 46.      217
 47.      316
 48.      317
 49.      318
 50.      319
 51.      313
 52.      314
 53.      317
 54.      315
 55.      314
 56.      317
 57.      318
 58.      409
 59.      408
 60.      410
 61.      407
 62.      406
 63.      409
 64.      405
 65.      409
 66.      411
 67.      410
 68.      412
 69.      408
 70.      407
 71.      PROC  PRINT;
 72.        TITLE  ONE-WAY  ANOVA  SAS  EXAMPLE;
 73.      PROC  ANOVA;
 74.        CLASS  GROUP;
 75.        MODEL  SCORE=GROUP;
 76.        MEANS  GROUP/SNK;
100.      //
101.      /*
```

Lines 71 and 72 cause data to
be printed with the title
indicated.

Lines 73 to 76 cause an ANOVA
to be conducted, using the
CLASSification GROUP as defined
in line 6, the MODEL SCORE =
GROUP defines the one-way
ANOVA. The MEANS GROUP/SNK;
indicates that the means are to
be presented and that the
individual comparisons are to
be calculated using the Newman-
Keuls procedure.

Two factor between ANOVA SAS
INPUT

```
1.      // JOB
2.      // EXEC SAS,REGION=500K
3.      //SYSIN DD *
5.      DATA;
5.1         INPUT   ANXIETY 1 STRESS 2 SCORE 3-4;
5.2         CARDS;
20.     1108
21.     1104
22.     1100
23.     1210
24.     1208
25.     1206
26.     1308
27.     1306
28.     1304
29.     2114
30.     2110
31.     2106
32.     2204
33.     2202
34.     2200
35.     2315
36.     2312
37.     2309
39.     PROC PRINT;
40.         TITLE TWO-WAY ANOVA SAS EXAMPLE;
41.     PROC ANOVA;
42.         CLASS ANXIETY STRESS;
43.         MODEL SCORE=ANXIETY STRESS ANXIETY*STRESS;
44.         MEANS ANXIETY STRESS ANXIETY*STRESS/SNK;
45.     //
46.     /*
```

Lines 41 and 44 define the two factor ANOVA and the comparisons to be made as well as the individual comparisons and tables of means to be printed. The statement 43, MODEL SCORE=ANXIETY STRESS ANXIETY*STRESS defines the two factor ANOVA.

SPSS-X is the latest release of SPSS. It is very different from and a great improvement over the previous releases. Like BMDP and SAS it has a standard organization. Again the line numbers in the illustrated input have little meaning, they are used for convenience.

Lines 1-4 and 554 are JCL unique to the system on which the jobs were run.

Line 5 indicates the title to be used on the output.

Line 6 indicates how many records (data cards or lines) per subject. In this case each subject has 5 lines of data. (We are only using data on two of the cards.)

Line 7 defines the fields of the data to be read and identifies the variable for each field by name. The entry /2 indicates that the data following are to be found on card number 2 for each subject.

Lines 8 and 9 assign labels to the variables.

In SPSS-X jobs the first procedure to be executed, in this instance, LIST VARIABLES, comes before the data. Additional procedures or sub-programs come after the data.

Line 40 indicates that a "0" is a missing value. You can tell the program, in another statement, if you wish, to include or exclude the missing data in some or all calculations.

Line 53 causes the program to print out the cases and the values for each variable.

Line 56 tells the computer that the data is coming.

Lines 57 to 551 of this input contain the data. In the data included lines 57-61 are the data for subject 1, lines 62-66 are the data for the second subject.

Line 552 tells the computer that the data is ended.

Lines 552.1 to 552.4 is a subprogram to descibe the data, to print values for given percentiles, to provide a histogram for each variable, and to print the requested statistics.

Line 553 is the FINISH card which indicates that the program is over. There could be system cards, // and /* as in the other programs by the system used to input these programs generates its own cards.

Descrip. stats. with histogram
SPSS-X
INPUT

```
 1.    // JOB
 2.    //*MAIN LINES=10
 3.    //EXEC SPSSX,REGION=512K,TIME=3
 4.    //SYSIN DD *
 5.    TITLE DESCRIPTIVE WITH CHOICE OF VARIABLES ON SPSS
 6.    DATA LIST RECORD=5
 7.    VARIABLE /1 VARA 7-9(2) VARB 56-58(1) /2 VARC 26-28(1) VARD 32-34(1)
 8.    LABELS VARA 'ITEM A' VARB 'ITEM B'/VARC 'ITEM C'/
 9.    VARD 'ITEM D'
40.    MISSING VALUES VARA TO VARD (0)
53.    LIST VARIABLES=VARA TO VARD
56.    BEGIN DATA
57.    2002883208291532703005772690112270300505316305214305272690120
58.    2064512004076220151306091660129217525221254352122115240101052
59.    2064530200100010000183200206120130020000241310001823110310100
60.    2064541823118231000002430000024313000024113555241310045524131000
61.    2064552503063203031551531272200586573012008161312107466700115
62.    2067520090709126310040160300124210175431012442322111324303070751
63.    2067530001000100000026526000000000000002643126431178312643100
64.    2067541783100010000073111318843120000000000555506131328
65.    2067550000611316831000002443100001613122224124110612094
66.
552.   END DATA
552.1  FREQUENCIES VARIABLES=ALL/
552.2  PERCENTILES=25 33.3 66.7 75/
552.3  HISTOGRAM/
       STATISTICS=MEDIAN SEMEAN MODE RANGE DEFAULT
553.   FINISH
554.
```

```
                      Independent t-test   SPSS-X
                             INPUT


      1.         // JOB
      2.         //*MAIN LINES=10
      3.         // EXEC SPSSX,REGION=512K,TIME=3
      4.         //SYSIN DD *
      5.         TITLE T TEST SPSS-X EXAMPLE
      6.         DATA LIST RECORD=1
      7.             /1 GROUP 1 SCORE 2-3
      9.         VARIABLE LABELS  GROUP 'TREATMENT CONDITIONS'
     14.         VALUE LABELS  GROUP 1 'EXPERIMENTAL' 2 'CONTROL'
     18.         T-TEST GROUPS=GROUP(1,2)/VARIABLE=SCORE
     18.2        OPTIONS 2 4
     18.3        STATISTICS 1
     19.         BEGIN DATA
     20.         109
     21.         110
     22.         112
     23.         114
     24.         115
     25.         108
     26.         107
     27.         115
     28.         112
     29.         113
     30.         114
     31.         113
     32.         115
     33.         216
     34.         215
     35.         214
     36.         217
     37.         214
     38.         212
     39.         209
     40.         215
     41.         214
     42.         216
     43.         214
     44.         215
     45.         210
     46.         217
   1500.         END DATA
   1501.         FINISH
```

Lines 1 to 14 are as previously described.

Lines 18–18.3 define the t-test procedure. Line 18 defines the groups as 1 and 2 and the dependent variable as the defined score. Line 18.2 defines the options to be in effect, 18.3 the statistics to be calculated and reported.

```
 1.   // JOB LINES=10
 2.   //*MAIN LINES=10
 3.   //EXEC SPSSX,REGION=512K,TIME=3
 4.   //SYSIN DD *
 5.   TITLE PEARSON PRODUCT MOMENT SPSS-X EXAMPLE
 6.   DATA LIST RECORD=1
 7.   /1 VARA 1-2 VARB 3-4
 8.   VARIABLE LABELS VARA 'VARIABLE A'/VARB 'VARIABLE B'
 9.   PEARSON CORR VARA WITH VARB
10.   STATISTICS 1
11.   BEGIN DATA
12.   2 6
13.   3 5
14.   3 9
15.   7 7
16.   6 8
17.   5 4
18.   6 9
19.   7 8
20.   3 6
21.   5 7
22.   END DATA
23.   SCATTERGRAM VARA WITH VARB
24.   OPTIONS 4
25.   STATISTICS ALL
26.   FINISH
```

In the case of this job there are two procedures. The first is the Pearson Correlation procedure (lines 9–10) the second, coming after the data, the scattergram procedure, lines 23–25.

```
178.        1 0    TITLE PEARSON PRODUCT MOMENT SPSS-X EXAMPLE
179.        2 0    DATA LIST RECORD=1
180.        3 0    /1 VARA 1-2 VARB 3-4
181.   THE ABOVE DATA LIST STATEMENT WILL READ  1 RECORDS FROM FILE INLINE .
182.        VARIABLE REC START  END      FORMAT WIDTH  DEC
183.        VARA     1    1      2          F      2     0
184.        VARB     1    3      4          F      2     0
185.
186.   END OF DATALIST TABLE.
187.        4 0    VARIABLE LABELS VARA 'VARIABLE A'/VARB 'VARIABLE B'
188.        5 0    PEARSON CORR VARA WITH VARB
189.        6 0    STATISTICS 1
190.
191.   *****PEARSON CORR PROBLEM REQUIRES    48 BYTES WORKSPACE *****
192.
193.
194.   03 JUL 84   PEARSON PRODUCT MOMENT SPSS-X EXAMPLE
195.   11:25:39    CUNY / UNIV. COMPUTER CENTER   IBM 3081 / 3033  OS/MVS JES3
196.
197.   VARIABLE   CASES      MEAN      STD DEV
198.
199.   VARA        10       4.7000     1.8288
200.   VARB        10       6.4000     2.2706
```

```
- - - - - - - - - - - - -   P E A R S O N   C O R R E L A T I O N   C O E F F I C I E N

                VARB

VARA         .7011
            ( 10)
            P= .011

(COEFFICIENT / (CASES) / SIGNIFICANCE)              " . "  IS PRINTED IF A COEFFICIENT CANNOT
03 JUL 84   PEARSON PRODUCT MOMENT SPSS-X EXAMPLE
11:25:39    CUNY / UNIV. COMPUTER CENTER    IBM 3081 / 3033   OS/MVS JES3

PRECEDING TASK REQUIRED     0.06 SECONDS CPU TIME;       1.77 SECONDS ELAPSED.

   8   0        SCATTERGRAM VARA WITH VARB
   9   0        OPTIONS 4
  10   0        STATISTICS ALL

***** GIVEN WORKSPACE ALLOWS FOR     3567 CASES FOR SCATTERGRAM PROBLEM *****
```

(LINES 225-286   SCATTERGRAM ON NEXT PAGE)

```
STATISTICS..
CORRELATION (R) -      .70107           R SQUARED -      .49149
STD ERR OF EST -      1.38320           INTERCEPT (A) -   1.08621
PLOTTED VALUES -        .10             EXCLUDED VALUES-      0

                                 '********' IS PRINTED IF A COEFFICIENT CANNOT BE COMPUTED.
03 JUL 84   PEARSON PRODUCT MOMENT SPSS-X EXAMPLE
11:25:40    CUNY / UNIV. COMPUTER CENTER    IBM 3081 / 3033   OS/MVS JES3

PRECEDING TASK REQUIRED     0.08 SECONDS CPU TIME;       1.05 SECONDS ELAPSED.

                                                   SIGNIFICANCE  -      .01195
  11   0     FINISH                                SLOPE (B)     -      .56466
  11    COMMAND LINES READ.                         MISSING VALUES -          0
   0    ERRORS DETECTED.
   0    SECONDS CPU TIME.
   6    SECONDS ELAPSED TIME.
        END OF JOB.
```

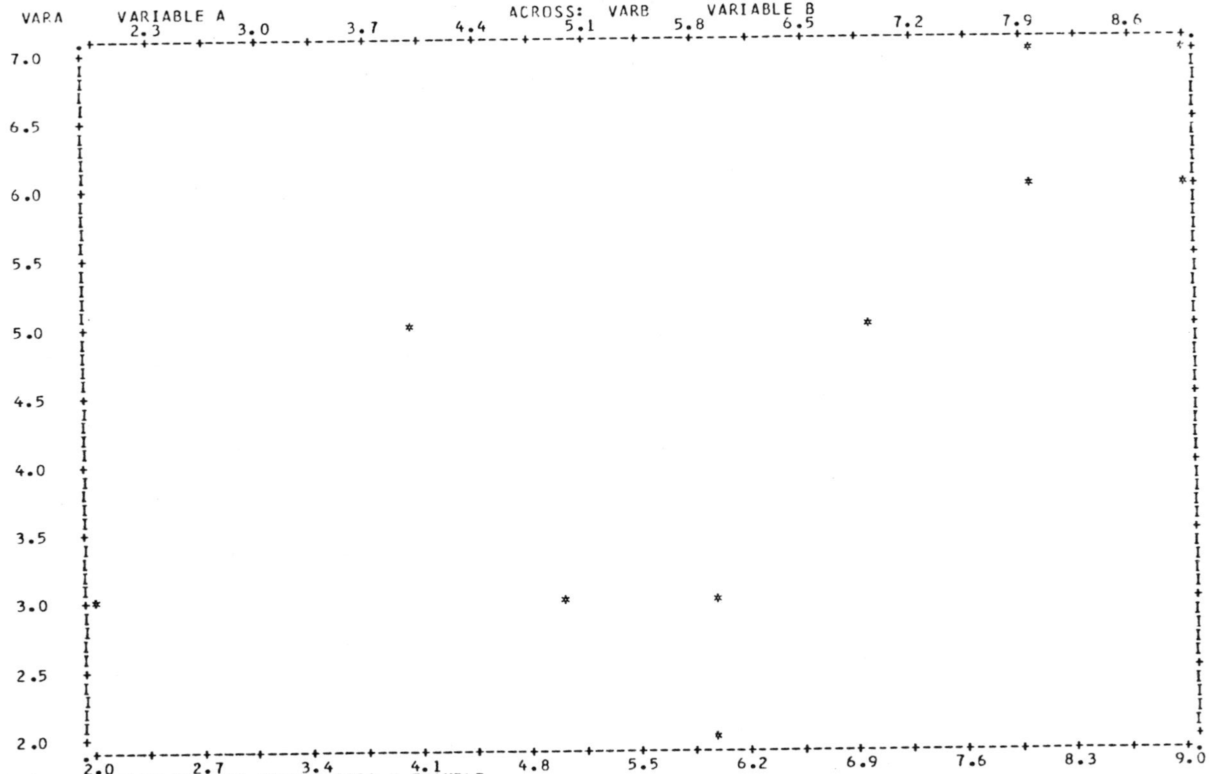

Two-factor chi-square SPSS-X
INPUT

```
 1.      // JOB
 2.      //*MAIN LINES=10
 3.      // EXEC SPSSX,REGION=512K,TIME=3
 4.      //SYSIN DD *
 5.      TITLE TWO-WAY CHI-SQUARE EXAMPLE
 6.      DATA LIST RECORD=1
 7.          /1 SEX 1 RANK 2 DEPT 3
 8.      VARIABLE LABELS   SEX 'SEX'/RANK 'ACADEMIC RANK'/
 9.                        DEPT 'DEPARTMENT'
10.      VALUE LABELS   SEX 1 'MALE' 2 'FEMALE'/RANK 1 'LECTURER'
11.                 2 'INSTRUCTOR' 3 'ASSISTANT PROF' 4 'ASSOC PROF'
12.                 5 'PROFESSOR'
13.      MISSING VALUES SEX TO DEPT (99)
14.      RECODE RANK (1=2)
15.      CROSSTABS TABLES=SEX BY RANK/SEX BY DEPT
16.      OPTIONS 3 4 5
17.      STATISTICS 1
18.      BEGIN DATA
19.      141
20.      241
21.      231
22.      131
23.      231
24.      131
25.      231
26.      121
27.      221
28.      221
29.      211
30.      211
31.      211
32.      111
33.      211
34.      211
35.      211
36.      111
37.      211
38.      211
39.      211
40.      111
41.      111
42.      211
43.      111
44.      111
45.      111
46.      211
47.      111
48.      211
49.      211
50.      111
51.      211
52.      152
53.      152
54.      252
55.      142
56.      242
57.      242
58.      242
59.      142
60.      242
61.      142
62.      153
63.      143
64.      143
65.      243
66.      143
67.      243
68.      143
69.      133
70.      133
71.      154
```

```
72.      154
73.      154
74.      154
75.      154
76.      154
77.      154
78.      154
79.      144
80.      244
81.      144
82.      144
83.      144
84.      234
85.      145
86.      235
87.      235
88.      135
89.      156
90.      156
91.      156
92.      156
93.      156
94.      156
95.      256
96.      146
97.      146
98.      146
99.      146
100.     146
101.     136
102.     END DATA
103.     FINISH
```

The procedure CROSSTABS is the procedure that calculates chi-squares. It is defined in lines 15-17. The unique statement is in statement 14. This enables the user to combine values. In this case there were too few cases in rank 1 so 1 and 2 were combined by recoding all 1's as 2's.

One factor ANOVA SPSS-X

INPUT

1.
2.
3.
4.
5.
6.
7.
8.
9.
10.
11.
12.
13.
20.
21.
22.
23.
24.
25.
26.
27.
28.
29.
30.
31.
32.
33.
34.
35.
36.
37.
38.
39.
40.
41.
42.

```
// JOB LINES=10
//*MAIN LINES=10
// EXEC SPSSX,REGION=512K,TIME=3
//SYSIN DD*
TITLE ONE-WAY ANOVA SPSS-X EXAMPLE
DATA LIST RECORD=1
  /1 GROUP 1 SCORE 2-3
VARIABLE LABELS GROUP 1 'TREATMENT CONDITIONS'
VALUE LABELS GROUP 1 'GROUP A1' 2 'GROUP A2' 3 'GROUP A3' 4 'GROUP A4'
ONEWAY SCORE BY GROUP (1,4)/
  RANGE=SNK/
STATISTICS 1 3
BEGIN DATA
109
110
112
114
115
108
107
115
112
113
114
113
115
215
214
217
214
212
205
214
216

 43. 214
 44. 215
 45. 210
 46. 217
 47. 316
 48. 317
 49. 318
 50. 319
 51. 313
 52. 317
 53. 315
 54. 314
 55. 318
 56. 408
 57. 408
 58. 410
 59.
 60.

 61. 407
 62. 406
 63. 405
 64. 405
 65. 409
 66. 411
 67. 410
 68. 412
 69. 408
 70. 407
100.
101.
END DATA
FINISH
```

The unique statements in this program, which calculates a one-way ANOVA, are 10-12. Line 10 indicates that the procedure ONEWAY is to be carried out with SCORE as the dependent variable by GROUP as the independent variable with a minimum group code of 1 and a maximum of 4. Thus, the program knows to look for 4 groups. Line 11 indicates that the program should perform individual comparisons using the Newman-Keuls procedure. Statistics 1 and 3 are to be calculated.

333

Two factor between ANOVA SPSS-X
INPUT

```
1.    //  JOB  LINES=10
2.    /// *MAIN  LINES=10
3.    //  EXEC  SPSSX,REGION=512K,TIME=3
4.    //SYSIN DD*
5.    TITLE TWO-WAY BETWEEN SUBJECTS ANOVA SPSS-X EXAMPLE
6.    DATA LIST RECORD=1 FACTORA 1 FACTORB 2 SCORE 3-4
7.    VARIABLE LABELS  FACTORA 'PERFORMER ANXIETY'/
8.                     FACTORB 'IMPOSED STRESS'
9.
10.   VALUE LABELS  FACTORA 1 'HIGH ANXIETY' 2 'LOW ANXIETY'/
11.                 FACTORB 1 'HIGH STRESS' 2 'MOD STRESS' 3 'LOW STRESS'
12.
13.   ANOVA SCORE BY FACTORA (1,2) FACTORB (1,3)
14.   STATISTICS 3
15.   BEGIN DATA
16.   1108
17.   1104
18.   1100
19.   1208
20.   1206
21.   1308
22.   1306
23.   1304
24.   2114
25.   2110
26.   2106
27.   2204
28.   2202
29.   2200
30.   2316
31.   2312
32.   2309
33.   END DATA
34.   FINISH
```

In this job the line which
defines the test is number 12.
It defines the procedure ANOVA
and indicates a two factor
analysis by the statement SCORE
(the dependent variable) BY
FACTORA (minimum 1, maximum 2)
FACTORB (minimum 1, maximum
3).

```
178       1  0
179       2  0
180       3  0
181  THE ABOVE DATA LIST RECORD=1
182       /1 FACTORA 1 FACTORB 2 SCORE 3-4
183  THE ABOVE DATA LIST STATEMENT WILL READ 1 RECORDS FROM FILE INLINE
184       REC START  END  FORMAT  WIDTH  DEC

185       FACTORA   1    1            F       1     0
186       FACTORB   1    2            F       1     0
187       SCORE     1    3    4       F       2     0

188  END OF DATALIST TABLE.

189       VARIABLE LABELS  FACTORA 'PERFORMER ANXIETY'/
190                        FACTORB 'IMPOSED STRESS'.
191       VALUE LABELS FACTORA 1 'HIGH ANXIETY' 2 'LOW ANXIETY'/
192                    FACTORB 1 'HIGH STRESS' 2 'MOD STRESS' 3 'LOW STRESS'.
193       ANOVA SCORE BY FACTORA (1,2) FACTORB (1,3)
194       STATISTICS 3
```

'ANOVA' PROBLEM REQUIRES   624 BYTES OF MEMORY.
03 JUL 84 TWO-WAY BETWEEN SUBJECTS ANOVA SPSS-X EXAMPLE
11:30:45   CUNY/UNIV. COMPUTER CENTER IBM 3081 / 3033   OS/MVS JES3

* * * C E L L   M E A N S * * *

SCORE   PERFORMER ANXIETY
BY FACTORA
FACTORB   IMPOSED STRESS

TOTAL POPULATION
  7.00
(18)

FACTORA   1   2
  6.00   8.00
(9)   (9)

FACTORB   1   2   3
  7.00   5.00   9.00
(6)   (6)   (6)

	FACTORB 1		2		3	
FACTORA 1	4.00	(3)	8.00	(3)	6.00	(3)
2	10.00	(3)	2.00	(3)	12.00	(3)

335

03 JUL 84   TWO-WAY BETWEEN SUBJECTS ANOVA SPSS-X EXAMPLE
11:30:45   CUNY/ UNIV. COMPUTER CENTER IBM 3081 / 3033   OS/MVS JES3

* * * A N A L Y S I S O F V A R I A N C E * * *

        SCORE   PERFORMER ANXIETY
BY   FACTORA   IMPOSED STRESS
        FACTORB

SOURCE OF VARIATION	SUM OF SQUARES	DF	MEAN SQUARE	F	SIGNIF OF F
MAIN EFFECTS	66.000	3	22.000	2.491	0.110
FACTORA	18.000	1	18.000	2.038	0.179
FACTORB	48.000	2	24.000	2.717	0.105
2-WAY INTERACTIONS	144.000	2	72.000	8.151	0.006
FACTORA FACTORB	144.000	2	72.000	8.151	0.006
EXPLAINED	210.000	5	42.000	4.755	0.013
RESIDUAL	106.000	12	8.833		
TOTAL	316.000	17	18.588		

18 CASES WERE PROCESSED.
0 CASES (0.0 PCT) WERE MISSING.

03 JUL 84   TWO-WAY BETWEEN SUBJECTS ANOVA SPSS-X EXAMPLE
11:30:46   CUNY/ UNIV. COMPUTER CENTER IBM 3081 / 3033   OS/MVS JES3

PRECEDING TASK REQUIRED   0.04 SECONDS CPU TIME;   1.20 SECONDS ELAPSED.

11 0   FINISH
    11 COMMAND LINES READ.
     0 ERRORS DETECTED.
     0 SECONDS CPU TIME.
     4 SECONDS ELAPSED TIME.
       END OF JOB.

Appendix C

Review of
Mathematics Skills and Symbolic Directions

Earlier, in Chapter 1, it was noted that statistics requires little more mathematics ability than that needed to add, subtract, divide and multiply. Thus, once you can **read** the language of statistical notation, the symbolic notation that is used to communicate operations and their sequence, you should have little difficulty using elementary math principles in solving problems. Perhaps the greatest difficulty students face in courses in statistics and research methods is in interpretation of the research. The format of this book is planned to make that aspect of the topic easier.

This appendix is intended as a review of the ways in which you will be asked to apply addition, subtraction, division and mutliplication as well as an introduction to the ways in which some of the operations are expressed in statistical notation. The appendix is also intended to help you diagnose your problem areas so that you can ascertain where you need assistance and clarification. It is important that you review the problems so that in later portions of the work you can concentrate on the logic aspects of the problems you are doing rather than on the mathematical skills you need to arrive at the answers.

If you experience difficulty it may be because:

1) you haven't used your math skills in a while and simply need some practice.

2) you are working too fast and too haphardly and so are making unnecessary errors.

3) you don't really understand the mathematical concepts involved.

If your difficulties are related to 1 and 2 then a brief review and practice should be all you need. If 3 describes your problem you should get assistance **immediately**.

MATHEMATICAL PRINCIPLES

Fractions

A fraction consists of two parts: a numerator, the top or first number, and a denominator, the bottom or second number. Their relationship may be expressed in a number of ways:

$$\text{numerator/denominator}$$

$$\frac{\text{numerator}}{\text{denominator}}$$

$$\frac{\overline{}}{\text{denominator/numerator}}$$

$$\text{numerator} \div \text{denominator}$$

337

These are all shorthand ways of indicating the process, division, to be used in our calculations. The denominator indicates the total number of parts in the fraction and the numerator indicates the number of the parts of interest.

There are several rules which govern the use of fractions. While you should know these rules for later work it is probably easier to convert fractions to their decimal equivalent. This is done by dividing the numerator by the denominator as in:

$$3/4 = .75$$

or

$$4/3 = 1.33$$

These decimal equivalents can then be added and subtracted more easily.

The rules for dealing with fractions are:

1. When multiplying fractions, numerator is mutliplied by numerator and denominator by denominator.

2. You may multiply the numerator and denominator of a fraction by the same number without changing the value of the fraction.

3. You **cannot** add or subtract the same number, the value of the fraction will be changed.

4. Wherever possible change fractions to their decimal equivalents.

5. To divide fractions, invert the divisor and then handle as multiplication.

Decimals

It has been suggested that fractions be converted, wherever feasible, to decimals by dividing the numerator by the denominator. There are several rules governing decimals that should be followed.

1. When adding and subtracting decimals, line up the decimal points within the problem and place the decimal point in the answer directly under the decimal point in the problem.

2. When multiplying decimals the answer should have as many decimal places as there are in the total problem.

3. When squaring a number which is less than 1, the product will always be less than the number. E.g., $(.5)^2 = .25$; $(.7)^2 = .49$. When taking the square root of a number which is less than 1, the product will always be greater then the number. E.g., $.81 = .9$; $.64 = .8$

4. When one decimal number is divided by another the number of decimal places in the answer will equal the number of places in the numerator minus the number of places in the denominator.

Proportions

A proportion is a share of the whole, a ratio of the part to the whole, a decimal equivalent, a percentage of the total. We will be dealing with proportions when we consider the normal curve. There are several guidelines for dealing with proportions:

1. To find the proportion for a given part of the total divide the part by the total.

2. To change a proportion into a percentage multiply by 100. (To
multiply by 100 move the decimal two places to the right.)
3. To find the proportion represented by a percent divide by
100. (To divide by 100 move the decimal two places to the left.)
4. To find the part of the whole that the proportion represents
multiply the total by the proportion.

Signed Numbers

Negative numbers can be used to indicate values below a given
reference point. Usually that value is zero (as we will see in
the chapter on the normal curve which considers z-scores).
Signed numbers are also important in conceptualizing the
notion of the standard deviation, which relates to the squared
deviations from the mean. Some rules for working with signed
numbers will be helpful.
1. To add numbers which have the same sign, sum them and attach
the common sign.
2. To add numbers which have different signs, take the difference
and attach the sign of the larger of the values. (When there are
many numbers you may wish to add those with common signs and then
proceed.
3. To subtract one number from another, regardless of sign,
change the sign of the number to be subtracted and add. (This
means that if the sign of the number to be subtracted is positive
to start the resulting sign will be negative. If the sign is
negative to start the resulting sign will be positive.)
4. To multiply or divide signed numbers: numbers with the same
sign give a positive result; numbers with different signs give a
negative result.

Rounding

Regardless of how many places you are rounding to the rules
are the same:
1. If the next digit is less than 5 the last digit is left as
is.
2. If the next digit is more than 5 the last digit is increased
by 1.
3. If the next digit is exactly 5 the principle "round to even"
is in effect. That is, in the number 3.435, you would round to
hundreths by dropping the 5 and rounding to even with 3.44. If
the number was 3.665 you would drop the 5 and leave 3.66. Thus,
the remaining number after the 5 is dropped is even.

In general, your answer should have no more than one place
more than your original data. Thus, if running times are
recorded to the nearest hundreth of seconds your answer could,
legitimately, be expressed in thousandths.

Order of Operations

In almost all statistical formulas the order in which
operations are to be carried out is indicated by parentheses or
brackets. All terms within brackets or parentheses should be
reduced to a single value first and then remaining operations
carried out. The most common error that takes place in treating
complex equations is sloppiness in work and resulting failure to

carry terms and symbols through the entire problem.   In
addition, exponentiation (squaring) **always** takes precedence.

A Simple Test

1. Perform the following:
   a. 1/5 X 1/5 =
   b. 2/5 - 3/4 =
   c. 1.38 X .02 =
   d. (.435)(.34) =
   e. 112/.61 =
   f. -8 + -5 =
   g. 6 + -10 =
   h. 7 + 12 =
   i. 10 - 13 =
   j. 15 - (-5) =

2. Round the following to the nearest hundreth:
   a. 24.0467
   b. 35.235
   c. 62.674
   d. 70.865

3. Find the square roots of the following:
   a. 21
   b. .89
   c. 144
   d. 456.27
   e. .091

4. Square the following numbers:
   a. .9
   b. 3.8
   c. 5.02
   d. 34

5. Solve the following:
   a. $(9+3)5$
   b. $(3 \times 4)+(5 \times 7)$
   c. $(4^2+6)7$
   d. $(3+4)^2+7(2+3)$
   e. $(4-3)(3-6)^2\ 2(4-7)$

SYMBOLIC OPERATIONS

In the first part of this appendix reference was made to the
language of statistics. This refers to a shorthand or notation
system for detailing the operations to be done to a set of
numbers. There are very few symbols which are used and a brief
introduction should suffice.

$$\Sigma = \text{Sum of}$$
$$X = \text{a score}$$
$$N = \text{number of cases}$$
$$\bar{X} = \text{average (mean score)}$$

These symbols are also used in different ways to signify different operations.

$$(\Sigma X)^2 = \text{Sum the scores and square}$$
$$\Sigma X^2 = \text{Square each score and sum the squared scores}$$
$$(X-\bar{X})^2 = \text{the score minus the mean squared}$$

These symbols are also combined to yield different statistics.

$$\sqrt{\frac{\Sigma X^2 - N(\bar{X}^2)}{N}}$$ = the square root of the sum of the scores squared minus the number of cases times the mean score squared divided by the number of cases. (Equals standard deviation.)

$$\frac{\Sigma XY - N\bar{X}\bar{Y}}{(s_x)(s_y)}$$ = the sum of the cross products of X and Y minus the number of cases times the mean of X times the mean of Y divided by the standard deviation of X times the standard deviation of Y. (See above for standard deviation.)

$$\frac{s}{\sqrt{N}}$$ = the standard deviation divided by the square root of the number of cases. (Yields the standard error of the mean, SEM.)

All problems in statistics can be reduced to their component parts. This book takes this approach and works from one step to the next in explaining the procedures for the different tests. Your learning will be eased if you study the examples and then work through all of the problems given in the chapters and in the appendix.

WORKING WITH EQUATIONS AND FORMULAS

Each equation or formula that you will encounter in your study and use of statistics can be broken into parts. By solving each part and then <u>carefully</u> substituting the solution into the entire equation or formula you will arrive at an answer with minimal difficulty and maximal accuracy. In the previous section you were given the formula:

$$\frac{\Sigma XY - N\bar{X}\bar{Y}}{(s_x)(s_y)}$$

Although it seems complicated at first if you break it down into parts it becomes simpler. To find the sum of the cross products of XY for example you must:
1. Multiply each X,Y pair and get a product.
2. Sum the cross products of the pairs.
3. This answer is the sum of the cross products of X,Y.

To find the value of $N\bar{X}\bar{Y}$ you must obtain:
1. The sum of the X scores divided by N to get $\bar{X}$.
2. The sum of the Y scores divided by N to get $\bar{Y}$.
3. The product of N times $\bar{X}$ times $\bar{Y}$.
4. The answer is the product of $N\bar{X}\bar{Y}$.

To find s_x:
1. Calculate the sum of the squared X's.
2. Use the mean of X calculated above.
3. Determine the number of cases, N.
4. Substitute in the formula for standard deviation:

$$\sqrt{\frac{\Sigma X^2 - N(\bar{X}^2)}{N}}$$

To find s_y:
Repeat the steps above using scores for Y.

Now subsitute the values into the original formula, carry out the appropriate operations, subtraction, multiplication, and division and obtain the answer.

Every formula in the book is approached in similar fashion, that is the examples show how to break it down into component parts, solve for each part and then substitute into the original formula to obtain an answer. The exercises given below will help you to become familiar with breaking down and working formulas.

Exercises

1. 2,7,6,8,5,4,3,9,12,3,14,15,14,12,12.

    Find: $\Sigma X, \Sigma X^2, N$.

    Substitute appropriately in:

    $$\bar{X} = \frac{\Sigma X}{N}$$

    $$s = \sqrt{\frac{\Sigma X^2 - N(\bar{X}^2)}{N}}$$

2. X = 2, 3, 4, 5, 2, 10, 12, 14, 16, 12, 13, 10
   Y = 4, 4, 5, 7, 3, 9, 8, 9, 12, 11, 16, 11

    Find: $\Sigma X, \Sigma X^2, N, \Sigma XY, s_x, s_y,$

    Substitute appropriately in:

    $$r = \frac{\Sigma XY - N\bar{X}\bar{Y}}{(s_x)(s_y)}$$

Individuals who feel they need more review and assistance with mathematical concepts and equations might consult an excellent book which uses a similar approach to problem-solving:

WHIMBEY, A. and LOCHHEAD, J. Developing Mathematical Skills. New York: McGraw-Hill, 1981.

Appendix D

Page 31

Data Set	Mean	Median*	Mode	Range	IQR	s
1	19.3	19.5	20	24	8.50	5.85
2	15.17	15	15	11	4.92	2.46
4a	7.5	7.70	8	4	1.46	.92
7c	4.5	4	2	7	3.92	2.25
8b	77.6	19.29	19	51	13.70	11.50

*precise estimate of median using formula

Page 109

Problem

1a	$z = -1.00$
1d	$z = 2.00$
2a	$x = 22$ (note: $s = 3$)
2d	$x = 31$
7d	$z = .75$; area above (smaller area) $= .2266$
7i	prop. $= .1667$; $z = -.965$; $x = 62.140$
9	95% conf. int. $= 94.02$, 95.98

Page 118-119

Problem

3   Mental practice: mean = 9.7 s = 1.676: sem = .53
    Phys. practice mean = 4.625: s = 1.653: sem = .58
    t-ratio = (9.7-4.625)/.7856 = 6.43
7   mean difference = 1.55; standard error of difference = .499
    t-ratio = 3.11

Page 135-136

Problem

2   r = .814

6   rho = .6625

Page 143-144

Problem

2   chi-square = 3.125

5   chi-square = 9

Page 151-152
Problem
2   mean a = 11; mean b = 12.625; mean c = 15.625

Source of variation	SS	df	MS	F
Total	269.83	23		
Between Groups	88.08	2	44.04	5.08
Within Subjects	181.75	21	8.65	

Page 158-159
Problem (The solution was obtained using BMDP 2V)
2
means
color = 13.00   suit = 21.733   pic-num = 13.53

Source of variation	SS	df	MS	F
Total	1255.63	44		
Between subjects	403.64	14	28.83	
Within subjects	851.99	30		
Treatments	718.97	2	359.48	75.67
Residual	133.02	28	4.75	

Page 170-171
Problem
1
means

	B1	B2	
A1	14.33	12.5	13.42
A2	8.67	11.5	10.08
	11.5	12	

Source of variation	SS	df	MS	F
Total	166.50	23		
A	66.67	1	66.67	20.33
B	1.5	1	1.5	1.00
AB	32.66	1	32.66	9.96
Error	65.67	20	3.28	

Page 189-190
Problem (The solution was obtained using BMDP 2V)
1
    means

		Learning	Retention	
	Mental	7.2	8.4	7.8
Open Ski	Physi	9.8	10.2	10.0
	Men-Phy	12.6	12.6	12.6
	Men-Phy	10.8	12.6	11.7
Clos Ski	Physi	14.4	15.0	14.7
	Men-Phy	16.8	17.2	17.0
		11.93	12.30	

Source of variation	SS	df	MS	F
Total	900.60	59		
Between subjects	858.60	29		
Skill Type	281.67	1	281.67	21.11
Practice	255.10	2	127.55	9.56
Skill X Prac	1.63	2	0.82	.06
Error	320.20	24	13.34	
Within subjects	42.00	30		
Test	8.07	1	8.07	6.77
Test X Skil	0.60	1	0.60	0.50
Test X Prac	4.63	2	2.32	1.94
Test X S X P	0.10	2	0.05	0.04
Error	28.60	24	1.19	

Pages 200-201
Problem (The solution was obtained using BMDP 2V)
1
    adjusted means
  cycling = 5.81   jogging = 7.23   variety = 7.73   control = 3.86

Source of variation	SS	df	MS	F
Total	91.05	31		
Between Groups	70.02	3	23.34	31.12
Error	21.03	28*	0.75	

*Technically the df for error should be 1 less because 1 df is
lost for the covariate. In the chapter, however this was not
done. BMDP will do this and will also provide the regression
coefficent.

AUTHOR INDEX

Ahtola, O. T., 192, 201
Allen, J. F., 270, 280
Alter, J. F., 271, 280
Anderson, W. G., 252, 274, 280
Ariel, Gideon, 270
Apter, M. J., 280
Arkin, R. M., 252, 253
Arnett, B., 44–5
Arnold, R. K., 73, 75, 94, 219, 249, 250–2, 255

Bangert, R. L., 254
Barlow, D.A., 279, 281
Barrette, G. T., 252, 274, 280
Bayliss, P. A., 279, 281
Baz, A., 270, 281
Benedict, J. Q., 281
Berger, B., 67, 75
Boettcher, J. W., 271, 281
Brodinck, R., 216, 252
Brown, M. J., 253, 265, 281
Busse, T. V., 219, 255
Butts, B. O., 281
Byatt, S. E., 256

Cacioppo, J. T., 282
Campbell, D. T., 61, 75
Capobianco, C., 250, 251
Carlberg, 248
Castellan, N. J., 281
Cervino, J., 250
Ceurvorst, R. W., 256
Chaffin, D. B. A., 226, 270, 282

Cheffers, J. T. F., 252–3
Chrobock, K., 250
Cicciarelli, C. F., 281
Cochran, A., 270, 281
Cohen, J., 82, 83
Cohen, P. A., 248, 253–4, 281
Cook, T. D., 253, 254
Cooper, H. M., 249, 253
Cox, D. R., 44, 45

Dalby, J. T., 273, 281
Dearborn, D. E., 258, 281
Diamond, D., 54, 59
Diamond, S., 30, 32
Dickson, W. J., 66, 75
Dillman, C. J., 270, 281
Donnelly, J. E., 271, 281
Drayton, M. A., 220–1, 225, 229, 253
Drew, C. J., 60, 64, 70, 75

Ebeling, B. J., 248
Eddington, E. S., 253
Efron, B., 68, 69, 75
Engelhorn, R., 264, 273, 281
Eysenck, H. G., 219, 253

Feltz, D., 229–30, 239, 240, 253
Fiske, D. W., 254
Fishman, S., 253
Fleishman, E. A., 54, 59
Fraleigh, W. P., 216, 218, 253
Friedman, P., 281

Gage, N. L., 220, 253
Gallenstein, J., 270, 281
Gallione, J., 250
Gallo, P. S., 219, 253
Glass, G. V., 9, 11, 219–20, 221, 228, 241, 247,
    248, 249, 253, 255
Gormezano, I., 282
Gray, J. A., 270, 281

Haertel, E. H., 256
Haertel, G. D., 256
Hall, J. A., 247–8, 253
Hall, J. L., 253, 265, 281
Haring, M. J., 256
Hartley, S., 248
Hedges, L. V., 231, 253–4, 256
Hempel, W. E., Jr., 54, 59
Hoffman, S. J., 216, 254
Homans, G., 65, 75
Hopkins, K. D., 9, 11
Hunter, J. E., 254
Huston, R. L., 270, 281
Hutton, S. R., 281
Hutton, S. S., 281

Jackson, G. B., 254
Jones, L. V., 254
Johnson, D. W., 248, 254
Johnson, M. A., 273, 281
Johnson, R., 248, 254
Jorgensen, L., 270, 281

Katz, L., 273, 281
Kavale, K. A., 230, 240–1, 243, 248, 254, 256
Kay, E. J., 256
Kerchner, M., 256
Kerlinger, F. N., 47, 56, 59
Kinney, C., 256
Kneer, M., 216
Kolditz, T., 252
Kulik, C. C., 248, 253, 254, 265, 281
Kulik, J. A., 248, 253, 254, 265, 281
Kushner, J., 250

Ladas, H., 254
Landers, D., 229–30, 239, 240, 253
Langa, F. S., 281
Lash, R., 250
Laubach, S. A., 254
Lehman, R. S., 282
Levison, M. E., 254
Leviton, L. C., 253–4
Ley, K. I., 216, 218, 255
Licht, M. H., 219, 255
Light, R. J., 255
Locke, L. F., 216, 255
Lynn, E., 219

Matsuda, F., 282
Mansfield, R. S., 219, 255

Marshall-Goodell, B., 273, 282
Maruyama, G., 248, 254
Matsuda, F., 282
Matsuda, M., 282
Mattson, D., 230, 241, 243, 254
Mayhew, J. L., 275, 282
McGaw, B., 219, 228, 253, 255
Menosky, J., 270, 282
Miller, D. I., 270, 282
Miller, R. I., 216, 255
Miller, T. I., 248
Miller, W., 256
Mizerik, P., 250
Morris, C., 68, 75
Morgenegg, B. L., 255

Nelson, D., 248, 254

Okum, M. A., 256
Olkin, I., 232, 254

Paul, G. L., 219, 255
Phillips, J. L., Jr., 10, 11
Pillemar, D. B., 255
Proshansky, H., 75
Putnam, R. R., 256

Quigley, B. M., 270, 282

Ramey, M. R., 270, 282
Rankin, B. A., 275, 282
Rawlings, R., 282
Rich, S., 54, 59
Richards, J. G., 264, 282
Richter, M. L., 256
Roethlisberger, F. J., 66, 75
Rosenthal, R., 67, 75, 220, 227, 228, 243, 249,
    253, 255, 263
Rothstein, A. L., 34, 39, 73, 75, 94, 216, 220,
    225, 240, 255
Rubin, D. B., 67, 75, 243, 255
Rushall, B., 255

Scandrett, J., 282
Schmidt, F. L., 254
Schmidt, R. A., 34, 39
Sealy, D., 270, 282
Seay, M. B., 256
Seidenberg, B., 75
Seidentop, D., 216, 255, 256
Seireg, A., 270, 282
Sidman, M., 37, 39
Skon, L., 248, 254
Sloan, M., 216, 256
Smith, M. L., 219, 248, 253, 256
Smith, P. V., 255
Sohn, D., 256
Sparling, P. B., 240, 243, 256
Stadulis, R. E., 63, 75, 216, 256
Stanley, J. C., 61, 75, 241

Stewart, D. M., 269, 282
Stoan, S. K., 266–267, 282
Stobbs, J., 270, 282
Stock, W. A., 231, 254, 256
Strube, M. J., 256
Suhor, C., 258, 282

Thorne, M. P., 282

Vatza, E. J., 256

Walberg, H. J., 256
Westby, G., 280
Wildt, A. R., 192, 201
Williams, D., 270, 282
Williams, G., 254
Williams, H. G., 50, 59, 275
Williams, P. A., 256
Wilson, V. L., 256
Winer, B. J., 186, 190, 203

Zeigler, E. F., 216, 256

SUBJECT INDEX

(Italicized pages are definitions)

Analysis of covariance, 191–201
  adjusting treatment means, 198–99
  calculating sums of squares, 196–98
  choosing a covariate, 192–93
  decision-making, 194–199
  definition, 191–92
  explanation, 191–93
  organizing data, 194–96
  presenting results, 197, 199
  use, 192
Analysis of variance (See also specific tests)
  covariance, 191–201
  design layouts, 161–63
  follow-up tests, 202–15
  foundations, 160–65, 172–77
  interactions, 186–89
  one-way between subjects, 145–52
  one-way within subjects, 153–59
  repeated measures, 172–90
  two-factor between subjects, 160–71

Biomedical Programs (BMDP), appendix B

Cause and effect, 46
Central tendency, 12, 15–22
Chi-square, 137–44
  decision-making, 139–40, 143
  expected frequency, 137, 142
  one-way, 137–41
  two-way, 141

Computers, 257–83
  bibliography, 280–82
  definitions, 259–61
  hardware, 262–63
  literacy, 257–59
  introduction, 261–62
  programs, 263–64, appendix B
  software, 262–63
  statistical software
    BMDP, 257, 280, appendix B
    SAS, 257, 280, appendix B
    SPSS, 257, 280, appendix B
  use in
    analysis of data, 274–77
    biomechanics, 267–69, 269–271
    exercise physiology, 267–69, 271–72
    instruction, 279
    literature search, 264–67
    motor learning, 267–69, 272–73
    research, 267–69
    research on teaching, 274
    sport psychology, 267–69, 273–74
    word processing, 277–78
Correlation, 121–36
  pearson product moment, 124–26, 127–28
    calculating, 125, 127
    decision-making, 128
  rank-order correlation, 126, 128–30
    calculating, 126, 129
    decision-making, 130
    ranking raw scores, 128–29, 131
  scattergram, 121, 122–24

Correlation (*cont.*)
  use in reliability, 132–33
  use in validity, 133–34

Decision-making procedures
  analysis of variance
    covariance, 194, 199
    follow-up tests, 211
    mixed design, 185–86
    one-way, 150
    repeated measures, 156
    two-factor, 168
  chi-square, 139–40, 143
  general model, 89–92
  pearson product moment correlation, 128
  rank-order correlation, 130
  t-test, 115, 118
Degrees of freedom, 91–92, 161
  analysis of variance
    covariance, 197
    follow-up tests, 211
    mixed design, 184
    one-way, 146
    repeated measures, 157
    two-factor, 169
  chi-square, 139, 140, 142
  pearson product moment correlation, 124
  rank-order correlation, 130
  t-test, 113
Deliminations, 41
Descriptive statistics, *3,* 12–32, 92

Effect sizes, 82–83, 221
  calculating, 228–29
  interpretation, 229, 230–31
Error, 29–31
  Type I, 81–83
  Type II, 81–83
  variance, 47, 58–59
Experimental design, 43–45
  avoiding systematic error, 44
  control, 40, 46–59
  generalizable results, 44
  precision, 44
  prediction, 40
  simplicity, 45
Experimental research, 40–45
  elements, 40–43
  goals, 40, 60
  hypothesis, 42
  plan, 42–43
  problem, 41
  variables, 41
External validity, 71–75, 91
  threats to
    Hawthorne effect, 74
    interaction of treatment and subject, 72
    multiple treatment interference, 74

    pre-testing, 73
    representativeness, 72

Factorial designs with repeated measures,
    172–90
  calculating, 181–83
  decision-making, 185–86
  degrees of freedom, 184
  extension of design, 186
  interaction, 186–89
  organizing data, 172–77
  preliminary steps, 177–81
  presenting results, 184
Follow-up tests, 202–15
  evaluating ordered means, 206
  individual comparisons, 202–03
    Duncan Multiple Range, 207–08
    Newman-Kuels, 204–07
    Scheffe, 208–10
    Studentized range statistic, 203–04
    Tukey, 207
  presenting results, 215
  simple effects, 210–15
    decision-making, 211
  unequal n's, 208, 209
Frequency distributions, 12–15

Hawthorne effect, 65–66, 74
History, 61–63
Hypothesis, 89–91
  research, 89
  statistical, 89, 115, 118, 128, 130, 139–140,
    143, 150, 156, 168, 185–86, 211
  testing of, 90, 115, 118, 128, 130, 139–140,
    143, 150, 156, 168, 185–86, 211

Inferential statistics, *4,* 92–94
Instrumentation, 66–68
Internal validity, 60–71, 191
  threats to
    differential subject selection, 45, 69–70
    experimental mortality, 70–71
    Hawthorne effect, 65–66
    history, 61–63
    instrumentation, 66–68
    maturation, 63–65
    pre-testing, 65
    statistical regression, 68–69

Limitations, 41

Maturation, 63–65
Mean, 1, 4, *15,* 16–17
Measurement, 1, *2,* 5, 8
  and inferential statistics, 92–94
  interval, 8
  nominal, 5, 8

Measurement (*cont.*)
  ordinal, 6–8
  ratio, 8–9
Median, 4, *15*
  calculating, 17–22
  case vs. score, 18
  for grouped data, 19–22
Meta-analysis, 216–56
  analysis of game statistics, 250–52
  bibliography, 252–56
  calculating effect sizes, 228–29
  cautions, 219, 231–32
  definition, 218–19
  description, 219
  examples, 229–40
  findings, 240–48
  importance, 217–18, 249–50
  interpretation, 229, 230–31
  methods, 220–25
    advantages and limitations, 226
    Bayesian approach, 221, 225
    combining results, 220–21, 227
    critical factors, 220
  procedure, 225, 227–28
Mode, 4, *16,* 22

Normal distribution, 98–109
  computing z-scores, 99–100
  confidence intervals, 107–09
  percentages, 98–99
  properties, 98–99
  using z-table, 101–06

One-way between subjects analysis of var-
    iance, 145–52
  calculating, 147–50
  comparision with t-test, 145–46
  decision-making, 150
  degrees of freedom, 146
  F-ratio, 151
  interpretation, 150–51
  presenting results, 149–50
One-way with subjects analysis of variance,
    153–59
  calculating, 155–58
  control of individual difference, 153–54
  decision-making, 156
  design, 155
  partitioning variance, 155
  presenting results, 157
  problems, 154

Pre-testing, 65, 73–74
Probability, 56–58, 95–98

Range, 4, *22,* 22–23
  interquartile range, 4, *22,* 23–25

Ranking, 6–8
Reliability. 9, 130, 132–33
Repeated measures, 153–59, 172–90
Research, 1, *2,* 33–39
  accuracy, 75
  control, 40, 46–59
  experimental, 40–45
  process, 35, 36–39
  precision, 44
  program, 34–35
  puzzle, 33–35
  representativeness, 75
  simplicity, 45
Research and practice, 216–17
Research design, 1, 38–39, 43
Responsivity to change, 11

Sampling, 76–81
  differential selection 69–70
  population, 76, *77*
  problems, 79–81
  random assignment, 2, 56–58
  sample, *76*
    cluster, 78–79
    proportional, 79
    simple random, 77–78
    size, 81–83
    stratified, 78
    systematic, 78
  volunteers, 45
Scientific method, 36–39
Score, 2, 29–30, 131–32
Sensitivity, 10
Standard deviation, 4, *22,* 25–29, 87, 88–89
  calculating, 28–29, 114
Standard error of the difference between the
    means, *87,* 88–89
  calculating, 89, 114
Standard error of the mean, 85–87, 88–89
  calculating, 89, 104
  confidence interval, 107–09
Statistical Analysis System (SAS), appendix B
Statistical control, 54
Statistical inference, 25, 84–89
  nonparametric tests, 84, 93–94
  parametric tests, 84, 92–93
Statistical Package for the Social Sciences
    (SPSS), appendix B
Statistical power, 81–83
Statistical regression, 68–69
  Stein's paradox, 68–69
Statistical significance, 59, 91, 191–92
  follow-up tests, 202–215
Statistics, 1, *2*
Subjects
  differential selection, 69–70
  matching, 50–54

Subjects (*cont.*)
  mortality, 70–71
  volunteer vs. paid, 45
Sum of squares, 25–27
t-test, 110–120
  assumptions, 110–11
  dependent groups, 113. 115–18
    calculating, 116–17
    decision-making, 115
  independent groups, 110–113, 114–115
    calculating, 114–15
    decision-making, 115
  t-ratio, 110–11

Theory, 1, 33–34
Two factor between subjects analysis of variance, 160–171
  calculating, 160, 164, 166–69
  decision-making, 168
  degrees of freedom, 169
  extending design, 164–65
  follow-up tests, 202–15
  interpretation, 170
  presenting results, 169, 170

Validity
  external, 71–75
  internal, 60–71
  of measurement, 130, 133–34
  statistical, 9
Variable, 5, 41
  adding to control variance, 49–50
  control, *41*
  dependent, *41*
  independent, *41, 47–49*
  intervening, *41*
  levels, 146
  organismic, *41*
  subject, *41*
Variability, 12
  measuring, 22–29
  understanding, 29–30
Variance, *22*
  calculating, 27–28
  control of, 46–59
  controlling extraneous, 49–58, 160–61
  maximizing treatment, 47–49, 160–61
  minimizing error, 58–59, 160–61, 191–92
  partitioning, 147–150, 155, 161, 166, 174